To Bob & Cynthia
with the memories
of a grand evening
at Columbia

Feb., 2014

Paris

in the

Age of Absolutism

OREST RANUM

Paris
in the
Age of Absolutism

AN ESSAY

revised and expanded edition

THE PENNSYLVANIA STATE UNIVERSITY PRESS
UNIVERSITY PARK, PENNSYLVANIA

Je voy bien que la vérité qu'on nous demande
est bien plus difficile à trouver qu'à escrire.

RACINE TO BOILEAU IN 1687,
WHEN BOTH WERE ROYAL HISTORIOGRAPHERS

Library of Congress Cataloging-in-Publication Data

Ranum, Orest A.
  Paris in the age of absolutism / an essay
  Orest Ranum.— Rev. ed.
        p.   cm.
  Includes bibliographical references and index.
  ISBN 0-271-02221-3 (alk. paper)
  1. Paris (France)—History—Louis XIII,
  1610–1643. 2. Paris (France)—History—
  Louis XIV, 1643–1715. I. Title.
DC729 .R3 2003
394.261—dc21   2002009846

This is a revised and expanded edition of the 1968
book *Paris in the Age of Absolutism: An Essay,*
published by John Wiley & Sons, Inc.

It is the policy of The Pennsylvania State University
Press to use acid-free paper. Publications on
uncoated stock satisfy the minimum requirements of
American National Standard for Information
Sciences—Permanence of Paper for Printed Library
Materials, ANSI Z39.48–1992.

FRONTISPIECE: *The Baker's Cart*, by Jean Michelin.
The Metropolitan Museum of Art, Fletcher Fund,
1927 (27.59). Photograph © 1983 The Metropolitan
Museum of Art. All rights reserved.

Contents

France in 1648

Introduction:
Parisian History as Part of French History

You politely, almost fearfully, asked for another piece of bread. Your father simply stared at you coldly. You are perhaps fifteen, maybe sixteen, you are not sure which. The soup had been hot, but thin; the eggs watery and vaguely sulphurous, a sign that they should have been eaten weeks earlier. The gnawing in your belly was almost as strong after supper as before it. Your older brothers had sat in silence, not quite staring the other way, but deliberately avoiding your eyes. Your exhausted mother is heavy with yet another child.

The next morning, you packed your other shirt in a little canvas bag, put on your hat, and set off alone on the road to Paris, some eighty miles away. A three- or four-day walk. Finding a straw stack last night was no problem, for the harvest has just ended. A cousin on your mother's side of the family, who is a cook and lives with a printer's family on the rue Saint-Jacques, can be counted on to put you up for a few nights when you reach Paris. Somewhere, somehow, you will find someone who needs wood hauled to the attic, a cellar cleaned out, manure loaded onto a wagon, water carried upstairs, or ashes removed from fireplaces. You walk along the dusty road in the August sun. When the cousin had gone to Paris, they had had to find someone with whom she could travel; for only women of ill repute, or the very poor and the aged, walked the highroad alone. Your name is Jean.

Are you fictional? Are you historical? The answer is: A bit of both. Until you marry, or more accurately, *if* you marry—or until you commit a major crime and get caught—no one will ask you for your surname: Jean will suffice. You lack the cash to be apprenticed to an artisan, so your only hope is to become a household servant, somewhere in the capital. Work in an inn is a possibility, or work in a stable.

Are you part of history? Yes, but not the high, lofty type of history that centers on battles and politics. Thousands of young people left their homes and villages to, as the phrase went, "seek their fortune" in the capital. Their parents had loved them, but by the time adolescents were fifteen or sixteen, they were considered more than grown-up; and there simply were too many mouths to feed every night. The Parisian population in the seventeenth century was not yet self-sustaining, that is, more infants died than reached childbearing age. Without the steady arrival of teenagers such as Jean, the population of the capital actually would have declined; and since that population is known to have roughly doubled over the seventeenth century, there clearly were thousands of young migrants such as Jean. There is something startlingly contemporary about teenage migration to Paris in the seventeenth century; for today it still occurs, legally, vaguely legally, or downright illegally, around every great urban center of the world.

Normans, Picards, Bretons, young people from the Beauce and from Champagne who know how to take care of babies, make fires, rub down horses—all with regional accents, colloquial turns of phrase, and some sense of pride at hailing from a particular market town or province—came to Paris in search of work. If a foreigner asked them where they came from, "France" was the immediate reply; but if a French person asked the same question, the name of the province of their birth was the answer. These young migrants would seek out relatives, often not all that close, or other young people from their village, and would beg for shelter; and as in all cultures of poverty, the hospitality they received was often accompanied with a warning that it was temporary. It was discouraging to walk the streets, looking for work or for a handout. On each street, in each quarter, the artisans, their apprentices, and the common laborers knew one another: they drank and caroused together. Merchants and their wives conversed as they set up their stands, all the while eyeing passersby or "idlers," to ensure that they did not filch a sausage. It was not easy for a new arrival to worm his way into the street sociability of the capital. Knowing someone, and being introduced, was almost indispensable.

At certain hours, traffic was horrendous. Coachmen shouted, "Make way for the Duchess of Such-and-Such," and in reply arms would fly up, with an obscene gesture. Clergymen, judges, attorneys, and physicians—in the gowns and caps appropriate to their profession and rank—majestically skirted the slop-filled potholes in the street, their trains or capes held up by livery boys dressed in the colors of their master. Wearing livery was a source of pride, not servitude: it indicated that the wearer belonged to a household, that he ate regularly, that he had a roof over his head.

Street scenes certainly changed over the course of the seventeenth century. As the decades passed, there were more richly gilded and carved coaches than ever before. Sedan chairs proliferated, as did great two-wheeled carts loaded with huge barrels of wine. The number of beggars, hawkers, flower-girls, prostitutes, magicians, jugglers, and pickpockets soared, despite police efforts to arrest them, make them pay for licenses, or chase them into the suburbs. Young people coming to Paris for the first time could not, of course, measure the changes brought by increased population and greater luxury consumption; but change there was.

In times of epidemic, food shortage, or extreme cold, the city fathers and the churches and monasteries of the capital would make little-used cellars, stables, and partially abandoned chapels available to the poor. There would be serious epidemics, that is, plague, in the first quarter of the century, and in the 1680s cold weather ruined wheat crops and drove up the prices for flour and bread. When bread prices climbed, the city fathers would legislate to keep them down, and they would post militia guards at flour and bread markets, to reduce the danger that the hungry poor would riot. Monasteries and prominent, well-off, and devout Parisians would open soup kitchens. The typical Parisian cared little about the power relations between the city fathers and the king's ministers, but they closely followed decisions about bread prices, excise taxes on wine, and regulations concerning the places where one could work and the hours during which work could be done. Over the century, a more hands-on regulatory administration would be created, along with special police and judicial powers and officials. Heaps of legislation, decrees, and orders had been pasted on walls or announced by town-criers, but enforcement remained ineffectual until well into the 1660s.

The laws regarding work rules, marketing, quality-control in manufacturing, acceptable or unacceptable street behavior, and even drinking, gambling, and loudness in *cabarets,* were much more coherently promulgated and enforced in the reign of Louis XIV than they had been over the previous centuries. Parisians had little choice but to conform to these state-enforced rules, most of which came down from high, that is, from the king in council through the office of lieutenant of police, created in 1667.

The word *police* in seventeenth-century France was a very general moral and legal concept that extended far beyond simply repressing criminality and assuring that laws were enforced. *Police* meant not just the good society, but the way to live the good life together, in community, according to divine and natural laws. On the one hand, *police* meant the government's duty to lift up the wayward, protect any and all persons and provide them with charity, and repress all threatening, violent, and heretical behavior *and* thought. The laws establishing *police* were not only moral but religious and political. They all came down from the king for the good of each and every one; and individuals had little if any right to challenge, in court, the royal definition of the best life-style and the best community.

For almost two centuries, historians have used the term "absolutism" to characterize this new regime of laws and *police* power, be it for Paris in particular or for the entire realm. The word, in its political and legal significance, simply means total, complete, without appeal, unquestionable. Royal power was not only deemed to be legitimate and divinely ordained; it was absolute. There were no legal or spiritual grounds for disobeying it.

Confronted by the lieutenant of police's coercive powers to legislate and enforce a virtually religious utopia in the form of a safer, cleaner, morally conformist, and more regimented and more prosperous Paris, the old city officials saw their power decline and their functions become largely ceremonial. Political emasculation in the name of absolute legal and royal authority? Yes, in a sense. While the old, late-medieval oligarchical city government run by merchants, lawyers, and guild officers had not been democratic, there had been at least a modicum of citizen participation in the Paris Hôtel de Ville.

Could some medieval centuries actually have been more "democratic" than the Parisian governance prevailing in the seventeenth century? This idea challenges our one-directional sense of progress involving civic rights for individuals and government by laws established by and for the people. Such was the case, however, in the history of Paris, in no small measure because the sixteenth-century movement not only to attain but also to increase individual civic rights became linked to a zealous Catholic religious reform movement that had as its principal aim the conversion, the exclusion, and finally the execution or murder of Protestants. The blending of the religious with the political community of civic rights occurred to a degree of intensity that made it "thinkable" to contemplate the murder of entire families in one's neighborhood, prompting a paroxysm of violence in the capital known as the Wars of Religion.

The coins that young people kept carefully pinned in their shirts as they walked the streets of Paris were of copper, crudely minted *liards* and *sous,* each with its royal portrait and identification (in Latin): "Henry IV, by Grace of God King of France and of Navarre." As kings aged, their portraits on coins aged with them, monarchy being of two living bodies, the body of the king and the body of the laws, the institutions and the solemn coronation oaths. Beyond the seasons and the times of day (not the hours, for many clocks still could not measure such small units of time)—morning, noon, afternoon, and night—the French measured time by the name of the reigning king and the number of years he had reigned.

Be it from portraits on coins or from shouts issuing from inns on holiday evenings, young people were familiar with the name of the king who had the power of life or death over them. Each king also brought a quick mental association, a discrete fact: he was the one who had been assassinated (Henry III, Henry IV), he was the one who lost a big battle in Italy and was taken hostage by the Spanish (Francis I), he was the one killed when a lance entered his visor during a joust (Henry II). The reigns of two of Henry II's sons—Francis II (1559–60), Charles IX (1560–74), assisted by their mother, Catherine de Médicis—blurred with memories of the Wars of Religion, the massive processions organized by the Catholic League, and the terrible, not-to-be-talked-about Saint Bartholomew's Day Massacre of Protestants (August 23–24, 1572). The third son, Henry III (1574–89), was remembered for being stabbed and killed by a zealous monk.

While in his death agony, Henry III had recognized as his heir Henry of Navarre (1589–1610), the Huguenot and lay head of the Bourbon branch of the royal family. The divine seemed to be playing tricks on the French, by allowing three male Valois kings to die without legitimate heirs, thereby leaving the throne to this Protestant! Henry of Navarre would not be recognized as a true king by many of his more zealous Catholic subjects. Slowly at first, and then more rapidly, he defeated the rebellious Catholic aristocratic armies that opposed him; and then in 1593, with great solemnity, he accepted religious instruction and abjured Protestantism at Saint-Denis, an event that was followed by his coronation at Chartres and his entrance into an exhausted and hostile Paris the following year. These military successes were at least partly the result of Henry's arbitrarily taking command of the royal fiscal machine, thereby acquiring money to pay his troops. Still, an entry into Paris was unthinkable until Henry's carefully staged and politically informed conversion.

After long negotiations, on April 15, 1598, he promulgated an edict in Nantes, a city in western France, giving Protestants rights to worship in certain designated areas (not in Paris!), hold royal offices, and own property. As the violence and polemics subsided, and as Henry ordered vitriolic preachers arrested or silenced, a reestablishment of the royal government took place via the law courts and actions of the Council of State. For just over a decade, Parisians lived between fears that civil war would again break out and hope for peace at any price. True, the city fathers had lost much of their power, but this seemed a small price for order and public safety. Then, on May 14, 1610, Henry IV was assassinated by Ravaillac, a man of humble birth who acted without accomplices and who believed himself called by God to carry out this heinous crime.

Henry IV's death left the kingdom to his nine-year-old, morose, stammering son, Louis XIII (1601–43), and a regent who governed in his name: the boy's Florentine mother, Marie de Médicis, daughter of the great patrician family that ruled Tuscany. Henry IV had not been all that popular with the Parisians while he lived; his son Louis would be just barely tolerated, and would be feared by many. Philosophers often posed the question: Is it better for a king to be loved by his subjects or feared by them? And which produces the greater political stability? Louis XIII—known as "the Just" because of his harsh, categorical use of the courts to try and execute his political opponents—never won the love of his subjects. In the realm generally, Louis became known for insisting on his divine-right, absolute authority. When his minister, Cardinal Richelieu, wrote about some provincial towns that had been in rebellion but were now "subdued," and that "the king is now absolute in that region," he meant that there were no grounds for appeal in any court against the king's divinely sanctioned authority. Though he was devout, something had occurred in Louis' childhood that weakened his sense of humanity, his willingness to overlook little signs of disobedience. A long list of political opponents and aristocratic plotters would rot in the Bastille, flee to England, or be decapitated. Fervent royalists blamed Louis' ministers, especially Richelieu, for this harshness, but it was Louis himself who signed the warrants for imprisonment, torture, and execution. His personality seemed in synchrony with the psychological need for a sense of order and increased political power to keep the peace that came like a shock wave after the violence of the Wars of Religion. By February 1643, Louis sensed that he was dying, but he willed himself to live until May 14, the anniversary of his father's assassination—no mean accomplishment.

Louis XIII's son by his queen, Anne of Austria (1601–66), the sister of King Philip IV of Spain, was born in 1638, after twenty-two years of childless marriage. The child, Louis XIV, "the God-given," was only four when his father died. There would be a special aura about this child, this boy king, and then this conquering king, owing to his arrival late in his parents' marriage and his own poise, presence, and capacity to observe and remember every mark of respect—or, God forbid, every lack of respect.

The regency government of his mother, Anne, faced growing rebellion owing to the high taxes enacted to pay troops for the long, bloody war with Spain that had been declared in 1635 and that did not end until 1659. The naturally less royal authority of regents—Catherine de Médicis, Marie de Médicis, and Anne of Austria—prompted princes, nobles, peasants, and royal officials to attempt to reverse the legislation passed by the king and his councillors to reduce their privileges and force payment of the high taxes that were being levied in arbitrary ways. Peasant rebellions and Protestant revolts as early as the 1620s in the West, forced royal armies to fight a three-front war: in the Alps, in the border regions to the north, and against rebels such as the Croquants in the Southwest or the Huguenots at La Rochelle. For well over a century, the Monarchy's highest priority had been foreign policy and military force. Foreign war and new threats to internal stability, especially after the declaration of war with Spain in 1635, fostered a political climate of arbitrariness and coercion, for, when necessary, troops were used to subdue and/or execute rebellious subjects. Not just city-governing elites, but high-ranking nobles felt the iron glove of state power, especially if they contested it.

With the end of civil war, the clash between the faiths took new, surprising directions. Some leading Catholics, and Richelieu was one of them, rejected the use of force and argued in favor of an exemplary Catholicism. The moral and community lives of Catholics should be so pure and so clearly in conformity with divine laws that heretics would be uplifted and would rejoin the ancient fold. The spiritual and moral, even social, impulses unleashed by this approach would fundamentally alter Parisian culture over the next half-century and would provide the new political energies that underlay the absolute state of Louis XIV. To be sure, there were ancient Roman precedents that would be grist for the public lawyers' mills of legal-police reform, but these merely deepened and justified what was the Roman Catholic spiritual and moral program for an ordered society. French spiritual vitality would provide the woof in the creative cultural fabric, including the arts, the sciences, and philosophy, a new vision of humanity grounded on the doctrinal orthodoxy of a revived Thomism.

The years 1648–52 were years of rebellion in most major French cities, except Lyons, while the countryside seethed with rage against royal tax officials. Paris underwent a "Fronde," that is, a series of destabilizing, even revolutionary popular shows of force and confrontations within the high-ranking law courts, while Bordeaux descended into a profoundly radical attempt to create a new urban social order and political community grounded on the principles of charity of the Early Church—a sort of League program not unlike the one that had occurred in Paris in the 1560s–1590s, but lacking the fanatical concentration on destroying Protestants.

These waves of civil war were followed by the shocks of "restored" and intensified royal power from 1598 to 1610 and again in the 1640s; but in the 1650s stability finally left French governing elites disoriented and eager for a kind of apolitical life centered on the worship of Louis XIV, partly from fear of disorder and partly from the psychological pain that resulted from profound religious differences and from the violence they had produced.

Worship of Louis XIV? Church teaching forbade it, but the Church's distinction between worship and veneration often became blurred, when preachers and poets sought to elevate the majesty and magnanimity of royalty. No one questioned that the king's authority had divine origins, and that it was his duty to uphold Catholic teachings and, if necessary, use force to bring his subjects to conform to them.

Monarchy can inspire the human gamut of emotions in a people. Love and good feelings burst forth at the time of royal births and marriages, while royal deaths bring grief sometimes combined with a sense of "good riddance." The long soap-opera relations of Henry IV and Louis XIV and their mistresses fascinated and titillated, while priests were castigating that very behavior. For the more educated Parisians, the royal family was in some sense *their* "family": they were a source of gossip and rumor, but they were to be cherished, especially when the head of that royal family was a boy who obviously was trying to do what was expected of him.

In this atmosphere, royal officials had virtually a free hand to create an absolute, divine-right monarchical state, a state with essentially a "new" capital in Paris, a capital that was policed in order to enforce proper morals, to regulate working conditions, especially for the manufacture of luxury products, an illustrious, luminescent setting for prestigious monuments to the king. During Louis XIV's mature years, and during the service of his aloof, brilliant, and visionary minister, Jean-Baptiste Colbert, a New Rome was created. By 1715 the city was very different from what it had been in 1590. Building on and extending what Henry IV had begun, there now were large geometrical public squares with statues of the king at their focal point, there were arches of triumph, hospital-prisons, a new and gigantic wing on the Louvre, handsome stone bridges, streetlights, and massive stone quays along the Seine.

In their Latin classes, educated Parisians, especially male Parisians, had been taught awe for ancient Rome. The military conquests of Rome's generals, its legal codes and its literature, philosophy, architecture, and engineering had constituted a "Golden Age" like nothing before or after it. There was simply no way, no critical perspective for the seventeenth-century French to be negative about things Roman—save, perhaps, for the fact that Christians were known to have been thrown to the lions in popular entertainments in the Coliseum. Absolutist governmental powers and the vision of creating a New Rome came together in Colbert's mind; and though French elites were politically emasculated, a dramatic, coherent, and virtually all-pervasive, mimetic Roman moment came into being from the 1660s to the 1680s.

The creative impulses unleashed by the end of civil war were not the same as those that the image of ancient Rome had inspired during the previous century. No longer so literalist in their attempts to write Ciceronian Latin or design buildings with Vitruvian ornamentation, the French after 1660 had some understanding of ancient rhetoric, classical poetic meter, the mathematics used by Roman architects, and the evolution of Roman law. Thus they could extrapolate from ancient "theories" and apply them to contemporary French buildings, laws, painting, and vernacular literature. These classicist impulses had, as their foundation, principles or "theories" that were consciously studied, articulated, and codified into laws for a given "art"—be that "art" grammar, governmental administration, painting, architecture, or music. During the reign of Louis XIV, these laws became highly coercive cultural impulses. Above all, mathematics, and its new, post-Galilean stepchild, physics, satisfied the psychological need among the learned for certitude that religious faith had filled prior to the Reformation.

The monuments of ancient Rome had been built pell mell, wherever space was available; the Forum was a marble labyrinth of temples and tombs. Thanks to mathematics, to theories of perspective, and to proportions between the number of columns and their width and height, the New Rome that was seventeenth-century Paris had the potential to surpass ancient Rome in beauty, in grandeur, and perhaps—and most of all—in durability. Colbert dispatched commissioners to study the stone from various quarries around Paris, to find a stone so excellent that the new monuments to the king would last for thousands of years. The realm was searched for marbles (Lacaune) as beautiful and as hard as those of Italy.

Classicism had as its deep, fundamental principle the recognition that humans wanted the memory of themselves and of their accomplishments perpetuated forever. This essentially religious and ontological dimension had been present in the culture of the sixteenth century, but it often had been dampened by the Christian-Augustinian doctrine that pursuing immortality on earth was the vanity of all human vanities. The classical creative generation of the seventeenth century—Poussin, Mansart, Racine, Le Brun, and Boileau—all, at least momentarily, pursued immortality through their creative impulses; and these impulses often were focused on the image of the divinely ordained person of the monarch. The pursuit of immortality through religious faith in grace and redemption no longer seemed to suffice. Smitten by the myth-histories of Caesar Augustus, Alexander the Great, Hadrian, Trajan, and Constantine, French poets, artists, and state administrators almost obsessively set out to do for their sovereign and Paris what ancient writers and artists had accomplished for their heroic, bigger-than-life conquerors and emperors.

Called "Louis the Great" by the poets who praised him to the skies—and likened to Apollo, the Greek god of the sun known for his powers as punisher (he carries a bow and arrows), prophet, enchanting singer, and protector of domestic animals— the boy king who had early been educated to do his duty grew to manhood while attempting to live in conformity with the images created for him. The Sun King slowly changed from an awkward, conscientious adolescent into a domineering, rule-bound adult.

Apollo in the new Paris and in Versailles was depicted as a beautiful young man, the symbiosis of the youthful monarch and the divine driver of the four horses who pulled his chariot across the sky each dawn. The Apollonian myth had, quite simply, elegant and erotic youthful meanings of power, fertility, and creativity. As the young king matured, fell in love—and in 1661 married a Spanish princess whom he honored but never loved—the French hoped that war was at last behind them.

Such would not be the case. French armies, in the name of glory for the king, began to suffer serious defeats at the hands of the sturdy Dutch in the 1670s. The wars of the 1680s, 1690s, and 1702–13 were more costly still in blood and treasure. In the eyes of Europe, France had become a bully. And the shelling and burning of Heidelberg by French troops in 1688–89—a deed perhaps more morally outrageous than the Saint Bartholomew's Day Massacre way back in 1572—indicated that the old structural consequences of a monarch's use of overwhelming military force could unleash feelings of guilt at home and outrage abroad that would last for at least a century.

Clouds from war and defeat were not the only deeply negative consequences of Louis XIV's authoritarian manner of governing. In 1685, having become convinced that there were really no Protestants left in the realm, or so few that they did not matter, the king revoked the Edict of Nantes. Here was a perfect illustration of what absolute sovereignty meant in practice: by absolutist principle, Louis XIV was not bound to honor the solemn promises made by his grandfather, Henry IV. Authoritarian, certainly, and in response to disorder, riot, and revolt, but not totalitarian. The legal system provided some protection for all who were born within the realm. But unlike some harsher twentieth-century regimes, there were no residence cards, no identification cards, nor even a centralized system of recordkeeping by the courts or the police.

The revocation of the Edict of Nantes was followed by an intensified effort to convert the remaining heretics, some of whom were rewarded financially for their outward conformity; but many Huguenots, and not the least skilled among then, fled the realm. Troops were used to break up any assembly of Protestants and to arrest those who wrote, shouted, or in some way protested the royal decision. In the far-off Cévennes mountains of Languedoc, peasants and nobles alike refused to convert and did not hesitate to kill royal troops who had been sent to disarm them and destroy their churches. A kind of guerrilla war followed in which Huguenots made surprise attacks upon armed soldiers. The English, once again at war with France, sent weapons and money to the Huguenots in the Cévennes and at home mobilized public opinion against France for these persecutions. The Huguenot communities in the Cévennes were never really defeated, though the government in Paris eventually declared a trumped-up victory.

The administrative power structures set in place between 1660 and 1690 would force French society to live according to the rules that had been established for their "benefit," whether they liked it or not. For another century, this rule-based absolutist machine would run even more quickly and more forcefully in and through society. Paris—and the culture first elaborated around royal monuments and around the veneration of literature and the arts—was among the wonders of Europe in the eighteenth century. Despite subsequent efforts to open avenues of political consultation and to weaken the system of laws that had assured elites of their social privileges in lieu of tax exemption, the French government fell almost entirely out of synchrony with the newer demographic, intellectual, and economic changes occurring in Paris itself during the eighteenth century. These changes prompted the rise of debates among the elites, and a mood of suspicion among artisans and laborers—a suspicion that the royal government was actually profiting from the dire material conditions that prevailed in the capital during the 1780s. Yes, the roots not only of the French Revolution of 1789 but also of the Terror of 1792–95 lay in the triumph of the visionary-utopian, rule-creating authoritarianism of the absolute state that had been created out of religious reform and New Roman images as an answer to social disorder and religious pluralism.

Chronology

1639 Popular revolt in Normandy

1641 Vouet's *Presentation in the Temple* for the altar of the Jesuit Novitiate

1642 Death of Richelieu; Poussin ends his stay in Paris; civil war breaks out in England

1643 Death of Louis XIII; Minority of Louis XIV; Regency of Anne of Austria; battle of Rocroy; Arnauld's *Fréquente Communion*

1644 Le Vau completes the Hôtel Lambert

1645 Construction begins on Val-de-Grâce

1646 Lully arrives in Paris; Le Brun returns to Paris after a four-year stay in Rome

1648 The Fronde; Peace of Westphalia; Poussin's *Ashes of Phocian;* founding of Academy of Painting

1649 Mademoiselle de Scudéry begins publishing *Artamène ou le Grand Cyrus;* execution of Charles I of England

1652 Condé's troops attack the Hôtel de Ville

1653 Mademoiselle de Scudéry creates Sappho-centered historical utopia; Pope Innocent X condemns the *Five Propositions*

1655 Construction begins on the church of Saint-Sulpice

1656 Founding of the General Hospital; Pascal's *Provincial Letters*

1657 Fouquet begins Vaux-le-Vicomte

1659 Peace with Spain

1661 Fouquet's disgrace; Champaigne's portrait of his daughter and Agnès Arnauld

1664 Colbert becomes superintendent of buildings; Louis XIV undertakes a large building project at Versailles; Molière's *Tartuffe; Plaisirs de l'Île enchantée* at Versailles

1665 Colbert named controller-general of finances; Bernini presents plans for the Louvre; La Rochefoucauld's *Maximes*

1667 La Reynie becomes lieutenant general of police; Perrault façade of the Louvre

1668 La Fontaine's *Fables* (I–VI); Turenne converts to Catholicism

1670 Pascal's *Pensées*

1672 Franco-Dutch war; crossing of the Rhine; construction of Porte Saint-Denis; Lully chooses Quinault as librettist for his operas

1673 Death of Molière

1674 Porte Saint-Martin

1677 Founding of the Invalides; Racine's *Phèdre*

1678 La Fontaine's *Fables* (VII–XI); Mademoiselle de Lafayette's *Princesse de Clèves*

1683 Death of Colbert; Girardon begins the equestrian statue of Louis XIV for the Place Louis-le-Grand

1685 Revocation of the Edict of Nantes

1686 Place des Victoires

1687 Charles Perrault reads *Le Siècle de Louis XIV* before the French Academy; Bossuet gives the eulogy at the Grand Condé's funeral

1688 La Bruyère's *Les Caractères*

1697 Bayle publishes his *Dictionary*

1699 Place Louis-le-Grand (Place Vendôme)

1701 Rigaud's portrait of Louis XIV in coronation regalia; War of Spanish Succession

1703 Jules-Hardouin Mansart's chapel is completed at the Invalides

1710 Destruction of Port-Royal-des-Champs

1713 Treaty of Utrecht; bull *Unigenitus* condemns Jansenism

1715 Death of Louis XIV

PART ONE

The Medieval Burden

Paris in the Age of Absolutism

A Traveler's View in 1600

Imagine a circle of gray stone walls a mile and a half in diameter lying on a green, rolling plain. This circle of walls, cut by the meandering Seine and surrounded by the distant "mountains" of Passy, Montmartre, Montparnasse, and Valérien, embraced an artificial mound of aged houses, churches, and monasteries. This medieval painting come to life was Paris, principal fortified city of the Île de France and customary residence of the French kings.

Towers and spires rose above the walls from a hodgepodge of stone and half-timbered buildings, all squeezed together. Merian's engraving of Paris in or around 1600 depicts a still-medieval town. The buildings seem piled on top of one another, teetering, out of proportion, unrepaired, situated at every angle, and walled-in as if their builders were oblivious of their neighbors.

The city walls were two parallel rows of cut and mortared stone filled in with rubble to make a solid mass six feet thick and about twenty-eight feet high. Towers jutted out and up to break the circle's course every two hundred and twenty feet. Gates, moats, bridges, and massive bastions with trees growing out of their turrets still guarded the dozen major entrances in the walls. At the four points where the walls came down to the Seine rose tall, quite neglected towers, from which heavy iron chains could be suspended across the river at both extremities of the city to prevent enemy ships from sailing into Paris during a siege.

The Medieval Burden

Outside the walls, rows of houses and *hôtels* lined the roads leading out from every gate, forming the city's *faubourgs* or suburbs. Between these roads, monasteries rose to encircle Paris with a belt of cloisters, refectories, churches, and gardens. The abbey of Saint-Germain-des-Prés, the most illustrious and extensive of these establishments, occupied what were to become the most fashionable parts of Paris in the eighteenth century.

Beyond the monasteries stretched the unbroken patchwork quilt of tiny vegetable gardens, vineyards, quarries, and pastures cared for by the Parisians themselves on Sundays and saints' days. Such holiday gardening seems not to have been forbidden or, if it was, neither the priests nor the magistrates sought to enforce the prohibition.

The traveler passing through these fields in 1600 would come on what still appeared to be an independent political entity. Its fortifications were still intact and essential for protection, the gates were locked and guarded at night, and the cannon of the Bastille stood primed and attended. Robert Dallington described Paris in about 1590 as "reputed not only the capitall city of France, but also the greatest in all Europe. It is about the walls some ten English miles: these are not very thick, the want whereof is recompenced with the depth of the ditch, and the goodness of the rampart, which is thick and defensible save on the south side, which no doubt is the weakest part of the town." For Dallington, the "greatest in all Europe" signified the largest population on the continent, and this large population and the Seine River were also the most impressive things about Paris for Giovanni Botero, the Italian author of the *Greatness of Cities*.[1] There were probably about a quarter of a million souls living in Paris in 1600. This made it the largest urban center in France, the most populous country in Europe.

Why had Paris become so "great"? The reasons are mainly geographic and political, though the fact that it was the largest university town in Europe also counted.

Paris is situated in a fertile valley just about halfway between the places where the Oise and Marne rivers flow into the Seine. Together these three rivers link most of northern France, and their tributaries reach south and east, to Montargis, Auxerre, Troyes, and numerous lesser towns. Paris had become a natural capital for trade early in the Middle Ages, and it never lost this primacy. The Seine was an ideal river. Its broad

---

1. "And Seine, mean river in France, beareth ships of such bulk, and carrieth burdens so great, that he who sees it not will not believe it, and there is not a river in the world that for proportion is able to bear the like burden. So that although it exceed not a mediocrity and be but a small river, yet notwithstanding it supplieth wonderfully all the necessities and wants of Paris, a city that in people and in abundance of all things exceedeth far all other cities whatsoever within the scope of Christendom."

and deep currents were not too swift, and hard turf or stone instead of swamps lined most of its banks. Some of the early descriptions of Paris comment on the extraordinary capacity of the waters of the Seine to support heavy loads. Tanners, dyers, and drinkers alike praised its sweetness.

The Seine enabled Paris to dominate trade in the North the way Lyons on the Rhone did in the Center and Bordeaux on the Garonne and Nantes on the Loire did in the West. France therefore did not have a single, exclusive economic capital until the nineteenth century, when canals and rails gave Paris the lead over other French cities.

In the beginning, the ease of fortifying the city made Paris as attractive to feudal lords as its rivers were to traders. Stone quarries lay close at hand. The Seine, smaller rivers such as the Bièvre, and the deep ditches around the walls, made Paris almost an island. The oldest part of the city, of course, was the *Île de la Cité*, a real island, where Notre-Dame and the *Palais* had been built on the foundations of Roman buildings. This island had offered men protection since the beginning of civilization.

The political reasons for Paris's greatness are more difficult to discern. In 1600 it was fashionable to assert that the kings of France, ever since the days when they lorded over only Paris and the tiny Île de France, had favored the city's prosperity by granting merchants special trading privileges and had honored the city with their presence. Humanists and jurists served up this royalist propaganda without ever examining critically whether or not it was true. The Capetian kings had unquestionably supported the claims of Parisian merchants to control the Seine trade, especially in feuds with the Dukes of Normandy, who controlled Rouen and the mouth of the river; but their motives may have been less to make Paris prosper than to make other towns suffer.

The king was the lord of the city, its defender, judge, and principal resident. He was the first Parisian, from whom all bounty flowed, or so thought seventeenth-century historians of the city. He possessed the largest, strongest, and finest palaces and châteaux, received more guests, held a finer Court, had more prayers said for him, and bought more than anyone else in the city. The purchases of arms, furniture, clothing, silver, relics, and works of art by the king's immediate family and the rest of the Court stimulated the city's growth and helped orient its manufacture toward luxury goods and *articles de Paris,* as they were called all over Europe.

The construction of the Louvre and other royal palaces, law courts, chapels, and *hôtels* for members of the royal family, favorites, mistresses, and officials maintained a steady flow of money into the city in the form of salaries for masons, plasterers, carpenters, roofers, wood carvers, cabinetmakers, gold-leaf workers, and so on. Most of this money

P A

1. La Bastille a Porte	4. Le Condelière.	8. S. Catharine.	12. S. Geruais	16. Porte du Temple	19. S. Iaques de la	22. S. Sulpice	26. Porte de.
S. Anthone.	5. S. Victoire.	9. S. Anthone.	13. Le Temple.	17. S. Seuerin.	Boucherie.	23. S. Magloire	27. S. Germain
2. L'arsenale.	6. S. Paule.	10. S. Bernhard.	14. Nostre Dame.	18. La S. Chapelle	20. S. Inocent.	24. S. Nicolas des Champs.	28. S. Germ
3. Bicestre.	7. Les Celestins.	11. S. Genouiesue.	15. Host. de Ville.	au Pallais.	21. S. Augustin.	25. S. Martin	29. S. Eti

Map of Paris, by G. Merian. This somewhat imagined hilltop view shows the Hôpital Saint-Louis in the foreground and the Temple Gate. The castle to the west is the Bastille. In the seventeenth century, these walls on the northern side of the capital were in somewhat better condition than the ones on the south side.

Louure.	34.	Porte S. Martin		38.	S. Roch.	42	S. Laurent	46.	les Bonhomes	50.	S. Pierre	54	Le pont de la
ueur.	35.	Porte S. Denis.	et Faub...	39.	le Faulans.	43.	les Recolles.	47.	Le Pont des Tuilleries	51.	L Hosd de la Royne.		Tournelle
ore.	36.	Porte Montmartre.		40.	les Capuans.	44.	S. Lazare.	48.	Faubourg S. Germain	52.	Prez aus Clerc	55.	Faubourg S. Iaq...
e du Louure.	37.	Porte S. Honore.		41.	Iacobins reforme	45.	la Riuiere de Seine	49.	les Filles Dieu	53.	les Chartreux	56.	La Sorbone

came either from excise and income taxes collected from the realm, or, in the case of lesser builders than the king, from seigneurial dues and the sale of grain or cattle. Year after year, century after century, the expenditures for construction by the Court remained very high, for such buildings as the Louvre, other royal residences, and private *hôtels* were periodically refurbished in the latest style or had new apartments added on to them. Thus both the privileges granted to the city's merchants by the monarch and his presence caused Paris to grow by pumping outside wealth into the city in the form of salaries. In an agrarian economy such expenditures represented a major market for imports and manufactured goods.

From the thirteenth century on, the presence of the University on the Left Bank (the Sorbonne was the college of theology) had caused that part of Paris to grow rapidly and become very populous; but in the sixteenth century and throughout the seventeenth century the number of students declined. However, the numerous new monastic foundations established as a consequence of the Catholic Reformation, and the growth of royal courts, added new and costly buildings in many quarters of the city and provided a new source of expansion. They also added inhabitants.

In the mid-sixteenth century, Rabelais' giant, Gargantua, came from the provinces to attend the University. Annoyed by the Parisians swarming around his giant feet, Gargantua sat down on the twin towers of Notre-Dame, facing west on the *Île de la Cité*. The streets beneath him were extremely narrow, some only six feet wide, and all were lined with medieval houses. Some were half-timbered, with each succeeding floor built out over the other, until the streets seemed tunnels beneath peaked roofs. Beyond the little open space before the cathedral, and past the first narrow streets, Gargantua could see the Hôtel-Dieu, the central hospital for Paris, just to his right, then the Marché Neuf, and finally the tall stone buildings of the Palais de Justice enclosing the lacelike Sainte-Chapelle. The yet-to-be-constructed Pont-Neuf would one day span the end of the island, beyond the gardens of the *Palais*.

Raising his head even further, and looking to the right, the giant could see the Louvre, unfinished and disparate, with its mixture of Gothic and Renaissance styles. On the left was the old Tour de Nesle, located where the walls came down to the Seine. The great Italian silversmith Cellini would soon establish his workshop there. Outside the city walls, Gargantua glimpsed the three tall spires of Saint-Germain-des-Prés and the fields beyond.

Notre-Dame is on the southern side of the *Cité*, so when Gargantua decided to wash away the annoying swarm of Parisians by urinating on them from his cathedral stool, those who could fled across the Petit-Pont and the Pont Saint-Michel to the Left Bank. Rabelais states that Gargantua drowned two hundred thousand Parisians, or nearly half the population. Escape from the torrents of urine would have been difficult in the narrow streets, and the Pont Notre-Dame and the Pont-au-Change leading to the Right Bank might both have been too crowded or too far away for escape. People, horses, carts, hawkers, beggars, and bankers jammed these bridges from morning until night. Garbage, manure, and mud lay as much as a foot deep on the surrounding streets. But for those who could take their eyes off Gargantua, there were other things to see.

There was the cathedral itself. Robert Cerceau (d. 1560), Bishop of Avranches, proved that in length, width, and breadth the dimensions of Notre-Dame exceeded those of the Temple of Diana at Ephesus "so much praised by the ancients." This gave a venerable and out-of-date monument a new, but unneeded, status. Most contemporary writers still found Notre-Dame "very beautiful, great, and majestic" despite the critics who condemned the Gothic style as vulgar. But all unanimously disliked the huge statue of Saint Christopher on the façade. Was the statue simply too "primitive"? Notre-Dame had long since become a shrine for all of France. Something holy and supernatural enveloped it; even its construction was a subject of mystery and wonder. Notre-Dame had neither sagged nor cracked inside or out; the "forest" of huge beams and rafters above the vaults humbled the little artisan who worked with his hands. It was long believed that Notre-Dame had been built on giant pilings, until excavations in about 1700 proved this to be untrue. One more miracle was refuted.

From the façade stared the statues of twenty-eight Old Testament kings, symbolizing the union of the Church and the monarchy, a favorite theme of guidebook writers under the Bourbons after Henry IV's abjuration of Protestantism.

Marie, Jacqueline, Gabrielle, Guillaume, Pasquier, Thibaud, and the "Sparrows"— the bells great and small—were rung on a schedule worked out over the centuries. There were smaller bells in the *flèche,* the spire over the crossing of the nave and the transepts, and there was a wooden bell too, which rang "only after dinner [noon] on Maundy Thursday and continuing until Easter morning." People of the *Cité* would not be deprived of their bells at the most solemn moment in the church year when bronze bells were silenced to commemorate Christ's death.

In 1600 the cathedral stood higher by several steps than the *parvis* or open space before it. Its mass seemed to rise higher then, because it was impossible to stand far away to view the whole above the much lower roofs. Inside all was darkness, candles, gold, and incense. There were no long vistas, except upward toward the vaults. Chapels, tombs, chantries, and a rood screen crowded the floor around a great choir until canons in the eighteenth century pulled them down. When the king was at war, battle flags captured in former victories were suspended to invoke God's help again. Or were they to remind Him and the king's subjects of past blessings showered on the monarchy? Notre-Dame symbolized the Gallican Church, unfettered by Rome and royalist. The bishop had been nominated by the king since the early Middle Ages. Seven popes had come from the chapter. Innumerable cardinals, bishops, royal councillors, jurists, theologians, poets, and missionaries proudly claimed that they came from Notre-Dame.

As late as 1742 the revenues of the chapter were thought to be 180,000 *livres,* not including the canonical houses. Notre-Dame itself, with its 150 chapels, was reputed to yield 700,000 *livres* a year. The diocese included 22 chapters, constituting 31 abbeys (10 in Paris), 66 priories (11 in Paris and the *faubourgs*), 184 monasteries (84 in Paris), 474 parishes (59 in Paris), 256 chapels (90 in Paris), and 34 hospitals, of which 5 were in Paris and the *faubourgs*.

During festivals, when people's thoughts turned to the problem of whether their souls were destined for heaven or for hell, nuns from a nearby foundling hospital brought orphan babies into Notre-Dame and placed them in a straw-lined box for all to watch. The offerings for the hospital thus increased in proportion to the obsession with sin and the compassion for these babies that gripped the faithful. Guidebooks in the seventeenth century never mention the beautiful stained-glass windows that made Notre-Dame very dark inside. In the eighteenth century, for the sake of light and splendor, the lower ones were knocked out and replaced by blue glass, so that the long rows of columns, now free of tombs and central chapels, could be admired by all. But in 1600 the gloom was interrupted only by the points of candle and lamplight before statues of Our Lady and the saints, each one invoked for a special problem or malady. Notre-Dame was still something of a religious marketplace in which sinners wandered, searched, and shopped for solace.

Notre-Dame was a busy place. Students filed in noisily to write examinations in the nave while the great organ played to inspire them. And to the regular rhythm of matins, vespers, and masses for church holidays was added the bustle of city functions, ceremonies of the courts of justice, guild celebrations, weddings, and funerals.

Between this religious capital of France and the judicial capital at the western end of the island stood a quarter full of old houses, with religious establishments and parish churches. There were more than twenty churches on the island. Along the rues de la Lanterne, de la Juiverie, and du Marché Palu, all torn down in the nineteenth century, stood many medieval houses, by then subdivided into several dwellings, in which lived bourgeois and notaries. There, too, was the "Pine Cone," a famous cabaret and favorite haunt of Racine, Boileau, Molière, and Lully.

Beyond rose the *Palais,* a sprawling maze of chiefly Gothic buildings and court-yards, which had once served as a residence for French kings. It still was a residence, in theory, but since the fourteenth century the sovereign courts had expanded to use all the space. Housed there were the Parlement, Chambre des Comptes, Cour des Aides, and Cour des Monnaies, together constituting the highest courts in the king-dom. The Sainte-Chapelle, built in the thirteenth century as a vast reliquary for a thorn from the crown of thorns, stood in the center of the great courtyard, its *flèche* rising higher than all the buildings around it. In 1600 the interior was still little changed from what it had been in Saint Louis' time, except that many relics and altar-pieces had been added to this royal chapel, endowing its wealthy, aristocratic clergy with a rich treasure. The lower chapel served as a parish church for those living in the *Palais* and nearby streets.

To the *Palais* scurried a population as diverse in interests and status as Paris itself. There were probably four or five thousand magistrates, clerks, copyists, and minor officials such as *huissiers* (doorkeepers) who together made up the personnel of the sov-ereign courts. In addition to these, merchants, booksellers, paper and ink sellers, prostitutes, singers, letter writers, and beggars, among others, daily set up shop or fre-quented the dozens of stalls displaying such items as cloth, mirrors, dolls, knives, lace, and purses. In this maze of corridors and chambers the principal attraction remained the *grande salle* itself, with its marble floor, heavy columns lined with statues of French kings, and gold ceiling. It was considered smart to go to the *grande salle,* for it was a favorite meeting place for distinguished people or for those who wanted to see them and buy luxury goods.

From the gates of the *Palais* the street led north past the Tour de l'Horloge, across the Pont-au-Change to the Châtelet and the *ville;* or south across the Pont Saint-Michel to the University. The Right Bank, called the *ville* in medieval times because it was the commercial part of Paris, had lost this special significance as early as the fourteenth cen-tury, when merchants settled on the Left Bank, or University, around the Place Maubert.

Before reaching the Right Bank, one passed under a fortress gate. The Châtelet was originally built as a castle to guard the bridge to the *Cité,* but very early it came to house the courts and prisons of the *prévôté* of Paris. Jurisdiction was both civil and criminal, equivalent to that of a *bailliage* in the provinces, nominally under the control of the *prévôt* of Paris (not to be confused with the *prévôt des marchands*), who rendered justice in the king's name in the city and who, in processions, marched right after the president of the Parlement and before the nobility. By 1600 the Châtelet had come under the Parlement's control, through the *lieutenant civil,* who directed its functions. Despite repairs under Francis I, from the fifteenth century on the Châtelet was partly in ruins, as shown in a Silvestre engraving of about 1650.

Beyond the Châtelet stood the central commercial and marketing section of Paris. After Philip Augustus established the Halles there as a kind of perpetual fair, the Right Bank became the stronghold of commercial society in Paris. Street names were usually functional: the rue de la Savonnerie (soap), rue de la Chausseterie (stockings), rue de la Cossonnerie (fowl), and rue de la Lingerie (linens). There merchants, as many as two dozen strong, would gather along a street to sell the same products. The rue de la Fripponerie contained many clothing shops where one could bargain, trade in the clothes on one's back for some others, either used or new, and pay the difference.

Up the rue Saint-Denis from the Châtelet, and west along the rue de la Ferronnerie, stood the Church and Cemetery of the Innocents. The chapels, galleries of charnel houses, lamps, crosses, frescoes of the Dance of Death, and the open common graves aroused the morbid curiosity of visitors in 1600. Some parts of the cemetery were reserved for the dead of special corporations, such as the hospitals of Sainte-Catherine and the Hôtel-Dieu, the chapter of Saint-Germain-l'Auxerrois, and the Châtelet, but most of it contained common graves for Parisians from every part of the city. The earth of the Innocents was said to be remarkable, because it could *manger son cadavre en neuf jours* (consume its cadaver in nine days). When graves had to be dug again in the same spot, the bones were pulled out of the earth and stored in piles along the walls. Two or three common graves stood open at the same time.

Adjacent to the cemetery on the northwest were the Halles, a series of pavilions where merchants rented stalls to sell chiefly grain, leather, cloth, and meat, and where articles were sold retail and wholesale to merchants (foreign and domestic) and consumers alike. The apparent confusion on market days belied the stringent laws and customs regulating sales, the use of land in the nearby streets, and the organization of produce by its place of origin. The Normans tended to put their stands together in one part of the market, to stay in the same inns, and to travel together, as did merchants from other provinces and foreign countries. Commerce was still familial and provincial. The houses in the market parishes of Sainte-Opportune, Saint-Jacques-de-la-Boucherie, Saint-Martin, and Saint-Denis were both commercial and residential, with their ground floors invariably a shop, either for sales or manufacture, and the upper floors living quarters for merchant or artisan families, servants, and apprentices.

In the midst of these stands, pavilions, inns, and houses stood several monasteries, each with its own cloister, refectory, school, and gardens. They varied in size and function, but like the parish churches they were filled with chapels, windows, tapestries, and altars given them by various guilds over the centuries. These chapels served as meeting houses for guilds and for weddings and funerals of the members. Paid masses on behalf of the living and deceased members of their company were said in the guilds' own sanctuaries, often decorated with trowels, scissors, or some other instrument serving as their emblem.

This commercial section was bounded on the west by an aristocratic quarter, beginning with Saint-Eustache and the Hôtels de Soissons and Longueville. It extended on the east as far as the Hôtel de Ville and the Place de la Grève before it. The Hôtel de Ville was an unfinished palace in the French Renaissance style in 1600, but it served as the meeting place for the *bureau de ville*—the elected officials of the bourgeois of Paris— and for receiving members of the royal family and visiting dignitaries, such as ambassadors. The registers of the elections and business and legal proceedings of the *prévôt des marchands* and *échevins* were kept there, as were arms for the militia, the seals of Paris, and its official weights and measures. The Place de la Grève was then much lower than the present square and was frequently flooded by the Seine. In the minds of Parisians, *La Grève* evoked the numerous public executions that took place there—decapitation for the nobility, hanging for commoners, and burning for heretics and sorcerers. People living on the square rented out their windows on days of public executions.

Except for the area bordering the quays, Paris beyond the Hôtel de Ville and the Church of Saint-Jean-en-Grève was mainly aristocratic. The *Marais,* or parishes of Saint-Gervais and Saint-Paul, was the most fashionable and wealthy part of the city. Since the late Middle Ages, when the royal residences of Saint-Pol and the Tournelles had attracted numerous aristocrats and clergymen to build in the area, the *Marais* had been the most homogeneous and solidly aristocratic part of the city. After the demolition of the old palace of Saint-Pol under Francis I and the sale of its land to a president of the Parlement, who built the Hôtel de Carnavalet, numerous judges and new aristocrats also bought and built in the area between the Hôtel de Ville and the Bastille. But the princes still set the tone. Diane de France, and later Charles de Valois, built and

The Medieval Burden

A market scene in seventeenth-century Paris. A dispute between two women led to the spilling of little pies or cakes onto the pavement. Some women fishmongers, in the right middle-ground, shout as a hatted and cloaked man feigns disgust and implies that the fish are not fresh.

The Hôtel de Ville and Place de la Grève, after Claude de Chastillon. Cannons are fired as the bonfire celebrating Saint John's Day (June 21) blazes toward the sky. Note the carriages of the well-to-do. The Île Notre-Dame and the Tournelle are in the distance.

lived in what is now the Hôtel Lamoignon; the Guises had built a little to the northwest of them; and later, Sully settled in the rue Saint-Antoine not far from the Duke of Maine. The medieval Hôtel de Sens had served as a kind of headquarters for the Leaguish plots. Most of the favorites of the last Valois king—d'O, Gondy, Vitry—had installed themselves there, as had the Jesuits who built Saint-Louis. Gardens stretched back to meet each other; the new streets were wide enough to let carriages pass. Though the least medieval section of Paris in 1600, several monasteries, the Hôtel de Sens, the Bastille, and the Temple still assured the inhabitants that they were in the old city. The Temple was a walled-in, turreted, and crenellated fortress that served as a residence for aristocrats, artisans, and debtors seeking to avoid the police of Paris. Artisans could work there free from the restrictions of a guild because the *grand prieur* defended the independence of the Temple against both the city and the monarchy.

The city was still very sparse west of the Halles. From the north the walls built by Charles V came down abruptly to the gates of Montmartre and Saint-Honoré, to disappear under the Grand Gallery of the Louvre. Outside were fields and windmills, just four or five narrow streets away from Saint-Eustache. This church, begun in 1532, rose high and spacious, reflecting the wealth and status of the merchants west of the Halles, and of the courtiers who lived in the houses and inns near the Louvre. Richelieu was baptized there in 1586, while his father was attending Henry III at Court.

Long fashionable because of its proximity to the Louvre, the area became a European center of art and culture in the late sixteenth century. Catherine de Médicis built a large *hôtel* there, later called the Hôtel de Soissons (all that remains of it is the astrologer's column between the Bourse de Commerce and the Halles), and by this means attracted numerous favorites to an otherwise mercantile and monotonous district of the city.

The rue Saint-Honoré, leading west from the Cemetery of the Innocents to the city gates of Saint-Honoré, was lined with late medieval houses and inns, where courtiers who had to follow the Court stayed when the king was in the Louvre. The Porte Saint-Honoré, with its turrets, drawbridge, and guardians, still stood about where we today find the little square between the antique shops of the Louvre and the Comédie Française. The Hospice of the Quinze-Vingts, founded for the blind by Louis IX, occupied a big piece of land along the street, reaching back to where the rue de Rivoli now is. In addition to the blind, numerous artisans lived there in order to be under the protection of the Hospice and thus escape the restrictions of the guilds. Judging from the inscriptions on the tombs of the Quinze-Vingts, the neighborhood around it must have housed some of the first families to move from commerce into the service of the Crown. Referred to simultaneously as *noble homme,* merchant, and notary to the king, those interred so near the Louvre must have been some of the first *robe* families of the fourteenth and fifteenth centuries.

Several streets ran behind the hospital, between the Louvre and the walls, approximately where Napoleon was to build the Arc du Carrousel.

After demolition of the *donjon* and the south entrance of the Louvre under Francis I, one gained access to the Louvre from the east side, in the rue d'Autriche, which descended from just east of where the Oratoire now stands, down between the palace of the Petit Bourbon and the Louvre, to reach the quay of the Seine. This postern entrance had been built by Charles V as a part of the flamboyant, even fanciful Gothic residence into which he had transformed the old fortress of Philip Augustus. After crossing the drawbridge over the moat and passing under the east wing, one entered a courtyard crowded with people, carriages, and horses. The people had either come out of curiosity or to beg, steal, or otherwise seek their fortune in the Louvre, for the court-yard was open to anyone wishing to enter.

The Gothic walls of the "old" Louvre on the north and east sides of the courtyard must have been in sharp contrast to those facing the Seine and the west. These latter had been built in the last half of the sixteenth century in the Renaissance style. Instead of conical roofs and gargoyles, there was a balanced play of classical columns, windows, and statues carved after the manner of the ancients. These two wings were much as we see them today, though without the more recent central pavilions—the western one built under Louis XIII by Le Mercier and the southern one under Louis XIV by Le Vau.

Tourists from all over Europe marveled at the beauty of these wings, forming an L, designed partly by Lescot and decorated, in the *salle des cariatides,* by Goujon. Judging from the number of travel accounts that include descriptions of the rooms, it must have been relatively easy to visit the interior and even the royal apartments. In both the old and new parts, the rooms on the ground floor were very long and wide, with huge painted beams and supporting cross beams painted with arabesques and monograms of the last Valois kings. On the floor above, the ceilings were even more magnificent, done in the Italian style of plaster and panels, covered with gold leaf and frescoes rep-resenting scenes from classical mythology. Only one of these ceilings has survived in its original place, tastefully restored and made beautiful again by the birds of Braque. Some of the older galleries, with their massive fireplaces and dark, smoked-up ceilings, looked much like the interiors we can see today in the much-restored Hôtel de Cluny, built a hundred years later. Tapestries covered the walls from floor to ceiling. The monu-mental fireplaces and the small windows and doors, cut through here and there at ran-dom, were reminiscent of a fortress and gave these rooms a somber dignity outmoded by the bright, sensual, regular style of the Renaissance wings.

On the south side of the Seine, opposite the Louvre and up a hundred yards from the bank, stood the richest abbey in the Île de France. Founded by Childebert in about 543, Saint-Germain-des-Prés grew under the double aegis of the Benedictine order and royal favor. The abbots were high-ranking feudal lords, usually of royal blood. The Faubourg Saint-Germain, extending from the lands of the Luxembourg Palace west to the Seine, where the Eiffel Tower now stands, was completely under the juris-diction of the abbey court. The monastery contained one of the largest prisons in Paris and was the scene of many public hangings.

Standing almost alone beyond the walls in 1600, Saint-Germain still possessed all the characteristics of a medieval stronghold. Surrounded by a wide ditch, high

The Saint-Germain Fair on the Left Bank. Opening each February 3 and continuing until the Saturday before Palm Sunday, the fair was frequently prolonged. Artisans and merchants actually worked all year long in the roofed-over stalls, which specialized in luxury products such as prints, silver, and scissors. Small theatrical companies, jugglers, magicians, freaks, gambling sharks, and prostitutes vied for the odd change that jingled in purses.

crenellated walls, towers, drawbridges, and gates, the abbey remained as independent of Paris physically as it was legally.

The abbey church housed numerous relics and a vast treasury of altar vessels and manuscripts. Its three towers (only one survives) dominated the entire Left Bank below the "mountain" of Sainte-Geneviève. Within the walls were chapels, a large and a small cloister, a bakery, a refectory, storehouses, numerous gardens, stables, and a new palace for the abbot constructed in about 1690 (now 3, rue de l'Abbaye). Saint-Germain-des-Prés was vast, encompassing many city blocks. It collected revenues from the produce grown by farmers on its lands and from the owners of *hôtels,* who paid an annual *cens* even after they had bought the land from the abbey. Its erudition, aristocratic tone, and venerability still made Saint-Germain-des-Prés a formidable ally or a dangerous adversary for the monarchy.

In 1482, Louis XI restored the abbey's rights—lost in 1176—to hold a fair near the monastery. Beginning a fortnight after Easter and lasting for three weeks, but often prolonged, the fair was one of the outstanding commercial and social events of the capital throughout the *Ancien Régime*. The main pavilion was nearly two hundred feet wide. Its stone walls and massive, high roof sheltered the principal stall-lined alleys, named Normandy, Paris, Picardy, Chauldronnière, Mercière, and Lingerie for obvious reasons. In fact the fair included all kinds of merchandise. Merchants rented stalls and built stands in the nearby streets; the houses all around the fair also contained shops. The fair was a very fashionable and also a very wild place to go. The Parisians showed off their new clothes, while young noblemen would gallop through the fair on horseback, pushing over carts and displays and picking up girls on the way. Saint-Germain's fair was a favorite haunt for pickpockets and merchants selling goods of poor quality. Prostitutes gathered there in search of provincials and Parisians.

Near where the east wing of the Institute now stands rose the Tower of Nesle, where the decaying wall of Philip Augustus ended at the Seine. Though not so high or so strong, as Dallington observed, this still-unbroken southern wall was bordered by a ditch. It stretched south from the Porte Saint-Bernard, just east of where the Tour d'Argent restaurant stands today, encompassing the Sorbonne and the monastery of Sainte-Geneviève and ending on the eastern side of the rue de Seine.

Until the twelfth century, little except monasteries nestled among the vineyards and Roman ruins of the Left Bank. When Abélard fled the buildings of Notre-Dame to escape the jurisdiction of the bishop who sought to drive him out, he settled there near the abbey of Sainte-Geneviève. Crowds of students, excited by his brilliance and radical way of teaching Aristotle, followed him and collected in the open air to hear lectures. Colleges were founded which in 1200 became the University of Paris when Philip Augustus granted it a charter. What had started as an exciting intellectual experience became institutionalized into quarrelsome and competing colleges and faculties. The ancestor of the modern university was the University of Paris.

The University's independence from the Church, and the interest engendered by a new and radical theology taught there, brought about a strong urge to donate money for scholarships and colleges. The University grew rich and the Left Bank became an international community of students and scholars. Parisians called it the *Quartier Latin* because of the habit of writing and conversing in that language which prevailed in the colleges, inns, and streets until the eighteenth century.

The character of the quarter changed little, though there were fewer students in 1600 than there had been in 1300, and the University was less independent and less influential in secular affairs than it had been before the reign of Louis XI. The religious quarrels and the civil war caused the Sorbonne to sink to a new low as an old-fashioned, even reactionary institution of higher learning. The Collège de France, founded on humanistic principles of the study of Greek and Latin literature, had also withered because of the civil war. But at the same time, the new Jesuit Collège de Clermont, founded on a similar classical discipline but with the underpinnings of rigid Catholic orthodoxy, grew rapidly in numbers and prestige. Intellectual discipline prevailed there in lieu of independence of thought or originality of argument; Clermont posed a threat to the medieval schools, but not to their intellectual stature. Though slumbering and losing students to Clermont, the Sorbonne had met Aquinas before.

The abbey of Sainte-Geneviève vied with Saint-Germain-des-Prés in size, age, and wealth. The monks possessed the relics of the patron saint of Paris, who in the year 450 had convinced the Parisians that they had nothing to fear from Attila and the Huns, who would bypass the city. Saint Geneviève had been right. Indeed, whenever a drought, plague, or some other divinely ordained catastrophe descended on Paris, the inhabitants would clamor and pray that the *prévôt* or the king make the customary offering to the abbey, in order to have the relics carried in solemn procession, with monks and representatives from the courts and guilds accompanying them, in hopes of warding off disaster. The influence of these relics upon Parisians remained strong until the eighteenth century, when rioting and speeches came to replace prayers and veneration of Saint Geneviève. The procession would make its way to Notre-Dame while all the bells of Paris tolled. Flowers would cover the streets, and tapestries would hang from the housefronts.

The abbey constituted a typically medieval ensemble of buildings serving every function performed by the monks. The bell tower of its Gothic church, torn down in the eighteenth century, still stands, as do some of the other buildings, now part of the Lycée Henri IV. The parish church of Saint-Étienne-du-Mont was constructed adjacent to it during the sixteenth century. Unfinished until the reign of Louis XIII, Saint-Étienne was already remarkable for its Renaissance stained-glass windows, given by parishioners who were part of the University, and for its *jubé* or rood screen, destined to be the only surviving one in Paris.

North and east of Saint-Étienne-du-Mont a belt of colleges and elegant houses built by judicial families made a half-circle from the Convent of the Cordeliers on the west, which stood just inside the walls from Saint-Germain-des-Prés, to the commercial and bourgeois section of the Place Maubert. Princes, abbots, and bishops had settled there in the fourteenth and fifteenth centuries to be near the Court, and had built fortresslike *hôtels,* of which Cluny is the only surviving integral example from among the many of the same type. Though much restored, it still evokes the flamboyant Gothic atmosphere of the *hôtels* and colleges of the Left Bank in 1600. Many of these buildings, however, were either renovated or were cut up in the sixteenth century. The Hôtel de Fécamp on the rue Hautefeuille, cut up and denuded of gardens and walls, illustrates the fate of medieval houses and *hôtels* on the Left Bank. They must have resembled some of the lanes in Oxford, except for the peppershaker towers jutting out at the corners of the houses to set off and add dignity to aristocratic residences such as Fécamp.

Lawyers and judges were next to settle on the Left Bank. From the fifteenth century, merchants' sons trained in the law began to assume not only the private judicial obligations of the king's vassals but also their duties in the Parlement and other royal courts. These were the ancestors of the *noblesse de robe,* because they were no longer mere merchants and bourgeois, nor were they yet *gentilshommes.* They built *hôtels* around the parish churches of Saint-André-des-Arts and Saint-Séverin. Their residences reflected their wealth, learning, and culture; and though somber when compared with noble *hôtels,* they had the dignity of being designed in the latest Renaissance pastiche of the ancients. Inside, fine libraries, works of art, silver, and furniture provided the owners with a unique environment that was neither simply bourgeois nor an imitation of a noble residence. The rues Hautefeuille and Saint-André-des-Arts were lined with residences belonging to the Loyseau, de Thou, Joly, and similar families, which were really dynasties of judges. The chapels encircling the now-demolished Church of Saint-André-des-Arts abounded with their tombs, one of which—that of the de Thou family—is now in the Louvre. Jacques-Auguste de Thou, with his robes of red marble and his head of white, evokes the bust of a Roman senator, and certainly not by accident. The Church of the Grands Augustins, a convent with buildings vast enough to house the Estates General and the church assemblies, was also a favorite burial place for robe families, who in addition frequently left it endowments. Saint-Séverin was a favorite too, but it had aristocratic and bourgeois parishioners as well, owing to the proximity of the Place Maubert and of the noble *hôtels* to the southeast.

The mixture of colleges and *hôtels* stretched eastward across the rues de la Harpe and Saint-Jacques, to the Place Maubert. There was no social frontier between, say, the rue Hautefeuille, where the judges lived, and the Place Maubert, but only a gradual *embourgeoisement*. Approaching the Place, one found progressively more shops, artisans, and butchers mixed in with the students and clerics, and fewer lawyers or royal officials, especially beyond the Grands Augustins. Furetière (d. 1688) called the Place Maubert the most bourgeois part of Paris. By this he meant that the families living there still behaved, talked, dressed, and married like merchants. Few of their members had adopted the high-blown courtly language so characteristic of social climbers in either merchant or robe families. The families around the Place Maubert were rich, and proud of it. Molière's Madame Jourdain might well have come from their midst.

The frontier between courtly and bourgeois styles was most marked between the wholesalers, who aped the latest fashions and language, and the retailers, who did not. The wholesalers and minor royal officials were a more homogeneous group, taking their cue from the aristocracy and the *parlementaires*. The retailers were something else, at the summit, as it were, of the artisanal and commercial corporations, which were beneath them in status and wealth. The Place Maubert remained more retail throughout the seventeenth century than, say, the districts around Saint-Eustache and north of the Halles.

The Place Maubert witnessed sporadic burnings of heretics in the sixteenth century. Was the choice of this site for burning Protestants, among the bourgeois and the students, accidental on the part of the monarchy, which in good medieval tradition believed that punishments should be public so that the example of what happened to heretics would be publicly known and felt? The stakes and ashes on the Place Maubert impressed students and citizens tempted by Calvinism, but fear alone could not have kept Paris from going Protestant. Fanatical preaching and sober thinking on the part of clergy, judges, and merchants attached to the Crown and to Spain helped give the emotional horror of public executions an intellectual basis.

The circle of abbeys surrounding the Left Bank began again at the Seine, just a few streets east of the Place Maubert. Inside the walls rose the Cistercian college called "the Bernardins," in honor of the founder of the order; and also Saint-Jean-de-Latran, the residence of the Knights of Malta. Outside the walls, and in a location on the east side of the city corresponding to Saint-Germain-des-Prés on the west, stood the abbey of Saint-Victor, where the faculty of science building is now. Ever since the quarrels leading to the collapse of the cathedral school and the founding of the University, the Benedictines of Saint-Victor had been known for their erudition and teaching. Their library was probably the richest in Paris. Rabelais dares to be ironic about the wisdom purported to be in its books, when he has Pantagruel come to Paris to study the seven liberal arts. The giant finds the food of boiled bones from the Cemetery of the Innocents mediocre and the books of Saint-Victor one absurdity after another.

But apart from the new humanistic learning of some judges and theologians, a few Renaissance buildings, and the aping of Romans (ancient and modern) at Court, Paris and the Parisians in 1600 remained about what they had been two hundred years earlier. In taste, buildings, and style of life, this was not by choice. Parisians having the means willingly pulled down their Gothic residences or transformed them in an effort to live in the Renaissance style. Indeed, nowhere can one find property owners anxious to preserve the architectural achievements of their ancestors. Only a lack of funds and of leadership during the sixteenth century had prevented the demise of the medieval city.

An Explosive Political Climate

Paris in 1600 comprised no real social or political community. The Parisians lacked a common heritage, common institutions, and common prejudices and ideals. How many had migrated from villages and seigneuries in search of work or public relief? The population of Paris still did not sustain itself by natural means, by an equal number of births to deaths. Only the influx from the countryside of thousands with their own regionalism and particular interests kept the population of the capital from declining.

To be sure, the people who happened to be living in Paris shared the same bad air, but apart from this and a mutual fear of plagues and the devil, what else did they have in common? Their speech varied immensely, not only because of regional dialects and "foreign" languages such as Breton, but also through patterns of speech peculiar to certain social groups. As late as 1660, Molière still characterized peasants, bourgeois, and nobles by their inflections, pronunciation, and terms of politeness. Furetière, in his *Roman Bourgeois,* demonstrates how persons were conscious, often painfully conscious, of their socially inferior speech. Furetière has the gentleman, in seducing a bourgeois girl, speak the fashionable language of courtship, whereas the girl cannot. But these and other differences might not have counted for much had there been a strong public ethos in Paris to which non-Parisians could conform. This did not exist. Public issues did not reach every group; there were no common taxes or even common sources of food and water.

The Parisians lived in closed, stagnant corporations within a compartmentalized society that was still medieval, elitist, and above all hierarchical. And, of course, the rule of celibacy separated the entire clergy, regular and secular, from the rest of society. How could there be a public ethos when men and women still thought of themselves first as monks, nuns, lace makers, merchants, artisans, or royal officials, and only after-ward as Parisians? These major groups had very little to do with one another, and yet all Parisians, save beggars and servants, belonged to one of them. These groups—clergy, merchants, artisans, and royal officials—lived oblivious to one another in exclusive cor-porations, notably chapters, guilds, and courts. Each corporation had special functions and privileges, guarded from time immemorial, to assure the status and survival of all its members.

The fact that the Parisians lived together deceives those who live in an age when individuals depend so much on one another. Their residences, abbeys, *hôtels,* and even bourgeois houses were built like fortresses, with high walls, barred windows, and iron-reinforced doors. The character of these residences would indicate that the Parisians never believed that the city guards would or could protect their property; it also reflects an extreme distrust for neighbors. Their foodstuffs and water were not procured from common sources. Monks and the *gens de bien,* the men of property, "imported" these products from their farms in the country to consume them in the capital. One never reads of a judge or abbot who suffers from want of bread in a famine. When plagues developed, these same *gens de bien* went their own way to seek survival by shutting themselves up or, if possible, by abandoning the capital for residences in the country until the contagion was over.

Monks, nuns, and the secular clergy—the priests, canons, deacons, and the bishop—made up one quarrelsome major group in Parisian society. The merchants, subdivided into guilds wholesale and guilds retail, and the artisans, each in his or her own guild, formed another; and the royal officials—chiefly from the Parlement and the other sovereign courts, but accompanied by hundreds of lawyers, clerks, and hangers-on—constituted the third separate community in Paris. Each had its own hierarchy, his-tory, leaders, and particular monopoly from which it drew an income. For example, the clergy, headed by the bishop and the abbots of Saint-Germain-des-Prés and Saint-Victor, lorded over the entire clergy and, if necessary, negotiated for its thousands of members with the *prévôt des marchands* and the *échevins,* as the city councillors who dominated the guilds were called. Occasionally the first president of the Parlement came in to represent the royal officials in negotiations with the leaders of the other two groups. Paris was therefore not a body politic but a three-headed monster, whose heads and members, in periods of tranquillity and prosperity, each pretended and acted as if the others did not exist.

When Parisians "rose" or crossed over from one exclusive group, whether royal, religious, or artisanal, to another (as opposed to crossing over from guild to guild, court to court, or chapter to chapter), they hastened to conform their behavior to that of their newly adopted group. In this atmosphere of separatism, heavy with envy and suspicion, there was little place for a public ethos. Dress, marriage aspirations, style of speaking, education, parishes, and cemeteries absorbed the climber soon enough, helping him to forget his past in his new obsession with the quarrels over precedent and functions of his newly adopted group.

Technically, Paris was not a *ville prévôtale* but a commune, a city with a royal charter granting citizens certain liberties. It had no charter of liberties; rather it was under the direct civil and military jurisdiction of the Crown. Royal power, represented by the *prévôt* (not to be confused with the *prévôt des marchands*), had declined, however, but the office and jurisdiction remained to add one more layer to the government of Paris.

The economic and social welfare of the city was left to the guilds, and to a kind of superguild called the *bureau de ville,* headed by the *prévôt des marchands* and four *échevins*. These officials, plus councillors and local officials at the quarter level, moved through a labyrinth of elections and customs. There was no chance for an individual to move up through these offices to reach the top in his lifetime. If the grandfather had started at the lowest level, as a *cinquantenier,* had served in the militia, donated heavily to his parish, and made a proper marriage, the father might become a *dizainier* or even a *quartenier,* the highest office in a quarter. There he would administer the militia, distribute the burden of municipal taxes on bourgeois, inspect the streets, count and tend for the poor, and generally watch over the activities of the quarter. Then, after a lifetime of service, good fortune, and possibly royal favor, he might see his son elected councillor for the quarter to represent it in the *bureau.*

How many families constituted the oligarchy that controlled the guilds and municipal government of the capital? The figure was perhaps as high as two hundred at the end of the sixteenth century. The massive sale of royal offices had increased the number of patricians, as new families moved up to fill the ranks of those definitely assimilated into the robe or the nobility of the sword. For how many generations did a family on the rise maintain some influence in municipal politics? From the time royal offices first appear in a family, usually two or, more rarely, three generations lived and died in the halfway house between patrician and low-ranking legal professional status. Once a family ceased to hold offices in one of the six major guilds, and had divested itself of offices in the royal government having to do with finance or taxation, its patrician status and power were assured. Now that they were patricians, they bought more prestigious royal offices in the law courts or royal offices in Paris that were not restricted to that jurisdiction.

Thus the *bureau* represented only one group of Parisians, the property holders. It was just another corporation, endowed with privileges to regulate trade and to tax, and burdened with providing services such as defense, police, street cleaning, water, building regulations, and facilities for investment, better known as *rentes*. These powers and services are considered primary and crucial to us in the twenty-first century, but in 1600, with France still predominantly agrarian and aristocratic, they were matters to be cared for by inferior men unqualified to meddle in affairs of state, religion, or arms.

Then, too, the *prévôt* and his aides did not have exclusive control over these services. Without exception every jurisdiction overlapped in the government of Paris. The King's Council meddled in its finances, and the governor of Paris (appointed by the king) did the same in military and police affairs, as did the Parlement, Cour des Aides, or bishop on other aspects of administration. The striking thing about municipal government in that age is the persisting confusion of powers and the consequent political stagnation. Parisian politics, with the exception of a few years under Henry IV (1598–1610) and the personal reign of Louis XIV (1661–1715), scarcely ever rises above interminable quarrels over authority. Each official and institution sought to preserve power, principally by stopping all initiative by other groups. Reform, therefore, was condemned as an infringement upon the rights of others. Not even in the grave crises of the League in the 1580s and the Fronde in the 1640s did any Parisian official rise above trying to take advantage of momentary conditions to humiliate his ancient competitors. Everyone remained content with government as it was, with no effort for change.

The problems of the Parisians in the late Middle Ages were quite different from anything known in the modern Western world. The effects, the terrible effects of subsistence living, death by exposure and epidemic, and despair over corrupt taxation, harsh justice, brutal police methods, unemployment, civil war, and fanatical religion, taken all together, cause one to wonder why violence and sedition were not more frequent. Why were there not more outbreaks of stealing, rioting, witch-hunting, pillaging, murder, and rape, considering the terrible living conditions and compartmentalized social life of late medieval times? If there was little notion of public welfare and no strong, centrally controlled police, what kept crowds of illiterate and hungry Parisians from falling on wealthy monks and merchants? What filled the void of social cohesion? Certainly it was not the Crown's direct intervention or police surveillance, and certainly it was not ecclesiastical leadership, for abbots and bishops lived nobly aloof from it all in cloistered forts. True, prelates imbued with the spirit of reform and charity would slowly assume greater power in the church over the century, but in 1600 almsgiving remained little more than routine.

Who or what kept in check the energies of a large, superstitious, and often subsistent, floating, propertyless population? The answer may well be nothing, except that ignorance of other groups and of the wealth they possessed, plus the absence of a common forum for propaganda that kept the Parisians calm despite the scourges they endured. This much is clear: Parisians of every social group accepted as a fact of life the conflicts over essential services for the poor and sick in the capital; the struggles over charities remained similar to those pitting monastic chapter against monastic chapter, guild against guild, or royal court against royal court. The absence of reformist ideas in the slogans of rioters and criminals reflects how politically stagnant and humanly explosive the climate had become by 1600. There were no regularly appearing newspapers to articulate social and political opinions. To cry out "usurer" or to demand justice was scarcely a program for change.

The formal corporate organization of Paris remained essentially what it had been in the thirteenth century. To be sure, some changes occurred, but the Golden Age, the time that in 1600 was looked back to as one of greatness, remained the thirteenth century. Officials spent their time searching for precedents in ancient charters to justify or render needed changes legal. A seventeenth-century author of a handbook on eloquence satirized this tendency by saying:

> What does the King's Advocate mean by amusing himself with writing books? It is a waste of time that cannot be excused. It leads me to believe that the affairs at the *Palais* leave him with a little too much leisure, and that he gets bored with waiting before the Bar. But in addition, what does he want me to do with the first "race" of our kings, and with his Latin about the Salic Law? If he were to send me the marriage contract of Pharamond and the Testament of Merovaeus; or even better, supposing he made me a present of the original Twelve Tablets;

The tavern. The man on the left holding a tankard lewdly touches the woman who is scolding the man at the right. The children play. Someone relieves himself in the corner. A notice glued to the wall states that there is no credit for drinks. The arbor and vine were associated with conviviality and drinking.

of the autograph copy of the Laws of Solon, of the manuscripts of Lycurgus and of Charondas; so many beautiful and rare things would not be enough to awaken my dormant curiosity, would not give me the least temptation in the world to become more scholarly than I am.[1]

But what seemed like idle pastimes was serious business for the jurists. For if some precedent for a proposal could not be found, or if the terms of some ancient charter

1. Obscure precedents, including the Salic Law, were attributed to the legendary French king Pharamond, and to a successor, Merovaeus. J.-L. Guez de Balzac, *Lettres Choisies* (Paris, 1658), Letter VIII.

could not be distorted without raising some opposing party, then innovation was blocked. Consequently little could be solved; litigation went on like waves in the sea, rising and falling with each new generation of officials and judges who earned fortunes by trucking out the same old arguments and precedents all over again.

Only one man, the king, possessed the power to break up this web connecting the political scene in 1600 with several centuries of the past. Precedents could be broken by the royal prerogative, but kings often chose not to intervene or, when they did, they were ignored. Outright disobedience rarely occurred, but laxity of enforcement, "forgetfulness," and delaying tactics made absolute power a feeble thing. Recourse to the king's courts remained frequent in the sixteenth century, and sometimes privileges were revoked, new charters were granted, and the hierarchy and marching order of medieval corporations was actually changed. But this was exceptional. It is difficult for us to imagine the importance of signs of prestige, even to groups low down the scale in Parisian society. Processions and funerals occasioned fully as many fistfights between chandlers and shoemakers as between monks from different chapters and royal officials from different courts.

Preoccupied with foreign war, religious controversy, and managing aristocratic factions, the last Valois kings (Francis II, Charles IX, Henry III, who reigned successively from 1559 to 1589) and their ministers either ignored or pretended to ignore the Parisians and their serious economic and ideological difficulties. Royal councillors, usually the chancellor or superintendent of finance, would mix flattery with blackmail, or at any rate show an interest, when it was time to wrest "loans," higher taxes, or troops from one of the major groups; but apart from this and the processions, Parisians counted for little in the royal administration, focused as it was on war and pleasure.

In levying taxes, royal councillors bargained with the leaders of each group independently, seeking special terms with each, and counting on them not to communicate with one another. But in emergencies a general subsidy became imperative. Then in a solemn assembly of the most powerful clergy, judges, and merchants, the chancellor would present the king's financial needs. More of an occasion than an institution, these assemblies were invariably poorly attended because everyone knew for what purpose they had been called. Under the Valois, assemblies became consultative in name only; decisions emanated from the royal councils.

More important for understanding the Crown's impact on Paris, however, were the notoriously poor public relations of the last Valois kings. Without exception, they treated the judges and merchants rudely, which in itself might not have been significant;

but, when rudeness was combined with a failure to inspire confidence, royal power over Paris declined. As civil war approached under the last Valois kings, royal officials resorted to distortion of the truth. Ministers denied or simply distorted statements and facts that were available and could be verified by the judges and merchants. Now, it is possible to argue that these Valois kings and Catherine de Médicis had the best interests of the Parisians at heart, and that these distortions had become necessary for royal policy; but the failure to inspire confidence, as much as anything else, caused the disintegration of royal power. The royal lie upset the judges, whose minds were caught in webs of precedents and historical truths. What ministers called absolute power could appear as lying to his educated and wiser subjects.

But the worst blunder was that the last Valois kings, particularly Henry III (1574–89) and his courtiers, all displayed genteel largesse by spending vast sums of money on "trifles" and by giving it away carelessly. Meanwhile, their chancellors solemnly harangued the merchants and judges on the need to make sacrifices and to accept cuts in their incomes. Paris was too small for these disparities to remain hidden for long, and for some of the more sober Parisians the question was not moral but political. With a large population living at the subsistence point in the 1580s, a life of courtly splendor was, more than anything else, poor politics.

Though Henry III's own sexual behavior and that of his *mignons* was no more scandalous than his father's or his grandfather's, he faced the fanatical opposition of clergymen and laymen in a resurgent and reformed Catholic Church. The invectives of the priests against adultery, sodomy, and general sexual permissiveness (including intercourse between married couples during Lent) fell as heavily on the Court as on any group in the society. Henry III failed to realize that in fanatical minds intellectual and physical libertinism were indistinguishable from heresy. During the crisis of civil war, with broadsides, pamphlets, and priests to stir up crowds, lewd portrayals of courtly behavior reached more subjects than in periods of calm. The king's life and habits became a matter of widespread concern, because, after all, was he not going to save them from heretics, starvation, and devils? Many thought so. As civil war grew out of Court squabbles, more eyes turned to the king as a symbol of stability and leadership.

Henry III seems to have made no attempt to maintain a climate of assurance and confidence with the leading families of Paris. Like the circle in Castiglione's *The Courtier,* he and his *mignons* seem to have sealed themselves off from the political reality outside the palace. When a *prévôt* or a judge went for an audience with his sovereign, he did not know whether to expect knighthood or imprisonment. Henry III's aim seems to have been to make these men feel inferior by never so much as asking them to sit down, rise from a prostrate position on the floor, or drink in the royal presence. Both Louis XI and later Henry IV, as authoritarian in Paris as any kings, treated these officials with dignity and generosity, to the point of occasionally dining *en bourgeois.* Judges and merchants were used to being scorned as bourgeois, but when their efforts to administer the city collapsed, the collapse invariably followed a period of hostility and humiliation for the city fathers in their dealings with the Crown. These men possessed the highest honors their birth permitted them to attain; they were learned, upright, cultured, and often had more ready cash than the king. Yet the king broke his word to them and treated them as common domestics.

Despite his intelligent and sound education, Henry III never developed the personal authority needed to rule, but this was scarcely his fault. His mother, and former regent, Catherine de Médicis often said that her son the king alone made all the decisions, but in fact she deftly controlled power through the influence of the chancellor and secretaries of state who, when faced with contradictory orders from Henry and his mother, usually opted to execute those of the latter. Appointments to command in the army were countermanded, and ambassadors received contradictory orders; even the king's verbal orders were ignored, thus humiliating him before his household servants. Lost self-esteem, conflicting advice, a climate of suspicion, and his inability to produce an heir despite periods of intense devotion and strident sexual activity depressed Henry to the point that he took violent action.

We shall learn in the next chapter of Henry III's fateful decision to have his household guards entrap and execute the Duke of Guise and his brother, the cardinal. (Absolute royal authority included powers of life or death over any subject.) He also ordered all his principal councillors to leave the Court, thereby ending his mother's shadow powers over the monarchy. A structurally similar *coup d'état* from above would occur in 1617, when young Louis XIII ordered his guards to waylay and kill his mother's powerful favorite, Concini, who held the highest military rank, marshal of France, but who had never commanded in a battle! Louis had his guard seize Concini as he entered the Louvre and kill him outright (execute him!)—after which he would be tried for treason.

The leading families of the *gens de bien,* principally judges and some wholesalers, constituted one homogeneous but quarrelsome group that controlled the royal courts, the municipal government, the parish *fabriques,* and the hospital boards, sat on the royal councils, and played a part in provincial politics as well, because they owned country estates. They had purchased offices, run importing houses, owned *rentes,* lent money, speculated in real estate, patronized the arts, and built chapels to the greater glory of God. Qualified as *bourgeois,* if their offices were of the clerk or *greffier* variety, and *noble homme* (never *gentilhomme*) in marriage contracts, they bound themselves together by their involvement in the affairs of state and by their purchase of offices. But even within this group the drive to form a narrow elite, composed solely of the presidents in the Parlement, the *procureur général,* the *prévôt,* and the *échevins,* tended to raise these men and their families above the others, usually with their hands no longer sullied by commerce.

The women in these bourgeois families, while unable to hold royal or city offices, did much more than assure the morally upright behavior of the members of their household of both sexes, and the servants as well. In seventeenth-century Paris, much of the energy for intense devotional fervor within families can be traced to the strong presence of devout women. They were the principal donors and activists in parish charities; they had a hand in numerous confraternities, and they gathered around the new convents for women to assure their financial health and their success in recruiting novices.

One of the characteristics of a social group tending to form an oligarchy is its compulsive division into councils of, say, thirty, ten, eight, or six, with individuals being co-opted from one to the other until the top consists of a small group of only five or ten men. This general characteristic of oligarchical politics marks much of what went on in Paris, particularly in the progression from *cinquantenier* for one of the quarters of the city, on to *dizainier,* on to *conseiller,* and finally on to the offices of *échevin* and *prévôt des marchands* for the entire city. Another of the characteristics of a social group tending to form an oligarchy is that families tended to remain fixed at a particular level, in a particular council or office, and to perpetuate themselves in power by passing their offices down to their sons or nephews. In Paris, generation after generation, the same families controlled the highest offices in the Parlement, the *bureau de ville,* and the less prestigious Chambre des Comptes. Such families as the L'Huilliers, Séguiers, de Thous, Achilles de Harlay, Nicolays, Bragelonnes, Hotmans, and Hennequins show up on list after list of offices, be they municipal, charitable, or royal, because they were pluralistic and dynastic, forming a single group at the top that joined together the merchants and judges.

But an oligarchy is not necessarily an "Establishment," if the latter implies a tacit agreement by the few to maintain control over the many. There seems to have been no tacit agreement among illustrious Parisian families, but rather efforts to form marriage alliances with equally or even more illustrious families. On the whole, however, they remained divided, competing with one another and respectful of one another, more out of fear and caution than out of agreement. Their elitist minds do not seem to have been closed, intransigent, or uncompromising except on matters of property, offices, *gages,* and *rentes;* when these were threatened by royal policy, they nearly always stood together. Like their English brethren in the Commons, they remained blind to the significance of international politics and war, especially when there was a question of paying for them; but they were more obsessed than the Commons by the desire to maintain unity of membership in their corporations. They feared corporate schism in the Parlement or the *bureau de ville* and were ready to attack royal policy rather than run the risk of splintering the Parlement or the *bureau de ville.*

This fear of schism and the consequent respect for the rules and customs of each corporation also caused them anxiety when the Crown intervened to invalidate the results of a legally held election. Time after time the king would choose as *prévôt* or *échevin* a man who had only the second-highest or third-highest number of votes. Yet the king dared not impose a candidate on the oligarchy, for his creature would have been either ostracized or ineffective as spokesman for the Crown. Hence he chose that candidate who seemed to be the most amenable to royal policy and made him *prévôt* or *échevin.* The Crown's intervention in municipal elections had become customary long before the last Valois kings, but in times of general discontent with the Crown it became still another grievance. Did Henry III come to realize that he was undermining his power by excessively favoring the de Thou family? Around 1580, the de Thous, three brothers, held the offices of *prévôt,* first president, and bishop of Chartres, while relatives such as the Hotmans held offices almost equally as high. Was it envy of the de Thou monopoly of power on the part of other oligarchs that moved Henry to leave the municipal elections alone from 1582 until 1586, only intervening again in an attempt to stop the coup by the League?

But despite its monopoly of power in the 1580s, the oligarchy failed to control Paris. A Catholic revolutionary movement rose up, cutting across corporations and hierarchies to rally monks, priests, artisans, merchants, and some judges into the so-called Holy League and to undermine the oligarchs' power in the capital. Seen from the distance of time, Parisian politics appears as something born out of crisis, out of common needs and fears. If ever Parisian politics was intense and communal, it was in a period of rebellion.

League? This abbreviated name for the Holy League, or Holy Union, was made up of Parisians from all social groups who answered the call of zealous preachers and the heads of the aristocratic Lorraine family. The Guise branch of the family, headed by Henry, Duke of Guise, known by the affectionate and chivalric sobriquet *Le Balafré,* "Scarface," and his brother Louis, Cardinal of Guise, deftly transformed vague reform feelings and fears of disorder and heresy into a powerful faction with considerable military strength. Their supporters in the Church and in various governments extended all over the realm. Guise remained outwardly respectful toward Henry III, but in fact he acted as if he himself were king. In Guise and his faction, King Philip II of Spain saw the opportunity to weaken France's military and foreign policy capabilities, particularly as these were, or were not, deployed in the war in the Low Countries, which pitted the Dutch against Spain. The Holy League, Guise, Spanish support, and papal approval came together in the late 1580s to reduce Henry III's power to the point that the king risked being taken prisoner by his own subjects (the Holy League) in his own capital, Paris.

Then there were issues of general public concern, mass meetings, propaganda, and centralized political power, first in the *Seize,* the Sixteen, the rebel leaders of 1588 and their supporters, and then in the Six, a still smaller directorate drawn from the Sixteen. But how were the oligarchs overthrown, and what was the Crown's responsibility in their undoing?

Religion gave Parisians a rhetoric after fears and anxieties had aroused them from their isolation and mental torpor. The capital was inundated with inexpensive publications, mostly about the Protestant danger and the corruption of the Court. These *cahiers* and pamphlets, however, are lengthy not because of what they say about religion, but from their detailed listing of economic grievances. Bankrupt government, military defeats, failure to pay *rentes* and *gages,* failure to stop pillaging in the countryside, new taxes, increased sale of offices, the high price of bread, unemployment, the poverty of the peasants, the collapse of commerce, the immorality of the age, and the fear of invasion were all spelled out in a heady, fanatical outburst against authority, both royal and oligarchical. The League placed the burden of France's misery and her civil war not only on the king, whom they thought to be a heretic, but also on his ministers, judges, and municipal officers.

The rhetoric of rebellion was quite objectively based on terrible emotional and physical conditions. The Parisians believed themselves to be abandoned by God, their king, their employers, and their customers. Inflation, drought, high bread prices, and the brutality of tax officials and mercenaries made the situation explosive.

These intense, murderous feelings that grew up between the two religious communities arose over the years, as a result of what one community perceived as threats from the other. "Little incidents" such as the beheading of a small statue of the Virgin located quite high up on the corner of a house—too high for it to be a childish prank—prompted questions about what the Huguenot heretics were up to. Was it not their belief that neither the saints nor the Virgin could really intervene with Christ on behalf of the sinner? Windows were broken and manure was smeared on the doors of houses where Huguenots were known to have worshiped. The solemn processions by Catholic confraternities, hooded and flagellating themselves, became frightening in their devotional intensity. Religious from various orders, including the Jesuits, armed themselves, and League militiamen fired their muskets into the air. Preachers aroused the faithful to white-hot intensity by declaring that this was the end of the world and that the Judgment Day had come. Pins were stuck into a doll with Henry III's features, to bring about his death by voodoo. Certainly the few Huguenots remaining in the capital after Saint Bartholomew's Day were threatened and terrorized in every possible way. Ironically, the great League processions taking place in the late 1580s were ostensibly intended to convince the Huguenots of the futility of their beliefs; but their effects were far greater, as they whipped up religious fervor among Catholics who had not as yet joined the League.

If there was a doctrinal divide between Catholics and Protestants, and there was, it was less important as a source of violent conflict than as a force for devotional practices, for example, prayers for the dead. The late-medieval Church had fostered popular beliefs about prayers for the dead, burning candles before the statue of a saint while asking for help in saving the soul of a deceased loved one, and paying for masses for the same reason. These practices were at the very foundation of Parisian religious life in the sixteenth century. The Catholic community stretched from the living through the clergy and prayers, to include the dead, the saints, the Virgin. It seemed "natural" to seek their help for the salvation of a loved one.

Though it was never completely articulated or fully practiced, the Huguenots adopted a radically individualist doctrine regarding prayers for the dead—which were held to be of no utility. They held that, to assure salvation, the sinner was obliged to live a life of faith before death. The dying Huguenot relied solely on the grace emanating from Christ's supreme sacrifice. Perhaps predestined for salvation by an all-knowing God, or perhaps not, the Huguenot could not rely on the prayers of loved ones, or on the intercession of the saints. When Huguenots broke religious sculptures they were therefore not technically committing vandalism: they were doing a necessary act that would oblige sinners to seek salvation by their own prayers and charitable deeds.

The often-quoted remark that the Sixteen—that is, the leaders of the League—"were not of this world" makes them one of the most misunderstood groups in history. Instead of being religious, self-denying ascetics, they were worldly, rich merchants, minor officials in tax administration, and undoubtedly tax farmers or persons who speculated in government tax contracts. Henry III's defeats, combined with the effects of crop failures and inflation on royal revenues, caused "those not of this world" to lose a great deal of money. *Gens de bien* they were, but not, save for a few exceptions, men of the long robe, of the Parlement. The Sixteen and their cohorts seized power in May 1588 in order to oust the judges from their control of the Hôtel de Ville. Having done that, they turned to attack the Parlement itself. They wanted high-ranking royal offices for themselves; this envy became all too apparent to Guise, and later to his brother, Mayenne, who finally had to purge the Sixteen in order to save the Parlement, for he knew there was no hope of his being made king without the judges' support. Nothing could stop the Sixteen from seizing power.

The Parisians had a pathological fear of the presence of troops in the capital. The mercenary army was the scourge of both the land and the city in the sixteenth century. None fighting in the Wars of Religion had been paid what had been promised. These armies and their officers had no choice but to plunder or disband. Royal officials had been informed time after time of the danger of sending troops into Paris, but this advice was ignored in 1588. Henry III ordered troops into the city in May of that year to thwart a plot. The immediate result was rebellion and complete loss of control, defeat, and finally humiliation for the king and the troops.

In 1588, despite Henry's halfhearted support, the quite energetic *prévôt*, Pereuse, had the city in hand and commanded the militia until the royal troops were sent in. Pereuse, representing the oligarchy, certainly had not been in a strong position for several months, but at least he was on top of the situation until the power of the militia melted away into the night of May 12. Governor Villequier and the *prévôt* had quarreled over the strategy to be used in keeping order; but then, in a single night the militiamen left their posts, claiming that they wanted to guard their own houses. Two *enseignes* of Swiss and one of French troops had arrived on the 10th, and late in the afternoon of May 11 two more companies of Swiss and three more of French arrived. Henry made no early effort to explain or to reassure the Parisians as to the purpose of these troops in Paris, and when he finally did he made up something that, for being obviously untrue, added to rather than reduced the anxiety.

On May 12, with the Swiss and French troops strung out on the bridges and beginning to raid butcher shops near the Place Maubert, a clash occurred between the troops and the militia that caused hysteria to envelop the capital. In only a few hours the merchants closed shop, built barricades of barrels, paving blocks, boards, and almost anything else at every intersection and around each quarter of Paris. Paris in barricades became a group of independent fortified areas, where the logistics of the areas and the confidence of the *gens de bien* in the militia colonels actually determined where the barricades were to be built.

Henry III fled Paris, while the *prévôt* and other municipal officials either escaped or were imprisoned. Then the triumphant League, in trumped-up elections, installed their own men in the Hôtel de Ville, purged the militia, and took over the Châtelet, the Bastille, and Vincennes. The royal authority had evaporated everywhere in the capital save in one place, and there it was at once unattackable, unsupported by the Crown, and therefore impotent. This was the Parlement, where, after Achille de Harlay had hoped to make a fight against the League and had failed because Catherine de Médicis had refused to support him, there was nothing left to do but listen to the brilliant oratorical lamentations of Guillaume du Vair. Lamenting the blindness, selfishness, and inactivity of the judges, du Vair clearly illustrates how compartmentalized and explosive Parisian politics were, that is, until a general movement came to sweep the oligarchy's authority away and to render its opposition to royal authority pale and selfish. It would not be long before the League would turn greedily to attack the Parlement itself.

Once the Parisians had barricaded themselves up in quarters, and once they believed their misinformed king had decided to make war on them, they turned in search of some savior, a protector, some leader who could reassure them that there were no troops and that they were not going to be looted. In 1588 this savior was Guise, who immediately after the barricades walked about the capital as if it were his, cheered by everyone. The Parisians would have made him king instantly because he had succeeded in doing what Henry III could never do: exude confidence, good spirits, and fatherly protection.

But the League in power had been no more effectual in solving problems than had been Henry III. Fanaticism was not the same as confidence. Their new *bureau de ville;* the savior, the Duke of Guise; the trumped-up king, Cardinal de Bourbon; and Lieutenant General Mayenne failed to restore order and prosperity in Paris. Trade did not improve, credit was not restored, the Protestants were not all massacred, and the problem of the succession remained unsolved by the "Spanish solution." But deeper, and more telling, religion in the form of daily sermons and penance served only as a temporary substitute for bread and *rentes*. For the moment, the Parisians remained transfixed in fanaticism. A solution had to come from the outside.

The Necessity of a Capital

The history of Paris in periods of crisis is only intelligible when seen in the context of French or, indeed, of European history. The events of 1588 that we have just described occurred as part of a deep national and European crisis of political disintegration and fanaticism. What had caused the Parisian revolt was echoed all across France, and the ultimate reason for the return to stability—royal power—could only come from Paris.

The Day of the Barricades and the establishment of the Sixteen in the Hôtel de Ville encouraged pro-Guise, pro-Spanish, and ultra-Catholic forces throughout the realm. Royal power existed in name only as Henry III fled for his life from the capital.

Broken, destitute, and without an army, Henry reached Blois and promptly called an Estates General. Attempting once more to rally support against both the Huguenots and the League, Henry negotiated with every party. The Sixteen in Paris sent delegates whom Henry III promptly had arrested.

The character of the civil war itself eluded most of the participants. Though individuals talked a great deal about fidelity and religion, from the beginning, almost twenty years earlier, the violence had stemmed from the bickering and rivalry of two or sometimes three great aristocratic families, the houses of Montmorency, Guise, and Coligny. Before 1520 these families, with the exception of the Guises, had been insignificant nobility, but owing to the persistent favors of the later Valois they came to control much of the political power of France. Without apparently realizing it, the kings of France had allowed all the profitable and powerful offices in the realm to fall into the hands of a few men. By the 1570s the Guises controlled the army and much of the Church, as well as entire provinces, towns, and hundreds of castles. Loyal to the Guises, the military forces were unwilling to do the bidding of the king who paid them. Catherine de Médicis had sought to control the Guises and other families by playing them off against one another, making them compete for royal favor; but instead of strengthening royal power, the religious fanaticism and foreign subversion by Spain strengthened the Huguenot and the Guise ultra-Catholic factions until they were as strong as the state.

In the chronicle of events for more than twenty years, the war itself became a ceaseless flux and reflux of campaigns, maneuvers, treachery, and commanders changing sides. This was not total war but annual marauding involving paid troops under the control of commanders who had in mind their own fortune rather than national or religious aims. In the society as a whole the nobility had, at least in numbers and wealth, a small basis of support. But there was no other force, either military or civilian, that could succeed in restoring peace without a changed political and religious climate. A military solution proved to be impossible. Henry III, Guise, Henry of Navarre, and countless lesser nobles, each of whom had the freebooter or *condottiere* in him, sought military victory, while the vast majority of Frenchmen watched on the sidelines, shifted allegiances and even religions more readily than historians have previously thought, or suffered from the presence of barbaric, pillaging troops in their fields and houses.

Henry III struggled vainly to stand between and surmount these factions, but he failed. He created a new chivalric order whose members had to swear fidelity to him and strict adherence to orthodox religion; but oath-breaking seems not to have bothered these power-hungry noblemen. Henry also promoted rapidly into the high nobility some young and promising men who would be obedient to him, his *mignons* as League members called them; but this group never gained the political force necessary to counterbalance the Guises.

Henry also knew that in combating the Guises he was attacking Philip II of Spain, who had infiltrated the League and was supplying it with money. But his knowledge helped him little, for he proved incapable of rallying the traditional, patriotic forces in the realm, namely, the judges and merchants of the third estate. Plans for 1588 were grandiose: a great Armada would sail from Spain, destroy the English fleet, and supply the Duke of Alba with money and supplies to deal a knock-out blow to the Dutch rebels.

Trying once more to rise above the Guises and impose his will on France as a Catholic king, Henry declared to the assembled Estates: "Certain *grands* of my kingdom have formed such leagues and associations as, in every well-ordered monarchy, are crimes of high treason."

The Duke of Guise, sitting beneath Henry when he spoke these words, accepted the challenge and, by a clever device of proposing a solemn edict of union, once more thwarted Henry's attempt to restore royal power. The king suffered defeat at Blois almost without his subjects' knowing it, for the political issues had become so confused that delegates believed they could simultaneously support Henry III and Guise. The responsibility for the prevalence of such an illusion must be laid to Henry, for either out of social snobbishness or out of lack of political acumen, he failed to make clear to the delegates that they had to choose between their king and Spanish-aristocratic disorder.

Beneath the thick veneer of religion lay the cunning and reason of state of sixteenth-century court politics. Mentally severed from subjects and vassals, Henry III and Guise both tilted on without regard for public opinion, traditional morality, French interests, or chivalric decency. Guise deceived or ignored his League partisans in Paris as much as Henry III mishandled his most loyal subjects. Having narrowly escaped Guise's clutches in Paris, and still smarting from his defeat at the Estates, the king resolved to have Guise assassinated.

On the morning of December 23, 1588, Henry staged the assassination. Invited to attend a royal council, Guise was stabbed by gentlemen whom Henry had admitted to the chamber and whom he had provided with daggers. With Guise lying before him, cut to pieces, Henry is reputed to have said, *"Le roi de Paris est mort"* (The King of Paris is dead).

If Henry III had consciously tried to increase the power and unity of his enemies in the League, he could not have committed a more efficacious act. All over France and particularly in Paris, the assassination of Guise confirmed in the minds of the ultra-Catholics that Henry III was indeed a heretic. Their savior had died a martyr, trapped and murdered by Henry. The fanatical Sixteen in Paris purged not only their own enemies, the persons loyal to Henry III, but also those seeking to be neutral. Scarcely anyone save the fanatical League members could be sure of his life and property after the assassination of Guise. Again the question is, why did not Henry foresee the consequences of such an action? The answer lies in the indifference, brutality, and isolation of a tiny group, the Court, which, though theoretically invested with supreme power, lost all sense of political reality. To rule Paris and France required more than a life of pleasure, conversation, hunting, and letter writing.

The balance of forces had long since tipped against Henry III, but after Guise's assassination he had no recourse but to ally himself with the Huguenot leader, Henry of Navarre. Together the two heretic kings marched toward Paris, each outwardly friendly and inwardly suspicious of the other. Soon after the beginning of their siege of League-controlled Paris in the summer of 1589, a Dominican monk named Clément asked for a private meeting with Henry III. The monk bent over to speak intimately with the king, thrusting a dagger into his bowels. The surgeons said it was only a superficial wound, but in a matter of hours it became clear that Henry III would die. Henry of Navarre visited him and received his blessing. Then, after the dying king had obliged the nobles present to swear to accept Navarre as their lawful king, he beseeched Navarre to become a Catholic.

The Parisians received the news of Henry III's assassination as if they had known it would happen at any moment. The outburst of delirious celebrating that followed should have shocked all of Europe, had not most countries been undergoing similar catastrophes. Henry III had been stabbed by a monk. Everyone sang the praises of the Dominican order for its remarkable son, who had delivered them from a heretic king and tyrant. Had not Clément received orders from Heaven to put the knife to the last Valois?

The king's assassin, who had himself been murdered by the king's guard, now became a hero and martyr. Sermons in his honor were preached throughout the capital, and in churches candles were lighted around hastily carved statues of the "liberator." Clément's mother was invited to Paris, lodged in the *hôtel* of Madame de Montpensier, presented with gifts, and honored by the Sixteen for having given life to such a holy man.

The Parisians celebrated collectively the assassination of their king, whom they condemned on false grounds. Henry III was not a Protestant or in any other way a heretic. We have seen that as a monarch he was a failure, but since when had incompetence been a basis for regicide? Henry was heirless and virtually powerless when he extended his recognition to Henry of Navarre. But the Parisians were neither interested in the subtleties of power politics nor sympathetic to the dead king's efforts to steer a middle course between two powerful religious and revolutionary forces in the realm. They wanted no balance; only victory over heresy interested them.

Henry III's assassination caused France to cease as a state, and to dissolve into territories more or less under the control of revolutionary parties. There was no prince to crown. The Leaguers wanted either a Hapsburg prince or the coronation of old

Cardinal de Bourbon, who would have been a tool in the hands of Philip II of Spain. The Protestants wanted Henry of Navarre, the dead king's own choice; but the Parisians believed that he was subhuman and an agent of the devil.

For the moment the hero of Parisian crowds was the Duke of Mayenne, brother of Guise, who wanted very much to be king himself, but who possessed enough political acumen to know that opposition to him was too strong in other parts of the realm to have himself crowned. He knew that France was more than Paris, and that in order to become king he would have to defeat Navarre's forces without much help from Spain. Soon after Henry's assassination, Mayenne found himself in just such a predicament of trying to gain national approval without Spanish help or Protestant support.

Contenting himself with the pretentious title of *lieutenant général de l'État royal,* Mayenne—principally aided by the Church and Spain—raised the money and arms needed to campaign against Navarre. His activities, like those of all leaders in the civil war, show an energetic and an extremely subtle political sense. Not an element, psychological, personal, or institutional, was missing in the play of forces produced by all parties, which was in strange contrast to the wild, spontaneous behavior of mobs and armies during the war. Navarre and Mayenne sparred with each other, half hoping for a political victory and half trying for a military victory.

In March 1590, Henry of Navarre defeated the French Catholics and their Spanish allies at the Battle of Ivry. Victory for Protestantism seemed at hand. A Huguenot prince was conquering France without abjuring Calvinism. After Ivry, only one great obstacle remained; Henry prepared to overcome it by following the strategy that wars were fought "not with walls but with men." Paris had to be conquered. Bewildered by defeat at Ivry, the Catholic Leaguers saw their only hope for salvation in the walls of Paris.

Ivry was four days' march from Paris. Henry dallied, perhaps overconfident, perhaps waiting for more troops from the South; but his purpose was to conquer Paris. The allegiance of its citizens, judges, and financiers was necessary if he wished to become King of France. Paris stood alone, with no army between her and Henry of Navarre. The Parisians, certain that, come what may, God and the saints would never permit a heretic king to walk their streets, prepared to defend their city. Hour after hour priests and fanatics prepared the rich and poor, noble and beggar, for a trial sent from God in the form of a siege. The devil incarnate was Henry de Bourbon, King of Navarre, and heir to the vacant French throne.

Henry attacked the Faubourg Saint-Martin, the northern side of the city, early in May 1590 with twelve thousand troops. The Parisians turned Henry's invasion into a rout. After this defeat, the only strategy left for Navarre to pursue was starvation. He camped and waited for conditions in the town to deteriorate, forcing the capital to sue for peace.

By July, horses of fine quality, donkeys, rats, cats, dogs, grass, tallow, and skins were scarce inside the walls. Cannibalism broke out; women told their husbands that they "would prefer to eat their children than to surrender for lack of food." The League reportedly ordered that bones stored in the charnel houses of Parisian cemeteries be ground up and added to the bread. Henry's army grew in strength, but the walls, guarded by monks and diehards, stood between them and any compromise with the Parisians. The city hung on as Europe watched.

The Duke of Parma, commander of the Spanish armies in the Netherlands, decided to save Paris from certain submission to Protestant Frenchmen. Parma marched south. Henry, with his smaller and inferior army, now understood that walls had prevented him from becoming King of France. Bourbon troops withdrew, Parma sent food, and Paris was saved—unconquered, righteous, and certain of Spanish victory.

Henry de Bourbon had failed to conquer Paris. He had made a maximum effort, but, like Philip of Spain, he lacked the forces needed to impose his will on Paris. Neither party succeeded in its aims; neither Counter-Reformation Catholicism nor Protestantism was acceptable to Paris.

Time and severe hardship finally broke the alliance of ideology and violence. As is often the case when warfare and rebellion cross national lines, only time could break the jumbled ideas and armies into pieces that could be put together in different ways by moderate leaders. Frenchmen had been killing each other to the detriment of the nation and to the advantage of the king's "true enemies." But until Henry of Navarre abjured Protestantism, and Paris was conquered, the party of the *bons Français,* a party of compromise placing France above religious quarrels, made little progress.

Three years of skirmishes, negotiations, hardship, and broken promises followed. They seemed necessary to break the deadlock. Patriotism revived in France and even in Paris, where people were becoming fed up with Spanish ways. The *politiques,* the *bons Français,* grew more numerous and more powerful. But still something more was needed.

By the summer of 1593, Henry knew that he must abjure his Calvinist faith if he wished to become King of France. His own salvation preoccupied him little, but he realized that, were he to renounce Protestantism too quickly, his Catholic subjects would mistrust him all the more and would accuse him of being Machiavellian and insincere. After a suitable delay, a ceremony was arranged in which he would become a Catholic. Henry stood before the Basilica of Saint-Denis, where, after being received into the Catholic Church, Roman and Apostolic, he heard mass and knelt among the tombs of Dagobert, Philip Augustus, Louis IX, and Philip the Fair. Ceremony followed ceremony: soon afterward he was crowned and anointed with holy oil at Chartres. But neither the oaths nor the blessings were enough; Henry knew that only the acclamations of the Parisians would make him truly king.

In March 1594, Henry's Parisian followers grew bolder. They left two city gates open for his troops. At about 6 A.M. on March 22, Henry IV appeared at one of them, riding slowly toward Notre-Dame. He proceeded solemnly to the cathedral. There, while he heard a *Te Deum* sung, Henry's followers ran through the streets, proclaiming the king's arrival and promising peace and amnesty to all. Then the king bravely went through the streets, jostled and greeted by the curious, who poured out to see him. *Vive le Roi!* was heard over the tumult. Spanish troops filed out of the city almost unnoticed. Some Parisians were surprised to find Henry quite human, normal physically, and friendly, for the preachers had not portrayed him that way. At the time, nobody knew that peace and the Gallican monarchy had been reestablished in France. Rebels were in the wings with plots and Spanish gold, waiting for Henry IV to blunder, but he did not. The war dragged on for four more years, but Henry was now the only solution; partition was impossible, for France was something more than just a name for a few jealous provinces. Was France to become another Germany?

Living conditions in the capital had become unbearable. The siege, mob violence, and the continual guard duty imposed on many citizens had caused shopkeepers to shut their doors and workers to cease producing even the necessities of life. Commerce, according to L'Estoile and other contemporaries, had ceased when the siege made land and river traffic impossible. Henry's first act had been to show his fidelity to the Catholic Church, and virtually his next was to order that shops reopen and work resume. Soon the pope's acceptance of Henry's conversion would help mollify the Catholics.

During the decades of war and rioting, the city's survival had become endangered by the neglect of public fountains and streets. With each year of the war, contamination of water supplies increased and the peril of epidemic grew greater. Plague was an annual occurrence in the last years of the sixteenth century; and even though responsible Parisians knew the water was contaminated, the municipal government did not prove up to the task of restoring the fountains to good working order. Many fountains had ceased to flow at all, and in others the conduits leaked, flooding cellars and privies

Henry IV enters Paris, March 1594, contemporary woodcut. Surrounded by troops in armor, the king rides through narrow streets to attend mass in Notre-Dame, seen in the distance.

in nearby houses. For lack of water the Parisians turned back to the old wells and river water, both of which were contaminated.

The streets were covered with a thick mud of decayed garbage, ashes, urine, and feces, animal and human. The uncobbled streets of the city became impassable during rains, and even on the paved streets the holes were so deep and full of mud that horses risked breaking their legs in them.

The registers of the *bureau de ville* covering the years 1595 to 1600 reflect the *prévôt*'s preoccupation with these problems, but lack of funds blocked even the most essential

projects. Officials knew what had to be done, but being independent of public facilities themselves, they saw no reason to tax themselves for the general welfare of Paris.

Henry intervened to coerce the bourgeois to rebuild Paris as soon as his own position was secure. By 1600 he had achieved peace with Spain, and the Huguenots had
quieted down in their demands after the Edict of Nantes two years earlier. As ex-
Leaguers struggled to forget the spiritually and politically intoxicating events of the
1580s, the Edict of Nantes could only mean defeat. The clauses guaranteeing the
Huguenots the right to worship, own property, and hold office would have little
effect on the remnants of a community that had survived the Saint Bartholomew's
Day massacre in Paris. On March 11, 1601, the very day Henry IV received news that
Savoy too had signed a peace treaty, he informed the *bureau de ville* that "now that
there was peace, we must look to beautifying the kingdom, and principally to com-
pleting the work begun by his predecessors, the Pont-Neuf and the fountains."

Henry IV shied away from being an overt innovator, for he knew that his subjects
would respond more quickly to projects evoking the past or earlier beginnings.

The registers of the *bureau* from 1600 on record the burst of activity that followed.
The monks of Saint-Martin-des-Champs received orders from the city fathers, at
Henry's instigation, to repair their fountain, lest it be repaired for them at their own
expense. Paving contracts and orders for repairing walls, fountains, bridges, and royal
residences demonstrate Henry IV's leadership in building the capital. The city fathers,
still dragging their heels and vainly seeking to avoid paying the bills, suffered defeat
after defeat at the hands of this strong monarch.

PART TWO

Foundations of Modernity

FOUR

Early Bourbon Absolutism

Henry IV's victory over Paris in the civil war marked the end of what little independence and pride the bourgeois had maintained in the late Middle Ages. They were finished. Participation in city politics, tainted by the League, diminished family prestige in the eyes of those who had gone through the civil war; new families waited, testing the wind, before committing themselves to municipal rather than royal careers in politics. What had been confused before the civil war had now become clear: choosing a career in city offices, except for diehard families, meant a slower climb to higher status through royal offices (that is, non-city ones). The old appeals of liberties for the Parisians against the Crown rang hollow after having been fraudulently magnified in the years under the League. Never again did the ideology of lost liberties serve effectively to rally the Parisians against the Crown.

Henry IV's pragmatic politics in Paris concealed his aim to have absolute control over every aspect of its government. He made few speeches about the theoretical superiority of royal power, or about its divine sanction or supremacy over customary law, but the Parisians soon understood that he believed all this to be true. Henry acted as an absolute ruler. For sheer political genius, Henry was France's greatest ruler.

In Paris his strategy sounded as if he wished to "forgive and forget," but beneath the soft talk Henry pushed hard to neutralize those who would not obey him. When he could not do that, he invariably threw all his weight behind the individuals whom he thought most inclined to serve him. Few were purged and even fewer were publicly rebuked. The cohesion of the *corps* permitted neither. Except for the Jesuits, banished in 1594, men of the League found their places in the *bureau de ville,* Parlement, and other institutions. Not even the University was purged. Henry seemed to remember the positions and acts of every city father; he knew who their relatives were, their wives, their favorite charities, and, most important, their religious predilections. His letters are filled with references to the most infinite and intimate details on the character and life of anyone of political importance. This knowledge came naturally to him, permitting him to judge the political climate of Paris, to know what he could or could not do without stirring up trouble.

Fond of reminding the Parisians of the years of misery and hardship caused by the civil war, Henry consciously posed as a symbol of force and leadership to all. This device of reminding them of their past condition and mistakes served to humiliate anyone having notions of challenging his leadership. Every year, on the anniversary of Henry's "conquest" of Paris, the *prévôt des marchands, échevins,* and the entire *bureau de ville* received orders to attend a solemn *Te Deum* for the deliverance of Paris from the scourge of civil war. Henry noted who attended and who did not through observers, for he never went himself. In effect this *Te Deum* was a kind of penance for past sins of independence against divine-right monarchy. Similarly, Henry quietly went about rehabilitating the last Valois kings, his "predecessors," in the minds of the Parisians. This enabled him to pose as the legitimate successor to them, and strengthened the power of the monarchy.

At the end of the civil war, Paris was in terrible physical and mental condition. Buildings were falling down, roofs leaked, fountains had ceased to flow, ashes, manure, and garbage lay piled up and decaying in the streets and courtyards. Some of it had been there for years. The siege had uprooted and divided families, ruined merchants, and disrupted the arrival of foodstuffs in the city. Hospitals, poor houses, and schools run by the religious and subsidized by the *bureau de ville* had seen their incomes cut by more than half in some cases by civil war and international inflation. Patients went uncared for and even unfed at the Hôtel-Dieu, Paris's great central hospital, because there was not enough money to buy grain at the exorbitantly high prices. In this paralysis caused by spiritual conflict and physical depravity, Paris faced the imminence of more bread riots and pillage, which throughout the siege had been constrained by sermons and Spanish troops. Henry had "conquered" a city on the verge of starvation and massive civil violence.

The modern capital, established by the absolute power of Henry IV, was born in this crisis and because of it. The old centers of power, now so weak and discredited,

Henry IV. The king wears armor, a starched ruff, and the cross of the Order of the Holy Spirit.

dared not resist the imposition of absolute power. Henry trampled on merchants, clergy, and his own royal justices in order to get the necessary functions in Paris going again. The most important acts of absolute power were Henry's control of the police, criminal courts, press, and sermons. As feudal lord, the king theoretically controlled all except the sermons, and he had no intention of allowing vital functions to be controlled by League diehards.

One of the often-unnoticed reasons for Henry IV's success in Paris was Jean Séguier, the Civil Lieutenant. He had remained at least nominally in charge of all these crucial administrative functions. Pragmatic, above the ideological struggles, Séguier had sought to maintain law and order. After the "conquest," Séguier came over to Henry's side, and thus the new king gained control of the most vital services for maintaining law and order in the capital. Thanks to Séguier, Henry's first orders of curfews, guard duty, food and water regulations, and restrictions on public gatherings had some chance of being enforced. The Châtelet, or central criminal courts and prison, thus came under Bourbon control. The rest of the capital would soon follow.

In 1552 Henry II had established the legal body known as the *présidial,* under the authority of the *prévôt* of Paris; but this congeries of jurisdictions became familiarly known as the Châtelet because its courts and prisons were in the old castle with that name, situated at the northern end of the Pont-aux-Changes, whose southern end led to the *Île de la Cité.* An officer known as the "civil lieutenant" had jurisdiction just one jurisdiction below that of the Parlement; and a bevy of judges, *commissaires,* notaries, and *procureurs* reported to him on matters both criminal and civil.

A family quarrel or a brawl in the streets or in a cabaret typically prompted the immediate call for a *commissaire* to come and take evidence from the parties involved and from witnesses. Like the militia colonel, a *commissaire* could order someone arrested and detained, pending further charges. *Commissaires* were required to live with their families in the quarter to which they were assigned. Gowned and followed by a clerk carrying a quill pen, paper, and ink, and by a valet, the *commissaire* was considered to be on duty at all times of day, throughout the year, though in practice *commissaires* shared their responsibilities with a colleague and therefore could often escape to their small country houses during the summer heat, like virtually all higher-ranking members of the nobility of the robe.

The civil lieutenant was the single most important royal official in Paris. Descending from the feudal *prévôt* of Paris and nominally under the control of the Parlement, the civil lieutenant's jurisdiction grew rapidly under Henry IV and his successors. The power of the *prévôt des marchands* to influence the civil lieutenant's decisions declined in the seventeenth century as royal power increased. For some decades after the civil war, the offices of civil lieutenant and *prévôt des marchands* were held by one person, François Miron being a good example.

When Séguier died in 1596, Henry named François Miron to succeed him. There had been no safe Bourbon candidate for this critical post, but Miron was the best of the lot. *Maître des requêtes* in the Parlement, he had fled the capital rather than submit to the League. Miron's greatest qualification was that his father had been a civil lieutenant, who, it was rumored, had been poisoned. Henry needed someone who had influence with the *gens de bien* and the Parlement. Miron had the confidence of both.

In December 1596, about six months after taking office, Miron had to prove himself. One of the wooden bridges spanning the Seine, the Pont-au-Meusnier, collapsed, throwing its 160 or more inhabitants into the river. The bridge had been swept away by currents many times. Earlier in 1596, an alert, probably a tremor, had occurred, and the *voyers* or municipal inspectors had warned the owners of houses on the bridge that it might collapse. The owners themselves must not have lived on the bridge; at any rate they did nothing to repair it. When the *voyers* charged them with negligence and took them to court, the owners made appeal after appeal to avoid the costs of repair.

When the bridge finally collapsed, Miron himself took charge of the rescue operations. He ordered guards placed over all the wreckage to stop pillaging and then began the task of prosecuting the guilty parties, the owners of the bridge. The incident might have set off a general riot.

Miron also imposed restrictions on the bearing of arms in the street; he enforced old restrictions on begging, prostitution, and other petty crimes. He attempted to improve conditions of prisoners in the Châtelet and, above all, increased facilities for the sick and indigent at the Hôtel-Dieu.

Every summer, Paris became plague-infested and was faced with a shortage of food, particularly bread. Miron undertook to raise money to pay for care of the sick and destitute. Lacking the authority to tax, early in his efforts Miron had to rely on the cooperation of the *prévôt des marchands* and religious, the former to find the money and the latter to supply the facilities and labor to care for what amounted to from five thousand to ten thousand, perhaps more, sick and dead Parisians. Lacking resources to care for themselves, the sick stormed hospitals, convents, and the residences of the rich in search of aid. Conditions grew worse—almost uninterruptedly from the summer of 1596 to the summer of 1605.

Even with the free labor of the religious, welfare costs went way beyond what the taxable property holders, the bourgeois, were willing to pay. The *prévôt* had, on several occasions, assessed special taxes for the relief of the poor, but the demand still far exceeded the available care. Bourgeois and "persons of quality," including some living on the rue Saint-Honoré, refused to pay these emergency taxes. The lists of persons owing back taxes lengthened even while epidemics ravaged the poorer Parisians.

Faced with this emergency, and recognizing the failure of the *bureau de ville* to meet it, Miron turned to the king. He made a special plea for funds. One courtier stated that "he had never heard of raising money for the administration of the city, and that

The Baker's Cart, by Jean Michelin. Bakers from small towns around Paris, such as Gonesse, regularly baked bread and carted it into the capital to sell at lower prices than the bread made by city bakers. The woman has made wild-rose water and has collected herbs to sell for "pin money." The man at the left has a frame for carrying bread, or perhaps firewood. Note the torn clothing, a characteristic of poverty noted by foreign observers. The Metropolitan Museum of Art, Fletcher Fund, 1927)

this proposition was new and impertinent." But Henry granted relief, this time to be administered directly by Miron.

These years of crisis kept the Parisians aware of the need for royal power. It was indispensable to the welfare of the capital. During these years Henry IV arranged several ceremonies at which every *corps* was requested to be present. Either he or his chancellor reminded the Parisians of how God punished sinful men, chiefly by "withdrawing their kings." They got the point. Already the *menu peuple* looked to Henry for help; it remained for the *gens de bien* to learn. In the case of the administration of welfare, as in others, Henry IV did not so much undermine the old administration of the city as replace it through Miron after it had proved inadequate.

By cooperating with the Parlement, Miron also managed to weaken the Sorbonne's control over the censorship of books. There were test cases, bitter quarrels, threats of appeal to Rome, and no clear victory in sight, but at least Miron began to reassert royal control against the learned doctors who were very pro-League. Censorship actually came to be a secondary issue in the debate over whether the decrees of the Council of Trent should be published in France, and whether the Jesuits should be permitted to return. Henry IV managed to find a middle course by rejecting the former and accepting the latter. Then with Jesuit help and Gallican support from the Parlement, the censorship of books became a royal function. Miron cooperated too with the Parlement in ostracizing inflammatory preachers, this time by claiming that their harangues endangered public tranquillity.

The next major victory of absolute power was control of the *bureau de ville* itself. Here the strategy had to be different. None of the offices was royal. The key, of course, remained control of the elections, chiefly those for *prévôt* and *échevin*. Earlier kings had nominated city officials by "suggesting" the names of certain patricians to outgoing officials, but Henry IV's consistent control was much tighter than even the "tyranny" of Louis XI or the sneering disdain of Henry III. He manipulated every election, and when someone who displeased him was elected, Henry simply refused to give the oath of office to the lawfully elected individual and presented someone else to the city as duly sworn in. A note in the *Mercure François* of 1606 made public what members of the *bureau* had known since the end of the civil war, "that the *prévôt des marchands* and the *échevins* are elected in mid-August, but everything is done according to the king's will."

The emergency over, Henry IV kept right on controlling elections. The crucial years were 1598, 1600, 1602, and 1604, years when Henry's own candidates were elected. After this the Parisians grew accustomed to being controlled.

In late 1599 and in 1600, Henry deluged Paris with orders to: elect as *prévôt* a certain Charmeaux who could be counted on to do the king's bidding; "reform" the *rentes,* or bonds; relieve the city of authority over guarding walls and gates; fix fountains and repave streets; and obey the orders of a newly created official, a *grand voyer* or chief overseer, who alone would authorize planning and construction in Paris. With the first assured, the rest became possible. Together these measures constituted the founding of a new political order in the capital. The king knew what he wanted; not being satisfied simply to restore Paris after the civil war, Henry sought to establish the Crown's complete political control of the city. He had a vision of Paris as an obedient city, beautiful, prosperous, and supreme in the realm.

Henry wanted to save appearances and yet to control the municipal elections. For the election that was to take place in August 1600, he wrote members of the *bureau de ville* in May that "after much consideration, and not being able to discover anyone more capable or of greater merit than President de Charmeaux, we have asked him to come to us so that he could hear what our intention is and our will that he enter into that office . . . we do not doubt that it should please your company that he render to us and to the public the fruit that we hope from him, and that under our grace and favor he should not fear to use his friends' voices to be elected and received in that office in the accustomed manner."

Charmeaux was elected. Henry picked the candidates and left the constitution of Paris intact.

During the civil war, the desperate Valois kings had ordered the *prévôt* to sell additional *rentes*. Even at the time of the sale, their value was dubious, owing to the precarious political situation; hence they bore exorbitantly high interest rates. In an effort to raise money by any means, Henry III had flooded Paris with inflated bonds. Some purchasers bought them in good faith, thinking that they were as safe as in periods of political stability, but most bought them to speculate on the probability that their value would increase.

Then, after the civil war, the question uppermost in the minds of bourgeois, speculators or not, was: Would Henry IV honor the terms of these bonds? Were he to do so, his popularity would increase immensely with investors, large and small, but at the same time such a decision would saddle the Crown with an enormous debt. The drama of a debt repudiation, of a refusal to honor the bonds, was that speculators and *honnêtes gens* alike stood to suffer. Some *rentiers* had received no interest in twenty years. This fact alone accounted for much of the political disturbances among the property holders in Paris. The Valois' failure to pay interest on the *rentes,* much more than any religious or political issue, had caused property holders to sympathize with the League and with artisans. Henry IV had before him the difficult decision of whether to court the most influential Parisians and a rather large number of artisans, or to lay the foundations for the future fiscal stability of the Crown.

In 1599 Henry ordered that the account books for the *rentes* be turned over to royal commissioners for "verification" so that payments of interest could begin. Sully, the king's Huguenot companion in arms and now in charge of finances, then bore the brunt of popular outrage by postponing public decision on what would be done.

About three years after *rentiers* had begun to hope that they would soon be paid, a royal commission produced new registers of all sales of bonds and then proposed to buy up, at drastically cut prices, most of the issues made late in the reign of Henry III. Other issues were canceled outright. *Rentiers* holding canceled bonds had no choice but to burn the parchment and seals they had bought. Bourgeois, judges, clergy, widows, nobles, and wealthy artisans protested vehemently the decisions of the royal commission. The losers joined in a common appeal to the *prévôt* that they had bought the bonds in good faith and were now the victims of injustice.

Bragelonne, *prévôt* from 1602 to 1604, during this period of crisis over the bonds, had been picked by Henry IV and elected with his backing. But as the storm over the bonds developed, he saw his chance to increase his influence and power in the *bureau* and in Paris generally by posing as an ally and supporter of the angry bondholders. Hoping to be reelected on a wave of *rentier* support, Bragelonne protested to Sully and the commissioners, presented a solemn remonstrance to the king himself, and waited to become the hero of the Parisians. Henry recognized Bragelonne's move for what it was, a test of royal power. At election time, the king nominated someone else for *prévôt:* François Miron, who had been doing so well as Civil Lieutenant. Would the councillors and *échevins,* those who lawfully elected the *prévôt,* bolt from royal control and support Bragelonne?

Miron won. The king had his way, and for the rest of the *Ancien Régime* royal control remained unchallenged, except for one election during the Fronde. Miron's brother, Robert, became Civil Lieutenant.

The principle that the *rentes* on the Hôtel de Ville were sponsored by the *prévôt* remained too, but only as a fiction. Henceforth their administration came under the office of the superintendent of finance. Sully was the first superintendent to have them as a regular part of his administration. The control of this important function by the Crown became final. The independent authority of the city government suffered its greatest single defeat in the battle over the *rentes.*

Sully went on canceling *rentes*. Soon after taking office, Miron was confronted by more petitions and threats to riot. He too made a humble remonstrance to Henry, but the tone of his remarks differed from Bragelonne's. He described the economic depression of

Paris and the suffering that cancellation of more bonds would cause. Placing the emphasis on the depression, however, had left the impression that neither the *bureau de ville* nor the *rentiers* had done much to restore commerce and prosperity. By appealing to the king to help the Parisians, Miron turned what started out as a remonstrance into royalist propaganda. In effect he condemned the *gens de bien* for not contributing to the city's prosperity. Henry and Sully made concessions; Miron's reputation survived, for, after all, he had remonstrated. But the outcome assured the cancellation of still more *rentes* and the improvement of the Crown's financial position. General fiscal stability and some decline in inflation became the principal benefits of these operations, something as desperately needed by merchants and *rentiers* as by the king and the artisans. The threats of rioting had not been empty, but public support for the king had proved greater than the appeal of a small but influential group.

Henry IV moved through the capital frequently. He flattered the Parisians in public speeches and, more important, listened to their complaints. Whether addressed by delegates from a guild or monastery, single individuals, or large groups such as the Huguenots or the nobility, Henry listened and appeared sympathetic. His personal magnetism became boundless as political stability reduced the fears in the hearts of former Leaguers, Spanish sympathizers, or diehard Protestants.

Willing to listen to criticism of his own behavior as a person and monarch, Henry posed as father to all the French. He had his faults. Sully scolded him constantly for spending vast sums on gambling and mistresses, but as with other critics, Sully's favor did not diminish because he dared to speak up to the king.

Indeed, it would seem that Henry IV always lost at cards. And he gambled nearly every day. But losing to influential subjects made a good bond of friendship. He may have won more Leaguers to his cause while gambling than on the battlefield.

Sully's objections were based on the expense rather than the moral issues involved in gambling or wenching. Henry had expensive mistresses, like the Marquise de Verneuil, but caught somewhere without Verneuil or some other regular acquaintance, it seems that any woman would do. Genteel daughters, bourgeois girls, barmaids, and peasant girls all might accidentally be requested to share the king's bed. Henry's love for women knew no bounds; neither age, political crisis, nor a new wife diminished his earthy sensuality.

The aristocrat *par excellence,* Henry was honest, generous, gallant, courteous, and spontaneous in everything he did. Nothing, no act or gesture or decision, seemed studied, worked over, or the result of earnestness. He remained natural, supremely sure of himself, and in command without the slightest degree of petulance. He conformed to the rules of the *gentilhomme* and yet forced changes in them. Violence for its own sake was repugnant to him, and he taught or sought to teach that respect for each individual according to his own merits and station was true honor.

"L'utilité publicque" became a refrain in edict after edict. It was his guide in choosing men for office. They could be Protestant, Catholic, or religious neutrals, moral or vice-ridden, noble or common, ambitious or disinterested, so long as they served his aims to the limits their station in society would permit. After the civil war he paid off his supporters handsomely and saw to it that his companions in arms got priority in appointments and pensions, but there is not the slightest indication of his having conducted a blood feud with any family, including the Guises.

His forceful talk about the public interest made it clear that the old claims of the *bureau* represented the narrow interests of a small number of wealthy Parisians. Further rebellion in the name of ancient liberties and independence for the city of Paris became impossible. The patricians hoped that, through obedience and cooperation on the king's public projects, royal funds would be employed to rebuild the city's fountains and bridges. But actually, through Henry's control of the *prévôt,* the patricians had to tax themselves to help pay for the projects he initiated. Through the *bureau,* therefore, Henry extended his power by using the power of the city fathers to tax.

While the king still campaigned against the League in the provinces, and after he had made peace with both the papacy and Spain, Parisians owning large amounts of property, chiefly the judicial and financial officers of the Crown, were rapidly becoming aristocratic in status and manner of living. They became nobles either through their royal offices, or through being elected *prévôt* or *échevin,* or through buying a fief in the provinces. The entire top stratum of Parisian society rapidly evolved from a purely communal, merchant, and bourgeois identity into the *noblesse de la robe.* Indeed, about seventy-five percent of the members of the *bureau de ville* constituted to elect Miron were officials in some royal court. They disliked Henry's absolutism and his violation of the city's liberties, but the majority of them were already more concerned about realm-wide affairs and their personal welfare as newly ennobled judges or secretaries, *procureurs, maîtres des requêtes,* or mere *greffiers.*

Because of this, the sale of offices by the Crown was as important to Paris as any action involving the *bureau de ville.* Henry began selling offices as soon as he had gained political control of France. How many he sold or how much they were worth is still to be studied, but the important fact is that they provided a great opportunity for many ambitious families to climb up the ladder at every level from the highest positions in the Parlement and Chambre des Comptes down to the most minor jobs, such as tax collectors and recorders. The center of this activity was Paris. The immediate result was a further reduction in the prestige of municipal officers at a moment when the stench of the League was still on them.

The Crown's insatiable need for money prompted the creation of new offices in the government, which would not quite be sold, although there was a guarantee that they would remain the property of the individual who had paid the stipulated amount of money. Vaguely defined in the late fifteenth century, this "sale," or "venality" of office as it was called, would be expanded considerably in the sixteenth century, and enormously so in the seventeenth. Virtually all but a few household offices would be venal by the reign of Henry IV. The *gages*—that is, the income from what we would call "interest" on the sum paid for the office—served as a kind of salary for the judge, treasurer, clerk, or sealing-wax-heater who held a venal office.

The king chose to favor the merchants and tax farmers who wanted to become part of the caste of ennobled families in Paris. He sold offices because he needed money at a time when new taxes would have been politically dangerous and disastrous for the economy. Then in 1604 he made both the old and new offices an unequivocally safe investment by permitting their holders to will them to some member of their family, in perpetuity. This edict of the *Paulette,* as it was called, displeased those who had already "arrived" because it guaranteed that the newly created officers would survive among them. If a tax farmer or merchant had the money, he could become a president in the Chambre des Comptes and join the company of the most prestigious families in Paris. If a merchant had only thirty or forty thousand *livres* to invest, he bought a cheaper office and became a *secrétaire du roi* or a *greffier* in some court. By selling offices, Henry IV not only reduced the luster of the old municipal offices but also forced open the closed companies that royal courts had become. The most important moves upward were, of course, made by families already holding minor royal offices, which they sold or passed to relatives when they purchased more important ones. After the *Paulette,* why should a wealthy Parisian strive to become *prévôt*? His tenure of office was customarily four years, if he pleased the king and was recommended for reelection after his first two-year term. Thus the sale of offices became a social foundation for the Parlement's claims to take over the functions of the *bureau.* With royal control, the Parlement's widening jurisdiction, and decreased interest in the holding of municipal offices, the ancient constitution of Paris became a relic cherished by many and respected by few.

Furthermore, this guarantee of their offices by the *Paulette* mollified the many persons holding both bonds and offices. After all, both were purchased, and in a certain sense families speculated in them. The last Valois kings had sold offices right and left to the consternation of existing officeholders, who saw the value of their own investments decline. Henry III had sold offices at ridiculously low prices, and many of those newly created offices offered little prestige or income. Coming together as they did, the *Paulette* and the liquidation of the *rentes* solidified the allegiance of aspiring *gens de bien* to the Bourbon house; at the same time, these measures reduced the wealth and prestige of the oligarchs and high judges. Though Henry IV's leadership assuaged these deep personal concerns of the upper stratum of Parisians, the king himself appeared much more interested in public projects.

Ever since the thirteenth century the Crown had appointed officers called *voyers* to oversee domains and rights, in order to stop encroachment by vassals. In an edict signed at Fontainebleau in May 1599, Henry IV created the office of *grand voyer de France* to oversee all the *voyers;* he named to it Maximilien de Béthune, Seigneur de Rosny, and, soon to be, Duke of Sully, his long-time favorite and adviser.

Sully accumulated three more offices in the same year, being named *surintendant des finances, surintendant des bâtiments,* and *grand maître de l'artillerie.* He thus became the single most important official in France. He could do something for Paris. His powers over the Crown's finances, buildings, and munitions supplemented his jurisdictions over public thoroughfares and construction. The final acquisition of power came in 1604, when the old office of *voyer* for Paris was joined to that of Sully's *grand voyer.* Henry's letter (dated June 1603; it was registered by the Parlement in the following year) explains indirectly Sully's task as Henry saw it: "The long wars that have afflicted this kingdom having obliged an individual to work rather for the preservation of his personal possessions than for the advancement and the utility of common concerns, caused all sorts of public works to be neglected to such a degree that almost none of them still remain intact."

The relationship between private gain and public suffering is recognized. Henry IV saw it as his duty to build public services in the interests of all Frenchmen irrespective of social status or religious and corporate attachments. Numerous political theorists in the sixteenth century argued that the advantage of an absolute monarchy was that power invested in the king might be employed in the interests of all. Henry understood his obligations in ordering public works in Paris, and he also understood that this could be accomplished only *if* individual interests were not allowed to block his initiatives.

In the edict of May 1599, Sully was ordered to "keep his eye on the aforesaid roads and passageways, preserve their open spaces, lengths, and widths, visit the buildings which are over streets and roads, keep the new buildings aligned, and [perform] all other related functions." Here are the elements of a modern city and of planned urban living. The monarchy had the power to override monasteries and noblemen, and it had a program to bring about the orderly construction of streets, houses, and shops according to the interests of everyone.

Sully ordered streets cut through so that carriages could pass and the traffic of merchants' carts would be eased. The carriage was not only the latest way for wealthy people to get around; it was also the latest status symbol. With streets made for them, the well-to-do were pleased. Living on a broad, straight street became a sign of social superiority. The *grand voyer* legislated for the convenience and aims of those having his own living standards and status symbols, thus setting one more precedent that urban planners have not hesitated to follow, either because they want to be respected by those in power or because they unconsciously want to bring the city into harmony with their own social group.

In 1600, on the advice of the *procureur du roi,* the *prévôt* issued a decree *"à son de trompe et cri public"* (to the sound of the trumpet and town-crier) through the streets of Paris, to the effect that all sheds, stands, and shops built out into the public thoroughfare must be torn down; that carpenters and others could no longer store timbers in public ways; that tanners and others could not dry their products in places where it would slow down traffic; and that property owners had to replace missing cobbles before their houses at their own expense. In addition, articles 21 and 22 stated: "All carters carrying and conveying manure, materials emptied from privies, mud, and other filth, are forbidden to unload elsewhere than in ditches and gutters designated for this purpose . . . and also all persons are forbidden to throw any water, filth, or garbage from the windows onto the aforesaid streets and thoroughfares, either in the day or at night, under penalty of two crowns' fine and prison."

The Parisians had heard similar ordinances before, it is true; but, as with every public law, the mixture of education and policing leading to its enforcement had constantly varied. The king and Sully started afresh and in several things, notably in the paving of Paris, found that it was not enough to revive and enforce old legislation. More drastic means had to be taken. Conditions were bad. Sully wrote: "I returned to my quarter in the dark, so drenched by the rain and so covered with mud that I was no longer recognizable." Yet paving, sewers, and lighting would soon make Parisian streets something of a marvel for provincials and foreigners.

Apathy extended to large-scale public works. Some required more power than all of Sully's high-sounding offices actually gave him. Henry IV had to propose to the *bureau* that the Pont-Neuf be completed and public fountains be repaired. Two assemblies, consisting of the *bureau* itself, prominent ecclesiastics from Notre-Dame, the abbeys, and the University, and representatives from the royal courts, were called to discuss completion of the bridge. They had to be canceled because so few attended. This apathy came, of course, from the fear of higher taxes and the unwillingness to levy more. But Henry persisted. The negotiations lasted throughout the spring of 1601. At one point Henry threatened to abandon the entire project because Parisians were so unwilling to pay. Finally a new tax to pay for the Pont-Neuf was levied on every measure of wine brought into the city. This tax struck everyone, to be sure, in the upper groups of Parisian society, but it fell especially hard on those families with lands and vineyards around Paris, who were accustomed to bringing their own wine into the city free of taxes. During the negotiations the *prévôt* dared to ask that the king extend the levy to the countryside to help defray the cost for the Parisians, whereupon Henry replied that "when he wished to tax his inhabitants of the countryside he would do it without them, the municipal officers of Paris."

In affairs of state, Henry did not mince words with the municipal government or with the Parlement. He understood the philosophy of absolute monarchy. Often, however, he had to temporize. The civil war and the collapse of royal power under Henry III had brought heady claims by the *bureau* that it represented the capital, and by the Parlement that it represented the realm. Contrary as these notions were to absolute monarchy, Henry did not engage in an outright ideological or even political battle with either. Content to do what he could to render them obedient, the king strove to recover the ground lost by the monarchy during the civil war. Henry IV lived long enough to sap the strength of those groups that had caused Paris to rebel against Henry III, and to emasculate the *bureau de ville,* but the Parlement was another matter. In 1610, the year of Henry's assassination, the power and claims of the Parlement were as great as ever. This was to have grave consequences for the capital.

The bridge was built. Work was resumed in the summer of 1601. Some time later Henry came down to inspect the work and, seeing the other side of the bridge so near, just across an uncompleted arch, he drew back, ran, and jumped across the Seine, to the enormous pleasure of the workmen and passersby. Other projects went rapidly ahead. Much new paving was laid, at the Crown's expense, and the fountains were repaired.

To increase the wealth of France, Henry and Sully sought to apply mercantilist ideas, largely those of Laffemas, and to build a national economy. (Laffemas was an ex-Huguenot whose mind bubbled with ideas on how to increase French wealth and, in turn, the power of the state.) Obsessed by the drain of gold from France to Italy and the Low Countries, Henry set up high tariffs on all products, chiefly luxury cloths, imported into France. Then, to cut the market for these fineries, the king reinforced the sumptuary laws legislated under Henry II to stop what could be considered the inflation of dress. It became illegal to wear certain silk cloths, buttons, ribbons, and stockings, which were available in France almost exclusively as imported products.

In the sixteenth century the tendency for all wealthy people to dress alike, and to dress like ladies and gentlemen, was very upsetting to France both economically and socially. The effect was to reduce the status of gentlemen, for *parlementaires,* bourgeois, merchants, and money changers all dressed as the nobles did. And worse, gentlemen often lacked the means to keep up, that is, to follow the styles of clothing. They saw themselves surpassed by people who were their social inferiors but who had more means to *"s'habiller à la mode"* (to dress in style) than they. Sully was a staunch defender of the sumptuary laws, mainly it seems for these social reasons rather than for economic ones. His intense disdain for the social climber represented the prejudices of his caste.

Henry IV, however, was more sensible. He legislated sumptuary laws, but—much more important—he sought to found "manufactures" that would supply French-made exotic cloths, furniture, and jewelry so that mercantilist aims would be attained. Sully disagreed. Time after time they clashed over whether fineries should be made available to Frenchmen. Perhaps Sully's Protestant background was more influential on his moral attitudes than was Henry's. At any rate, the mercantilistic legislation caused the king to clash with the city fathers. High tariffs cut down profits for the wholesale merchant, and artisans (such as the drapers) were irritated by the king's insistence on establishing new factories and companies of workers for luxury cloths.

The implementation of a mercantilistic economy showed how regional the French economy still was. Lyons, rich and connected to the international market stretching from Antwerp to Florence, fought the high tariffs, while Tours, less rich and with manufactures that were threatened by foreign competition, favored high tariffs. Cities throughout the realm reacted according to local interests; Paris also took a stand. Though the

LE COVRTISAN SVIVANT LE DERNIER EDIT   LE LACQVAY

Bien que sans mentir ie cherisse   Puis que le luxe m'incommode,   Sur ma foy cette broderie
D'auoir du clinquant dessus moy;   J'aprouue fort ce changement;   N'a desormais plus d'entregent,
Il faut pourtant que j'obeisse   Lacquay sers moy donc'a la mode,   Si ce n'est à la friperie,
Aux defences qu'en fait le Roy.   Et serre cet habillement   Où lon en tire de l'argent

le Blond excud Auec Priuilege du Roy

Conforming to sumptuary law, by Abraham Bosse. Royal legislation forbidding ribbons, silver buttons, and other frills was frequently promulgated but rarely enforced. Here the young man has cast off his beribboned, presumably silken, clothes in favor of a simpler outfit.

subject is complex, it does seem that Paris came down on the side of protection. If so, this would be very significant as an indication of the general political climate of the merchant oligarchy in the capital. Because protectionism implied hostility to the Low Countries, the economic aspect of Paris's pro-Spanish and pro-League sympathies becomes much clearer. League cities were generally protectionist, but often for contradictory reasons.

Shortly after 1600 a merchant from southern France wrote the *prévôt* asking for permission to set up a factory and to train workers for making velvet in Paris. The *prévôt* did not deign to reply for a year, so the merchant sought the king's help. Finally he received permission. The *prévôt* was clearly being an obstructionist. The first, negative reply from the *prévôt* noted that the velvet made at Tours was excellent; and, as it was available in Paris, he saw no reason to set up a factory to make a similar product in Paris.

The wholesale merchants in the capital undoubtedly sought in every way to maintain their control over the high-profit, luxury trade. They saw no advantage in bringing more manufacturers to Paris, because their market for "imported" goods would slacken. Moreover, they themselves wanted less and less to do with manufacturing, or even with retail selling. The wholesaler fancied himself superior in status to both, and indeed he was. The crucial step up from merchant to royal official was most often made as a wholesaler. In the seventeenth century this barrier between the wholesaler and the rest of those dealing in trade or manufactures becomes greater and much more significant. But it was already present in 1600.

Henry IV's efforts to introduce silk manufacture into Paris were slowed by the interested groups in the capital. But he imported artisans, gave them quarters, incomes, and, above all, protection against the guilds. After completion of the Louvre's Grand Gallery, he invited jewelers, silversmiths, carvers, sculptors, and painters to live there and produce works of art, which would be free of the regulations of their respective guilds in the capital. The resistance to these innovations was very great. No wonder that all of Henry's royal manufactures collapsed after his assassination. Few Parisians had any economic or social interest in their survival.

The Birth of Modern Paris

I

Some kings are builders; some are not. Henry IV was a builder. In what was short for a Bourbon reign, Henry revolutionized the concept of urban living, largely by his radical initiatives in Paris. He alone of French kings made the general improvement and beautification of Paris the principal objective of the Crown. No château on the Loire bears Henry's monogram,[1] and the inexpensive additions at Fontainebleau and Saint-Germain-en-Laye resulted as much from his attempt to please mistresses and to complete work already begun as from his own initiative. Nor did he spend his resources acquiring works of art to be hidden away in a country residence where they could be enjoyed only by the Court and visiting dignitaries. What building Henry did was in Paris, and, more important, all his creative energy went into planning and political reorganization in the capital. Not even a great church or monastery stands as the result of his patronage; the Trinity Chapel at Fontainebleau, begun in 1609, after completion of the big projects in Paris, belongs more to the following reign than to Henry's, for he was soon to be assassinated.

Henry IV had come to Paris in March 1594; by September he had begun work on the Louvre and on the tombs of his "ancestors," the Valois kings, which lay unfinished in the abbey church of Saint-Denis. The intent of these projects was obvious: beginning work on the Louvre would give work to hundreds, perhaps thousands, of unemployed artisans

1. Henry started to build at Blois in a new style, but work never went beyond a long arcaded gallery and a pavilion, which collapsed in the eighteenth century.

and laborers. Châtillon, one of Henry IV's engineers, remarked: "The great monarch, Henry IV, intensely admired architecture, and brought it back to life to take on more luster than it had had in past centuries." Such a remark about a patron is typical, but Châtillon then goes on to describe how Henry was "motivated by a just desire to do good for everyone, to provide work, and to increase the incomes of the common people." The king's aims showed a blending of aesthetic, political, and humanitarian qualities. And then the new Louvre, as it rose out of the ground, became tangible evidence of the new power of the monarchy. Building the tombs helped too, for they soothed consciences, reduced guilt, and brought together that party of servants who traditionally supported the Crown. Judges, merchants, and *négociants* would be impressed by these marble monuments, while for Henry IV their iconography and his subsidy blended together, grafting his dynasty onto the dead one.

Though still desperately in need of money, in September 1594 Henry allocated a congeries of feudal dues for the construction of a series of galleries which, when finished, would stretch some two thousand feet between the Louvre and the Tuileries palace. Catherine de Médicis, builder of the Tuileries, may have planned these galleries, and Charles IX may have begun one of them, but it was Henry IV who projected and built the ensemble of buildings connecting the residences.

Galleries had become fashionable, first in Italy and then in France during the early sixteenth century. Virtually every royal palace and residence of any dignity at all had one and sometimes several galleries. Long, high, fearfully drafty and cold rectangular rooms, they served to show off works of art and to hold banquets, ballets, and other court functions. But what Henry built at the Louvre differed from the traditional galleries. By placing gallery after gallery, the effect was to have, at one stroke, the longest and most spectacular gallery in Europe. Any royal guest would be invited to make the trip through them, of course, and would be duly impressed, especially when the monarch was Henry IV, who had a habit of conducting affairs of state when on a walk.

Since this use of art as propaganda was already more than enough reason for the existence of a long gallery, Henry's other possible reason for building it may have been overlooked. Henry III had almost been captured right in the Louvre on the Day of the Barricades. The new combination of galleries offered an escape route from the Louvre and from Paris, permitting the king to leave the city unnoticed by the back way, through the galleries, to the Tuileries, and into the countryside beyond. Tallemant des Réaux, in whose gossip there is always some truth, believed firmly that Henry IV built the galleries as an escape route from Paris in the event of another rebellion. The galleries crossed the city walls, the windows were high above the ground, and more-over, there were, as there are even now, few stairways from the first to the second, or main, floor of the gallery. As an architectural and political precedent, there was of course the *galeria* in Florence, which Catherine de Médicis knew as having been only recently completed in her lifetime. It linked the Uffizi to the Pitti, on the other side of the Arno.

The actual construction was begun at both ends. First the pavilion of Flora, the high, pointed structure with huge monumental chimneys, brought the Tuileries down to the Seine. Then came the Little Gallery, then called the Gallery of Kings and later named the Gallery of Apollo when the original was replaced after a fire in the reign of Louis XIV. Begun by Charles IX, it brought the Louvre down to the Seine, almost directly up the river from Flora. All that remained was to connect the two.

At this point, either through accident or genius, a blunder was avoided. The over-all effect of the Grand Gallery might have been a monotonous, interminable building with uniform roofs and façades. But there was and is (there have been many changes, chiefly under Napoleon III) a kind of controlled decorative variety and structural uni-formity that combined to make a harmonious ensemble. The sheer mass of the Grand Gallery, seen from a distance, imparted to the Louvre a monumental quality that it had not had before, and up close the different orders and variety of decorations broke up the impression of massiveness and avoided a repetitious effect. The order is single or colossal near the Flora pavilion, whereas it is multiple near the Louvre; the pedi-ments, which serve no real structural function, break the roofline into regular semi-circular and triangular forms. But not even these are the same size on the Grand Gallery. Those nearer Flora are larger to blend in with the colossal order. The Lantern Gallery, with its own roof, separated the two parts of the Grand Gallery, dividing the different orders and again breaking up the long façade and roofs. Only the part of the Grand Gallery nearest the Louvre retains some of the original decoration. The statu-ary, garlands, proud *H*'s, *putti,* and columns evoke the so-called Lescot wing of the Louvre, and as such the Grand Gallery must be viewed as the final creation of Renais-sance architecture sponsored by the Crown.

When Marie de Médicis came to France in 1600 to marry Henry IV, she found the Louvre dark and full of "vile" furniture. Something had to be done. Sully called on Antoine de Laval to refurbish some apartments and to make designs for decorating the new galleries. Laval's plans for the Little Gallery, which were carried out, made it a kind of pantheon of Old Testament prophets and kings, classical gods, and sixty-three

French kings, all depicted together in painting and sculpture. Laval believed his creation came "close to that which the Romans observed . . . and which Vitruvius calls Megalography." The effect was that of a hero gallery where French kings were raised to both Christian and pagan divine status.

Henry built for his own glory, certainly, but there was always something more sober, less expensive, even more useful about the results than the work of the last Valois kings, or, for that matter, the work of his successors. For instance, the king installed artists and master craftsmen in the lower Grand Gallery. This vast cavern of vaults, once divided by partitions, made excellent studios and decent living quarters for the artists whom he patronized. Their installation in the Louvre and their special treatment by the king caused animosity to swell into open quarrels between these artists and their counterparts in the guilds. In 1608 Henry regularized the status of these artists and granted them special protection from other artists belonging to guilds.

Unlike most Renaissance princes, who either accepted as true the flattering dedications written to them by poets or who claimed to make the arts flourish through their own standards of taste, Henry IV attributed the revival in his reign to the new peace after a long civil war: "Since among the infinite good things caused by the peace, that which comes from cultivating the arts is not the least, and [because the arts] having greatly flourished as a result of the peace, and being of very great convenience to the public, we have decided in the construction of our gallery of the Louvre, to design the building in such a way that painters, sculptors, silversmiths, watchmakers, jewelers, and other masters of excellent art can be comfortably lodged in it." So read the Letters Patent. As if this were not enough to put Parisian guildsmen in their place, the king decreed that any apprentice having served satisfactorily in the Grand Gallery for five years was entitled to admission to his appropriate guild in any city in the realm without further questions or examinations. After some months of stand-off, which took the form of delays in adding new names to the rosters, the new apprentices were accepted. This stimulus attracted fine young craftsmen who, as long as Henry lived, almost exclusively supplied works of art and furnishings to the Crown.

II

The impetus to rebuild sections of Paris also came from Henry himself. He set about making his capital—which had the reputation of being a "common sewer"—an attractive place in which to live, at least for some. In building the Place Dauphine and the Place Royale, Henry IV established a precedent of leadership by his direct intervention into the construction, finance, and design of private housing.

Sully does not deserve all the credit for these projects. He made plans, negotiated contracts, and inspected the work, but the initiative came from Henry himself. For example, in 1607 the king learned that houses were being built between the Pont-Neuf and the Porte de Buci, south of town; so he wrote Sully: "I would be very pleased if you would see to it that those who are beginning to build in the aforesaid street make the façades of their houses all of the same [architectural] order, for it would be a fine ornament to see this street with a uniform façade from the end of the bridge. Farewell, my friend, Henry."

Who had informed the king that the rue Dauphine was being built? Did the idea of uniform façades come from Henry? We do not know. But Henry's enthusiasm for a new Paris, ordered and inspired by the latest architectural principles, fixed at one stroke the future urban character of Paris. He wanted a new and radically different kind of urban ensemble. His letter contains, in vague language, two fundamental principles: the first concerned the design of buildings, the second the arrangement of streets and monuments. Building façades were to be uniform, not one story higher or one story lower in jagged confusion. And streets should be aligned geometrically to form vistas that would complement monuments judiciously placed at their ends. Henceforth Paris would be built according to legislated notions of taste. It would cease to grow on the basis of judicial decisions determining which monastery owned what parcel of land, or where public thoroughfares were to be. Until Henry's impetus, public thoroughfares had as often as not been what was left over, land unclaimed or land that could be bought cheaply, regardless of convenience, design, or taste. Buildings zigzagged around jurisdictions, streets turned corners or curved to avoid some private field or dwelling. But Henry could not transform Paris in a day. His efforts influenced areas that had not been built up, but they changed little those older parts already laid out. But why had the king been obliged to inform his *voyer* of such an obvious chance to beautify the city, or why did he think it necessary? Sully's *Mémoires* indicate that his own *gloire,* or failure to attain it, was in finance. Indeed, his scant references to Paris, and his failure to boast about his responsibility for the capital's beautification, raise many doubts about his importance as *voyer,* other than as executor of the king's commands.

On April 6, 1607, one month before Henry's letter to Sully about the rue Dauphine, the building grant for the square to bear the same name was registered by the

Parlement. What is so important here is that Sully did not drag his feet. He battled obstructionism with relish, in the name of his king and friend, Henry. The king strove to give Paris a grandiose urban development consisting of a bridge, houses, shops, and streets, all in the classical style tempered by the French fondness for high roofs. He was successful, though one would hardly think so now; for the eastern side of the Place Dauphine has been torn down, and additional stories have been added on top of those houses still standing, making them so high that the harmony between the size of the square itself and the height of the houses is destroyed.

Built on a low, uneven, and muddy area between the *Palais* and the Pont-Neuf, the Place Dauphine stands at the western end of the *Cité*. Achille de Harlay, First President of the Parlement, had been granted 3,120 square *toises* (about 19,000 square feet)[2] of the royal domain to build on in accordance with the plans in the hands of the *voyer* (road supervisor) of Paris. Harlay followed them. When completed, the Place Dauphine constituted not merely buildings and streets, but a harmonious ensemble of spaces, buildings, statuary, and bridges. A formless mass had become a triangle of elegant buildings set off by the wide new bridge.

Though the name of the designer of the Place Dauphine is unknown, we do know he was an appointee of the Crown. What he designed must have pleased Henry IV. The houses, each four stories high, were built in rows to form a triangle. Constructed of brick, with heavy beveled stone quoins at the corners to fill in the courses of brick, these houses were nothing more than row houses dressed up by classical decoration and situated in a way that maximized the space around them. Their cornices, windows, doors, and dormers were all alike, regularly spaced to create the illusion of infinity.

Row houses with uniform façades had never before existed in Paris, in fact had never before existed north of the Alps. And what a harmony of color they made against the sky and the Seine. The brownish-red of low-fired brick combined beautifully with the golden Seine-valley limestone of the trim. Owing to these materials, the houses exuded a kind of warmth rarely achieved in classically inspired architecture. And their cost was moderate.

The roofs gave comfort to the traditionalists. Of gray Anjou slate, they stretched high into peaks almost two stories above the last floor. These roofs had a beauty of their own, an important factor for the overall success of the design in a country where roofs had been one of the principal vehicles for artistic expression since the fourteenth century.

---

2. One *toise* equals about six feet.

This ensemble made an impression on the Parisians, living as they did in houses built in different styles and shapes along streets sometimes only six feet wide. The Place Dauphine appeared more spacious than it actually was, as a result of the application of Renaissance experiments in perspective to urban planning. This fascination with perspective, uniformity of design, and arrangements by squares, circles, ellipses, and triangles, the pure geometric forms, had its first concrete expression in Paris in the Place Dauphine. Henceforth architects would strive to realize perspectives wherever and whenever possible and over the centuries would make central Paris into an urban unity that seems much bigger than it actually is.

Whether standing at the north or south end of the Pont-Neuf, or looking west from the *Palais* through the apertures in the triangle of houses, the observer found his eye naturally attracted to one central spot. This high rise in the Pont-Neuf, marking the end of the *Cité* and the sharpest point in the triangle of houses, drew the eye from along the façades, bridges, and nearby quays to the spot where an equestrian statue of the victorious Henry IV was placed in 1614. Marie de Médicis had ordered it made in Italy at a time when French artisans still lacked the skill to make such a large casting in bronze.[3] With the erection of this statue, the first of its kind in Paris, the Place Dauphine became the first complete urban ensemble in the capital. It was the most important construction since Philip Augustus built the city walls in the thirteenth century. Royal power had intervened again, this time to establish a new style in urban living. Cramped streets winding into more cramped streets became old-fashioned, while a style of residential spaciousness, previously unknown in Paris to all but kings and princes, was made available to wealthy judges and oligarchs, for the Place Dauphine had a bourgeois and robe tone.

Building the square undoubtedly added to Harlay's prestige and wealth. Henry had not coerced him into undertaking the project; there is a letter from the king to Sully stating that if Harlay does not wish to engage himself in the project, that he, Sully, should find someone else who would. Henry, with this idea in mind, established the rules of how private capital could be utilized for the benefit, good health, and prestige of numerous Parisians.

This blending of absolute monarchy with classical principles of architecture to lend dignity to what were essentially bourgeois houses resulted in new strength and support for Henry and the monarchy. Henry fused political leadership with innovation

---

3. The present statue is a modern copy, the original having been melted down during the Revolution.

A view of Paris toward the west, from the Pont-Neuf. To the left of the equestrian statue of Henry IV, the Collège des Quatre Nations dominates the quay opposite the wing of the Louvre designed by Louis Le Vau. The Grand Gallery of the Louvre stretches into the horizon just above the Pont Royal.

and vitality in architecture in an age when aristocrats and oligarchs placed value on patronizing the arts. The king recognized that architecture was an indispensable complement to power; his decision to build in Paris rather than in the country demonstrates his awareness of where he should manifest his power. When Sully informed the king of some remodeling being carried out in the chapel at Fontainbleau, the king sent more money than Sully requested in order that *"quelque chose de beau"* (something beautiful) might be built. That little phrase epitomized the aristocrat's commitment to art. Not, of course, that the aristocracy or Henry believed art to have intrinsic merit or to be good for its own sake. Rather, art, objects of beauty and devotion, whether sensual or ascetic, assured the patron immortality in this and the other world. Henry IV assuredly did not understand the fine points of this view, but he was for art, for the

The Pont-Neuf looking toward the Right Bank. The houses at the point of the Place Dauphine rise opposite the equestrian statue of Henry IV. Coachmen intimidate people whose rank is inferior to that of their masters or mistresses, insisting on their right to pass without regard for a left-right (or a right-left) traffic pattern.

impressive and tasteful. His commitment to Renaissance ideals of taste was unsophisticated and unaffected. Henry felt the breath of Roman emperors while remaining a *"bon Français"* and unconcerned about a conscious imitation of an adapted imperial court style for his capital.

Without waiting to discover whether the Place Dauphine would be a success, Henry went ahead to sponsor and direct the construction of the Place Royale, known since the Revolution as the Place des Vosges. The same principles of control over style, materials, and standards of spaciousness were applied here to a project twice the size. But how was construction of such a large square possible so close to the center of Paris?

In a sense the Place Royale may be classified as "renewal." There had been a palace there, the Tournelles, until Catherine de Médicis ordered it torn down after her husband, Henry II, had suffered a fatal accident while jousting in a street just next to the palace. Except for occasional horse auctions, the land lay vacant throughout the civil wars.

Henry's first thought was to build a structure there to house his prize silk workers; and over Sully's strong objections, a large, well-built structure was erected for this purpose. Then, after having seen this handsome building, the king decided to move the silk workers elsewhere and to add three more rows of buildings to complement the first and to form a true square. Sully takes credit for convincing Henry that this site offered many more possibilities than the housing of mere silk workers, and well he might have, for his more narrowly aristocratic sensibilities might have caused him to combat the housing of artisans in the most aristocratic, "smart" quarter in Paris. Princes and dukes had originally built in the *Marais,* this fashionable quarter, in order to be near the royal residence of the Tournelles; but if the former palace area were now to house silk workers, the character and appeal of the area would change.

The Place Royale remains today a picturesque if not quite grand Baroque space, with its geometrically laid-out walks and its fountains and flowerbeds that bear honor to the (replaced) equestrian statue of Louis XIII in the center. Shops and restaurants long ago encroached on the residences themselves to transform them from a would-be genteel residential ensemble into a commercial neighborhood.

Originally the vast gardens of the *hôtels* of the *Marais* stretched back to those of the houses on the square, forming a buffer between the residences. The whole—that is, the square itself, then the residences around it, and finally the gardens and *hôtels* of the *Marais*—constituted the finest expression of urban residential living in the seventeenth century.

The law prohibiting the subdivision of houses on the Place Royale again shows Henry IV's desire to guarantee the spaciousness of urban living, and also his desire to please the aristocrats living in the *Marais.* Because neither floors of a house nor single rooms could be sold to another person, the Place Royale would remain in the hands of wealthy merchant, robe, or sword families, and would therefore not decline in social prestige. Thus most of the houses on the Place, unlike many *hôtels,* remained integral and aristocratic to the end of the *Ancien Régime.*

The Place Royale, as engraved by Israël Silvestre. A favorite place to stroll and to see or be seen in new clothes, the treeless central space enhanced the domineering effect of the equestrian statue of Louis XIII.

Henry had built one side consisting of nine pavilions at his own expense and then sold them to robe families, chiefly in the Parlement and the Chambre des Comptes. Like those on the Place Dauphine, the houses are four stories high, of brick, with arcades, stone pilasters, and high slate roofs "with leaden trim . . . made in the form of vases, from which emerge leaves and fruit," which have since disappeared. An equestrian statue of Louis XIII, placed there in 1639 by Cardinal Richelieu, completed the ensemble.[4] The king appeared *en empereur romain,* like a statue of Marcus Aurelius in Rome.

The addition of the central statue to the square made the Place Royale the model for numerous other squares built in the provinces—at Charleville, for example, and in foreign cities. Massive wrought-iron gates, added in the eighteenth century, reserved the central park exclusively for the owners of the houses on the square. The breadth

---

4. Revolutionaries melted down the original statue, leaving King Louis Philippe the task of ordering another.

and spaciousness of the square were a source of wonder and amazement to the Europeans who came out of their medieval cities and off the land. As yet not even in Rome could be seen so much space, taken away, as it were, from inchoate nature and shaped by man into a geometrical form.

Henry had other plans—such as the Place de France, which was to be a gigantic residential semicircle near the Temple—but he did not live to complete them. The striking thing about the first Bourbon was his political genius for controlling construction being built with private capital. Both the Place Dauphine and the Place Royale were largely private projects by "new rich," or more often by "new status," to whom Henry gave enlarged dignity by establishing for them royal standards of residential elegance near an aristocratic quarter. Thus Henry's promotion of the robe by the *Paulette* was complemented by his extension of *gloire* to them. Was he successful? When Scarron wrote about the square in 1643,

> Adieu, belle place où n'habite
> Que mainte personnes élites[5]

he recorded the prestige and high status of those same families.

III

For Henry IV the poor and sick were a different matter. He was a Christian prince, and it was therefore his duty to ease the sufferings of his subjects. His acts to repair fountains, build hospitals, and increase the allocations to institutions caring for the destitute reflect as unified and as systematic an effort to deal with these problems as possible in a society where individuals not cared for by their families, guilds, or parishes were considered inferior and sinful. In Henry's acts there is neither religion nor moralizing, but only the frank recognition that people were suffering and that they could be better cared for than they were. Epidemics rather than hunger caused most of the concern.

During epidemics and droughts, peasants and unskilled laborers would pour into the capital to take advantage of the services offered by the hospitals and monasteries.

---

5. Good-bye, beautiful square / where reside / only numerous élite persons.

The Hôpital Saint-Louis. Persons infected with contagious diseases were isolated in the inner core of the buildings. Did the sick have access to the principal chapel, on the left?

During these crises, the bourgeois policed the city gates to keep out the poor, and officials rounded up beggars in each quarter regularly to find out whether they were officially enrolled Parisian poor. These brutal acts resulted from the laws and traditions requiring each parish or town to care for its own. The poor in Paris had to wear a red and yellow cross attached to their sleeves to signify that they belonged in the city. This was their protection against officials ordered to eject the poor who had migrated to Paris in search of jobs or relief. In grave crises, the inadequacy or failure of local government to meet the needs of individuals, either resident or migrant, could only lead to tension and violence.

The Hôtel-Dieu had been founded to care for "every sort of poor sick people from every nation, age, sex, and condition." But this medieval ideal could not be realized, especially after rampant inflation reduced the purchasing power of the hospital's endowment. Then, after the Reformation, quarrels between religious orders intensified and tended to reduce the number of nuns and brothers willing to devote their lives to caring for the sick. By the end of the civil wars, services for the poor and needy in Paris reached a nadir unequaled since the Hundred Years' War.

Again Henry IV did what everybody knew had to be done. The plan or conception for a new hospital reserved for contagious persons dated from as early as 1496; but nothing was accomplished. Then in a burst of activity from 1606 to 1608, Henry founded two new hospitals, Sainte Anne's (better known as *la Santé*) on the south side of the city, and the Hôpital Saint-Louis, on the north, beyond the Faubourg Saint-Denis. Saint-Louis was specially designed for patients with leprosy or plague. Named for the saintly King Louis IX, who died of the plague, and honoring his namesake, Henry's first-born son, soon to be Louis XIII, this impressive construction boasted the latest innovations, largely Italian in origin, designed to prevent the spread of contagion.

To the modern eye the Hôpital Saint-Louis resembles a prison. The complex of buildings designed by Châtillon is a square within a square, originally connected only by guarded bridges. Fierce dogs roamed the grounds to discourage escape. Each part was closed off from the others, but as a whole the hospital provided all the services known to be beneficial to the leper. The pharmacy, kitchens, laundries, storerooms, quarters for the nun-nurses, and the chapel, constituted a community that sealed off the contagious from the outside world. Like the squares of elegant residences in town, the hospital was built of brick and stone with the same high roofs and classic dormers. Certain pavilions were, in fact, set aside for bourgeois or noble patients. The wards had large windows, high ceilings, and double exits to allow maximum comfort for those suffering from rotting flesh and maximum convenience and safety for those devoted to caring for them. A spacious formal garden, separating the central contagious wards, freshened the air and evoked a residential garden.

As was the case with the Hôtel-Dieu, Henry appointed eminent and rich members of Parlement to preside over the finances and administration of the two hospitals. Achille de Harlay, First President of the Parlement and "builder" of the Place Dauphine, also governed the Hôtel-Dieu. His task was to raise money for it. One entire wing of the new Hôpital Saint-Louis was built from the gifts of Pomponne de Bellièvre. He, like Harlay, had been one of Henry's friends during the civil wars; after the peace, he was showered with offices and honors in return for his support. But what Henry gave with one hand he took away with the other, by prodding such persons to serve the public need.

Additions were also made to the old hospice of Saint-Germain-des-Prés, which cared for the aged and infirm; and finally several wards were added to the old Hôtel-Dieu so that it extended beyond the island to the Left Bank and occupied the bridges connecting the two parts.

Most of the actual care of the sick was still done by the religious, mainly by girls aspiring to become members of the various orders, each occupying itself with different

Henry IV performing the ritual of the Royal Touch, contemporary engraving. Medieval and early-modern kings believed that they possessed divinely ordained powers to cure subjects of scrofula, a disease that produced infected boils. Henry's performance of this ritual further consolidated his reputation as a sincere Roman Catholic.

charities or hospitals. The following description of the "little" laundry of the Hôtel-Dieu gives some impression of their task. The head has

> under her six girls called little laundresses, whose daily task is to wash in the river all the sheets removed from the beds of the gravely ill; since it is impossible to boil the laundry every day, they settle for simply rinsing them out and drying them before the fire, especially during the winter, to such a degree that it is the hardest job of all, for they must at times work day and night and the amount spent on wood is unbelievable, and they must dry more than three hundred sheets, and all six of them are assigned this job for a full year.

This was part of a novitiate, or preparation for becoming a full member of a religious order.

Nevertheless, conditions in the hospital remained terrible even to the eyes of contemporaries. But there was some awakening. The efforts to improve both the patients' physical condition and morale shows something of the desire for improvement present in the early seventeenth century. In 1612 a brother said: "It was an urgent matter to remove the other sick from the beds of the dying, in order to avoid any apprehensions they might have, and the odor [the dying] might spread while dying; the *compagnie* [hospital administration] ordered that whenever a sick person is being given extreme unction, the other paupers lying in bed with him are to be removed and put elsewhere until he has given up his soul to God."

Perhaps this represents not so much a new sensibility as a return to some past ideal. Nevertheless, to perceive and to act in accordance with these humane principles came as an innovation after so long a period of decay.

In the Hôtel-Dieu the maternity wards were run by different nuns and were separated from the rest of the hospital. The *office des accouchées* had under its jurisdiction the control of the Tower of Limbo, "which is a square tower where they throw stillborn children that are brought there, from the entire city of Paris as well as from the *faubourgs* and other surrounding areas, in with which they toss a measure or so of quicklime, in order to burn them and prevent too great an odor."

The urgent public services remained in the hands of those who also cared for men's souls. There seems to have been little difficulty in recruiting women to join the nursing orders, particularly the white sisters. However, the brothers of the Hôtel-Dieu died out. No novices were admitted after 1608. Why? Though the order had very stringent and rigorous rules, some other explanation must be sought because other strict orders flourished. It seems that the increased powers of the lay administrators and of the Crown so infringed upon the customary functions of these brothers that the last of them preferred extinction rather than submission to royal control. No more novices were found to be "capable" of the burdens and responsibilities after 1608. The last brother, Frère Bourgeois, died in 1661 and, with him, the order. The Hôtel-Dieu thus became a *de facto* royal hospital.

In founding new hospitals, increasing their revenues, and giving greater power to lay administrators, Henry IV acted in the tradition of those of his strong predecessors. Louis IX and Louis XI had also broken with tradition in order to do what needed to be done. The strong monarch, at least in the last centuries of the *Ancien Régime,* could not be so much innovator as executor of plans and hopes long present in the public mind.

The Neighborhood Builders

No spectacular upsurge in either residential or royal construction had occurred in Paris in the two centuries before Henry IV. This stagnation resulted from the lack of good, cheap land on which to build, the timidity of speculators and builders, and political strife. The last major additions of land to the capital dated from the fourteenth century, when new walls had been built on the north. This fenlike land surrounded the Temple and extended toward the Seine in a region called the *Marais.* Actual building in these fields had come slowly, not only because of the poor drainage but also because of the great expense involved. A prospective builder had to negotiate for years and pay dearly for this second-rate land, owned chiefly by monks. Each boundary, *lods, cens,* and title presented something of a trap for speculators, and income, of course, for monks and lawyers. Speculators were in a hurry; the monks could wait until doomsday. Thus the *Marais* lay vacant until about 1550.

In order to have ready cash, French kings leased (it was called "farming out") the right to collect excise taxes. Once the tax "farmer" had paid the sum stipulated in the contract, he pocketed any and all surplus revenue that he by right could collect. Tax farmers had capital, and so they speculated in *rentes,* in real estate, and in special secret loans to the Crown. Their activities pushed them into spending great sums on luxury goods, in order to show outwardly that they were indeed wealthy and therefore financially able to honor the contracts they had signed. Only Court favorites and tax farmers could afford to pay the exorbitant cost of construction in the *Marais.* In the century following 1650, these two groups developed it into an exclusive, aristocratic or would-be-aristocratic neighborhood. Building *hôtels* (that is, very large private residences) rather than houses, each tried to outdo the other in splendor and spaciousness. Only favorites and tax farmers had the necessary money or influence to speed up negotiations with the abbots and priors. Purchasing tracts adequate for fifteen or twenty bourgeois houses, they constructed a single *hôtel*. The population density was therefore lower in the *Marais* than in any other quarter.

These residences were not urban in character. Designed to shut out the prying eyes of outsiders, and supplied with foodstuffs and water directly from the provinces, these *hôtels,* like their medieval namesakes, were really châteaux in town. Symbolizing aristocratic independence and power, the *hôtel* presented to the city a solid, windowless wall, broken only by one monumental door. Their construction, important as it was to Parisian cultural life, did not constitute new growth. Few in number, the *hôtels* of the *Marais* filled in the unoccupied fringes of the capital.

The Place Dauphine and the Place Royale broke the long stagnation by opening up the possibility of new housing for a different social group. The *pavillon* on a square was less expensive than a *hôtel,* yet was smarter and more pleasant than a typical bourgeois house. The *pavillon* symbolized some commitment to urban life and at least a tolerance for neighbors. Residents strolled under the same galleries, sometimes shared a garden, and could peek through one another's windows. These residences appealed greatly to those royal officials who, for psychological as much as financial reasons, preferred not to assimilate directly into the aristocracy by building an *hôtel*.

Probably more important in the long run, however, were the financial arrangements that Henry IV established for the squares. He made the plans and then private capital met most of the construction costs. With royal sponsorship, the fear of bankruptcy diminished. With royal backing, wealthy bourgeois, royal officials, and perhaps even gentlemen invested in large-scale housing projects that would otherwise have been risky. This combination of royal initiative and private capital outlived Henry IV to become the chief stimulus for the construction of three new quarters.

After Henry IV's death, the prime mover was almost always an engineer with daring and dreams. Looking at vacant wasteland, these men envisioned bridges, markets, churches, quays, and dozens, even hundreds, of houses, all built at once. Their desire for profit must have been considerable, but judging from their boldness in risking their capital and from their modest way of life, their chief desire was to build and build, rather than to make money.

The prestigious architects of the day, so far as we know, did not so much as glance at these projects. They were busy designing châteaux or *hôtels* for rich clients. But some, such as Christophe Marie, with an engineer's knowledge, could undertake to design and build all the structures comprising a neighborhood. These engineers often had little capital themselves, but they knew how to raise it. They also knew how to negotiate successfully with the chancellor of France and with other influential Parisians.

THE ÎLE SAINT-LOUIS

In 1577, at a meeting held in the *hôtel* of Christophe de Thou, rue Saint-André-des-Arts, the *prévôt* and *échevins* decided to request that the king choose a site for a new bridge "capable of carrying wagons." There had been discord at the meeting. Nicolas L'Huillier, president in the Chambre des Comptes and *prévôt,* wanted the bridge built from the Right Bank to the *Île de la Cité,* just behind Notre-Dame. Antoine de Nicolaï, president in the Chambre des Comptes, argued that the bridge should be built to the *Île aux Vaches,* the "Cow Island," because it would encourage "the building of houses" there. Henry III read a summary of the arguments and decided in favor of the project that would have placed another bridge on the *Île de la Cité.*

Nothing came of these deliberations until 1610, when Christophe Marie, engineer and bridge builder, proposed to Henry IV that the Crown sponsor a bridge and housing development for the *Île aux Vaches.* The king died a few months later. But Marie did not give up. In 1611 he received royal backing for a stone-arch bridge to be built to the *Île aux Vaches.* The capital was to be furnished by one Lugles Poulletier.

The canons of Notre-Dame, owners of the island, had watched these negotiations from a distance, but now they pounced on Marie to have the project annulled. On the pretext that Marie's proposed new bridge and quays would increase the strength of the river currents about the *Île de la Cité,* the canons insisted that Marie build quays around the southern end of the *Cité* before they would consent to the construction of the new bridge. Their claim represented just the sort of intangible yet real consideration that could slow up, if not stop, construction for months, even years, if the courts moved slowly. The canons had made trouble before and sentiment against them ran high among the robe officials and the bourgeois of Paris. Finally, after lengthy negotiations, the Crown bought the island, gave it to Marie and his financial backers free of rent for sixty years, and ordered quays to be built around the *Cité* at the Crown's expense. Royal sponsorship helped, but, as we shall see, it was not enough. The canons appealed. After 1617, the year in which they lost one of their numerous legal appeals against the Crown, the canons seemed defeated, at least momentarily. Work finally began, however. Six years had been lost. Furthermore, there had been a loss of public confidence in the project.

To Marie and Poulletier's great dismay, little land on the island had been sold, owing to the uncertainty of whether the Crown or the canons would win in the courts. Marie's contract included deadlines which, because of the lack of capital from the sale of land, he could not meet.

Between 1617 and 1622 things moved rapidly, but not rapidly enough to avoid a financial crisis for Marie and his backers. During these years the entire western half of the island was sold off into tracts of irregular sizes and shapes, but the bridges and quays still had not been constructed.

It is difficult to discover whether the first to purchase land were merely speculating in real estate or were sincerely interested in building residences and living on the island. One of the earliest buyers was a *trésorier extraordinaire des guerres,* from a family just newly belonging to the robe and probably still attached to the wholesale merchants. He doubtlessly had profits to invest. Most of the early purchasers were of this sort, except for some who were higher in the robe and others who were rich artisans. There was a Jérôme Séguier, president in the *Grand Conseil;* a *receveur du domaine;* a master carpenter; a *trésorier de France;* an *intendant des gabelles* (address, Place Royale); a *conseiller d'Etat;* a *secrétaire du roi;* and a *trésorier des ligues suisses.* At best, these families were on the fringe of the robe; they would have to be divested of their interests in finance before they would be fully accepted into the group. In the years following 1617, Marie saw those like himself buying in for a share of the profits, but without sharing his high costs. Squeezed between creditors, construction costs, and slow land sales, Marie sank deeper into financial difficulties. The entire project resembled a modern financial operation in that success and high profits depended entirely on the timing. Had Marie managed to build the bridges and streets in time, the sales of land would have increased and would have enabled him to pay his creditors. He had borrowed heavily on a short-term basis. Thanks to the canons of Notre-Dame, Marie's time ran out, leaving him paralyzed by debts.

Marie and Poulletier went bankrupt in 1624 and were replaced by a man named La Grange, backed by a new group of moneylenders. The new contract resembled the old one, except that La Grange had even fewer years in which to complete the work.

It also stipulated that the island be renamed to honor the memory of the king's patron and ancestor, Saint Louis.

The surveyors and assessors started all over again to measure and fix the value of all the available land on the island. This took more than two years. Only a bridge to the *Cité* had been built before 1627, when a new financial crisis occurred. This time La Grange dropped out. The Crown signed a second contract with Marie.

Such vicissitudes on the Île Saint-Louis continued for twenty more years, until all the houses and bridges had been completed. The canons raised new difficulties, the Crown switched the *lods* and *cens* owed to Notre-Dame from its own accounts to those of Marie, masons encountered financial difficulties, and so forth.

We know little about the actual builders and speculators themselves. They left no letters, account books, or memoirs, but only a record of their dealings in the notarial archives. Marie's bridges at Neuilly, Lyons, the Île Saint-Louis, and the one from the Tuileries to the rue du Bac (predecessor of the Pont Royal) attest to his ability as an architect. The Pont Marie, its classic simplicity hiding its massiveness, is not unlike the work François Mansart sought to do. Marie's wife could not write well enough to sign her own name. But her father was a master stonemason who, in cooperating with Marie to contract and build on the island, enabled Marie to keep more of the profits in the family than appearances indicate. Madame Marie's will indicates that she and her husband lived in bourgeois simplicity, with modest and inexpensive furniture, silver, and clothing, even after having amassed enough wealth and credit to undertake something as big as the project on the Île Saint-Louis.

Not so the tax farmers and judges. They spent as much as they could afford or borrow to build splendid *hôtels* on the eastern half of the island. The Pont Marie, at last finished in 1635—except for the tall houses, barely twelve feet wide, added later—attracted to the island people who had become rich in a hurry and who wanted to build quickly. Typical of these was Jean-Baptiste Lambert, who began as the son of a *procureur des comptes* and, through working for Claude de Bullion, Superintendent of Finances, soon became rich enough to buy an office of *trésorier de l'épargne*. He hired Louis Le Vau, a young and quick-working architect, to design the *hôtel,* which still bears his name. Work began in 1642. Le Sueur and Le Brun decorated the interior (Le Brun did the Gallery of Hercules), and Lambert moved in at Easter 1644, just a few months before his death at the age of thirty-six.

Even larger, better-situated, and enclosing the only real garden on the Île was the Hôtel de Bretonvilliers. Jean I du Cerceau designed it to take advantage of the full view east, up the Seine, from the very tip of the island; and Simon Vouet, the most fashionable painter in France during the 1640s, did some of the ceilings. The richness of the tapestries, furniture, and statuary, and the sheer amount of space occupied by Bretonvilliers, made it a showplace of avant-garde art, architecture, and society. It was the most aristocratic establishment on the island, reflecting the aspirations of its owner.

After Lambert and Bretonvilliers, other houses extended west along the quays. Though also magnificent inside, they were on the exterior more bourgeois and restrained. Today, as in 1650, when it was constructed, no one looking at the unassuming façade would imagine the richness and beauty inside the Hôtel de Lauzun. The builder, Charles Gruyn, a munitions supplier and tax farmer, must have been unwilling to pose overtly as a *grand seigneur,* as Bretonvilliers did. Son of a tavern keeper (who ran the "Pine Cone" on the *Cité*), Gruyn hired Le Vau to design his house. The architect was his neighbor. Le Vau's own house also has a plain façade. Perhaps it was Le Vau who subtly, through design, imposed the modest façade on Gruyn to preserve the sober harmony of the rich bourgeois houses that lined the Quai d'Anjou. Certainly Le Vau's own house would have faded into the background had he designed a sumptuous and monumental façade for Gruyn; as it is, the two harmonize very well.

Gruyn and his heirs had the ceilings, shutters, and panels painted by Le Brun, Le Pautre, Le Sueur, and other equally famous artists, to make the interior of the *hôtel* a veritable jewel box of intimate elegance. Lauzun is not monumental, but luxurious and delicate. The parties and ballets held there were of necessity small, intimate, almost familial, owing to the size of the rooms. It is not architecturally or stylistically an *hôtel* in the way that Bretonvilliers' was, with splendid sculptures and very large galleries. At Lauzun, Le Vau did not even use the customary devices for making the courtyard or the galleries seem bigger than they actually were.

By 1660, the island was nearly built up, except for the parish church of Saint-Louis, which was very long in building. Finally consecrated in 1726, when the ancestors of the builders had become *bonne noblesse,* it reflected an aristocratic tone that the island had originally lacked.

THE LEFT BANK

Christophe Marie was but one of the big speculators to add entire parishes to the capital. His contemporary, Louis Le Barbier, surpassed him in every way, from the boldness of his financial operations to the ingenuity of his schemes for selling land. Only one thing kept Le Barbier from being an unqualified success: he too went bankrupt. Le Barbier, perhaps more than Marie, had a sense for constructing elegant *quartiers.* His clients and financial backers were certainly of the robe, and therefore more prestigious than Marie's. Also, Le Barbier married the daughter of a *secrétaire du roi,* built his own very elegant *hôtel* (nos. 3–5 Quai Voltaire), and bought the Château of Mesnil (Seine-et-Oise). His connections with people high up in the government—the Loménies, Cornuel, and even Richelieu—provided the clientele and financial resources to undertake not merely one but two large urban projects. As speculators, Marie and Le Barbier really had only one thing in common: their power to conceive of and execute such projects. Apart from this, they were very different. Le Barbier, for example, showed no prowess as a designer.

Le Barbier and his backers first undertook to buy up and then sell off the properties accumulated by Marguerite de Valois. Sister of three kings of France and first wife of another, Marguerite undertook, as late as 1606, to build the last Valois folly in Paris. She decided to complement her mother's achievements in the Tuileries by building an *hôtel* and gardens on the Left Bank of the Seine, just opposite the palace. For this purpose she acquired, at enormous expense to her ex-husband, Henry IV, all the land between the rue de Seine and the rue du Bac, as far south as the rue Jacob and its continuation, the rue de l'Université. Those streets were little more than paths at the time, but the monks from whom she purchased most of the land had a good idea of what it was worth. The *hôtel* of Queen Margot and its dependences extended along most of the rue de Seine and included the monastery of the Petits Augustins; for, like Henry III, when Marguerite was not debauching or entertaining, she worried over the fate of her soul and went to pray. Marguerite's *hôtel* encouraged only a small number of aristocrats to build on the Left Bank, for she was excluded from power. But, like the land under the old Tournelles and the Hôtel Saint-Pol, the immense garden tract had just that aura of royalty that would make it attractive. Her debts were enormous, and after Marguerite's death in 1615 her eager creditors demanded payment. The Crown decided to sell the *hôtel* and the land, except, of course, for the Petits Augustins. Le Barbier and his colleagues bought it after long negotiations, fixing exactly which parts of the tract were to belong to which speculator. For neither the projects of Marie nor those of Le Barbier strictly resembled a company; each major investor had his own parcels of land to build upon or to sell.

The history of these sales and of the construction of quays, bridges, and houses resembled that of the Île Saint-Louis, except for one thing: Le Barbier was more imaginative than Marie. He built houses and offered them for sale entirely finished and ready for occupancy. Though it is impossible to discover exactly where these houses were, the fact that they are described as *"maisons,"* and the fact that Le Barbier also built and sold completed *hôtels,* would indicate that they were residences for people of differing social standing and wealth. He also erected a market to encourage merchants to move into the new Faubourg Saint-Germain. So while by 1675 the quays (now Malaquais and Voltaire), the rue de Bourbon (Lille), and the rue de l'Université were lined with elegant *hôtels* belonging to robe and sword families, the southern streets may well have contained some houses built by merchants. Malingre's few comments about these streets in 1640 would indicate that they were almost entirely built up and that they had few illustrious inhabitants; but the fact that he also mentions the existence there of several *académies de noblesse,* schools for gentlemen, indicates the presence of a clientele of would-be gentlemen from robe families, in the Latin Quarter and the University. The old parish church having become too small, a new Saint-Sulpice was begun in 1655 with Le Vau as architect. Its vastness reflects the aspirations of an ambitious *curé,* Olier, and the pretension of new wealth, which proved to be less great than had been expected, for through lack of funds the church was not completed until 1736. The façade, changed many times before the Revolution, was never really finished.

THE RIGHT BANK

With the exception of the Île Saint-Louis, the new quarters of Paris included both secular and spiritual refuges from urban life. The two were much more integrated in Le Barbier's other project, called the "Wall of the Yellow Moats," on the Right Bank, which attracted residents socially superior to those induced by Le Barbier to build in the Faubourg Saint-Germain. In spite of the aura of royalty conferred by Marguerite de Valois, the Faubourg Saint-Germain had to wait for the *Quartier-du-Palais-Royal* (first known as the Palais Cardinal) to fill up before it could attract the upper crust of noble and robe families.

In 1631, Louis XIII and Richelieu decided to complete Henry II's plans to extend the city's fortifications westward to include the Tuileries and the *faubourgs* of Saint-Honoré and Montmartre. Simultaneously, the Crown engaged a contractor to dig a canal wide enough and deep enough for boats, to extend around the entire circle of walls on the Right Bank. But this very ambitious proposal came to nothing. Nor did

Cardinal Richelieu, in a nineteenth-century engraving after a portrait by Philippe de Champaigne. The cardinal's reasoning about power and politics intimidated everyone, including Louis XIII.

Richelieu's plans to build new walls around the Left Bank get any further in the face of opposition by the *corps de ville,* an indication that the bourgeois of Paris preferred to be poorly defended rather than heavily taxed. But the new walls, dubbed the *"fossés jaunes"* (yellow moats), were built as much through Richelieu's personal interest as through Le Barbier's thirst for profit.

Born in 1585, the son of an ambitious minor nobleman from Poitou who at his death left his family in financially precarious circumstances, Armand-Jean du Plessis de Richelieu earned a degree in theology, became first a court preacher and then a bishop, and eventually gained favor with Marie de Médicis. Brilliant, self-confident, hard-working, able to argue effectively for the foreign and domestic policies he believed best for the kingdom, Richelieu became principal minister to Louis XIII in 1624 despite the king's hostility toward the prelate's domineering person. Named cardinal in 1622, and duke and peer in 1631, on the recommendation of Marie and Louis XIII, Richelieu quickly set about building a splendid *hôtel* in the capital, refurbishing his house and gardens in nearby Rueil, and building an immense château and accompanying model city (it was called "Richelieu") in Poitou. He loved fine things, enjoyed the theater, commissioned artworks, and had very little time to enjoy any of them. Nervous, sickly, but highly energetic, in his life and in his prose Richelieu refined and exemplified what the absolute state was all about. In his later years he believed himself to be an "instrument" divinely chosen to give peace to Europe and to reform French military and naval operations.

The cardinal had decided to live on the rue Saint-Honoré. In 1624 he bought a medieval *hôtel* (near the Porte Saint-Honoré, opposite the Quinze-Vingts), had it torn down, and hired Jacques Le Mercier to design and build a new and sumptuous residence worthy of a prince of the Church and a minister of state. The neighborhood was old, but fashionable, because of its proximity to the Louvre. Richelieu set out to modernize and enlarge the *hôtel,* seizing the opportunity provided by the construction of the *"fos-sés jaunes."* It is just possible that Richelieu promoted new city walls, not for the defense of Paris but to enable him to build an *hôtel* near the Louvre, in the heart of the city.

In 1631, Le Barbier signed the contract for the new walls, bastions, and ditches, to be built in the latest style, extending from the Porte Saint-Denis to the Porte de la Conférence on the Seine, approximately where the eastern end of the Orangerie is now. But where would Le Barbier make his profit? He was not a stonemason. The terms of the contract guaranteed him the right to sell the property under the old walls of Charles V and to negotiate the sale, at the expense of the owners and to his own profit, of course, of the land incorporated into the city by the new walls. Le Barbier cooperated with Richelieu, sold the land to whomever the cardinal wished, and expected great profits.

The *Quartier Richelieu,* or Palais-Royal, was born. Everything centered on the Palais Cardinal and its builder, who never ceased to acquire more and more land, until his death in 1642. Richelieu wanted his friends to build *hôtels* around his, so to please him several of his "creatures," who were high up in the government though subject to his control, bought large tracts from Le Barbier and made this part of Paris a veritable ministerial quarter.

Le Palais Roïal du côté de l'Entrée.

The Palais-Royal. Richelieu donated his magnificent Parisian residence on the Right Bank to the Crown, thus the name Palais-Royal. Note the corner shops on the busy square.

For the next two hundred years, Richelieu's grandiose plans for the Palais Cardinal determined the social tone, building style, and even the planning of the streets in the quarter. The immense rectangle situated between the rue Saint-Honoré and the rue des Petits-Champs, bounded by today's rues de Richelieu and Radziwill, became the heart of a new and almost aristocratic quarter. The *hôtels* put up by Richelieu's creatures appeared just as aristocratic as any built by a *grand seigneur*—there were *cours d'honneur,* galleries, libraries, fine furniture, spacious wine cellars, and formal gardens. But their owners were mere noblemen, not true gentlemen. In this neighborhood, status, even wealth, depended on the favor of one man. Together the Palais-Royal and surrounding *hôtels* formed a second-rate *Marais,* at least until about 1650. The quarter never acquired the latter's smartness nor its cultural vitality and boldness. Le Mercier himself seemed incapable of avoiding a dull heaviness in everything he built.

To put it bluntly, the cardinal's urban projects were self-interested in the extreme, and unimaginative when compared with those of Henry IV. Richelieu was a provincial man, a man who did not enjoy living in the city. He would flee Paris and his palace for his country place at Rueil (Malmaison) at every opportunity. No wonder that both the Palais Cardinal and his town of Richelieu (Indre-et-Loire) were destined to become failures as urban projects. Neither attracted investors once the cardinal's death had removed the possibility of gaining favor through building to please him. Politics had sustained architecture, not the reverse. This became apparent after 1642, the year of Richelieu's death, though the more odious aspects of the original designs were not removed until the palace was completely remodeled in the eighteenth century. Richelieu had wanted his garden to be surrounded by uniformly built houses. His palace was a kind of Place Royale turned inside out, making it the very antithesis of urban living. But the idea of an enormous garden, unshared and unglimpsed by anyone, appealed to Richelieu's country blood. He sought to realize this idea. But the little houses around the walled-in garden sold very poorly, for they were obviously only a scheme for reducing some of the immense costs entailed by the Palais Cardinal itself. Unlike the *pavillons* of the Place Royale, whose various residents could meet and admire the harmony of the uniform façades, the little houses of Richelieu's palace looked out onto magnificent *hôtels* and made their residents feel their obvious social and financial inferiority. Thus La Fontaine's lines,

> La plupart sont inhabités;
> Je ne vis personne dans la rue.
> Il m'en déplut; j'aime aux cités
> Un peu de bruit et de cohue,[1]

written about the city of Richelieu, also apply to the Richelieu quarter of Paris. They imply the existence of a spirit of urban living from which Richelieu remained aloof. The only justifiable explanation for the original conception of the *pavillons* and gardens of the Palais Cardinal is Richelieu's need to be protected from would-be assassins and rioters and his consequent fear of making the garden public. Indeed, the cardinal never went anywhere in Paris without forty guards. The bare walls around his garden also reflected a grand *seigneur*'s hostility to urban life.

In the 1630s and 1640s, the streets beyond the palace—such as the rues des Petits-Champs, Richelieu, Vivienne, the Square Louvois—and east, toward the old Hôtel de

---

1.
The majority are uninhabited;
I saw no one in the street.
It displeased me; in cities I love
A little noise and throngs.

Soissons of Catherine de Médicis, became lined with the massive residences of ministers and tax farmers grown rich and powerful under Richelieu and Mazarin. They hired the best architects, chiefly François Mansart, and spared no effects or money to build residences worthy of *grands seigneurs.* Visiting a man of power such as Mazarin, Colbert, or Louvois, foreign ambassadors were impressed (except the Italians, who thought the architecture terrible) by their host's magnificent *porte cochère, cour d'honneur,* central building, grand staircase, and formal gardens. With so many *hôtels* in the quarter, there was little room for smaller houses until the press for money in the eighteenth century forced their owners to sell the gardens and build living quarters behind the front walls, at the expense of the *cour d'honneur.*

Though restored and modified since the 1620s, number 8, rue des Petits-Champs, still preserves the size and typifies the sober monumentality of these residences. Begun by a Curet, who never lived to see it finished, it was bought by Tubeuf, an *intendant des finances* and confident of Bullion and Mazarin. Le Muet designed it to be worthy of a *grand seigneur,* as indeed it was.

The Hôtel Tubeuf and its neighbors are bigger and heavier than such Renaissance *hôtels* as the Carnavalet or the Lamoignon. The brick does add just a hit of fancifulness to the Hôtel Tubeuf, but in the *hôtels* built by Mansart during the thirties, even this disappears, leaving an all-pervading and cold classicism. Mansart's Hôtel de la Vrillière (now buried under later constructions of the Banque de France) and his monumental Hôtel de Nevers (58 bis, rue de Richelieu), built for Colbert, reflected his efforts to overwhelm onlookers by the sober balance of almost naked classical orders and steep slate roofs. Decoration was kept to an absolute minimum; Mansart's control over every element forced into mathematical harmony the solid, thick stone walls and pure lines in Nevers, as at Blois and Maisons-Lafitte. Mansart's deep devotion to the classical forms of architecture caused him to rise above other architects, to become independent of the judgment of his contemporaries, in a way not unlike the poet Racine. For Bérénice and Phèdre belong somehow to the *salons* of the now-fragmented Nevers, in a way that Madame de Lambert, the witty conversationalist of the Île Saint-Louis, never did. Then too, Colbert's love for the ancients made him a worthy owner of Mansart's masterpiece.

The names of the residents in the *Quartier-du-Palais-Royal* evoke most of the history of seventeenth-century France. Richelieu, Mazarin, Anne of Austria, Louis XIV (as a minor in the Palais-Royal), Séguier, Le Tellier, Louvois, Sublet de Noyers, Châteauneuf, Colbert, Seignelay, la Vrillière, d'Hozier, Chamillart, d'Hémery, and many of their relatives, who also held important offices, made the quarter the paragon of would-be-aristocratic living. The best painters decorated their ceilings; their fine libraries, collections of medals, classical statuary, tapestries, and furniture made by Boulle, now fill the museums of the world.

Richelieu's initiative was important, but his gift of the Palais Cardinal to the Crown proved to be even more significant for the development and social tone of the quarter. When Anne of Austria decided to raise Louis XIV in what soon was named the Palais-Royal instead of in the Louvre, the ministers of the next two generations decided to stay where their fathers, who had usually been Richelieu's favorites, originally had built and settled. Thus from 1620 until the 1660s this quarter remained the political and courtly center of France. Replaced by Versailles from the late 1660s until 1715, it became so again when the new Regent, Philip, long attached to the Palais-Royal, brought Louis XV and the court back to the quarter. When the royal family lived in the Palais-Royal, the king lived among his ministers, and not among his marshals or his judges. The fact that the parlementarians chose not to reside in the *Quartier-du-Palais-Royal,* and that with few exceptions the ministers chose not to live on the Left Bank, shows some delineation between these families. But ministers had relatives in the parlements.

West and north of the *hôtels* built by the ministers, new or much expanded old monasteries and convents extended to fill all of the space within the new walls and "yellow moats." Through royal favor, sisters, nieces, uncles, or cousins of the Richelieus, Mazarins, Colberts, and Le Telliers had become officials in these monasteries. Coislin, a nephew of Colbert, was long Abbot of Saint-Victor. One of Colbert's uncles headed the Feuillants. These ministerial families accumulated ecclesiastical offices for themselves and their relatives to increase their prestige, power, and revenues, but in the capital their extensions of power into the Church had a particular significance. The *Quartier-du-Palais-Royal,* with its mixture of *hôtels* and monasteries, resembles the social composition of those districts of Paris built up in the fourteenth and fifteenth centuries. The *hôtel du seigneur* was often not far from an *hôtel abbatial;* the builders might often be brothers. But in the seventeenth century the architecture differed, in that the streets were aligned and the façades more regular. But the agglomeration of secular and religious constructions in one quarter represented a type of urban construction, often repeated, of feudal Christian society.

It would be interesting to discover whether the new families of the seventeenth century actually spent a greater percentage of their total accumulated wealth on their urban residences than had their medieval predecessors. For like the latter, these officials all possessed magnificent châteaux and large domains in the provinces, with the exception, of course, of Mazarin, who set up his nephews-in-law instead of building a great domain, park, and château of his own. Mazarin was not only an astute politician but also was a devotee of city palaces; hence he never sought to pass himself off as a feudal lord in the French countryside. Moreover, he was a foreigner. The French Court never let him forget that.

To serve the new residents, a parish church was founded on the rue Saint-Honoré in 1633, the year in which Richelieu's initiatives in the *Quartier-du-Palais-Royal* were at their peak. His favorite architect, Jacques Le Mercier, was commissioned to design the Church of Saint-Roch. The actual construction went very slowly. The efforts of Nicolas de Malebranche, a tax farmer, father of the philosopher, and churchwarden of Saint-Roch, finally raised enough money so that in 1653 Louis XIV came to lay the cornerstone. The residents of the parish were clearly not heavy donors, probably because they had other worthy causes, either some provincial church near their château or a monastery. Saint-Roch was finally completed in 1740. The succession of rich chapels attached to the apse makes it almost as long as Notre-Dame. Corneille, Mignard, Le Nôtre, Chancellor Pontchartrain, some princes, a natural daughter of Louis XIV, d'Holbach, and Diderot are but some of the illustrious parishioners buried there; they reflect the mixture of aristocratic patronage of the arts and the aristocratic pretensions of those who built the new quarter.

In addition to the parish church, there were also numerous chapels, such as Notre-Dame-des-Victoires, founded by *confréries* who paid special devotion to the Virgin. Built on land given to the *petits frères* brought to Paris by Marguerite de Valois and then chased off her land in 1612, Notre-Dame-des-Victoires has a special political significance because of Louis XIII's vow to offer his kingdom to the Virgin for her protection. Founded shortly after the victory over the Protestants at La Rochelle in 1627, the *Confrérie* slowly collected the funds to build the church, completed in 1740. Lully is interred there.

The immense, stately Renaissance parish church of Saint-Eustache served the new residents who had built east and north of the Palais Cardinal. Obviously more desirable for its age and aristocratic tone, Saint-Eustache seems to have let the new men of wealth find their places right away. Colbert helped administer the parish finances; he donated money for a new façade, and, dare we say, almost in return Saint-Eustache honored him by letting him "donate" one of the most attractively located chapels in the church. Indeed, most of the great nobles of the period 1620 to 1645 built chapels in Saint-Eustache, of which often only the heraldic keystones high up in the side vaulting remain. Gaston d'Orléans, Condé, Longueville, Richelieu, and others of that princely ilk sidle up to the serpent on Colbert's arms.

Beneath the serpent stands Colbert's tomb, carved in white marble by Coysevox. Supported by Abundance on one side and Fidelity on the other, the great minister is portrayed kneeling in prayerful dignity. There is not the slightest indication by the artist of anything but the usual formal, Catholic piety, nor any indication that Colbert's claimed descent from an old aristocratic Scottish family was true. The robes of high office in the Order of the Holy Spirit that he wears evoke his power to command in the king's name, for Fidelity carries a seal bearing the royal *fleur-de-lys,* rather than the serpent. Colbert's tomb immortalizes an eminent figure who has won glory through royal service. It is in marked contrast to the tomb of Créqui in Saint-Roch, that of a true knight.

In all three new quarters, the Île Saint-Louis, Saint-Germain, and the Palais-Royal, the social composition of the builders was officially the same (Third Estate), but each quarter was on a different level and each was successively higher along the road to becoming part of the aristocracy. The Île Saint-Louis had more financiers than Saint-Germain, which had more judges, making it superior; and the *Quartier-du-Palais-Royal* had more ministers and *gentilshommes,* like Richelieu himself, making it higher still. But the builders in all three generally had two things in common: they held offices purchased from the Crown, and they sought to become part of the group immediately above them. Thus the general labels of robe and sword conceal important distinctions existing within each social category. For example, the tax farmer who became a tax official had climbed upward, as had Richelieu, who rose from being a titleless *seigneur* to become a duke and peer. But these distinctions were breaking down. Colbert was treated as a *grand seigneur* even though he was not one. Probably the best answer to this difficult question is found in Colbert's own words addressed to his son, Seignelay: "He must consider that he serves the greatest king in the world, and that he is destined to serve him in the highest of the high offices that a man of my social standing can have." Colbert was blocked by his birth from higher office. Satisfied, devoted, and eager to have his son attain a similar distinction, Colbert accepted the hierarchical order of society and seems to have had no illusions about being anything more than a mere servant of the king. Certainly neither he nor his master, Louis XIV, believed that the social hierarchy separating the *noblesse* from the *gentilshommes* was dead. Nor did Molière, in spite of his portrayal of the count in the *Bourgeois Gentilhomme* as corrupt. Molière's moral lesson is always that each group in the social hierarchy has its own particular virtue, and that he who tries to surpass his group is fated to scorn, ridicule, and failure. The count's corruption is his own, not that of his social group.

In the new quarters few artisans built houses among the tax farmers and parlementarians. There were merchant families, installed in shops to supply the needs of the new residents; but there seem to have been no streets where artisans clustered to form new manufacturing areas. From the beginning, the Île Saint-Louis had a marketing center where the main streets crossed. Saint-Germain, being just next to the Place Maubert, where "everything was sold," had only the new grain market built by Le Barbier, beyond the rue de Beaune. It was never really a success, probably because the population per house in the Faubourg Saint-Germain was low, and because many of those living in *hôtels* brought in livestock, wine, and dry vegetables from the farms they owned outside the capital. Richelieu seems to have planned no marketing section, nor did one develop in the seventeenth century, except for luxury goods on the rue Saint-Honoré. The proximity of the Halles again made the acquisition of necessities relatively convenient in an era when there were armies of servants in every *hôtel*. This separation of commercial and artisanal activities from residential areas was something new in the seventeenth century.

What struck contemporaries, however, were not these subtle distinctions in status, but the beauty, size, and richness of these new quarters. None other than Pierre Corneille grasped the force and boldness of these houses, streets, and gardens. In *Le Menteur,* first performed in 1642, Corneille flattered their builders:

> Paris semble à mes yeux un pays de romans.
> J'y croyais ce matin voir une île enchantée:
> Je la laissai déserte, et la trouve habitée;
> Quelque Amphion nouveau, sans l'aide des maçons,
> En superbes palais a changé ses buissons . . .
> Paris voit tous les jours de ces métamorphoses:
> Dans tout le Pré-aux-Clercs tu verras mêmes choses;
> Et l'univers entier ne peut rien voir d'égal
> Aux superbes dehors du Palais-Cardinal.
> Toute une ville entière, avec pompe bâtie,

Semble d'un vieux fossé par miracle sortie,
Et nous fait présumer, à ses superbes toits,
Que tous ses habitants sont des Dieux ou des Rois.[2]

All three quarters were idealized, and though the builders were clearly not gods or kings, those of them in the audience must have been proud.

The reigns of Henry IV and Louis XIII witnessed the greatest administrative expansion in the history of the monarchy. The number of officials serving the Crown doubled, at least in Paris, and the energy for social changes and residential construction released by this phenomenal growth gave Paris three new quarters. Thus the capital grew, not so much through increase of trade or manufacture as out of the needs of the state for a bureaucracy. The social composition of this new capital differed from the combination of commercial and ecclesiastical growth of medieval Paris.

But what of the rest of the Parisians? There were no new quarters built by guildsmen and artisans. Here a house, there a house, but construction of low-income housing was never intensive or located in any one area. And how do we explain the rise in the density of population in the artisan quarters of the city? Not by the construction of new houses. No speculator thought of building neighborhoods of low-income housing.

Artisans and merchants remodeled their old houses, cutting up large single apartments into two or three smaller ones to house sons and their brides; or they added entire stories and new roofs to their houses, or cut up their gardens into tracts on which new dwellings could be built. Overcrowding in old quarters inevitably developed as the number of rooms per family declined. This kind of "new construction" was often created to house a relative, or to increase one's earnings. Almost without

2. Paris to my eyes seems a storybook land.
     This morning I thought I was seeing an enchanted isle:
     I left it deserted, and find it inhabited;
     Some new Amphion, without the aid of masons,
     Into superb palaces has changed its shrubs . . .
     Paris sees these metamorphoses every day:
     In the whole Pré-aux-Clercs you will see the same things;
     And the entire universe can see nothing equal
     To the superb exteriors of the Palais Cardinal.
     A whole complete city, built with pomp,
     Seems by miracle to have come from an old moat,
     And makes us presume, from its superb roofs,
     That all the inhabitants are Gods or Kings.

exception a widow would keep one room for herself and would turn the rest of the house over to her sons; or if the family had the means to set up the sons in houses of their own, this same widow might still live in two rooms and rent the rest, so that she might preserve her inheritance for her sons. The love of gain predominated in artisan families, even to the point of going without the luxuries their fortune actually permitted them to enjoy. But the construction of partitions, little sheds in gardens or behind the gates of the *porte cochère,* and additional stories on houses went unrecorded by a notary. No exchange of property actually took place, yet more families were housed.

Though little new low-income housing was actually built, designs for modest houses nevertheless began to appear. In 1647, Pierre Le Muet published the *Manière de Bien Bastir pour Toutes Sortes de Personnes.* This was a handbook of designs within the comprehension of the barely literate artisans and merchants. Le Muet, who came from Dijon and was himself a very successful architect of large châteaux and churches, introduced standardized house plans to Paris and to France in general. Instead of merely revising Vitruvius, as did most seventeenth-century architect-authors, Le Muet developed thirteen different, complete house plans. Le Muet's houses could be built by any master mason without supervision, thus saving the prospective builder an architect's fee. Designed to be built in a mass, along streets identically laid out, Le Muet's houses are the ancestors of the single dwelling, uniform façade, "row" house. Le Muet sought to satisfy or to create a market for uniformly designed, small, and inexpensive housing.

Not that Le Muet's houses were to be flimsily built or designed to be replaced in a few years. No indeed. The notion of permanency in construction was so firmly entrenched in France that Le Muet stressed the need to use the best materials. Some of the little houses, such as number 6, rue de Seine, and number 28, rue du Bourg-Tibourg, which he either designed or inspired, stand today, run-down but solid. Nor did the ninety-nine-year lease, which led to poor construction in eighteenth-century London, ever become a favored device of Parisian landlords.

Even Le Muet's design for the smallest house evokes a kind of sober, classical dignity. The house was to be twelve feet wide and twenty-one-feet deep, with a cellar, three stories, and an attic. Every element of the independent residence was included, with a tiny open court barely five and a half feet square at the rear of the house, to contain a well and, a few feet away under the stairway, a privy. The fireplaces were included in the design, which also indicates the ideal location of a bed. No space for

Le Muet's model house plan. It occupied a lot of only about 320 square feet. Note that the privy is only a few feet from the well in the tiny courtyard.

either horses or a carriage was provided, for both were beyond the means of a family building such a small house. Nor was there a special room for cooking; this was done in the *salle* on the main floor.

From this first design, Le Muet goes on to present a dozen others, each more elaborate and occupying more land. The thirteenth plan really represents a château in miniature, with a central *logis* or living space, two wings, a monumental staircase, and some rooms as large as 48 feet long and 24 feet wide. This house was to be on a lot 101 feet wide and 45 feet deep, a far cry from Le Muet's first design. The ceiling for the second floor, *étage noble* (a phrase Le Muet avoids, perhaps because he wanted rich clients who were not noble), were designed to be fourteen feet, nine inches high, permitting a prospective builder to furnish his house with large tapestries, chandeliers from Venice, and the other monumental furnishings prevalent at the time.

At about the same time appeared Louis Savot's *Architecture Françoise* (first edition, 1624; second edition, 1642), which was often reedited and augmented to keep the work up to date. If Le Muet gave designs for moderate-income prospective builders (that is, law clerks, accountants, and skilled artisans), Savot gave them something equally if not more essential. His book is crammed with every type of practical information about building, including the types of stone, wood, tiles, and slates, and, to be sure, their prices. Savot presented the master builder's expert knowledge to the public or, as he put it: "non seulement pour les Bourgeois et Seigneurs . . . mais aussi pour beaucoup d'autres sortes de personnes." Anyone who could read and do a little arithmetic could, with Savot's help, learn how to measure in square feet (*toiser*) and, by that means, estimate the cost of a house on the basis of the desired materials and dimensions. Savot's treatise is a model of how to present the special knowledge of certain trades in a clear, understandable fashion. Indeed, any man wishing to build a house and possessing copies of Le Muet and Savot did not risk being gouged by an *entrepreneur bâtisseur*. But still one element was lacking before the prospective builder could work free of the master architect or artisan.

In the 1685 edition of Savot, much augmented by François Blondel, a brilliant architect, mathematician, and member of both the Academy of Sciences and the Academy of Architecture, the third and last essential element of technical knowledge needed for building was made available as common knowledge to the reading public. This was the building code of the city. In brief and precise statements we find the laws establishing the thickness or height of walls between houses and gardens; where windows could only be cut through with the consent of the owners on the other side; the location, construction, and number of privies, fireplaces, chimneys, and so forth—all worked out as the consequence of innumerable lawsuits, royal edicts, and proclamations from the *prévôt des marchands.* Henceforth neither the builders and architects nor the owners of new residences could claim ignorance of those laws decreed to maintain public health and to reduce the dangers of plague.

But the laws were not enforced. The fact that they were forever being reissued, like most legislation in the *Ancien Régime,* is clear proof that they were ignored at least by some. But the degree of law enforcement increased, particularly in the eighteenth century. After about 1660, more frequent references to visits to building sites by inspectors and *"les experts,"* to measure walls and approve the substructure of new constructions, indicate the rise of a new and forceful bureaucracy to enforce the building codes. The *maîtres des oeuvres,* or masters of works, had existed since medieval times as distinguished members of artisan guilds nominated by the *prévôt des marchands* to inspect all sorts of construction from bridges to housing. The *maîtres* were frequently called upon for advice on whether a bridge was about to collapse or whether the vaults of some medieval structure risked coming down.

The *maîtres* increased in number and in jurisdiction in the personal reign of Louis XIV. But even before that the Villedos, *maîtres des oeuvres* in the last years of the reign of Louis XIII and during the Regency, inspected much of the new construction on the Île Saint-Louis, in the Faubourg Saint-Germain, and around the Palais Cardinal. But it would seem that their work increased mainly because of the new owners' desire to avoid lawsuits with their neighbors, rather than through any desire to improve public health. With Savot in their hands, owners discovered rights of which they had probably been unaware. And in the *Ancien Régime,* the cliché about the passion for suing (the *procès*), so often evoked in the plays of the time, has much truth in it. Lawsuits may or may not have been more prevalent in the *Ancien Régime* than in other periods, but one thing is clear: urban life, with all the tensions derived from the struggle for space, when combined with elaborate social hierarchies that prevented families from dealing directly with each other, at least created a favorable climate for lawsuits.

With the lack of law enforcement (the *arrêt* forbidding inhabitants to dump chamber pots into the street was issued nearly every generation), the building codes and other laws enacted to protect public health and ensure privacy remain impressive even today. It is tempting to speculate that the reason Paris was, and is, an interesting place to live, despite the extraordinarily high density of population, remains above all the building codes, legislated in medieval times and elaborated upon to conform to changing standards of public health and privacy. Often violated and ultimately ignored by their authors (the bourgeois of Paris), in the hands of royal officials they became strong weapons to force the buildings of a capital into an orderly and monumental conformity.

SEVEN

The First Women Writers

Is a little learning a dangerous thing? A lot of men thought so in the seventeenth century, especially with regards to women. Learning to write and read were distinct skills that few women truly mastered prior to the rise of public education in the nineteenth century. Known as "arts," they were not automatically taught to daughters unless the fathers were legal or medical professionals, or skilled artisans. It has been estimated that as late as 1700 only 15 percent of women could actually sign their names on their wedding contracts, a skill not necessarily indicative of the ability to write or read. This percentage would certainly have been higher in Paris and in other larger urban centers, but perhaps not all that much given the fact that many women migrated from their poor peasant families to the capital, to seek work as servants, wet nurses, lace makers, and seamstresses. After considerable effort to find the proper wet nurse, poet Jean Racine and his wife were disappointed when her breasts dried up while the newborn was still very much in need of nursing. The Racines paid the wet nurse anyway, instead of just turning her out. What had happened was certainly not her fault, but it is interesting to note that she was paid, even though she could not fulfill her obligation. It is doubtful whether the wet nurse could read and write. Indeed, the lack of these skills may have prevented her from finding other employment.

The girls' schools founded by female religious orders, particularly the Ursulines in 1610, rue Saint-Jacques, made reading, writing, and counting skills, along with devotions and homemaking, the core of what can be considered a curriculum. In the mid-sixteenth century, Protestant reformers had emphasized reading for both boys and girls in order to be able to read the Word, that is, the Bible. But this impulse did not always carry over to girls, and in any event, after the Saint Bartholomew's Day Massacre the Huguenots were such a small minority in Paris that the number of their daughters who could read would scarcely have been statistically significant. Male (Catholic) moralists often asked in their treatises: Why should women learn to read and write? Their duty is to bear and raise children, to stay at home, cook, sew, and care for their husbands.

If women in the non-elite population could not read or write, how did they think or reflect upon their sense of themselves, and their relations with others? The non-reading-writing person—and there were many males in this situation as well—was, and indeed still is, restricted to what can be learned from oral exchange, sermons, and listening to others read aloud. Oral acculturation no doubt was and is extremely rich, complex, and influenced by learning from books that at one point or another come to be spoken. Proverbs, counting, and shop signs, along with prayers learned by hearing them repeated over and over again, could well contain a complex understanding of the social, religious, and craft skills that permitted persons to earn a living and interact with others. Shop signs were like primers for reading: animals, birds, towers, and so forth indicated the name of the shop. For example, a large gilded ruler was the sign for the *Règle d'or,* the "Golden Rule," a shop selling ruled music paper and music books.

Being a writer, especially a woman writer, meant pulling together a distinct identity out of very disparate, very gendered, male or female social and cultural practices. Note the infinitive "to be" in the word "being," signifying the self, the individual person in the strongest possible ontological sense. Readers, neighbors, journalists, publishers, and courtiers referred to someone as a "writer," or said that "she writes." Something deeper and that often was a long time in maturing, rather than a role or an activity that was expected because one is a woman or a man, the writer linked her own intellectual presence to a reader, to readers, to a public, a special recognition through her pen. The identity "writer," as it were, had to be constructed at the expense of other activities, duties, and conditions expected of them, some of which can be touched on here in the most general terms. The exemplary women writers, namely, the ancient Greek poetess Sappho and the late medieval moralist and adviser to princes, Christine de Pisan, would play consolidating exemplary roles in the second half of the century, after writers such as Madeleine de Scudéry and Marie-Madeleine de Lafayette had matured and had established literary reputations.

In all but the elite families, little girls learned household chores, starting with such tasks as peeling vegetables, folding linens, sweeping, and watching over younger brothers and sisters. There was always the danger that one of these might fall into the open fire that was the sole source of heat for cooking and comfort. Little Nanette Racine, the poet's daughter, nearly died from her burns when she fell into the fireplace.

As women matured, they heard their mothers and aunts tell stories about sicknesses and health, pregnancy and dying, stories filled with sighs of lamentation. "We cannot eat the soup before it is cooked" was a proverb that could be said in all sorts of family and non-family social situations, to indicate the need to be prudent or cautious, to wait and see. Knowing the "Hail Mary" and the "Our Father," the stories about the birth of Jesus or the courage in faith of the saints, typically but not exclusively female, linked non-literate women to the general cultural environment—this transcendental element being perhaps as much a source of fear or anxiety, as a feeling of shared experience with the more well-off women parishioners who belonged to confraternities and charitable corporations.

Beginning to read perhaps started with the letters on the names of cheap woodcut engravings of saints, the kind bought for almost nothing from the hawkers in the market, and tacked up on the wall, or leaned on the mantle. If the bedrock first reading experience for women and men was religious or commercial, the shaping of the letters in her own name to make her signature was the foundation of writing. The next experience would be to listen and watch, as a notary read out to her from documents that, once all interested parties had signed and fees had been paid, attested to her ownership of her own property (*propres*). This property might not be much, but it was truly and legally hers, inherited from her biological and other relatives. Individual family members with sums as small as five or ten *livres,* servants, and perhaps the majority of artisans and their spouses, and certainly all the retail merchants, and legal-medical families went to the notaries to recognize small debts or possessions, draw up marriage contracts, wills, and inventories of property after death. By law, children, including daughters, inherited equally from the estates of their parents, that is, the property spouses held in common.

Did female spouses find themselves in precarious financial circumstances as a result of their husbands' decision to transmit the family property directly to the children? While this could legally happen, and certainly did, it was quite infrequent. Indeed, spouses, male and female, typically made each other the executors of their estates, indicating a bond of trust and partnership within the couple. If a wife had a sizable estate in her own right (*propres*), her husband might then will his estate to his children, to be equally distributed (by law) among them.

If a couple had no children, however, the personal wealth of the female spouse (*propres*) went back to her surviving parents, siblings, and other relatives. Abraham Bosse's engraving of the older and younger couples in a notary's presence is idealized, but it conveys something of the legal solemnity of a marriage "alliance" between families in the *Ancien Régime.* Marriage without parental consent became increasingly a prosecutable offense. The prevailing idea of the family stressed that this obedience was simply "natural" because money and property were involved, not simply for the bride and groom, but for the two allied families. A marriage contract ended with the signatures of the greatest possible number of relatives and godparents, plus a few protectors and friends. Did the bride feel embarrassed when all she could do was mark an X, forcing the notary to attest that the mark was indeed hers? Without a doubt, and the result was that many women could sign their names, but that was about all—they could neither read nor write. Thanks to the survival of tens of thousands of notarial documents, "real" historical women can be learned about, making it possible to revise, question, and nuance the stereotypes found in sermons, moral treatises, novels, and plays.

Étiennette Charpentier was a "mistress *lingère,*" as her grandmother had been before her. A cloth-seller in a chapter on women writers? Yes, for every day Mlle Charpentier would, in her distinctive and basically phonetic French, jot down sales and charges in her account books. Well into her seventies in January 1709, she survived the coldest, most frightening months of that terrible winter, only to succumb in mid-March. At the request of longtime friend and executrix, Dame Françoise Ferrand, widow of the First President of the Parlement of Brittany, notaries arrived to seal all doors and cabinets in Charpentier's two-story lodging on the corner of the rue des Anglais and the rue des Noyers in the Parish of Saint-Séverin.

Described legally as an adult and having the rights of a merchant in clothes and linens, Charpentier had once sat on the *jurade* of her guild, an honor and certain indication of upright commercial practices. In the listing of all her personal effects, there is not only approaching familiarity with her but an understanding of what gave her pleasure and self-esteem as a woman and a merchant.

As was their habit, after noting that the deceased *lingère*'s body lay on the straw mattress of the bed, the notaries started the inventory, describing the fireplace utensils and the andirons topped by brass globes, the red serge curtains draped around the bed, the six chairs with red serge seats, a small tapestry-covered armchair, six tapestry-covered

Negotiating a marriage contract, by Abraham Bosse. The parents are working out the financial terms with the notary, while the prospective bride and groom hold hands. Her right hand on her chest signifies fidelity. The mask held by the boy who is frightening the girl suggests that all is not what it appears to be on this occasion.

stools, a chair covered with carpeting, twenty-four small engravings and four reliquaries (some with gilt frames, others with cedar ones), a small painting of fruit, a family portrait in a frame and another without a frame. Bergamo tapestry covered the walls of what had been the room where she received guests, slept, and perhaps read.

In the adjoining room there was a four-door *armoire,* or wardrobe, with two drawers, containing various articles of clothing and books, including Father du Pont's *Lives of the Saints* in two volumes, and a New Testament also in two volumes, and the *Imitation of*

Woman walking in the country, adapted from Abraham Bosse. Sometimes shown in church, and at others in the country, this elegantly dressed woman (often described as a widow) displays finery in the quality of the cloth rather than the cut of her dress, and the artist displays his skill in capturing an overall elegant image.

Christ as translated by Pierre Corneille. The remaining books went unappraised, as being of no consequence. Tablecloths, *serviettes,* nightcaps, and irons for pressing linens were listed, alongside an assortment of copper basins, pewter dishes, andirons, skewers, a dripping pan, two small candlesticks, two dozen small pewter plates, and a small copper water-reservoir (*fontaine*). A coffee mill, two sugar loaves, a tin coffee box, and two white metal coffee pots completed the contents of the wardrobe. Étiennette Charpentier apparently took her meals in the room with the *armoire,* and at least some of the cooking was done there.

The clothes in the *armoire* consisted of nine bonnets, five *gorgettes* (some plain, others with lace), six handkerchiefs, three pair of "stirrup" hose, four pairs of underpants, two lace-trimmed shifts, two striped dressing gowns of cotton, and an assortment of skirts, scarves, and coats, all of gray or black serge, silk, or wool. Six pairs of sheets, seven table-cloths, four camisoles, a dozen more *serviettes,* other bits of clothing, and small pieces of cloth completed the listing.

Her silver and jewelry consisted of two old silver candlesticks, a saltcellar, a goblet, a holy-water holder and crucifix, a sauceboat, a porringer, six spoons, six forks, 234 silver tokens (*jetons,* probably awarded for attending guild meetings), a gold ring with a diamond, and a gold pin with four little diamonds—objects either inherited or bought for the pleasure of owning, using, and wearing them. The shop was below these rooms, accessible from the street. An oak counter with two doors and two drawers contained just under 13 *livres* in various coins. A large canvas ensign showing a carpenter with his tools clearly served to identify the name of the shop owner. An old four-door *armoire* contained the stock; it must have been tall because there was a five-step ladder so she could reach the top shelves. Five low-backed, tapestry-covered chairs, five shelves of beech and pine used for displaying cloth, a small chiming clock in an oak case, a toilette mirror, a copper brazier, a spittoon of walnut, and a copper balance made up the rest of the furnishings. No andirons are listed: the only heating must have come from the brazier.

An assortment of common and fine linens of various dimensions and qualities was appraised as worth a little more than 6,650 *livres.* There was heavy ticking of hemp, muslin "from the mountains," gray Laval cloth, toweling, linen from Alençon, Rouen, Lisieux, and Troyes as well as from Holland and Frisia. Her personal effects, plus a labyrinth of small investments and money owed to her by relatives, would bring her heirs a total inheritance of some ten to eleven thousand *livres,* certainly not a huge sum, but not small either. Her niece, also a *lingère,* would receive almost nothing: her share of the estate would go to satisfy her creditors.

Étiennette Charpentier's lengthy will is in her own hand. She may have had some legal advice in drawing it up, but it remains deeply personal. She refers to her estate as the "property which God has permitted me to earn," and describes the time of death as "when my body is separated from my soul." Asking to be buried without pomp near the cross in the cemetery of Saint-Séverin, with six torchbearers who are poor, and with minimal bell-ringing, Charpentier distributes bequests for masses and charity to almost a dozen different confraternities, asylums, and convents (including Port Royal, where her sister was a nun). She instructs her executrix to put the money directly into the hands of the poor, evidently fearing that it will be absorbed by the general treasuries of those institutions. Two hundred *livres* are given to the Jesuits, in gratitude for their "instruction" when she was young, by which she presumably means religious instruction since girls were not admitted to Jesuit *collèges*. Her executrix and friend was to receive the gold ring with the diamond, as a token of friendship and an expression of gratitude for carrying out her wishes.

As a highly respected *lingère*, Étiennette Charpentier was part of the culture of reading and writing, irrespective of whether she had inherited her books or bought them. The books the notaries describe as having "no consequence" and her will in her own hand are the proof. She probably would not have owned books of no value unless she could read them. What were they? An almanac, a prayer book, books for teaching reading and writing, or perhaps a novel or two? It is impossible to answer the question, but it is possible that not only their usual lack of value but also male hostility to women's reading might account for their being listed as of "no consequence."

Étiennette Charpentier's furnishings, especially the pictures, books, silver, and the coffee service—suggest a taste for luxury consumption, and there seems to have been no apparent feeling of contradiction with very strong, highly institutionalized Roman Catholicism. What was once the preserve of aristocratic and legal professional families, and the tax farmers, was becoming a more available lifestyle in modest proportion in the seventeenth century. It is probable that merchant families increased consumption more slowly than royal officials, but the general trend was in the same direction. Charpentier's father had been a *maître écrivain,* or public writer, that is, he earned his living drafting letters for people who could not write. It is not impossible that, just as the father taught his two sons calligraphy, so he taught his daughters to write (Étiennette's younger sister had a lovely hand), so that they could help at home or earn extra money as copyists. We shall never know.

Étiennette Charpentier's brother, Marc-Antoine, had spent several years in Rome, perfecting his skills as a composer. When he returned to France, he composed devotional music for the princely House of Guise and for the Dauphin. During these same years, he wrote theatrical music for Molière and the troupe that kept his theater going after his death. He eventually moved on to the Jesuits at the Church of Saint-Louis, then ended his career as chapel master at the Sainte-Chapelle. He had borrowed money from his sister at a couple of crucial points in his career, and he did not repay these debts. Étiennette's heirs were the rapacious children of her late sister: Marie-

Anne Édouard-Mathas and Jacques Édouard, the former an indebted *lingère* and the latter a quite unsuccessful bookseller who kept a stall near Notre-Dame. They could scarcely wait for her to die, but she defended herself and her patrimony against their constant requests for "loans." Had her apartment not been quickly locked by the notaries and the contents put under seal, it is doubtful if the shop girl could have kept out the niece and her aggressive husband. The girl, simply described as a *"fille* to help in the shop," is willed two hundred *livres*. No name is given because Étiennette Charpentier was not certain who would be working for her at the time of her death. She specified that in order to inherit the 200 *livres,* the "girl" had to have worked for her at least four or five months. Like so many prices, rents, and wages in the seventeenth century, bequests to servants were scaled according to the social rank of the person making the bequest, rather than to the specific duties carried out by the servant. Had Étiennette Charpentier had a chambermaid, that domestic would not only have received a bequest in cash but the clothes of her late mistress, which she could decide either to wear or to sell, there always being a strong market for used clothes.

In Abraham Bosse's engraving of the parable of the wise virgins, six young women are depicted reading, their lamps and a flagon of oil nearby. Each virgin holds a small book, presumably devotional. Reading, indeed learning to read for a moral purpose, had had its defenders among learned humanists since at least the late fifteenth century. Reading for pleasure was, however, considered sinful because it was a waste of time. Frivolous reading challenged the social control by the Church. Writing was still more threatening, especially when done simply for self-expression or profit. When uncoupled from learning, in the sense of research into religious or scientific thought, writing was to be condemned. To be sure, men had written simply for pleasure, but no matter. In fact, not a few women writers would decline to put their names on their works—not just for fear of censorship, but for fear of social and religious ostracism. Male writers (Charles Sorel and the Duke of la Rochefoucauld, for example) also sometimes avoided notoriety by not signing their works. Thus the Catholic Reformation environment tested the mettle of writers as they began to raise the notion of "writer" to a cultural dignity which, in the nineteenth century, would come to be virtually equal to the moral authority exercised by priests.

In a city where a large percentage of the population still could neither read nor write, it was quite paradoxical to begin to read about, or to refer to, some men and women as "writers." The current usage, with the term "master"—the *maître écrivain,*

Nil vain obiet ne peut distraire
Ces Vierges, sages en tout temps ;
Aux Folles leur honeur contraire
S'entretient de plaisirs constans

La Nuict, quand les autres sommeillent
D'vn repos qui leur semble doux ;
Celles cy raisonnent et veillent
Attendant leur celeste Espous.

LES VIERGES SAGES.

Le Monde en vain leur fait la guerre,
Puis qu'il est certain que leur yeux,
Fermes aux Ombres de la Terre,
Ne s'ouurent qu'aux clartez des Cieux

Ce n'est que la seule Sagesse
Qu'elles se proposent pour but
Et que les guidant les adresse
Dans le vray chemin de salut.

le Blond excud auec Priuilege du Roy.

The wise virgins, by Abraham Bosse. The biblical parable is interpreted to teach the morals of preparedness and obedience.

the "master writer"—was known to everyone, and especially those who could not write: he was the man on the street corner with a little portable desk, ink, paper, and quills, whom one paid to write letters to relatives back in the provinces. The master writer earned pennies for his work, but his craft had corporate status and a monopoly over the occupation of writing from dictation.

Not savants, or philosophers, or men of letters, women who wrote and circulated their writings among friends and had them published came to be known as "writers" when the activity still had something pejorative about it. The term "woman of letters" never became current, largely because men of letters refused to apply it to persons who knew literature only through translation. For these men, the women had no "letters," a code word for education; they were mere scribblers.

Debates over a woman's capacity to learn, and whether she should learn if she could, continued throughout the century. But it is important to note that while in certain circles women came to be known as writers, that title had not yet assumed the prestige it would later have. Still, the lineage of Simone de Beauvoir, Colette, and Marguerite Duras begins with Mesdemoiselles de Scudéry and Montpensier, Marie-Madeleine de Lavergne (usually referred to by her assumed name, "Madame de Lafayette"), and Marie-Catherine Desjardins (known by her assumed name, "Villedieu").

The aristocratic rank that initially would be so important for female writers became less consequential as conviviality and rivalry, wit and charm, came to be definable social skills that women could learn. If genuinely witty, high-ranking, or if inspired poets, men survived in the new literary salons of the 1660s, but woe to him who displayed erudition or peppered his talk with Latin. The pedant became the butt of jokes and ridicule; only the very learned could understand him. The notion of being genteel also assured recourse to the general knowledge familiar to everyone from conversation. To say something heavy with references from lecture halls was a sign of lack of maturity. Conversation, an art that could be learned, turned on themes selected by hostesses, not hosts; and those who learned their rhetoric well in school often found this to be a handicap. After all, making a speech in a court of law or giving a sermon were not the skills most vaunted in conversation. Their lack of schooling turned to the advantage of women here, as it also would in writing novels.

How to measure the depth of the new literary culture in Parisian society? Novels, essays, and songs sometimes went through as many as ten editions, with print-runs of about a thousand each. Hence literary culture became part of luxury consumerism. Novels and essays were often not collected as books, but were passed on like newspapers—ending in privies. For males, especially the learned ones, encounters in various libraries, which still usually were monastic or judicial or had been constituted for a *collège,* remained preserves for the learned. Frequently celibate, and garbed in cassocks or in the gowns of the law courts or the medical faculties, these learned men met for verbal tournaments about points of scholarly controversy. With very few exceptions,

L'Almerinde. This frontispiece for a novel of intrigue and murder set in ancient Greece captures the heroine writing a letter confessing her imposture. She is in a *cabinet* where the walls are hung with tapestries; the table is covered with a *bure,* the root word for the word *bureau,* "desk."

painfully conventional verse, usually about inspiration from a muse, flowed from the pens of these celibate males, who read them before a shy group of listeners afraid of saying the wrong thing.

The *salon,* with its mingling of men and women, and the all-female gathering in a *cabinet* or some other quite private space, free from interruption, had very different social and gender dynamics. How could more socially modest women come together for conversation or a meal? The characteristic two-story *maison bourgeoise* did not really have a space where literature could be discussed. True, women received guests in their bed chambers, even in the *ruelle,* the space between the wall and the bed, which had intimate, even erotic connotations if a male friend was received there alone. But in general, when the lady of the house received larger groups of six to eight people while still in bed, it was a ceremonial event to receive congratulations after childbirth or to accept condolences. The *ruelle* was often one-on-one, except in high-status households; while receptions in the bed chamber were pretty solemn affairs, scarcely a time for talking about the latest poems or about the pangs the heart felt after reading about the love of shepherds and shepherdesses who were actually disguised nobles, not peasants. Bosse's engraving of women dining in the absence of their husbands is interesting in that the experience must have had some social and gender significance. Since the dining room had yet to be invented as a domestic space for the specific activity of dining, they are in a bed chamber, but it is not clear that their conversation centers on literary subjects.

In the newly designed luxury housing of the Île Saint-Louis, the Faubourg Saint-Germain, and the Place Royale and the surrounding *Marais,* there were rooms expressly designed for receiving small numbers of guests, say four or five, for conversation—the *cabinet* being the prime example. The aristocratic and vivacious Julie d'Angennes (the daughter of Madame de Rambouillet) received guests and inspired the budding poets of high social rank to write verse about her virtues and beauty. Needless to say, finding a place to hold small conversation groups in an aristocratic *hôtel* was not difficult, since *cabinets* and *galeries* had been part of their makeup since the mid-sixteenth century. But what about the social world of the wives and sisters of the legal professionals, the tax farmers, the merchants? Just like the *hôtels,* the new type of house would have a *cabinet* for the master of the house, another for the mistress, and small rooms, still called *salons,* for conversation.

Sometimes, when women met regularly each week, their conversations were referred to as *académies,* but over time that term gradually became reserved for the royal institutions with that name. By the 1660s the proliferation of such weekly gatherings began to alter the Parisian cultural landscape. Indeed, the old male, Latin-centered, and learned culture lost ground to both the women's groups and to *the* French Academy, still another place where learning had to be left at the door or worn lightly, in the form of rhetoric. To be sure, the French Academy had its place, hortatory for the king and ceremony-filled around controversy between ancients and moderns, but smaller groups became the arbiters of a more private taste.

Regardless of their social rank, women administered households, though males oversaw the procurement of larger supplies such as firewood, wine, candles, and dried fruit. Since the fourteenth century, women were often depicted with rings of keys on their belts, indicating that they alone had access to the storage rooms, *armoires,* and cellars of the house. Servants came and went, often engaged by the mistress of the house, who did not trust them. Supervision of the housework took hours and hours, and much patience—an educational and acculturation process of enormous importance for the teenage domestics who had fled the countryside in search of food and work. Repeated pregnancies shortened the lives of these women, the average length of a marriage being probably no more than fifteen years. Males remarried and had more children: the daughter from the first marriage—Cinderella—was sometimes an object of scorn and jealousy. Otherwise the story would not have had the romance it still possesses today, especially in the way it shares the dream of marrying not just a prince but a prince who loves her alone.

Except in grand Court portraits, the Parisian women of the seventeenth century, married or single, hold a book as they look out at us, dressed in black, bodice laced, and head covered by a starched white bonnet. The courtly young women depicted by Bosse have fewer buttons on their bodices buttoned up, and they are often in quite compromising positions, alone with young males (Touch), indicating an erotic, *galant* dimension to these prints that authentic portraits of women do not have.

Male moralists inveighed against women for wasting so much time reading novels, but no one seems to have noticed the profound contradiction between the portrait with the prayer book and the onslaught against women over novels. To be sure, the genre of the portrait had, and still has, a transcendental dimension, with thoughts about the passage of time and the fragility of life easily coming to mind. But it is tempting to think of women reading novels by candlelight in their beds (Tristan L'Hermite); and however paradoxical, there is evidence to suggest that the same women might read pious books and novels, irrespective of their age group, such being the power of reading in a society where large segments of the population had been deprived of it. Also, while women's education increased in the seventeenth century, largely through convent schools such as those run by the Ursulines, the daughters of judges and merchants perhaps were instructed by their brothers' tutors. Their reading may have been relatively free of the quite all-encompassing emphasis on piety in the schools.

There developed a pious fictional genre—Bishop Camus excelled in it—through which readers could share the devotional and the fictional all in one; but this combination never attracted as large a readership as the books that kept fantasies about love between dukes and duchesses at the Court of Henry II quite distinct from the devotional. To delineate the specific role of women writers in creating fictional courtly worlds in which historical figures revolved, it must be remembered that it was Honoré d'Urfé, a *gentilhomme* from the Forez and a contemporary of Henry IV, who, in the thousands of pages in his *Astrée,* updated the old chivalric notions of courtly love and moved them to a pastoral setting. D'Urfé's characters have very aristocratic and Neoplatonic currents of thought, clothed beneath the costume of shepherds and shepherdesses. Love and social relations are not generally violent, erotic but not sexual. Intimacy between the sexes is explored to some degree (verbal intimacy, hand-holding, and exchanging small gifts), as reputation and honor become shattered or strengthened by love. After d'Urfé, male writers tended to satirize this rural fantasy world, but not only did women take pleasure in reading *Astrée,* the novel also became a cult object through which memories and friendships could be built and sustained. Inspired by *Astrée,* women easily moved from conversations about the novel to imitations of the life it described—this in an age when imitation was not a derogatory approach to creating works of art.

In the gilded and painted *cabinets* of the new houses on the Place Royale, the Faubourg Saint-Germain, and the Île Saint-Louis, the novel undoubtedly was more frequently the subject of conversation among women, and exclusively among women, than it was in *salons* where learned men were present. Conversation and "portraits," those brief descriptions of a person's physical features that reveal character or personality, constituted the salient features of the aristocratic literary romance as it developed in the mid-seventeenth century. The locale remained quite vague, but it was always splendid and rich. There were isolated *pavillons* in the woods, and clothes reflected in candlelight and in pools in grottoes. There were secret *cabinets* that only the lovers could enter. Balls and receptions were described as ideal places where men and women could meet and fall in love. The narrative of seduction tended to be augmented by details about *décor* and clothes, but the same devices—the eye contact, the quickened pulse, and the blush—still remained characteristic of the most successful or unsuccessful novel. Intensity of sensual experience would, of course, go beyond the words available to express it, with love becoming ineffable. As the novel traveled thematically downward to include *bourgeoises* (Furetière), there were fewer tales of falling in love with someone of one's own sex who has cross-dressed.

In her *Artamène, ou Le Grand Cyrus,* written during the agitated political atmosphere of the Fronde, Madeleine de Scudéry set her contemporaries in ancient Greece and gave them pseudo-historical names, the "Grand Cyrus" being, of course, the "Grand Condé." And having compared *salonnière* Madame de Rambouillet with various Greek goddesses, Scudéry portrays her thusly:

> Furthermore, the mind and soul of this marvelous person surpasses her beauty by a lot, her mind being limitless in its extension, and her soul is without equal in *générosité,* constancy, goodness, justice, and purity. Cléomire's mind is not like one which has only the brilliance that nature gave it. She has cultivated it with care, and I think I am able to say that there is nothing of the lofty subjects that she does not know. She knows various foreign languages, and she knows just about everything that is worth knowing, but she knows it without seeming to. She always speaks admirably; . . . she has found the art of making a [living] space of only medium size into one of vast expansiveness. Order, regularity, elegance are to be found everywhere in her rooms, and all the furnishings are magnificent; even the lighting lamps are different from those others have. Her *cabinets* are filled with thousands of rare objects, . . . the air is always perfumed in her palace, and splendid baskets of flowers make for a perpetual springtime in her room.

The literature of courtly fantasy and the new consumerism that gained ground so rapidly in the late sixteenth and early seventeenth centuries complement each other effectively in Scudéry's novels.

As the princely Fronde stalemated, Condé's brutal attempts to wield power in Paris soured the heroic impulses among many writers, including Scudéry, who as a probable result made a brilliant, very attention-grabbing shift in her lengthy serial novel. Imagining a historical-mythical little ancient Greek female community composed of the "happy few" and devoted to literature and music under the leadership of the real-life Sappho, Scudéry offered images and ways of behaving that strengthened an inclination to value literature and writing as serious self-expression. Sappho's works survived only in fragments, but these fragments confirmed her high reputation in ancient Roman and Hellenistic literary commentary. A poetess who sang of love six centuries before the Christian era became an example to follow, a historical cultural moment that Scudéry could make still more utopian and feminist on behalf of women and writing. Sappho's love lyrics were interpreted as homoerotic by some writers, among them Plutarch and Longinus, a fact that stimulated seventeenth-century Hellenists to ponder deeply the grammar in the surviving lyric fragments, in order to make up their minds about whether or not Sappho was sexually attracted to women. This question may have stimulated interest in Sappho among the learned, including Pierre Bayle, who included an article on the subject in his *Dictionnaire;* but it was not Scudéry's principal concern. Neither a scholar nor an explorer of the ambiguities about sexuality that were frequently found in love poetry, she created a feminist cultural space centered on writing, conversation, and music that had parallels in the ancient Greek world and in her own. As we shall see, no writer quite accomplished for Christine de Pisan's reputation what Scudéry did for Sappho, perhaps because Christine's writings were not only numerous and extant, but also paid more attention to masculine pretensions for power.

Just as a specific area in the house had to be created before private reading and writing could take place, so the written description of these places in novels (and, after 1672, in the *Mercure Galant,* and eventually in the *Journal des Dames* of the eighteenth century) fundamentally altered Parisian elite culture. The third element was, of course, the portrait example of the courtly woman: learned but not pedantic, perfectly mannered, creating her own courtly lifestyle. This novelesque portrait paralleled the examples of learned, effective, and even pious women that were collected in the so-called "galleries of worthy women." Fiction and history were enveloped together in female cultural spaces and social relations. Learned males, from Sorel to Boileau, smarted; and though they satirized these literary works that established literary fashions, the effect was perhaps to advertise them, not cause them to fall into disfavor. Male command over literary trends declined abruptly after 1660 and would perhaps only return to dominance again in the nineteenth century. A public—a modern reading, theatergoing, conversing public—had come into existence in Paris in the 1660s to 1680s, and this public was neither the old political-legal public inherited through the growth of the monarchy after the Middle Ages nor the spiritual public of the church, Gallican or universal. Male writers in the eighteenth century took their cues from this literary public, adapting its "rules" into the quite influential combination of the female-directed *salons* and the Enlightenment.

With the *Princesse de Clèves,* published in 1678, the novel became a mature genre. It not only lost its awkward impression of being endless, but it started the trajectory of defining interpersonal relations in less aristocratic and courtly ways. Like virtually all seventeenth-century writers, Marie-Madeleine Pioche de Lavergne, better known as Madame de Lafayette, had no formal schooling, but she attended various *salons* and women's groups in Paris. With influential friends at Court, and easy familiarity if not intimacy with some of the other great writers of her generation, particularly La Rochefoucauld, Lavergne navigated between gendered literary worlds and strikingly different forms of conversation.

The Court during the reign of Henry II is depicted in gentle, almost youthful terms. No one sinister appears, no intrigue destroys, though human foibles, especially male ones, move history and the novel forward. Henry II insisted on just one more joust, despite attempts by several courtiers to convince him to stop. Just moments later an accident occurred that would prove fatal. Lafayette therefore makes Henry's hubris the reason for his death.[1] The Duke of Nemours, a perfect, upright, handsome leader at Court, falls in love with a married woman. His weakness is a moral flaw that causes his beloved pain and leads to her husband's death. Nemours cannot stop himself from overhearing his beloved admit to her husband that she feels an "inclination" for another man. He sinks deeper into passionate love when he recounts this conversation to a friend, who then gossips about it at Court.

The Princess of Clèves is a genuine heroine, one who watches her beloved in knightly combat but is married to a man she does not love. Her husband is upright, patient, and deeply in love with his wife; and he is, of course, a close friend of Nemours. Accidents, such as a lost letter found by the wrong person, prompt ever more intense feelings of love mingled with suspicion. Slight moral weaknesses in the men involved in this love triangle become larger faults as the novel progresses. Only the heroine remains com-

---

1. Lafayette offers a highly plausible account of the rise to power of the Cardinal of Guise and his brother, the duke, immediately after Henry II's death in 1559. Catherine de Médicis ordered the powerful Constable Montmorency to stay beside the late king's bier, and he may well have spent days there. By isolating him in this way, the Guises and Catherine effectively took over the government. To the late seventeenth-century reader, this brief account of the origins of what would culminate in a civil war would have great historical plausibility. Still, Lafayette offers no slippage from the world of Court life and gossip to the high politics of governing the fate of the realm.

pletely upright, intelligent, and compassionate as she refuses to betray the husband she does not love and refuses to enter her beloved's presence.

In addition to the Louvre, the Clèves' château of Coulommiers, with its lovely gardens and isolated little *pavillon* where intimate conversation can take place, and the heroine's house and garden in the capital are almost lyrically sketched to stimulate the reader's fantasies. The princess refuses to see Nemours, who unbeknownst to her has found a remote place on another property that provides a view onto her garden. Needless to say, the jilted lover spends hours in his hideaway, watching the princess. The rich, jewel-encrusted velvet clothes of the men are described, but there is little attention to women's garb. At one point, Nemours spies the princess through a window at Coulommiers: it is a hot summer evening, and only her flowing blonde hair covers her chest. In the *Princesse de Clèves,* Lafayette is an effective miniaturist in regard to the consumerist tendency that would gain currency among her imitators.

Despite her husband's death, which makes it possible to wed Nemours, the princess withdraws from society, her passion having subsided. This triumph of the will is exemplary: it teaches the truth that marriage must be grounded on friendship, as a sharing of souls, not just on falling in love. And the ideal of "retirement" is extolled; it is not a sign of failure or religious crisis. The princess is almost a pendant for the medieval knight who loves his lady intensely but never pollutes this love by violent seduction or marriage. To be sure, she is a princess, but she is above all a woman. Rank had been no impediment: she was every bit as aristocratic, and perhaps more so, as her beloved, the Duke of Nemours, who came from an immensely prestigious family. The novel always turns on movements of the heart and the will, not on social rank or wealth. Lafayette's accomplishment in so few pages was very great: it would not be equaled until Abbé Prévost's *Manon Lascaut* of 1753.

The most significant indicator of the depth of the new writing and consumerist culture that women had created would be the invention of new words, and new meanings for old words. In the very decades when learned male literary culture was deleting vulgar words and awkward usages and creating the French classical language, small circles of women conversationalists and writers were inventing euphemisms, those special meanings of words that veiled the intimate and the erotic, usually, and by association, luxury objects. The tiniest attention to gestures, eye movements, or a turn of the head, or to scarves, combs, and ribbons worn a certain way, stimulated and excited verbal exchange and writing. In novels, conversation was the principal narrative device. What came to be called *préciosité*—and especially the special words for friendship, love, and luxury living—finally confirms the impression that the feminine creative movement in the mid-seventeenth century ran deep. Some male friends of Mademoiselle de Scudéry also created new meanings for words, made puns, and worked out what was almost a jargon known only to a few friends; but in general, the *collège*-trained males ridiculed *préciosité* in their essays and in conversation. Without condemning the effort toward exploring enhanced powers of literary language, Molière attempted to draw the line between whimsical or witty word play and the creation of "affected" meanings for old words. Other learned males were far more harsh, but it was not really their criticism that caused the movement to decline. The rise of the literary public, and its acceptance as an arbiter of taste, brought about a poised, measured equilibrium between gender and literary expression.

Growing respect for what we know as "classical" French, with its uncluttered syntax, strict rules of usage, and academically "approved" vocabulary—combined with a decline in the insularity of small literary groups—was the inevitable result of the creation of the literary public. Certainly not a popular movement, the literary public nonetheless created the desire to see the plays and read the books being talked about; and the desire to be read by larger and larger numbers of people—authorial *gloire*—slowly pulled together literary concerns and the consumerist movement for selling books and luxuries. Criticism as a genre remained weak, so far as it can be learned about. Works were usually either demolished or praised to the skies, depending on the affiliations and the friendship networks to which a writer belonged. Theater criticism could be ugly, as it was over Racine's *Phèdre* in 1677, a major work so ridiculed by a small women's party at Court that the author gave up writing for the theater.

While Madeleine de Scudéry's famous *Carte de Tendre,* a map that shows emotions as stops on the journey to true love, is considered to be an expression of *préciosité,* it is really only a visual depiction of the terms about love and friendship that poets, composers, and novelists used when narrating intimate relations. The subject of hours and hours of conversation, the *Carte de Tendre* gave structure and hierarchy to the vocabulary of love. Feelings, not reason, are celebrated in the little villages. The Lake of Indifference heralds a distancing in human relations (it is always better to be less vulnerable to love's powers), culminating in the virtually cruel, exploitative mood that writers such as Choderlos de Laclos captured in the later eighteenth century.

The contrast sharpens between vague geographical distance and central place in the later novels of the seventeenth century. This is also true for memoirs, especially those of Mademoiselle de Montpensier, known to her contemporaries as the "Grande Mademoi-

The Carte de Tendre. The bucolic and still quite unstructured courtly relations in d'Urfé's *Astrée* (1608) tended to become less spontaneous after the mid-century writings and cartographies on the passions. The Scudéry *Carte de Tendre* was dedicated to Madame de Rambouillet.

selle." Speaking about the Grand Condé's descent into rebellion, she observed: "The intentions of the *grands* must be like the mysteries of the Faith. Men are not supposed to understand these mysteries. One must revere them and believe that they never are for anything but the good and the salvation of the fatherland [*patrie*]."[2] This apologia was not only heroic; it was ideological and a sincere expression of what she thought should be the attitude of everyone, not only toward Condé but toward herself as well.

2. "Il faut que les intentions des grands soient comme les mystères de la Foi; il n'appartient pas aux humains d'y pénétrer; on doit les révérer et croire qu'elles ne sont jamais que pour le bien et le salut de la patrie."

Montpensier pours out her heart in love for Lauzun, a love that ends in pain because neither she nor he can surmount the enormous differences in social rank that separate them. When she insisted that Lauzun's servants wear her livery, with the *fleur-de-lys* of France, instead of his, there was little room for him to demonstrate to the world his masculinity.

The Grande Mademoiselle had herself painted as an amazon, one of those strong women who fought like men, of whom ancient writers spoke and whom some presumed to find in the depths of Brazil. Was a woman's wearing of armor considered to be cross-dressing? The exchange of male clothes for female ones, and vice versa, had the usual "role reversal" implications of the "world upside-down," in fêtes, for example. The image of Joan of Arc in armor that is so strong in our minds was already known to the amazons of the seventeenth century. As the force of women's literary culture increased in the 1670s and 1680s, gender signs were increasingly contested, the result being more explicit and more apparent signs reserved for each sex. Women dressed more and more as women, and men as men, not because of Louis XIV's growing conformism (which was true), but because gender issues had been sufficiently public to make the outward signs of male and female sex specific. The *femmelette,* the man who liked jewelry and perfume, as Marshal Luxembourg did, was remarked about in ways he would not have been fifty years earlier.

The highly emotional, heartbreaking, tearfully intense narratives about falling in love so characteristic of seventeenth-century Parisian novels strike us as either trite or simply unbelievable, yet below their surface may be found a literary and psychological order that is primordial in Western culture. Feelings of being distraught, depressed, or even physically ill, all appear in the genre of the love narrative, as do reflections on cosmic forces, God, destiny, and fate.

The love letters that play such an important role in seventeenth-century Dutch genre scenes (and eighteenth-century Parisian ones) have rarely survived. In their brevity (including the very few authentic letters by Henry IV) and in the economy of their vocabulary—you are my heart, you are unique in the world to me, the thought of you uplifts my soul, and so forth—they are very similar to the fictional letters found in novels. When Monsieur Jourdain of *The Bougeois Gentilhomme* wrote *"Belle marquise, vos beaux yeux me font mourir d'amour"* (Lovely Marquise, your fine eyes make me die of love) and revealed his sense of inadequacy by struggling to improve the literary style of this love note, the resultant humor in no way undermines the convention of the love letter.

Indeed, Jourdain's attempt to fulfill a courtly lifestyle by forming a romantic attachment was typical of the day.

Letters had, of course, been an important genre for literary expression since at least the days of Petrarch and Erasmus, but their themes usually were spiritual and erudite, and were imbued with philosophical friendship rather than courtly love. In the early 1620s, Guez de Balzac published a volume of his literary and moral letters in French, promoted as and received as literature. The pioneering woman writer of the literary letter was Madame de Sévigné, a highly visible frequenter of *salons* and *précieuse* circles. In letters to her daughter, Madame de Grignan, and to her literary friends, she poured forth incisive social observation about the Parisians and the Court, with wit and some candor about herself. Not published in her lifetime but circulated in manuscript, her letters marked an important step in the movement for women's literary self-expression.

The Grande Mademoiselle's account of her very painful and disastrous love for the Marquis de Lauzun has an authentic air about it, yet it, like the love letter, has literary features. Daughter of the indecisive but charming brother of Louis XIII, Gaston d'Orléans, Mademoiselle de Montpensier grew up as the richest heiress in the realm. Her royal rank made her eligible to wed the highest-ranking kings and princes of Europe, including her own first cousin, Louis XIV. But after years and years of rumors and failed negotiations, the Grande Mademoiselle remained unmarried. In 1670, at forty-three, she suddenly experienced some sort of disquiet. Sensing that she really wanted to marry, she came to assert that, at her age, she could wed anyone she wished. Very punctilious about her high rank, she nonetheless hoped for, even longed for, an intimate love relationship with a man, believing that by her power and wealth she could raise up anyone on whom her eye fell, and that the king would approve the match.

The Marquis de Lauzun came from an old noble family, the Caumonts. He was an officier in the royal army and a likeable, respected figure at Court. When the Grande Mademoiselle's eyes fell on him, she pretended to seek his advice and help for marriage negotiations—a role he accepted. She idealized him, gazed at him at parties, took pride in his military command (Soubise had doffed his hat to Lauzun in military salute, not in courtly recognition of his rank, which was inferior to Soubise's). Occasional conversations between Lauzun and the Grande Mademoiselle took place while the army and the Court traveled north to the front, as war loomed. Finally, the princess told Lauzin that she would write on a piece of paper the name of the person she really loved and would give it to him. He had long suspected her inclination for him, but he had not dared to respond for fear that their relationship would become known, and that he would be ridiculed for daring to express his love for someone of a rank so far above his. The letter, written with her heart beating rapidly, simply said, "It is you." Lauzun interpreted this as making fun of him. In her thoughts about Lauzun, the princess had come to wonder whether God had predestined their union; she wondered what their horoscopes would reveal; and she thought of some verses from Corneille that captured her loving feelings.

Louis XIV did not immediately say no when she asked permission to wed. The possibility of a marriage with his recently widowed brother, Philip, was brought up, but the king did not stridently press the Grande Mademoiselle into such a union. She was at the end of her childbearing years and Philip clearly preferred intimate relationships with males. After wavering for a while in favor of her request to marry Lauzun, Louis XIV finally said no, to the despair and grief of the broken-hearted cousin with whom he had been raised. In refusing, the otherwise very absolutist king added the following words, as recorded by the Grande Mademoiselle, and raising his voice so that he could be heard by everyone in the room:

> "Kings [said Louis XIV] must satisfy the public. Assuredly you will
> sacrifice yourself to this [principle], because those who would see you
> making this [marriage] would make fun of you." [I answered:] "I ask
> your Majesty's pardon if I say this, but it is very true." He replied: "It
> is late. I shall say no more about it." . . . He embraced me and took
> me to the door, where I found someone whom I cannot recall. I went
> as fast as I could to my lodgings, where I cried out in shrieks.

What had happened? Lauzun had become entangled in contradictory advice from friends and relatives; but undoubtedly more important for understanding the king's decision was the opposition from the Condé branch of the royal family, a faction that included Madame de Longueville. Some of the king's closest councillors had advised the couple to wed quickly; but the details of court etiquette, titles, and the bride's great wealth had prompted opposition.

Despite her vast fortune and her lofty rank—and her often prickly temper—the Grande Mademoiselle narrates what could only be an embarrassment. Why? Without the account of her love for Lauzun, her *Memoirs* would have been stilted, if not distorted; so the fact that she included this incident not only testifies to her honesty but to the role that writing could play in self-expression and creativity for seventeenth-century women. To be sure, seventeenth-century men wrote memoirs; but affairs of the heart rarely appear in them, and when they do they take the form of brief allusions, as peccadillos in some instances. By narrating her love story, the princess made fiction become more real. By sharing her embarrassment, the Grande Mademoiselle opened the way to the more intimate private memoir, thereby prefiguring the *Confessions* of Jean-Jacques Rousseau. The princess never married: as she wrote her memoirs, she relived the joy and the pain of a true love affair.

Prior to 1660–70, there was a nonchalance about writing among women. They were almost all of aristocratic birth and, as noted previously, were often reluctant to sign their works. Authorship still had an odor about it: it was lower-class rather than commercial. Lafayette never generally admitted that she was the author of the *Princesse de Clèves*. From the beginning of her career as a writer, Marie-Catherine Desjardins wrote almost constantly, not only because she needed the income, but that was the way she was. To call Scudéry or Lafayette "professional writers" is to use the term very loosely. They earned *gloire* from writing, but they were not professionals in a Weberian sense of the word. Writers, male and female, were still socially defined as exercising a "craft," not a profession, because they usually sold the products of their pen to printer-publishers. The piecework aspect of the writer's craft often but not always prompted very high rates of literary production. Several writers of history produced between ten and twenty thousand printed pages in their lifetimes. The great women novelists, Scudéry and Lafayette, for example, were also very productive, but less so than some of their colleagues, say Villedieu, who occasionally wrote for a perceived consumerist readership.

Indeed, Villedieu *was* a professional writer, for her whole being turned on writing and she earned her livelihood with her pen. In Lafayette's writing there may still have been something of the aristocratic nonchalance. Not so in Villedieu. She has one of her heroines declare: "To begin with, I never knew who I was; I only knew that I am a person with a common (run-of-the-mill) destiny. My birth, my education, and my marriages have had the effect of being like extraordinary adventures." Her life fascinated contemporaries, but not everything written about her is true. Born out in Alençon (Normandy) in 1632, her parents were Parisian, her mother possibly being a lady-in-waiting for the Duchess of Montbazon and her father an attorney. There were rumors that as a girl she had to flee Paris because of a pregnancy. Portraits of her confirm her own self-description:

> I shall say that I have a happy and witty physiognomy, small black
> eyes, a big mouth, with beautiful teeth, which does not make opening
> it unpleasant; a complexion as pretty as can be after a nasty smallpox
> left its scars, an oval face, chestnut-colored hair, the bust and hands
> inclined to be beautiful; someday I will have some extra weight, but
> up to now my age and waistline have prevented it. . . . I love Paris very
> much and can have good times in the country. . . . I like to tease a lot
> and never get angry when I am teased back.

Is this the portrait of a straightforward professional woman? There are only the vaguest possible Neoplatonic resonances, and no aristocratic nose or noble forehead. As might be expected, Villedieu peoples her novels (the exception being her historical novels) with generally quite anonymous individuals with vague social ranks and looks, but the heroines and the heroes are always attractive and dashing. The reader is tempted to see the author projecting herself into her characters, even though the latter occasionally have well-known names. Love, disguises, orphaned and lost princesses and princes, ships lost at sea, sieges, and long dialogues between lovers show a remarkable talent for taking the tiniest shred of history and developing it into an entire novel.

Villedieu had a "natural" talent for writing poetry, and she earned a genuine literary reputation. One of her plays, *Le Favori,* would be produced in court in 1664–65. The story of a king who arbitrarily arrests a minister-favorite in order to find out who his true friends were, after which he has the minister released, is quite daring politically, coming as it did so soon after Fouquet's arrest and trial. Did Villedieu offer Louis XIV a way out of the moral dilemma he had got himself into when arresting Fouquet? The real minister-favorite spent the rest of his life in a prison in Pignerola.

In the later 1670s, Villedieu joined Scudéry in breaking with the novelistic tradition of setting a story in the French Court of the late sixteenth century. One of her novels would be set in Granada and another in ancient Greece, while Lafayette preferred the more conventional Spain, and Africa. Her sources remained quite obvious. She also wrote a history of the loves of great men, including, of course, Socrates, Caesar, and Bussy d'Amboise. In her *Disorders of Love* (1672), she borrowed from Tacitus and Suetonius to create a melodramatic love plot involving the Roman imperial family. Like the great Racinian tragedies where the whole fate of empires turns on personal jealousy, love, hate, and sex, Villedieu's fictional history laid the foundations for understanding those in high places as corrupt, luxury-loving brutes who would do

anything, even murder, to have their way. Villedieu implicitly instructed female readers in the art of high politics. Intercepted secret letters, disguised encounters, and
plots to disgrace the king's mother put considerable strain on a couple. Rumors, lies,
sexual favors, and political influence, not fidelity and honesty, seem to be the avenues
toward wealth, titles, and power. The image of "the family" is terrifying and not
unlike that of classical republican stereotypes about Caesar's despotism. For readers
unfamiliar with the history of ancient Rome or sixteenth-century Europe, were
Villedieu's novels historical? The possibility of drawing parallels with goings-on at
Versailles would build up over the next century of readers and imitators of Villedieu's
novels. Horrific accounts of murder, orgies, luxury, and supreme power had long been
the stuff of literature, with Boccaccio setting the example. But Villedieu gave the
lurid a new intensity for the "uneducated" reader. When Jean-Jacques Rousseau's
father read to the boy, it was not only late medieval romances but, perhaps, Scudéry's
and Villedieu's novels as well, which formed an indelible impression in the mind of
this supremely sensitive autodidact.

By 1670, Villedieu had become a legend of sorts: the *Recueil des choses diverses*
included this word-portrait, written several years earlier:

> At thirty years of age, she has a pension worth 2,000 *livres*. She rises at
> five in the afternoon, sees her friends or is seen by them, does not go
> out of her way to pay visits but is seen and receives them. She writes
> maxims about love, and novels. . . . She writes in bed. She wrote about
> orgasm [*jouissance*], which is very impertinent for a single woman. She
> writes with ease, is happy to be corrected, but she does not show her
> writings to others because she finds that they are always being criti-
> cized. Her fieriness appears in her passionate books. . . . She is impu-
> dent; she imitates La Fontaine's verse. D'Aubignac had a high opinion
> of her plays because she observes the rules.

In what ways did the major women writers who published their own works—
Scudéry, Lafayette, and Villedieu—break out of the routine-filled lives of their contemporaries? Evidence is scanty, but it is worthwhile to note that family demands
were thought to be natural for women, that is, commanding attention and time. Escape
from these affective constraints to do creative work was rarely possible, unless joining
a religious community could be considered an escape from family. Needless to say, life

in a convent scarcely gave autonomy; the rules to obey and the routines were probably as time-absorbing and distracting as family obligations.

By coming from the provinces, Scudéry, Lafayette, and Villedieu probably benefited from some geographical separation from their extended families, but this is not certain. During her formative, *salon*-attending years, Scudéry lived in the same household as her literary brother, Georges, who fled back to Normandy when Condé lost out in the Fronde, thereby giving his sister not only more privacy but also the opportunity to build her daily life around her chosen literary friends.

Lack of money, beyond the bare essentials required for paying a household servant to help with the cooking and washing, effectively impeded all three women from joining the parish women's charitable organizations, since participation in these groups required charitable giving and an outward life of piety. Having reached an understanding that would leave Madame de Lafayette responsible for raising their two sons in Paris, her husband retired to the provinces, where he battled creditors in order to raise revenues from his lands. From Paris, his wife helped with this litigation in every way she could, certainly a factor that could be psychologically time-consuming and that had the potential to distract her from writing about aristocratic love.

Like Scudéry and Lafayette, Villedieu also had family ties to Normandy, and little income from her family. Engaging and outgoing, Villedieu moved through numerous aristocratic circles and was genuinely respected and received as a friend. Clearly she was seeking protection, as is evident from numerous poems and dedications addressed to prominent persons at Court; but these gestures rarely yielded more than a present or two. Her recognition as a poet and her social flair attracted the attention of a secretary of state, Hugues de Lionne. A royal pension certainly helped the financial situation and gave Villedieu still more recognition. Of all the royal ministers, Lionne conformed least to the pious outward appearances that were supposed to characterize high royal officials. His support for Villedieu is evidence of a lively, youthful Court interested in literature and galantry, around a still-young king who supported Molière against the *dévots*.

A marriage late in her thirties and the birth of a son did not definitively sever Villedieu from her work. The husband did not live long, thereby freeing her but at the same time obliging her to pursue an inheritance out in the provinces. In fact, Villedieu's life is peopled with important affective relationships with males who die and leave her pretty much on her own.

The Grande Mademoiselle was immensely wealthy, and she certainly never thought of herself as a professional writer; nor did Madame de Sévigné, who, while lacking a fortune the size of Mademoiselle's, had the means to dower her daughter for the sum of 300,000 *livres* when she wed the Count of Grignan!

It has been estimated that there were some seventy books authored by women in sixteenth-century France, though this number may well increase as a result of further research. At least forty of these books were produced by Parisian publishers. Some bear titles indicating that they were devotional; others were literary, poetic, or medical (gynecological). But the absence of editions of ancient authors done by women indicates that Humanistic learning, which revered and edited the ancients, remained scarcely more accessible to women than was the university education from which they were totally excluded. Some of these were princesses, Marguerite de Navarre being the prime example; and Louise Labé's stature as a poet could scarcely be contested by the most misogynist of readers; but only one woman author came to play a major exemplary role, and this more than two centuries after her death. This was Christine de Pisan (1364–1430), whose writings ranged from the most serious and important of themes to romances, that late-medieval genre in which the fictional and the historical, the realistic and the fantastic, were combined in lofty narrative. Her great feminist work, the *Trésor de la Cité des Dames,* was written in response to attacks on women's intelligence by learned men. It may seem incongruous to reach back to a fifteenth-century author in a chapter about women and writing in the seventeenth century; but this is what women themselves did during the decades that followed the Fronde. The *Trésor de la Cité des Dames* saw three early editions, and numerous libraries owned manuscript versions; but Christine's writings remained unknown until there was a growing awareness, perhaps even a consciousness of the importance of writing by women as means to inspire women and to contest and refute the arguments that men were making about women writers. The pervasive silence in French literary culture of the sixteenth and seventeenth centuries about Christine's writings, including her poetry and her romances, is further evidence of the dominance of men, who allowed their familiarity with Latin and their experiences in a *collège* determine what should or should not be read.

The women feminists who began to collect and publish rosters of short, sometimes one-sentence biographies of learned, powerful, and saintly women included Christine, but they were unaware that she had done exactly the same thing two centuries earlier. Froissart, the chronicler who was Christine's contemporary, and some minor medieval poets would be edited and published in the seventeenth century, but not the *Cité des*

Dames. Christine recounts how she had been reading one day and was struck by Froissart's frequent, offensive, untrue, woman-hating remarks. This sense of injustice toward women prompted her to write the *Cité des Dames,* a complex work that not only demonstrates how women can use reason to refute misogynist attacks, but searches for and discovers women worthy of being praised and emulated. Some of these heroines were literary, others were devout, still others were artisans, including one of the women who painted the illuminated illustrations in her books.

Christine's strategy was like that which prompted women writers of the seventeenth century to begin collecting biographies of women: an impulse grounded on a sense of injustice. Boccaccio, whose gossipy, salacious work on women Christine knew and borrowed from, had none of the sense of the pursuit of justice for women that is Christine's central theme. Brantôme's *Dames Illustres,* written in the late sixteenth century but not published until the 1660s, perpetuated Boccaccio's gossipy, condescending tone, a distinctly male view of women written for male readers. The learned culture of the day represented by the Dupuy brothers, royal librarians, facilitated the publication of some of Brantôme's works, while Christine's *Cité* lay on the shelves of the royal library, with no new editions. True, her writing style would have seemed old-fashioned to the obsessively style-conscious Parisian readers of the 1650s, but editing scruples would not have prevented updating the style had the learned thought it desirable to publish.

A cursory exploration of the principal bibliographical directory of seventeenth-century writers (Cioranescu) lists seventy-eight women writers and their works. Sometimes only one publication is cited, perhaps a single poem or a devotional pamphlet; but it is clear that the scholars who are producing bibliographies have sought to include *all* writers, irrespective of their subject or the general significance of a work. About one-third of these women wrote devotional pamphlets or personal memoirs narrating their religious experiences. This high number is not surprising in the light of the pervasive force of the Catholic Reformation during the seventeenth century. Certainly there were lay women among these authors of devotional works, but there were also nuns, among them the Arnauld sisters—Agnès, Angélique, and Angélique de Saint-Jean—whose writings bore witness to the oppression by both the Church and the State as a result of their opposition to constituted authority and their reputedly heretical doctrines.

The women responsible for the administrative and financial welfare of the hundreds of venerable monastic communities across the realm, and the newly founded ones as well, carefully brought along two or three of the younger nuns, who could not only read and write but who knew how to litigate, keep accounts, and interact effectively with the religious, fiscal, and political figures who wielded influence on matters of property and investments. With these skills came privileges and, of course, power over others.

The last knightly heroes, who will be encountered in Chapter 9, and the first women writers of this chapter: a chronological and gender juxtaposition? Knightly and lady-like conduct had for centuries been as much a matter of literary and artistic imagination as social and political reality. Indeed, medieval social and gender roles, reshaped and transferred through a code of honor, would assure Louis XIV an almost endless supply of officers who came out of the provinces to pursue glory in his service by leading cavalry charges. The links between the chivalric romance and the seventeenth-century novel remained strong throughout the seventeenth century.

The fantasy world of the pastoral constructed by d'Urfé was both aristocratic and courtly, attracting readers to live vicariously, in love with princes and princesses. D'Urfé's chivalric fantasies had mostly lush green valleys (in the Forez) with streams of cool, crystal-clear water flowing through them. Conversing, and then writing in this fictional genre would give women ontological equality with men, that is, the right to be themselves, as individuals in groups of women, without the anxiety unleashed by attempting to enter the company of the learned—a quite exclusive culture where masculinity never really accepted Court culture, especially when there were questions about the androgynous nature of youthful, male, courtly love. The social power and production of humanist learning, especially legal and textual learning, declined rapidly after it had failed, by about 1570, to offer avenues out of religious conflict. Indeed, learning ancient languages, editing ancient authors, and practicing orations that Cicero might have appreciated, became priorities of a bygone era for the sons of the legal and medical families, the only ones where Humanism had the greatest impact. The lure of the muses—poetry in particular, plays, and their updated handmaiden, French rhetoric and prose rules—attracted the sons (and daughters) of legal professionals and state servants toward the courtly sirens of polite conversation, and the *salon*.

Religious fervor shifted toward devotional practice in and through the literary and visual arts, at the expense of the study of the Word and the history of the Early Church, facilitating a blurring between the sacred and the profane that already was none too clear. If pagan gods were dressed and closeted, the saints could radiate even more powerfully through their gold-framed portraits. Consumerist values and a culture of appearances, including religious devotions, went hand in hand. Bosse's engravings of a *gentilhomme* and a lady in church are as much about courtly gestures, fine clothes, jewelry, and hairstyle—and for the lady, reading—as they are about devotion. Indeed, these works are about fashion, displayed and legitimated by the atmosphere of emptiness in the Church.

While women who wrote novels and verse may not have seemed part of the feminist movement when they did not address the issue of women in their writings, they actually were. Aware at the outset of the high stakes for reaching recognition in small literary circles, female writers soon aimed at being recognized by the new literary public. Be they highborn, or not so highborn, all participated in the principal instrument used to gain recognition: collecting biographical data about worthy women, women who could be celebrated for their accomplishments as writers, for their political service, for their saintliness. Holding up worthy examples, heroic role models—that strong feature of medieval and Renaissance culture—pervaded the ethical and religious thought of European culture. French women were not at all pathbreaking or unique in this regard, except that the rosters of women did not include men. This separation made a medieval ethical genre at once more modern and susceptible to becoming secular. Integrating writing women into the canon of saintly women and stateswomen was facilitated by evoking the muses and antique heroines, notably Sappho.

Collège- and university-trained males participated somewhat in creating these rosters of worthy women, but in general they preferred to display their schoolboy learning by reasoning on a perfect subject, a binary subject: male versus female. The so-called "quarrel" about women in the seventeenth century is largely characterized by this recourse to simple logic, with few new facts or examples. Some largely male mental energy was absorbed, throughout the seventeenth century, by three possible assertions: (1) women are superior to men, which means pulling together some stories to support the contention; (2) men are superior to women, so muster evidence to support this contention; and (3) men and women are equal, which involves assembling supporting evidence to support this contention. Owing to the entrapping features of logical argument, these writings seemed important at the time and seemed more profound and more destabilizing of gender roles and rights than they actually were. By comparison with the movement to collect biographies of exemplary women, these logical arguments pale in significance. Derogatory clichés about women continued to be listed for the sake of argument, no matter how many times they had been previously refuted.

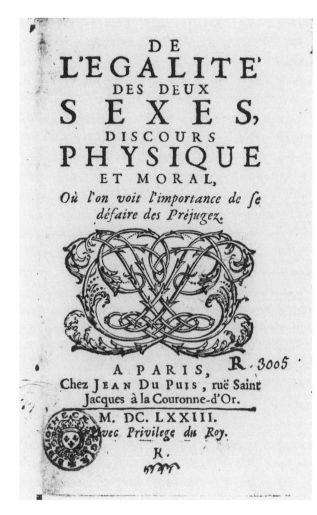

Title page of François Poullain de la Barre's book, "The Equality of the Sexes." Note the ordering of the subtitles. The first puts "physical" in larger letters than "moral," indicating that the former is more important. The second subtitle is in italic type and stresses activist elimination of prejudice.

The treatises on women, and on women's education, by Poullain de la Barre are an exception to this pattern, thanks to his Cartesian rigor and his willingness to undermine all antifeminist arguments grounded on biblical and religious authorities. Poullain is brilliantly unrelenting in demolishing arguments based on Eve's behavior in Eden, for example; and he tackles and rejects ancient and updated theories about body temperaments, which were being used to argue in favor of male superiority. True, Poullain attests to differences between the sexes, and when he asserts that women have more imagination than men it would seem that he has lost his way. The accomplishment was remarkable, however. Though his books went through few editions and only one translation, into English, his thought never undermined the general arsenal of arguments based on the Bible, which the clergy—and numerous writers—would use against equality for women even into the late nineteenth century. Poullain had no followers in France. Like Christine de Pisan, his thought was brilliant and pioneering, but ignored.

The literature written about strong women was like Christine de Pisan's initiative: reading fostered a sense of injustice about women by women, an injustice that would very slowly pull forward a revisionist history, and that at first would talk only of literary and saintly women. Unworthy women were simply not included in these biographical anthologies. Cleopatra and Catherine and Marie de Médicis would be pondered over and rehabilitated on occasion because they had redeeming features, as indeed they did, and do (being ethical as well as historical); but the positive would always be stressed, making Clotilda, the queen who converted her husband, Clovis, Blanche of Castille, mother and regent for saintly Louis IX, and Marguerite de Navarre, the poetess sister of Francis I, particularly eminent. Jean de la Forge and Marguerite Buffet published rosters of illustrious women in the 1660s, works that complemented the ones about "strong" women that had been written to enhance the legitimacy of Anne of Austria as regent.

The structural similarities between the lives of saints and the rosters of illustrious women seem more apparent to us in the twentieth century than they did to readers in the seventeenth century. The obscurity of their births (their parents usually were commoners) and the complete lack of knowledge about their education made them seem so similar to the women saints who founded orders, taught, and wrote that they were the most illustrious and saintly of all—except, of course, they did not die for their faith.

The forced conversions of the Huguenots stimulated devout women to reflect about education for girls. Young Protestant women were dispersed, usually to convents where they were "converted" either by force or by a slow inner "healing." In some devout Catholic circles, there was strong opposition to the use of *dragonnades* (troops) and to breaking up heretical families. This opposition was usually grounded on the belief that coercion did not work. It was soon discovered that putting young Huguenot women with Catholic girls of the same age was disastrous: the Huguenots, "being more experienced in controversy," would immediately start to convert the Catholic girls. Girls were believed to be particularly stubborn in their faith. When a crucifix was placed in the bedroom of one of these girls, she asked that it be removed, saying that it might be damaged when she was playing. It stayed in place.

The recognition that hundreds of girls from noble and "upright" families were growing up without education and had no hope of marriage because their families could not offer dowries prompted well-to-do devout women to found schools especially for them. Education grounded in spiritual devotion and courtly manners would, it was thought, make these girls marriageable, thereby reducing prostitution. With these principles in mind, Madame de Miramion founded the Daughters of Saint Geneviève. Very carefully supervised by the archbishop, and indeed by a bevy of prelates, her girls' school on the Quai de la Tournelle became a model known for its intense discipline and devotion. A teacher from Chartres recorded her observations about a day spent at the school, one of the rare documents that permits us to know what schools were really like in the seventeenth century.

In the morning, when she visited the class for girls of "middling" rank, all fifty stood up the minute she came in, greeting her but not making any noise. The mistress directed the class by signals, which every child obeyed immediately. Did "middling" rank mean a rank according to progress in reading and writing, or a social rank? Very probably the latter. The visitor to the class observed that, in contrast to other schools, here the mistress never shouted and that the catechism was taught continually, as were polite manners, while the girls were reading. The visitor observed that in order for this discipline to be effective, the parents also had to have a "good disposition" toward it. Punishment for minor infractions consisted of withdrawing little rewards: the maximum punishment for *dérèglement,* breaking the rules, was kissing the ground (floor?). Each girl had to have her dress-strings tied up, her face and hands washed, and her hair brushed back and out of her eyes.

The visitor attended a different class in the afternoon, one with forty children between the ages of six and thirteen. The same discipline prevailed. Three or four learning activities were going on simultaneously: while the older girls were writing, the little ones read. Two were being pressed to write to their mothers, who were in the country.

Did the members of the new literary public support such schools, or others? The answer is generally in the negative. Villedieu's readers would join with friends to hire private tutors for their sons, and would insist that a few lessons be given to their daughters; but good manners, playing the harpsichord, and dancing were often on a par with reading and writing. The age of girls' "schools" run by a single woman was about to become a general elite phenomenon. "Classes" would be held in her parlor for girls who had probably already learned to read and write at home. These "finishing" schools were certainly more secular than the schools run by the Ursulines and by

Madame de Miramion's teachers. They would enable young, well-educated women from good families to earn a living—a very important and modern alternative to convent life or a socially unacceptable or otherwise not-wanted marriage.

The *Trésor des Almanachs* for 1692 advertises that, in each quarter of the capital, there is a master and a mistress who teach "little schools" under the direction of the cantor of the archdiocese of Paris. The aim was to teach children of both sexes the catechism, Christian (*sic!*) prayers, reading in Latin and in French, and the principles of grammar, writing, and arithmetic. Sources about the teachers' qualifications and the enrollment in these schools are scanty. The cantor who directed these schools was none other than Claude Joly, the great friend of Cardinal Retz during the Fronde, now eighty-five years old. His treatise on education, published in 1678, stressed the importance of religious education to deter children from falling into petty crime and prostitution. It is difficult to imagine that only a few of the thousands of children who worked for their room and board, roamed the streets, begged, or simply did nothing, found their way into these classes for long periods in their lives.

The *Almanach* also lists classes given by writing masters teaching cursive, italic, and other "modern" French scripts, along with spelling and arithmetic—an education that required enough wealth to pay for it. There were also masters of arts who, in return for tuition fees, taught Latin, Greek, philosophy, and mathematics.

The riding and dancing schools, along with teachers of musical instruments, were far more numerous than the "little schools" discussed above. The author of the *Almanach* gave the names of all the teachers, plus a vague address, probably thinking that his readers would be more interested in these than in the more elementary classes run by the cantor. The long lists of teachers of these courtly skills testifies to the ever-extending influence of the Court itself in Parisian society, departed to Versailles but setting a standard that the families of royal officials, fiscal managers, legal professionals, and physicians were engaged in articulating in their own lives. Novels, engravings of stylish people, luxury goods, even a nascent fashion industry, pulled Parisian culture toward what came to be called "taste" and "refinement."

PART THREE

Medieval Revival

EIGHT

A Generation of Saints

The religious enthusiasms of the civil wars did not dissipate after Henry IV's conquest of France. Quite to the contrary. Religious feeling remained intense, coloring every aspect of life, but it did change its character. Casting aside wars and fanatical preaching, the Parisians turned to introspection, works of devotion, and charity. The main impulse of the Counter Reformation had aimed at either converting or exterminating the Protestants. The Parisians strove mightily to achieve this aim, and they failed. This defeat, combined with feverish emotions, became the basis for a culturally profound religious revival. Almost as if enthusiasm could be transferred, the enormous energies of the Counter Reformation became internalized into a realm-wide religious revival whose center was Paris.

After the Edict of Nantes, no serious, mentally stable Catholic would suggest that the Protestants be exterminated. That had been tried, and it had failed. Now the Parisians examined themselves to discover what had gone wrong. They accepted Henry IV, though in their hearts lay an uneasiness and guilt over memories of prayers for his defeat and death. Pens and prayers rather than swords, charity rather than burnings at the stake, would henceforth be their weapons; and quiet devotions rather than invectives would prevail. Henry's victory caused the Counter Reformation in France to change character, but this did not mean that Catholics had given up, or that they were willing to live and let live. At the Estates General of 1614, Richelieu, then Bishop of Luçon, set the tone for the new terrain on which Catholics hoped to win against the heretics:

> As for the others who, blinded by error, live peacefully . . . we think
> about them only by desiring their conversion. [We must] advance
> this by our setting a good example, teaching, and prayers, which are
> the only weapons with which we wish to do combat.

After all the invective and violence, this must be considered a position of moderation, but not defeatism. Nor had the Protestants backed down. After the Edict of Nantes, each church, in what was still a divided country, set out through different methods to triumph over the other.

What of the remnant that was the Huguenot community in Paris after the Saint Bartholomew's Day Massacre? It is difficult to measure its size, perhaps as few as three thousand in 1625, but clearly the community grew in the first half of the seventeenth century.

Forbidden by the Crown to have their own place of worship in the capital, the Huguenots raised funds to build an interesting, elegant church in Charenton, a village east of the city, along the Seine. A church in the round, with balconies, the "Temple," as the Huguenots called their churches, was easily reached by boat by the wealthier Huguenots. Others simply walked to attend the three-hour-long morning services and the two-to-three-hour afternoon services of sermons and psalm-singing. Sometimes *"garçons"* would pelt the Huguenots with snowballs as they climbed from their boats at the Place de la Grève. The boys claimed to be just playing, but they did not aim at Catholic passersby.

In this war of prayer and nerves, the religious revival among the Catholics was far richer than that of their Protestant foes. Their resources were much greater, for France was a Catholic country. Moreover, they had the support of the king and the capital. If we may trust contemporary accounts, a thorough reform, if not a revival, was long overdue in France.

While on visitation outside the Paris region, Saint François de Sales, in 1606, wrote the pope:

> It is extraordinary how the discipline of all the Regulars has lapsed in
> all the abbeys and priories of this diocese, except for the Carthusians
> and the mendicant orders: the wealth of all the others has reduced
> everything to dirt and changed their wine to poison whence they cause
> the enemies of the Lord to blaspheme when they say every day: Where

The demolition of the Temple of Charenton. Once ordered in October 1685, the demolition of the spiritual center and pride of the Huguenot community in the Île de France was completed in just a few days. This illustration is from a calendar for 1686.

is the God of these people? As for the ruins, while the two houses of Saint Clare are certainly in good order, the doors of the Cistercian convents are open to all, to the nuns to go out and to the men to enter.

In 1600 the French church still lacked vitality and efficient administration, largely because it had become the fief of the Crown and of a worldly aristocracy. A spiritual abstraction manifested on earth by small, petty, competing parties—the secular and regular clergy, chapters, colleges, hospitals, priories, monasteries, and chapels—it went on oblivious to the religious reform movement that was sweeping Europe. The wealthiest institution in Paris could never realize its potential power as long as prelates quarreled over ceremonies and tiny plots of land. Not even the religious revival of the seventeenth century would unite them in a common purpose. The upper clergy led comfortable lives at Court while many parish priests and hospitals lacked funds. The Church in Paris seemed united only for the negative purpose of fighting within itself, unless, of course, an institution such as the Parlement attacked the privileges of one of its members. Then the clergy stood together to protect its own interests. In Paris, more buildings, walls, gardens, courtyards, and fields belonged to the clergy than to any other group, including the royal family; but jealousy kept them from viewing this as a resource for further charitable or missionary activities.

Taken as a whole, the clergy, both secular and regular, was split into two groups. First there was the upper clergy, consisting of bishops, abbots, deacons, priors, and cardinals who either were princes or nobles or were so rich that they were rapidly becoming so. Through their control of the Church's wealth and through influence upon their aristocratic relatives, these churchmen had enormous political power. In general, the higher the Church office, the more prestigious the family name of the man or woman holding it. More courtiers, ladies, and knights than abbesses and prelates, in most cases these men and women knew little of the affairs of the Church. As often as not, these aristocrats filled the second-best positions that a family could acquire through royal favor, with the favored brother or cousin receiving a governorship or military office. As royal appointees, the vast majority of upper clergy lacked a deep commitment to the welfare of the faithful in their charge. Often ignorant of doctrine and of their own functions, they relied upon educated, common-born advisers to see them through what tasks they had to perform. There were exceptions, of course. There were reformers among them, but more frequently they were worldly prelates, relatives of a royal favorite. This upper clergy had been charged by the general decrees of the Council of Trent, not yet accepted in France, to reform the Church. Decades went by without much activity on their part in reducing corruption, pluralism, nepotism, or the other common vices of the late-medieval Church. More important, the sixteenth century had brought very little progress in the fundamental work of educating priests and administering parishes. Reform came late to Paris.

The second group consisted of the parish priests, monks, and nuns, beneath this aristocratic upper clergy. Here existed extraordinary variety and unevenness of commitment and capacity. The Parisians were unquestionably better served in their parish churches than were provincials. Yet, although the *curés* heading the organization of each parish were often well-educated, urbane, and able administrators—as we might expect a protégé of the upper clergy to be—political ambition and high living frequently made them indolent if not corrupt. Like their superiors, these men left their duties to be carried out by the socially inferior, often better-educated priests. Judging from the comments found in the letters of the great seventeenth-century reformers concerning conditions in parish churches and in monasteries, reform and missionary activity were essential to Paris. Only the more austere, ascetic orders, particularly the Carthusians and the reformed Franciscans (Capuchins, for example) seem to have provided real spiritual leadership to the faithful. At any rate, their religious impact was much greater than that of the upper clergy and most parish priests.

What began as mere reform quickly led to new growth. In many respects the latter is the more interesting, particularly because of its cultural importance. Like a medieval revival, the revival occurring in France after 1600 culminated in a monastic regeneration, a movement in education, the rise of private devotions, and large-scale charitable projects. All these elements, blended into one, permeated every aspect of Parisian life in the years 1600 to 1640. In Paris alone, forty-six new monastic communities for women were founded by the mid-century, and twenty-four for men. Some of these remained small, struggling to survive and financially precarious; others became quite large and prestigious, with beautiful buildings. Monasticism then enjoyed its last great expansion and provided leadership and unity of purpose for the other functions stimulated by the revival. After the 1640s this unity of purpose collapsed, largely because of doctrinal quarrels; but as long as the first generation of saintly revivalists (persons invariably born and influenced by the civil war) remained in control of the movement, its unity prevailed. Only after their disciples had begun to take over did cracks appear and doctrinal splintering, principally Jansenism, develop into something more than theological controversy.

At first, the inspiration and force for the monastic revival came from outside France. Jesuits and Carmelite nuns from Spain, through books and personal relationships, provided the models for the French monastic revival. Then, from Switzerland, the works and person of François de Sales (1567–1622) breathed into Leaguer and moderate alike some sense of God's love. Aristocratic himself in origin and manner, he gave the wayward nobleman hope for satisfaction in the Christian life.

The Spanish models differed from François de Sales in tone but not in doctrine. They stressed asceticism, strict obedience, and a mystical, almost physical union with

God through ecstasy, while François de Sales preached humility and love, leading to a generally relaxed confidence in God's mercy. These foreign models complemented one another, and laid the foundation for a new age of saints in Paris. In addition to Saint François de Sales, there were Saint Vincent de Paul, Saint Jeanne de Chantal, Saint Louise de Marillac, Saint Mary of the Incarnation (Madame Acarie), some of whom would not be beatified until considerably later, and other reformers including Saint-Cyran, Bérulle, Father Joseph, and Father Condren. Though of not quite the same age group, they were all intimately acquainted and, more important, were inspired to become more holy and zealous from personal contact with each other. They visited one another frequently or kept up active correspondence about their visions, prayers, sense of sin, and missionary activities. In a way, they set out as a group to remake the Church, believing that if they could triumph over their own sins they would receive divine power to help others do the same. The enthusiasm of this group grew with an intensity reminiscent of the eleventh and thirteenth centuries. Nearly all of them would found new monastic orders. In Paris alone their work was extensive, varied, and influential in diminishing the anxieties left by the civil war.

What exactly is a saint? There had developed in the Early Church a recognition among various communities of the faithful that some men and women lived in such totally devout ways, so filled with God, that they were special, they were the "holy ones," the "saints," from the Latin word for "holy" (*sanctus*). Their deaths often were so peaceful and filled with a sense of divine presence that fellow Christians faced with danger, illness, or the death of a loved one sought intercession with God through praying to or talking with a saintly person. Over the centuries, bishops developed formal proceedings to authenticate the accounts of miracles that had occurred as a result of prayers to one or another of these holy men and women. In time, only the bishop of Rome, that is, the popes, retained the prerogative to recognize formally a deceased holy person as having been a saint, on the basis of testimonials about miracles that followed prayers by the faithful.

In the tentative, halting search to recover from the spiritual wounds caused by the Wars of Religion, a generation of saints, and their associates and followers, would breathe new faith into the French Church.

The theologians of the sixteenth century had been at least partly responsible for all the violence committed in the name of religion; now it was the turn of the devotional practitioners, who would inspire the faithful to pray, to live in more peaceful communities, and to be charitable. The emphasis on devotional practice would be kept in strict accord with Church doctrine, in general the more specific teachings and practices approved by the church council held at Trent. The work of the generation of saints explored in this chapter would not, in most instances, be officially recognized until somewhat later, but the contemporaries of Saint François de Sales, Saint Louise de Marillac, Saint Jeanne de Chantal, and Saint Vincent de Paul lived intensely devout lives, in the belief that these individuals and their leadership in how to save their souls from damnation, were in fact saintly.

This dramatic shift away from theology, with its emphasis on logic and reason, to devotional practice, with its emphasis on what would later be called "psychology," had all-pervading consequences in general French culture. The sense that there was more to being human than the rational unleashed an interest in the emotional. Could religious faith be grounded on feelings—the passions—and the sense of one's own self and one's body? Attempts to restore religious unity by reasoning or by force had failed; the saints of the early seventeenth century, having observed that certain persons had a very strong faith not grounded on reasoning, had thus turned to devotional spirituality.

The Society of Jesus, known as the "Jesuits," was already a far-ranging, well-disciplined order in France before the crisis of the civil war that resulted in their banishment from France. Recognizing the need to win over former League Catholics, and needing Jesuit support in Rome, Henry IV readmitted the Society. Almost at once the Jesuits again became a power in France. Through their *collèges,* such as Clermont in Paris, reopened in 1618, they exercised the preponderant influence on French intellectual and political life throughout the seventeenth century. Some of the saintly revivalists—as we shall call the new saints—received Jesuit educations at Clermont. As long as they restricted themselves to reform activities, little real conflict developed between them and the Society. But when some of the revivalists came of age and developed devotional positions differing from those held by the Society, disputes occurred that ended the unity of the movement.

In 1602 Saint François de Sales came to Paris. His years spent as a student at Clermont, his success at converting Protestants in the Chablais region of Savoy, and his consequent influence upon the exiled Genevan Catholics had made him quite well known even before this return.

Saint François de Sales began preaching, first in the queen's own chapel, and then in the more fashionable parish churches. He became the preacher of the hour. Great crowds of princes, judges, and common folk rushed to hear him. The striking thing about his success was its effect on the upper aristocracy and on the royal family. They came to listen instead of merely to be seen.

His sermons captivated the Court by their direct and simple pronouncements about God's love for man. In elegant French, Saint François de Sales would exhort his listeners to recall the sufferings of Christ, His compassion for the unfortunate, and the beauty of the love of God for those whom He has created. This seemed like poetry to the Parisians, who for decades had heard nothing but invective and hellfire.[1] Saint François de Sales attacked neither Calvinist doctrine nor its proponents. In fact, there was little theology in his message. The impact of his sermons on the aristocracy and judicial nobles was immediate, and, thanks to his works, particularly the *Traité de l'Amour de Dieu,* published in 1616, the effect was often deep.

Written in spare moments over a decade, the *Traité* is a handbook about the choices men and women face every day. There is little in it that is political or social:

> When someone thinks with some concentration about the divine, he or she senses endearing feelings coming over them from their hearts. This testifies to the fact that God is the God of the human heart, and our understanding has more pleasure when we think of the divine, . . . if some shock upsets our hearts we turn to the divine. . . . This pleasure, this confidence that the human heart naturally has in God can only come from the union of this divine goodness with our souls. (*Traité de l'Amour de Dieu,* I, xv)

Saint François de Sales asserts that love is the basis for all thought and activity giving pleasure and peace of mind. This love is a gift of God, at once the same, yet transcendent, measured, and hierarchical, or "differing in perfection." A man's love for his dog is not or should not be the same as that for his brother, father, or wife. All these are in fact different loves, but at the same time each may be good and perfect. Love of God is the highest good because it fills man with unequaled pleasure and well-being. Physical love, therefore, is not evil or something to be suppressed; it is merely a lower kind of love.

Sales' work is filled with parables demonstrating how choices may be made on the basis of love. Many of these are paraphrased from the Old Testament, though the life

---

1. With the exception of du Perron's sermons.

of Christ is also used to demonstrate what total love may do in practice. A powerful work of religious ethics, to the sterner scholastics and reformers it appeared to be an apology for licentious behavior. Parts of the work shocked those who had committed themselves to asceticism. But what appeared as indulgence was a higher kind of religious idealism.

While in Paris, Saint François de Sales met Madame Acarie. Beautiful, young, widowed, and wealthy, she experienced ecstatic fits that caused her to appear dead for hours. Her highly emotional, mystical religious life attracted others seeking union with God, and a small group formed around her to share in her religious power. Intense devotions, flagellation, confessions, and fasting had already transformed Madame Acarie into a powerful woman of religion before her meeting with Saint François de Sales. Moved by her example, he too joined the little group, though from his recollections it is clear that he himself remained reserved, if not cold, to the physical effects of enthusiasm. He seems never to have doubted Madame Acarie's sincerity; he supported her efforts for union with God by the same kind of commonsense advice found in his sermons.

Though Madame Acarie knew little about the Spanish nun Saint Theresa of Avila, who had died some twenty years earlier, the saint in a vision asked the Frenchwoman to found a Carmelite order in Paris. Deeply moved, Madame Acarie discussed the vision with those in her group, including Saint François de Sales, Pierre de Bérulle, and Michel de Marillac. Together they assured her that she had had a true vision, and that it was her duty to attempt to found a Carmelite house.

In 1604, two years after the vision, Bérulle, who helped Madame Acarie more than the others, succeeded in bringing seven Spanish Carmelite nuns to Paris, housing them in austere quarters on the rue du Faubourg Saint-Jacques. Received and honored by the high aristocracy and Marie de Médicis, the Carmelites quickly became the religious center for highborn, devout ladies in the capital. By 1610, seven other houses had been founded in France, and by 1630 this number had reached forty-six. This phenomenal growth can only be accounted for by the magnetism that mystical, ascetic religion exerted upon aristocratic and judicial families at that time.

Both the Acaries had been fanatically pro-League and connected with the *Seize* during the civil war. Though some of her entourage had done the same, they were more typically League sympathizers who had stood on the sidelines during the violence. Marillac had remained loyal to royal authority and had held back; now that the violence was over he could commit himself fully to a religious revival. Then too, the younger members of the group had been influenced by the League but had not been directly engaged in it. Bérulle, for example, had attended Clermont in the 1580s, during the height of the League's influence, but being too young to take a more active role he spent his time in study and devotions. Born of a strange alliance between a degraded aristocratic family and an old judicial family (his mother was a Séguier), Bérulle had the opportunity to let his education guide his life. His father had died when he was very young. His extremely devout mother was a distant relative of Madame Acarie. The Séguiers held high offices in the Parlement, and, as Bérulle's guardians, they saw to it that the youth had the best available education. As an adolescent, Bérulle was pressed by these guardians to choose the legal profession. But his mother's encouragement and his Jesuit teachers' influence guided him to "dedicate his life to God." At seventeen he wrote:

> I will only accept God's gifts in order to belong more fully to Him, and I will use everything in Him and for Him: nothing to the world, nothing to my intimates, nothing to myself.
>
> I will love God in Himself, for Himself; and outside of Himself, I will love only for Him, only what He Himself loves, in the manner in which He loves, and because such is His will for me.

The process of total sublimation of self through mystical union with God progressed rapidly and continued throughout his life. His Séguier relatives ceased attempting to make a judge of him.

Deeply influenced by the friendship and works of Saint François de Sales, Bérulle applied himself to writing devotional works. In 1623, just seven years after the *Traité de l'Amour de Dieu,* Bérulle published his *Grandeurs de Jésus.* Couched in a language of devotion and piety instead of scholastic theology or biblical exegesis, the work became extremely popular. Struck by the majesty, suffering, and divinity of Christ, Bérulle pleaded that Christians accept the benefits available to anyone who would contemplate his life and death. Saint François de Sales had stressed the love of God, the latter conveyed as a metaphysical abstraction. Bérulle emphasized the person of Jesus as God and as man. In the *Grandeurs de Jésus,* the reader is swept up by what were termed *"élévations,"* poetic devices that made him feel a member of the "mystical body of Christ." For Bérulle, the entire Church was the body of Christ, and the saints too were its members. His theme becomes the identity of self with God through the person of Jesus.

Such an emphasis on Christ had been absent, except for the teaching of some spiritual Franciscans, since the High Middle Ages. At the time, Bérulle's message appeared radical, even dangerous. Not a few Sorbonne doctors, Dominicans, and sterner Jesuits objected to its sensual mysticism. Instead of being theology or mystical metaphor, the *Grandeurs de Jésus* presented a Man-God previously unknown to seventeenth-century Catholics.

Bérulle was also an able organizer and administrator. After helping to found Carmelite monasteries in Paris and then in other parts of France, he set about establishing schools to train priests. By 1616, after some early failures, his new school, the Oratory, had the funds to buy the old Hôtel de Bouchage (Petit-Bourbon) on the rue Saint-Honoré, across the street from the Louvre. The location was ideal. Bérulle helped build the first chapel himself, carrying up hods of mortar to the masons.

Here priests lived according to a rule prepared by Bérulle. Though ascetic by our standards, life in the Oratory was by seventeenth-century standards activist and outgoing. Priests studied some theology, but the main emphasis was on their personal transformation through prayer, confession, and the reading of devotional works. They learned to sing, preach, and minister to the needs of parishioners. Upon receiving permission from parish priests, the Oratorians would go to work baptizing, hearing confessions, teaching catechism, and preaching. Their impact on Paris was immediate, though, owing to lack of good parish histories, it is impossible to know its true extent. But the effort was made to breathe new life into the parish churches. Oratory schools were established in many parts of France, using the one in the capital as a model. Soon the old *hôtel* and first chapel became too small. In the late 1620s and the 1630s, a new Oratory was begun, of which the great chapel, designed in part by Le Mercier, still stands and is now a Huguenot place of worship.

One of the most successful preachers of the Oratory was Jean Le Jeune (d. 1672), a pupil of Bérulle's, who evangelized throughout France for sixty years. Parts of a sermon on charity, given in Paris, typify the appeal made by the reformed, better-educated clergy. Instead of the humble pietism of Saint François de Sales, the Oratorians, and Le Jeune in particular, used current political conceptions as analogies for defining God and man's relationship to Him. God was the king, the feudal lord and master; the faithful were his subjects and tenant-farmers: "A lord [*seigneur*] shows that he is master of a farm when he can give orders to the one who rents it: Give so many measures of wheat to this person, and so many of barley to that one. When God presents you with poor people, and you have the means to help them, these are the orders which He gives you to distribute to His friends the goods which belong to Him."

By elaborating upon the analogy, Le Jeune struck the hearts of the men of wealth and power:

> [God] shows His wisdom: a king or a minister of state shows his intelligence, prudence, and industry when he fosters commerce in order to enrich the realm, when he is inventive and finds easy, convenient means of transportation to far-off provinces, in order to transport from them those things his subjects lack. . . . Now what is more far-distant from Heaven than the earth? What commerce is thus more desirable, but more difficult, than that between Heaven and earth? See, for mercy's sake, the admirable ingenuity of God's wisdom: He established a bank, a changing house in this world, by means of which you can store up in Heaven all the goods which you have on earth . . . the poor are God's bankers.

At the end of the sermon, Le Jeune lashed out at special groups whose way of life provoked his accusations of hard-heartedness:

> Do you see, on the one hand, this poor person all covered with rags, living solely on alms, who sleeps on straw and who is devoured by vermin? Do you see on the other this count or marquis, riding by in a coach, followed by a large retinue, all covered with gold and silk? It is this poor wretch who provides for, who nourishes, and who enriches this marquis. . . . Here is the real cause of your lack of charity: you do not believe that Jesus Christ suffers with the poor.

Le Jeune turned every basis for self-esteem into a source of guilt. His imagery encompassed every group in the typical Parisian congregation:

> You work on weekdays for others or for your own body: work on Sunday for yourself and for your soul. You are a merchant, you have reckoned with your creditors all week long: now render an accounting to your God. You are a tailor, you have made clothes for men and women:

now make ornaments for your soul. . . . You are a lawyer, you have conducted lawsuits against other people: prepare one now against yourself, judge and punish your faults.

This stern radicalism stemmed from the moral and spiritual force of the leaders, the saints, who exhorted the less devout and less intelligent to exceed their capacities. The Church began to rise again above self-interest and social snobbery, to become a motor for changing the intellectual and physical conditions of society. Literature, the law, politics, and the arts thus were tempered by the revived religion.

Though Saint François de Sales had helped found the Carmelites and the Oratorians, neither order manifested his ideal of communal living. He exhorted another of his intimate friends, Saint Jeanne de Chantal, to found an order on the principles of the *Traité de l'Amour de Dieu*. Saint Jeanne came from a wealthy, eminent, and Gallican judicial family of Dijon, the Frémiots. Her father had opposed the League and yet had withheld support for Henry IV until the latter's abjuration of Protestantism. In this atmosphere the young bride of a soldier of Henry IV developed into a woman of intense devotion. Deeply depressed after her husband's death in a hunting accident, she gradually turned to reaching union with God through mystical experiences.

Saint François de Sales felt himself the chosen devotional guide of this still young, beautiful woman, and she, in turn, accepted every suggestion from her "dear Father," François de Sales. Their lifelong friendship was spiritually rewarding to both. Out of it grew the Order of the Visitation, established first in Saint François' own diocese of Geneva, then in Lyons, and finally in the rue Saint-Antoine of Paris, in 1619. The nuns of the Visitation shocked contemporaries by their nonconformity to the traditional patterns of religious life. Saint François wanted nothing to do with the almost militaristic tradition of monastic life propagated by the Jesuits and Carmelites. Rejecting the rigorous admission requirements for the spiritual and physical health of applicants, preliminary to excruciating novitiates, Saint François influenced Saint Jeanne de Chantal to admit older women, the sickly, and those who were still unsure of their commitment to the religious life. Shocking in itself, this was not all. Instead of fast upon fast (the Carmelites were reduced to an ounce of bread on certain fast days), the nuns of the Visitation ate good food with hearty appetites. Though they led a life of contemplation and devotion, they needed sound nourishment to accomplish their other work. Unlike cloistered nuns, they went out on daily missions to care for the poor and sick. They established regular schedules for going into the neighborhoods and into the

Saint Jeanne de Chantal, nineteenth-century engraving after a seventeenth-century original. From a Leaguer judicial family of Dijon, Jeanne-Françoise Frémiot married the Baron de Chantal and became a mother before a profound religious experience led her to found the Order of the Visitation, and to sainthood in 1767.

very homes of the poor. This innovation proved to be too much for the archbishop of Lyons, already suspicious of Chantal's foundation because of the relaxed standards for admission. He forbade the nuns to leave their convent. Saint François de Sales, Saint Jeanne de Chantal, even Cardinal Bellarmine, objected, but the archbishop won. The nuns of the Visitation conformed, though the innovation of permitting nuns to walk in the streets to help the needy did not die. Some twenty years after this defeat, Saint Vincent de Paul revived the idea for the Sisters of Charity.

In Paris the nuns of the Visitation attracted daughters from every social class, but the majority came from judicial and tax-farmer families. The first superior, Hélène-Angélique L'Huillier, member of a prestigious judicial family, learned under Saint François de Sales' direction to repress all feelings of class and all interest in clothing, literature, and personal beauty, in order to teach the novices the same lesson. Here, as in other generally upper-class religious houses, servants of these ladies would often join too, adding a leaven of truly popular origins to the Visitation. Receiving support from Noël Brûlart, relative of the former chancellor, the nuns built a large and beautiful monastery on the rue Saint-Antoine, adjacent to the very fashionable *Marais*. The central-space, domed chapel, begun in 1634, was designed by François Mansart. Only thirty-four at this time, Mansart revealed his immaturity in his mixing of Mannerist and classical elements. Still the design is just as successful as Le Mercier's Sorbonne chapel, built about the same time—and the latter architect was older and more experienced. In the rich setting, the nuns of the Visitation developed an identity of their own, original and independent of the Spanish models. The Spanish-influenced houses were, however, just as fashionable. They were to be found in the Faubourgs Saint-Honoré and Saint-Jacques.

In the Faubourg Saint-Jacques, almost a dozen monastic societies flourished south of the University and near the Luxembourg Palace: the Sisters of the Visitation's second house, the Ursulines (reformed Augustinians, founded by Madeleine L'Huillier); the Feuillantines; the English Benedictines (refugees from the Puritan Revolution); the Benedictines of Val-de-Grâce; the Capucines, or Capuchin nuns; the Carmelites; the Carmes, or barefoot Carmelite fathers; the Congregation of Notre-Dame-du-Calvaire (supported by Marie de Bragelonne, wife of Claude Bouthillier); and the reformed Cistercians of Port Royal. Occupying fields and gardens on both sides of the rue Saint-Jacques and the gardens of the Luxembourg, together they formed an entire new quarter of the city, which in extent, cost, and style was every bit as significant as the rise of the three new residential quarters described in Chapter 6.

These monasteries, each with cloistered courts, formal gardens, chapels, and magnificent apartments, became fashionable places of devotion and piety for members of royal, aristocratic, and robe families. Whether the rules were austere or indulgent, the surroundings were beautiful and particularly attractive to those feeling the need for devotion and the calm of the country. There was something aristocratic about these establishments, with their rural atmosphere and their exclusiveness in the religious garb and rules governing the activities of every member. The abbots or abbesses were

The façade of Saint-Louis, by G. Merian. The Jesuit church on the fashionable rue Saint-Antoine bears the royal coat of arms at the top, the IHS symbol for Christ in the middle, and Cardinal Richelieu's coat of arms with its three chevrons just above the central door. Louis XIII's and Louis XIV's hearts are interred in a chapel near the main altar.

almost invariably of the sword nobility themselves, and those from families of lesser social distinction rapidly assumed the aristocratic status of their colleagues in the order. The devotional routines of the contemplative communities could be interrupted by the visits of high-ranking and wealthy donors; but in general some devotional decorum remained. The nuns and monks who were socially inferior found their social and religious aspirations at once inseparable, unified in the edifying rituals, prayers, and mystical exercises centering on the *gloire* and *noblesse* of the soul found through humility, mendicancy, fasting, and flagellation. Most remarkable among these religious foundations were Saint-Joseph-des-Carmes, the Val-de-Grâce , and Port Royal, for each, independently and at different times, represented a dominant complex of religious and political tendencies among the ruling families of the seventeenth century.

First to come into their own were the barefoot Carmelite fathers. The Order of Saint-Joseph-des-Carmes was a French shadow of the newly revived Spanish order inspired by Saint Theresa of Avila. Intense devotion, self-abnegation, and general submission to the answers proposed by the medieval Church on doctrinal matters made them a strong force for Catholic revival in France. Founded just a few weeks before Henry IV's assassination, the Carmes suffered some of the reproaches and charges of regicide heaped upon the Jesuits, because their inspiration and general religious orientation were part of the movement for a strong, universal Church. No longer particularly pro-Spanish (in fact, they were more ultramontanist, that is, looking to the papacy), the Carmes, along with the Jesuits, became favorite subjects for attack by Gallican parlementarians who saw Spanish conspiracies in everything coming from outside France.

In 1611, Marie de Médicis began to support the Carmelite fathers, and a tax farmer named Nicolas Vivien gave them the land and money needed to build a new church. Cosmopolitan and leaning toward Rome, these Carmelites built a chapel in the style of Vignola's *Il Gesù*. It was the first of this style in Paris, caricature though it was, and the first Parisian church to have a dome. The chapels, frescoes, dome, and statuary (including a Virgin holding the Infant Jesus by Bernini) represent one of the best-preserved ensembles of seventeenth-century religious art in Paris, despite the iconoclasm of the French Revolution. The Carmes flourished when the triumph of the papacy over the purely Spanish forces for reform made it possible for Anne of Austria, the Séguiers, the Brûlarts, and the Viviens to build altars and chapels without being accused of pro-Spanish leanings, except by a fringe of zenophobic Gallicanists. Brûlart's chapel, built not as a burial place but as one to *"embellir et orner ses armes,"* epitomizes the combination of official piety and ambition in a robe family under Marie de Médicis' careful and intelligent balancing between the Spanish and papal forces in southern Europe during the second decade of the century.

Val-de-Grâce was chiefly the work of another Regent, Anne of Austria. Like so many Hapsburgs, Anne liked to retire among aristocratic nuns to pray, write letters, and avoid the strains imposed by court etiquette. She commissioned François Mansart to build the Val-de-Grâce in the Faubourg Saint-Jacques. Its very name conveys the personal, highly emotional spirituality that was Anne's. Never a center of great learning or

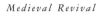

The beautiful alms-collector, by Nicolas Bonnart. The ironic observation, below the title, that one gives more to the church if the person collecting the money is physically attractive, is made stronger still when a member of the lower clergy is caught gazing at her as he puts a coin in the plate. He is not tonsured.

Marie de Médicis,
by Peter Paul
Rubens. Like
Catherine de
Médicis and her
son Henry III,
Marie de Médicis
clung to power
when Louis XIII
reached maturity,
thereby
stimulating plots
and rivalries for
power. Anne of
Austria created
no such problems
for Louis XIV.

even of ascetic devotion, Val-de-Grâce became a haven of sincere but moderate piety for the granddaughter of Emperor Charles V and the mother of the Sun King.

Begun in 1645 and completed in 1667, with Le Mercier, Le Muet, and Le Duc succeeding Mansart, Val-de-Grâce —along with the Collège des Quatre Nations (Institut)—became the most Roman Baroque ensemble in Paris. The chapel dome is an imitation of Saint Peter's, as is the altar, with its twisted marble columns; and the façade is one more variation of Vignola's *Il Gesù*. Mignard's fresco inside the dome teems with more than two hundred persons. Bernini suggested the perspective. Never

Val-de-Grâce, by Pérelle. As early as 1624, Anne of Austria started remodeling an older structure to house some Benedictine nuns brought from the country and her own private apartment. Sumptuous and inspired by Baroque Rome, the principal chapel looms over the more modest neighboring convents. Anne loved the solace that her stays there provided, and she willed that her heart be interred there.

before had such a grandiose ensemble existed in Paris. Anne had quarreled with Mansart and had finally released him before completion of the chapel. His successors were more subservient to her desires and more willing to build outside the French tradition by following the cosmopolitan style established by Rome. The rectangular courtyard, high slate roofs, mansard dormers, and clean, undecorated majesty of the cloisters and cells would indicate that Mansart's original design was somber and in keeping with traditional

French and Benedictine architecture, though the planned entrance gate had a theatrical quality as a junior-sized predecessor of the *piazza* before Saint Peter's. Anne's apartment was like a jewel box, a Renaissance cabinet; its sculptured panels covered with gold leaf set off religious paintings by Philippe de Champaigne. The Val-de-Grâce reflected Anne's and the monarchy's acceptance of an original interpretation of what was the current Baroque style.

The architecture of Port Royal was something different, something more original, and in a way more French than any of the other monastic houses in the quarter. The underlying force for originality was Jansenism, a religious thought and devotional pattern different from those of the Carmes. Initially Port Royal had stood in a low valley west of Paris; but the strong and indomitable Mère Angélique Arnauld brought her nuns to the Faubourg Saint-Jacques in 1625, as much for status as for anything else.

Apart from the theological controversies, which only began in earnest in the 1640s, the history of Port Royal is the history of the Arnauld family, first the daughters of Antoine, and then the sons. The majority of Antoine Arnauld's twenty children became committed to the religious life at one time or another in their lives. A member of Parlement who could instantly become hysterical over the question of readmitting the Jesuits to France, Antoine Arnauld gave his children a lust for God and status. Not all had much choice in the matter. His oldest daughter, known as Mère Agnès, became abbess of Saint-Cyr at the age of six and a novice at Port Royal at fifteen, in 1608, where her younger sister, Mère Angélique, had already become abbess in 1602, at the tender age of eleven. So it went with most of the family, not only during Antoine Arnauld's life, but later into the lives of his grandchildren.

All the Arnaulds, beginning with Mère Angélique, underwent deep religious crises in their adolescent years, during which they became "converted," as they said, to a life of contemplation and separation from the world. Mère Angélique's decision as abbess to close Port Royal to visitors, even members of her own family, resulted in the dramatic encounter of the *guichets* (the wrought-iron grills that separated cloistered nuns from the outside world) in 1609, when she told her father that he could no longer see her or her sister.

Then, proceeding frantically to educate her soul to the religious life, Mère Angélique sought the spiritual aid of the revivalist leaders, among them Saint François de Sales. Later she took Duvergier de Hauranne as her spiritual guide; it was through his teachings at Port Royal that the so-called rigid Augustinianism associated with the name of the Dutch theologian Jansen became connected with the monastery.

Port Royal of Paris. The chapel of the Cistercian convent of Port Royal is sober and almost without decoration, a sharp contrast with the Jesuit church of Saint-Louis.

Duvergier de Hauranne came from an old patrician family of Bayonne. Educated by the Jesuits, he seemed well on the way to becoming a successful, aristocratic ecclesiastic at court, until he underwent a religious crisis in the early 1620s. Coming under the influence of Bérulle and then of Sébastien Bouthillier and Saint Vincent de Paul, Duvergier de Hauranne, by then known as the Abbé de Saint-Cyran, turned abruptly to the study of ethics and theology.

Following in Bérulle's footsteps, Saint-Cyran experienced doubts about the overly mechanical administration of the sacraments fostered by the Jesuits and Carmes. He was particularly troubled by the practice of confession, absolution, and then immediate partaking of the Eucharist by a penitent. Saint-Cyran, like Bérulle before him, thought that there should be a pause, a period of reflection between absolution and communion. In Port Royal he had the opportunity to put his ideas into practice.

In the 1630s this simple practice became grounds for intense theological controversy. From what could be called the "party of contrition" developed the Jansenist movement; the Jesuits and Richelieu defended the attritionist position that sincere repentance over one's sins, when joined with absolution, sufficed as preparation for communion. The Jansenists insisted that in addition to love of God there must be something of an ethical-psychological cleansing of the sinner before he be allowed to take communion. From here it was not far to the subtler arguments on the nature of grace, predestination, and the number of the Elect.

The controversy would have blown itself out had not personal antagonisms, threats, and intimidations been used by both sides. Jansenism grew out of French thought, in fact out of the originality of Bérulle's conception of the suffering of Christ. No Dutch theologian was needed for the controversy to develop this far; but theses were defended and allies collected, and Jansen became associated in the controversy with Port Royal. Richelieu saw what was coming. Never quite able to understand the fervor of those who were reviving the Church, and blinded by his own conception of success, the cardinal offered Saint-Cyran a bishopric in hopes that he would accept and cool off. Saint-Cyran spurned the offer in humble righteousness. Meanwhile, Jansen had attacked Richelieu's foreign policy, causing the cardinal to associate the theological controversy with the opposition to his policy by the Spanish Netherlands. The Port Royalists moved further into what Richelieu, an avowed attritionist himself, could only consider heresy. He had Saint-Cyran arrested in 1638. Jansenism was helped by this near-martyr to the cause, but there were as yet no real political implications.

The entire Arnauld family rallied to defend the nuns and their spiritual adviser; Saint Vincent de Paul and other influential clergymen intervened to stop Richelieu from trying Saint-Cyran for heresy. From then on Port Royal was to know sporadic persecution until it was finally suppressed in 1664 and most of its buildings destroyed by Louis XIV in 1709. The dispute over Saint-Cyran broke the support for the religious revival in government circles; the unity and force of the movement dissipated slowly through the seventeenth century. True, the work of Saint Vincent de Paul was still mostly in the future, but the spiritual and ethical originality generated by the Jansenists became diffused into secular matters, science, and poetry; it did not generate further religious unity. After about the 1640s, the forces of reaction, unreformed upper clergymen and monks accepting more casuistical answers to the difficult problems of Christian doctrine—that is, the Jesuits and the Carmes—actively sought to stamp out the influence of Saint François de Sales and Bérulle, by ignoring, if not suppressing, their works. Henceforth charity, something that raised few theological disputes, would be the main outlet for revivalist energies. The Jansenists, like the Calvinists, would be considered outside the Church.

The architecture of the Port Royal chapel proclaimed the Order's independence from, even repudiation of the European Baroque style. In the first place the Jansenists chose an architect, Antoine Le Pautre, who was only twenty-five years old, inexperienced, and from a family not known for its architects. He lacked the father or uncle who so often advised the novice issuing from a family of architects. His youthfulness recalls that of the great Jansenists: the energetic young Arnauld sisters; Antoine Arnauld, who was only twenty-nine when he finished *De la Fréquente Communion;* Pascal, who at thirty-three wrote the *Lettres Provinciales;* and Racine, twenty-eight when *Andromaque* was produced. Begun in 1646, Le Pautre's chapel drew its inspiration from obvious sources, yet it came out differently, even disturbingly, as did Jansenist writings. The monumental porch, caryatids, great broken slate roofs, *pots de feu,* and freestanding statuary systematically rejected the overall effect sought by Vignola and his French imitators; and there was no dome. Le Pautre could have capped the interior dome by another on the exterior, but instead he used Mansart's recently refined solution of a modified trapezoid. The interior also showed a conscious rejection of the cosmopolitan style. Over the altar, a *Last Supper,* painted by Philippe de Champaigne, placed the figure of Christ and the sacrament of the Eucharist in the center of Jansenist religious life. Not the Virgin, not even the Crucifixion, rather the living God-Man had significance for the Jansenists. In the Faubourg Saint-Jacques, the Jansenists struck a discordant note. With all these monasteries just a few steps from one another, tensions developed on the streets of the quarter, for members of the various houses were clearly recognizable by their unique "uniforms," their habits. Some of the women were cloistered and were therefore never seen in the streets, but their assistants, the *converses* garbed in distinctive habits, could do errands outside the convent.

The third area of monastic growth was the Faubourg Saint-Honoré. Huddled together were reformed Dominicans, called the Jacobins; the Feuillants, reformed Cistercians, who built the biggest monastic establishment in the quarter; the Capuchins, reformed Franciscans, who included Father Joseph, Richelieu's chief diplomatic adviser; the Capucines, their female counterparts; the Dames de l'Assomption, a fashionable and pious retreat for widows (now the Polish church); the Daughters of Saint Thomas; and the Convent of the Conception, where Cardinal Retz, on visitation, frankly admitted that the presence of some eighty-five young women, many of whom were *"belles et coquettes,"* tested his vow of chastity.

In virtually the same years as the Feuillants, the Jesuits of the rue Saint-Antoine, with the help of Louis XIII and Richelieu, had built as a chapel what is now the parish church of Saint-Paul and Saint-Louis. When completed, the church looked something like the parish church of Saint-Gervais, finished about a decade earlier with a new Baroque façade that Voltaire later called the most magnificent in Paris. It would be in this Jesuit church that Louis XIII and Louis XIV would want their hearts interred, as a mark of special favor to the Society. Their bodies, on the other hand, were interred in the abbey church of Saint-Denis, the traditional place of repose for French kings. Some of Marc-Antoine Charpentier's most monumental masses were composed for this church. Together these three Baroque churches stamped the influence of Rome on Paris. Not until the completion of the Val-de-Grâce some thirty years later did Parisians see any buildings more "foreign" in design and decoration.

In all, about seventy monastic houses were founded in Paris between 1600 and 1650, and most of the older ones were reformed and often rebuilt. For the upper classes, the revival had manifested itself mainly in monasticism. These religious houses were socially a part of Paris and eventually became an integral part of it; but when they were built, in nearly every case on the edge of the city in the *faubourgs,* they provided an escape from urban life. Monasteries were the spiritual equivalent of the country château; the aim and dream of bourgeois and judicial families was to have one or the other for all of its members. Monasteries represented a kind of community profoundly un-urban and uninterested in the traditional preoccupations of townsmen: trade, man-ufacture, and administration. Their increase came at the ebb tide of religious revival and coincided with a new push for the aristocratic way of life in upper-class Parisian society. It is tempting to assert that the monastery was the judicial family's "château" for those members of the family who could not marry owing to lack of dowries. The monastery stood in the suburbs, surrounded by *hôtels,* pointing toward the country life and protecting its inhabitants from contact with social inferiors engaged in ignoble enterprises. Though this tendency was a far cry from the intention of the saints who had launched the revival, it was not far from the minds of at least some of the wealthy who chose the smart, not-so-austere regular life.

For the rest of Parisian society, what was the impact of the revival? The archbishop and his chapter seem to have done little to ensure effective administration in the parishes. This came later, however, but largely through the missionary activities and charitable works of Saint Vincent de Paul and devout laymen.

By the time Saint Vincent de Paul became acquainted with Saint François de Sales, Bérulle, and Saint Jeanne de Chantal, he was already deeply religious and on the way to becoming one of the most effective and original figures in the revival. Unlike the others, Vincent de Paul was of peasant stock, a child of the fields, nourished on boiled millet. Close to his own family, which had sacrificed so that he might be educated, Vincent de Paul never lost that sense of natural intimacy given him by hard-working, humble, and loving parents. Modest by nature, he did not have to go through a process of self-discipline or intellectualization of others' humbling experiences. His letters exude the faith and peace that the other saints strove to attain. It was natural for him to share what he had, or even to give it away. His early career also sets him apart from the other revivalists. Educated in what must have been mediocre schools, he set out at once to become a priest, and for a time he enjoyed the support of cardinals and politi- cally influential families—the Gondis, for example, where he tutored the children, including the future cardinal Gondi de Retz. His self-effacing manner and his spiritual presence attracted attention: years before he was officially recognized as a saint, his con- temporaries sensed that he was someone special. After spending some time studying theology in Rome, Vincent de Paul was appointed almoner to Queen Margot, first wife of Henry IV. Debauched and devout by fits, like all the later Valois, this queen's life in her magnificent *hôtel* on the Left Bank gave Vincent de Paul a glimpse into courtly life. But the call to evangelize in the fields and villages prevailed and kept Vincent de Paul from becoming a bishop or courtier.

Neither monastic nor mystical, Saint Vincent de Paul was above all familiar, a mem- ber of the family of mankind. This natural intimacy prompted persons of every social class to confess their sins, fears, and jealousies to him. Saint Vincent de Paul did not quiet the souls of the wealthy or proud by pleasant assurances. His letters to them indi- cate that he could be stern yet understanding. A strain of anticlericalism runs through his works, for he believed no ecclesiastic could be wealthy and still be true to his vows. On the other hand, more than once Vincent de Paul saw in himself and in the Poor Daughters of Charity, the sin of pride, the pride that came from showing the world that they were poor because they had given away their possessions to help the poor.

Saint Vincent de Paul's missionary activities consisted in visiting parishes that had been abandoned by priests, or where human misery was very great. He knew better than any minister or tax collector where to locate the pockets of economic depression and epidemics in France. In Paris he had started out as *curé* of Clichy, then a rural district of great poverty. He found the response of those who had been abandoned by the Church to be gratifying. Then, organizing missionary groups, he would go into the churches and homes of the poorest districts in France.

Though himself primarily concerned with rural evangelizing—he founded an order of missionary priests, the Lazarists, for that purpose in 1625—he did not neglect Paris or the other cities. There he relied to a greater degree on the help of well-to-do and pious laymen. In Paris, with the help of Saint Louise de Marillac, he transformed the informal *Dames de Charité* into the Order of the Poor Daughters of Charity. Composed primarily of daughters of poor and lower-class families, but directed by zealous women of judicial families, the Daughters of Charity struck the fear of God into those who had money, and His compassion into those who did not. They collected considerable sums of money and bargained well to purchase food and clothing, which were distributed to the poor. Again, it is impossible to know their precise impact on Paris, but their work, particularly in the poorest quarters, and among orphans, quickly became the most extensive of its kind in the capital.

To Saint Vincent de Paul and the Daughters of Charity, there could be no distinction between helping the "poor in spirit" and the "poor in body." Their emphasis lay where these were one and the same.

More than Saint François de Sales or Bérulle, Saint Vincent de Paul stirred rich Parisians to undertake large-scale projects to relieve the poor. *Confréries,* groups of laymen originally joined together for religious education and devotion, were transformed into charitable organizations through his prodding, and through worsening economic conditions. One of these, the Company of the Holy Sacrament, included among its membership some of the highest officials in the government. Michel de Marillac, keeper of the royal seals and brother of Saint Louise, headed the Parisian group in the 1620s. He and other men of power accepted the revivalist notion that helping the poor was spiritually edifying, though, like Saint Vincent de Paul, they emphasized preaching, confession, and obedience—the spiritual welfare of the destitute—as much as physical needs. It is doubtful that the motivations of these powerful men came from their fears of rebellion, but social and economic conditions stimulated their feelings of guilt and their fear of not being attentive enough to divine exhortations to clothe and feed the destitute. But at the same time, the preaching of obedience and the emphasis on work, which was making its appearance in some of the houses and hospitals supported by the Company, suggest that they were attempting to render society more stable. The task of seeing to the spiritual and physical welfare of all needy Frenchmen would prove to be too big a task for private projects or charitable orders. In fact, not even the royal government, which in the 1660s finally began serious efforts to cope with the problem of suffering, could meet the demands of the hundreds of thousands of destitute who seemed to appear from nowhere whenever crops failed.

In Paris, the Daughters of Charity and the worthy judges who gave alms to distribute at least had the merit of being aware of the problem. Their efforts undoubtedly reduced the suffering and tendency to violence, and for this latter end preaching and confessing were probably still as effective weapons as food and shelter. Saint Vincent de Paul offered no original answers to either man's spiritual or physical condition. Stressing the need for humble piety and charity, he struck deeper into the hearts and met the needs of more Parisians than any of the more original or more intellectually stimulating figures of the saintly revival.

The Last Heroes

The religious revival reduced the fears and violence in Parisian life, but it did not eliminate them. Though religion calmed widows, judges, and merchants, it had less effect on nobles and artisans. Tensions and physical violence would continue to reign in the streets throughout most of the seventeenth century, for religious fanaticism had not been the sole cause of the cataclysm in the 1580s. The nobles' style of life was based on violence, and the poor were driven to it by hunger and taxes. These social and economic conditions would not be changed by prayer alone.

The idealization of violence by the nobility made them the most unstable, vicious, and disturbing element in Parisian society. Not really belonging in the capital, the nobles came and went from their lands, leaving confusion, debts, and often death in their wake. The obsession with violence, manifested in hunting, war, and dueling, had increased and become formalized as a way of life in the sixteenth century.

The aristocratic resurgence and consequent influx of new families into positions of prestige and power that spread throughout Europe in the late Middle Ages infected France belatedly, but rather more deeply than in most countries. Instead of a few hundred courtiers behaving fancifully, and brutally as in medieval Burgundy, the entire second estate, the judicial social environment known as the "robe," and some of the bourgeois were swept up by chivalric idealism.

The preoccupations of the French aristocratic resurgence were war and politics, not the arts or love-making. The latter aspects reappeared strongly in the Wars of Religion, but even stronger were the rough and tumble of military campaigns and the conspiracies to gain power. The reason for this impetus is obvious. Campaigns to Italy occurred almost annually after 1494; then decades of Hapsburg-Valois fighting were followed by a quarter century of civil war, which threw French society back into the arms of professional soldiers. Knights, not bureaucrats or judges, earned the highest honors and pensions in the state.

No longer in the line, as at Agincourt, the knights had learned to command and recruit mercenary armies. Adapting themselves to this new kind of warfare without losing their rationale for privilege as defenders of society, the knights dominated society. Yet neither their ideas nor their way of life changed. They unleashed forces of violence, pillage, and misery to a degree unknown to their medieval ancestors.

The century of war before Henry IV had caused the extinction of many illustrious noble families and had inflated the status and power of the survivors. It had also surrendered the nobility into the hands of youths. Fathers and grandfathers of great houses had been killed or exiled, leaving adolescents to control entire provinces, armies, and the Church. An adolescent quality pervaded the nobility of Louis XIII and the aristocratic culture that developed to give the survivors and social climbers some meaning in life. In Paris, this new aristocratic culture tempered every aspect of life for the upper classes, at least until Louis XIV's new army regulations and the strict regularity of life at Versailles finally broke the nobility's obsession with violence. The civil wars of the sixteenth century had caused an aristocratic resurgence.

In 1600, or even in 1700, no alternative to the medieval rationale for society had yet appeared. "I pray for you, I fight for you, I labor for you"—though old and out of touch with developments in society—still seemed a legitimate maxim to Frenchmen. The failure of thinkers to give French society new ideals, aims, or notions of status was reflected in the aristocratic resurgence. Indeed, medieval conceptions so limited the imaginations of Frenchmen that political philosophy in France died immediately after the civil wars. Between Bodin in the 1560s to 1580s and Montesquieu in the 1720s to 1740s, we encounter no political philosophy of the speculative sort, but only elaborations and emendations of the medieval tripartite conception of society. This ideal maintained estates, not classes, as the warp of society; so long as this ideal persisted there would be a nobility, a warrior class whose *raison d'être* was violence. Of course, had there been no wars to keep them fighting, the nobility might have grown passive; but Richelieu, Mazarin, and Louis XIV not only believed in an ebullient nobility but, like the nobles themselves, idealized war and conquest. From the king on down to the politically inarticulate, reverence and adulation for the nobility, not contempt, predominated until the reign of Louis XV.

Poets, painters, philosophers, and scholars led the flight from reality by enhancing the place of the *gentilhomme* in society. He was their hero, the one who could do almost anything without reproach or arrest. Yet these noblemen did not quite know how to act the part of heroes. There was more to being heroic than mere fighting. The aristocratic style developed by the last Valois kings had failed politically and had been repudiated by the Council of Trent. Henry IV had served as a model, expressing his passion through women and buildings, until an assassin had struck him down in 1610. After that the nobility, led by the princes and Henry's own sons, legitimate and illegitimate, again resorted to intimidation, lawlessness, and violence. Condé, Rohan, Conti, Soissons, and Épernon never quite knew what to do with themselves. So they quarreled violently over points of honor. The early years of the reign of Louis XIII were rife with plots, sieges, murders, and pillage, even in Paris. A more stable style of life was essential, lest the nobility destroy itself. Richelieu knew this; poets and artists may have sensed it. By 1630 there were signs of a rationale for them to live by; in 1645 it was well developed, synthesized, and overt. Given to the *noblesse* mainly by sons of the robe, this rationale transferred violence from real life to the stage, paintings, and sculpture. The men and women who lived according to the dictates of Corneille, Rotrou, Poussin, and Champaigne constituted the last hero-obsessed generation in French culture. Like the new saints, these last heroes were believers—zealots in their efforts to lead truly noble lives.

More than anything else, nobility was a style of life, an ethos, a captivating fiction that gave life to the second estate. Neither subtle nor hidden beneath other social conventions, the aristocratic way was open, institutionalized, manifest in the law and in the minds of men. In every generation, nobility acted as a powerful magnet on the young: power, style, pleasure, and acceptance as an individual depended on it. In seventeenth-century culture, ambition and power became synonymous with acceptance as a gentleman. By the late 1630s the aristocratic style had developed originality, independence, and force, attracting the best minds and artists to its cause, to enrich and perpetuate it.

Often overlooked in this society is a certain openness. The last heroes clearly defined their status hierarchically, with not one, but two, barriers separating groups within the nobility. *Gentillesse* and *noblesse* were not the same; hence to assert that persons were either noble or bourgeois is to distort the clearly defined hierarchy. Socially anxious and politically angry nobles such as the Duke of Saint-Simon would later refuse to recognize these genteel-noble conventions, but the Bourbons, the law courts, and the poets had by 1645 rendered them impregnable.

Noblesse meant possessing virtue and strength of character. This strength derived from service or from physical triumph over other men. *Noblesse* could be acquired, but the higher *gentillesse* could only be transmitted by birth. Loyseau, the jurist, stated: "*Gentillesse* is native, the other is given . . . so that among us one ordinarily distinguishes the nobleman from the gentleman. . . . *Noblesse* and *noble homme* do not involve true *noblesse*." There seems to be a contradiction here, but if there was, the Parisians— and here we refer to the wealthy men of trade and of the law—would not have seen it. Loyseau had the task of "fitting" into the second estate a distinction that really was not there. He did this in a thoroughly unoriginal fashion by differentiating between the nobleman and the "true" nobleman, the latter being a gentleman. Louis XIII, Corneille, Racine, and Richelieu would all have accepted Loyseau's solution to a difficult problem. Not original with him, it had in fact long since become a cliché. Loyseau went on to describe what happens to an individual who is ennobled; it "purges the blood and the posterity . . . of the stain of *rôture* [being a commoner] or servitude, and puts him in the same quality and dignity as if his family had been nobles from the beginning of time." Not unlike baptism, ennoblement was a miracle.

The king might create a noble, but not even he could make a gentleman, though he was one himself *par excellence*. Blood could only be transmuted to this higher degree by deeds, heroic deeds, and by time. Two generations usually sufficed, though this convention lessened in the seventeenth century, partly as a result of the influence of Corneille and the other makers of the aristocratic style. Thierrot wrote in 1606: "New nobles are still affected by the nature of those who begot them. . . . Nobility is all the more excellent in proportion to its age; its force and its vigor are in its antiquity. . . . If it has a recognized beginning, that very knowledge weakens it; perfection consists in the forgetting of its birth." These legal definitions provided the underpinning for a style of life. Corneille, Racine, and Poussin took these definitions and personified them in medieval knights, Roman statesmen, and sons and daughters of judges. Nobility was a caste based on race and blood, two of Corneille's most repeated words. Race was not color, but stock or breeding, as in horses or dogs. Certain physical characteristics exemplifying noble blood were intentionally sought out and bred by prestige-conscious parents. The cult of physical beauty that accompanied the aristocratic resurgence led to an aesthetic ranking of individuals, though this was more important for females than for males. Men and women were judged and judged themselves by physical beauty. La Rochefoucauld, in his self-portrait written in 1659, remarks: "It would be very difficult for me to say what type of nose I have, as it is neither snub, aquiline, large, nor pointed, at least I do not believe so. . . . They used to tell me I had a chin that was a little too big." For La Rochefoucauld, detached and secure member of an illustrious family that he was, these criticisms of his features caused little anxiety. For the would-be gentleman they were a source of great concern.

These aesthetic judgments, combined with the conception of inherited virtue and the very hard-nosed politics of dowries, lands, and châteaux, established rules compelling children of dukes to marry only children of dukes or princes, and so on down the ranks. Abhorrence of *mésalliance,* or mismatching, pervaded French thinking; conversations in hushed voices in salons, at Court, or in shops, reflected the deep anxiety over it. Mismatch was dreaded like miscegenation. Genuine disgust and anguish flooded their minds when these nobles thought of "mixed marriage," an act more revolting to them than prostitution or homosexual relationships. It is important, then, to clarify exactly what was meant by *mésalliance:* a union between a family possessing *gentillesse* with one of the *noblesse* might be considered a mismatch of the first or lesser degree, abhorred but in practice accepted. What really shocked was the marriage into a bourgeois family of someone possessing *gentillesse.* There is little evidence that *mésalliance* of this second degree was very frequent in the *Ancien Régime.* Marriages of judicial families with "truly" noble families occurred frequently, but this type of mismatch could be covered up by the contradictions that were noted in Loyseau. Ennoblement by office was still ennoblement. Loyseau described it as "accidental, exterior, accessory, indirect, not being conferred on the inside to a person on his own account but transferred to him from the outside. . . . Now as the rays of the sun are stronger than those of the moon, which borrows its light from the former, so the nobility . . . of the man provided with the ennobling office is not so vigorous as [that] of race, which is a part of the person and is infused, if one may speak thus, in his blood." The metaphor was not the most original, but it served to capture convention. Corneille would make this the distinction between tragedy and comedy: gentlemen only could be tragic, while noblemen could be ridiculed in comedy. In his comedies, Molière would explore the corrupting influence of money on gentlemen. The second estate was becoming more and more explicitly stratified, with tensions at different levels caused by the different families' pretensions to ancient origins. Along with this, the prestige and identity of judges as learned men devoted to justice declined and almost disappeared. The force of this fiction of the nobility as *gentillesse* and *noblesse* would eventually fuse the two groups.

In the public mind, gentlemen were courageous, polite, and eager to defend the meek, women, and merchants. Not even the Parisians knew better, or, to be more precise, they did not want to know better. No matter how many nobles they observed who obviously displayed none of these virtuous characteristics, society refused to reexamine its idealized conception of the nobility. Corrupted perhaps, but to restore and purify rather than to eliminate the second estate was their aim. Reaching for a golden age, Frenchmen yearned for Roland, Gaston de Foix, Du Guesclin, and Saint Louis to come to life again. Chief among those longing for these legendary knights were the poets. But what astonishes is the great number of real-life Don Quixotes and would-be Don Quixotes from upper-class families of the capital who roamed the streets of Paris. Judges' sons forsook the law for poetry and the idealized chivalric life, portrayed in such books as Castiglione's *The Courtier*. Satirists poked fun at their behavior and at the brutality of the "true" nobles, but like Cervantes their moral was to reform and revive. For La Luzerne, Auvray, Mézeray, and Le Moyne mark a clear path to knightly virtue by pointing out the foibles and inferiority of the contemporary nobility. "Live as did your ancestors," they pleaded, reinforcing beliefs and hopes that a new golden age could be reached.

The mind of the late-medieval knight will always be an enigma. How much did he truly identify himself with historical and poetic personages? The boasting, etiquette, and exaggerated garb shocked some, like Sully, as affectation and effeminacy, but the chivalric ideal remained too strong an attraction for persons to change their ways. Almost as if unanimously refusing to live in their harsh surroundings, nobles and upper-class Parisians fled to ancient Rome, medieval Spain, and to the Capetian era. Escapism and fantasy through poetry and art nourished these, the last of the knights.

The violence of the Wars of Religion had perhaps momentarily submerged the male aristocratic obsession with dueling. In the first decades of the seventeenth century, it once again became a subject for ethical debate. Henry IV and Louis XIII issued decrees forbidding dueling, but if a *gentilhomme* who had challenged another *gentilhomme* to a duel obeyed the law and refused to duel when challenged, he sullied his honor. The exemplary trial and execution of notorious duelers such as Montmorency-Boutteville prompted debate, anger, and frustration among the younger, more hotheaded *gentilshommes,* who often were already hostile to the government for other reasons.

Manners slowly became less violent after 1600 as heroic impulses were turned to more refined modes of expressing violence, such as hunting, acting, ballets (including mock hunts and duels), and patronage of the arts. A curtain separates the aristocratic style of the Valois Court and the early *Marais* from that of Richelieu and the Place Royale. The Valois Court was more intense, sensual, and violent. A bas-relief on Francis I's tomb at Saint-Denis depicts the king high in the air on a rearing steed, fierce and triumphant at the Battle of Marignano. On the field opposite him stands a row of cannon belching shot and smoke. The sculptor sought to demonstrate heroic victory against the most formidable enemy then known to man. Fascination with death, incongruity, and lack of reality marked aristocratic resurgences. Consider the paintings in the château of Tanlay (Yonne) depicting allegorical nudes lined up on opposing sides. Diane de Poitiers as Venus and the Duke of Guise as Mars politely combat Admiral Coligny as Neptune and his brother as Hercules. For the aristocracy, the civil war had been a sport between the gods, a chance to prove their heroic natures. The ecclesiastics at Trent were not the only ones to be upset by the emotional and psychological implications of Renaissance art. Knights had entered the fantasy world of mythology. Valois court poets mentioned the Greeks as much to add erotic elements to their works as they did to display wisdom in ethics. Of what significance the upright, turgid codpieces that became fashionable all over Europe? Or the low-cut dresses with their tight bodices and flared-out hips? Velvet and silk clothing, furs, fancy hose, plumed hats, fine gloves, perfume, and quantities of jewelry adorned men. Aristocratic literature, dress, and manners unconsciously pulsed with youthful erotic appeal. Religious revival and the disillusionment following the civil war aborted these tendencies. Literature became more historically grounded, less concerned with the mythological; through imagination living people now identified themselves with dead heroes. The gods and men returned to their separate spheres. The aristocratic style of Louis XIII became decidedly more national as French art, theater, and handbooks on manners grew independent of Italian and Spanish influences.

But the most striking difference between Valois and Bourbon aristocratic styles is that the latter extended to a much larger segment of the population. No longer restricted to the Court or the Loire, the capital for manners, dress, and convention now shifted to Paris. Judges, bourgeois, and retail merchants reached up and accepted the morality of Corneille, adulating and aping the "true" gentlemen in their midst. Massive sales of offices had allowed perhaps several hundred Parisian families to slip from the commoner to the *noblesse,* which in turn pressed the existing *noblesse,* chiefly in the Parlement, to push on for acceptance as "true" gentlemen. At every stage, therefore, social change in Parisian society after the civil war required a synthesized, overt, aristocratic identity that would join *gentillesse* and *noblesse.* This was a real need in the society,

Medieval Revival

A ball, by Abraham Bosse. Dancing was a highly stylized and formal experience in courtly circles, with only one couple dancing at a time, while others watched for missteps and awkward gestures.

not unlike the anxieties over religion, which also needed to be calmed. Moreover, Parisians had the money required to construct their identities through the arts. If prestige could be bought, they would buy it even if it meant high expenditures for paintings, tapestries, gardens, clothes, riding lessons, and the theater. Status-seeking robe families poured a flood of money into the hands of artists and skilled artisans. Money that had previously gone into commerce or had been hidden away was now spent on culture, producing one of the richest cultural and consumerist movements in the history of Paris and of all Europe.

The heroic style was propagated in the theater, paintings, sculpture, furnishings, riding schools or *académies,* and *salons.* The latter replaced the Court in the extended

A tournament in the Place Royale, in Antoine de Pluvinel's handbook on riding. Young Louis XIII is shown learning to catch a ring with his lance. Throughout his life, the king loved to ride, hunt, and go on military campaigns.

aristocratic society. Gentlemen and would-be gentlemen and ladies could mix to show off their manners and prowess as persons of culture. Conversation developed into a refined art where words enabled persons to triumph over others, to impose their superiority as in the duel. Court tournaments, ballets, and jousts went on, of course, and it is clear that the number of both onlookers and participants increased until Louis XIV abandoned Paris for Versailles. Emphasizing youth, war, love, and politics—not poetry or painting for their own sake—the heroic style combined unity with articulated fantasy. Though the answers to the problems facing society may have been completely irrational, or even fantastic and dangerous, they were answers nonetheless.

By 1645, the foundations for this monumental cultural synthesis were laid. The long reign of Louis XIV that was just beginning would be an elaboration of the achievements made before 1645. The psychology, aesthetics, and social values canonized by

Corneille, Rotrou, Poussin, and François Mansart would remain unchanged in the works of Racine, Molière, Le Brun, and Jules Hardouin-Mansart. The latter were no less great for having accepted the canons of the former. But here there was a change of attitude, a loss of faith in the application of the heroic ideal. Instead of suggesting to contemporaries that they live like heroes, Racine made the hero a historical, bygone phenomenon. And by attracting all talent to himself, Louis XIV unconsciously transformed the heroic ideal in art into something heavy and applicable only to kings. The grimness of professionalized war would extinguish what had begun as such an appealing ideal in 1636, the year Corneille's *Le Cid* was first performed in the *Théâtre du Marais*.

In the 1630s, writers and artists met the needs of an anxious Parisian society. "True" nobles themselves did not know how to behave, or even what it was to be heroic until the oracle of the moment, Pierre Corneille, told them how to think and act. Though the impact of the theater on Parisian society after 1630 cannot be measured, it was by all indications very great. Richelieu had commandeered the best talent to write plays for him, but almost immediately and accidentally Corneille captured the imaginations of the Parisians, creating as he went along from play to play a dream world for them to live in.

The son of a minor judicial official from Rouen, Pierre Corneille (1606–84) projected his own aspirations in his theatrical works. Anxiety over a love affair may have prompted him to write poetry and eventually to create a complete system of courtly ideals and social values. It is a mistake to think of Corneille or his theater as bourgeois. He was himself of the *noblesse* just turning *gentillesse,* and so are his first comedies. The Parisians accepted Corneille's idealized view of social behavior, and Corneillian characters were eventually as prevalent on the streets as on the stage.

Corneille made the *grandes âmes* come alive. The term cannot be translated: they are supermen and superwomen, demigods and demigoddesses, men and women who are like other men but who are endowed with a greater degree of the qualities all men and women share. Every individual is capable of anger, ambition, or any other human attribute; the *grandes âmes* have these qualities in much larger quantities. They can hate more than others, or love, fight, and grasp for power to a measure beyond the ordinary individual. Kings, princes, gods, medieval conquerors, Roman statesmen and their wives and daughters, and saints were *grandes âmes*. In Corneille they reach degrees of intensity, obsession, even madness—stemming from jealousy, power, love, devotion, hate, incest, and pride—which simply could not be attained by ordinary people. This in essence was the psychology of the heroic style. The combinations were infinite, the psychology the same. Idealized, morals personified, the *grandes âmes* stalked the Parisian stages, loftier, more destructive, more terrifying to audiences than Everyman could ever be. Breathless with excitement, young people sucked in the violence and emotions of these heroes. No one was duped by the pseudoclassical dramatic rules. Even the dull-witted reeled at the duels, murders, rapes, and battles evoked but never seen. Aristocratic convention permitted not the slightest social or religious constraint on the *grandes âmes*. Corneille's plays made conventional morality an absurdity, and yet they tended to establish a new morality, more refined and less violent. Egotism and love, wound into politics, became the stuff of tragedy; the Parisians swooned under Corneille's power. Dynasticism, war, and love-making, the subjects of his tragedies, were mirrored in upper-class Parisian life.

Until Richelieu's influence, Parisian theater had been insignificant and bawdy, probably because audiences were predominantly lower class. The earthy quality of *Mélite,* Corneille's first comedy, was so quickly outmoded that Corneille changed, only two or three years later, some lines of this play. He first wrote:

> PHILANDRE: Cependant un baiser accordé par avarice
> Soulageroit beaucoup ma pénible souffrance:
> CLORIS: Prend-le sans demander, poltron, pour un baiser,
> Crois-tu que ta Cloris te voulût refuser?
> TIRCIS: Voilà traiter l'amour justement, bouche à bouche:
> C'est par où vous alliez commencer l'escarmouche?[1]

This would never do. How unlike the mature Corneille and the new, refined taste. So he changed it to read:

> PHILANDRE: Cependant en faveur de ma longue souffrance,
> CLORIS: Tais-toi, mon frère vient. . . .

---

1. PHILANDRE: However, a kiss, granted in advance,
     Would greatly ease my painful suffering.
     CLORIS: Take it without asking, coward, for a kiss
     Do you believe that your Cloris would refuse you?
     TIRCIS: That's treating love justly, mouth to mouth:
     Just where were you going to begin the skirmish?

TIRCIS: Si j'en crois l'apparence,
            Mon arrivée ici fait quelque contretemps.[2]

Corneille evoked the same emotions, but in a refined, elegant language acceptable to anxious elites, especially the young. As the genre became refined, the audiences increased and became more aristocratic. Paris had only the *Hôtel de Bourgogne* until 1600, when the *Théâtre du Marais* was established. Plays performed at Court or before the cardinal appeared immediately afterward at these theaters.

From its first presentation in 1636, *Le Cid*[3] stirred up the Parisians and moved whole audiences to tears, first of sadness, then of joy. It was fashionable to weep profusely and noisily in public. Corneille, writing thirty years after these first performances, recalled that at the moment of Rodrigue's appearance before Chimène after the duel, a *"frémissement,"* a shuddering or quivering came over the audience. Poetry chiseled the minds and stimulated the imaginations of gentlemen and bourgeois alike. Voltaire asserts that the Grand Condé wept at *Le Cid*.

By ignoring convention, Corneille gave the play a stern though happy ending. Technically everybody should have met violent death had the fashionable rules of tragedy been followed, but by making the plot as much a duel of words as of swords, Corneille makes honor, duty, and love triumph. Love is tested by terrible circumstances; yet as *grandes âmes* Rodrigue and Chimène love each other all the more because of the trial of honor and duty. Sensuality is not quite transparent; yet one senses that the hero and heroine are eager for the king to stop talking and the play to end.

No previous literary work had struck the Parisians so profoundly. *Le Cid* satisfied something. The lofty moral tone, the anguish, struggling, and passion did not appear to them as affectation, nor did the themes of the play, which were everyday topics, idealized and ennobled. Blood feuding, dueling, the role of the king in aristocratic society, genteel love-making, and crusadelike foreign wars (Father Joseph still hoped to free the Holy Land from the Infidels) made *Le Cid* realistic for Paris under Louis XIII and Richelieu. Costume and setting were contemporary; the evocation of medieval

---

2.   PHILANDRE: However, in favor of my long suffering,
                   CLORIS: Be quiet, my brother is coming. . . .
                   TIRCIS: If I am to believe appearances,
                                My arrival here is a bit inopportune.

3. Corneille was then thirty years old. He dedicated the play to Richelieu's powerful niece, Madame Combalet, Duchess of Aiguillon.

The stage of the theater in the Hôtel de Bourgogne, by Abraham Bosse. The stock characters, largely Italian in origin, were constantly adapted by players for over two centuries.

Spain deceived no one, nor was it intended to. Don Fernand, like Louis XIII, is well-intentioned but not truly heroic, yet he is kingly in spite of himself when he renders justice. Corneille supplied answers, solutions to the most pressing problems of upper-class French society.

Nor did the psychology seem affected. The idea that the self, or personal identity, depended solely on the opinion of others struck audiences in the 1630s as correct, even obvious. Reputation and *gloire* or *honneur* meant only one's image or appearance before one's peers. Therefore, identity, acquired by birth, had to be defended and, ideally, increased by virtue. Breeding alone did not determine a person's capacity to be heroic. At the same time, neither Corneille nor anyone else in Parisian society conceived of a

The theater in Richelieu's Parisian residence. In the foreground are Louis XIII, Anne of Austria, and, to her right, the future Louis XIV. The king's brother, Gaston d'Orléans, sits at the king's left.

peasant or bourgeois as heroic. Thus in Corneille we find exactly the same conceptions of society and behavior as in Loyseau. Except, of course, that Corneille made a religion of pride, of that *orgueil* which dominates the actions and thoughts of the true hero, who is never satisfied until he intimidates, kills, or in some way destroys other men. Reason and passion are the tools of pride; only lesser men, never the *grandes âmes,* suffer from conflicts between the two. Egotism sets reason to work, makes a hero cunning, while passion drives him on to death or victory. Fascination with death, success, and sex gives Corneille and the aristocratic style in general an adolescent quality. Over and over the theme of fear of old age is repeated in tragedy and memoirs, for in the heroic ideal it is old age, the inability to fight and love, not death, that is the enemy. How could all this be believed? Society's need for ideals and Corneille's poetic power made *Le Cid* come alive.

In the plays of Rotrou, Corneille's contemporary and chief rival, the same themes appear, though the worship of *grandes âmes* and violence is even more intense. The political overtones are heavier too, particularly in his great play, *Venceslas,* first presented in 1647, after Corneille's great triumphs of *Horace, Cinna,* and *Polyeucte* in the early 1640s had already imposed new rules for tragedy on the theater. But Rotrou was as independent and egotistic as Corneille; now, four years after the death of Louis XIII, new themes had become available. A king must be the noblest and most heroic individual in the society, or he becomes the cause of violence. Nobility as such cannot be at fault. Rotrou gave Creon these lines:

> Dans les dessins d'un roi, comme dans ceux des cieux,
> De fidels sujets doivent fermer les yeux,
> Et soumettant leur sens au pouvoir des couronnes,
> Quelles que soient les lois, croire qu'elles sont bonnes.[4]

These verses vulgarized absolutism and extended it by moralizing on the role of the king. Venceslas tries to rule and fails, because he takes merit instead of passion as his guiding principle. Losing control of power, then of his family, and finally of his subjects, Venceslas becomes a man condemned because he has not lived up to his ideal. For merit is a common, indeed a commoner standard of judgment, ignoble, and suitable only for bourgeois.

A favorite wields Venceslas' power, his son Ladislas rages, and, faced with his father's refusal to do so, finally attempts to murder the man who rules. The favorite had more merit than the king himself, but not more passion. Ladislas' conduct cannot be condemned, because he seeks to have his royal house live up to the *gloire* of its founders.

4.
In the plans of a king, as in those of the heavens,
Faithful subjects must close their eyes,
And subjugating their sense to the power of the crowns,
Whatever the laws, believe that they are good.

Then, as if this were not enough, Ladislas accidentally murders his own brother. Venceslas renders justice and, ruling according to merit, condemns Ladislas to death. This violation of pride and passion leads to Venceslas' fall. The moral, of course, is that kings who do not reign, princes who do not fight, or *gentilshommes* who lead base lives become propagators of crime, murder, and sedition. Venceslas, not violence itself, was at fault.

Comedy was something else. Relegated to second place, its concern was the daily life of the *noblesse*. The foibles of the social climbers or such bourgeois characteristics as piety, avarice, provincialism, narrow-mindedness, and bawdiness became the essence of comedy. Based fundamentally on ridicule, here persons were laughed at, not admired. Corneille wrote about tragedy and comedy: "[Tragedy's] dignity demands some great interest of the State, or some passion more noble and more masculine than love such as ambition or vengeance. It desires as its subject an illustrious, extraordinary, serious action; [comedy] stops with a common and playful action."

Corneille's comedies concern the failure of the social climber to be accepted as a gentleman. His clothes are right, his hair is properly trimmed, but something always gives him away. Would-be heroes usually become lovable through their foibles, as Corneille intended. The true hero is feared, admired, respected, but never simply loved. Corneille gives these would-be heroes fantastic names: Lysandre, Dorimant, Alidor, or Cléandre. Though failing at deception, they usually win the girl anyway. Love becomes *badinage* and adolescent enthusiasm for something never experienced. Corneille invariably suggests that it takes a gentleman to recognize a true *fille de qualité,* for often the would-be hero finds out that the girl he loves is not the genteel girl he thinks she is. Technically these are not bourgeois comedies but noble ones, in the sense that the family origin of the heroes and heroines is almost invariably judicial on the way to becoming *gentillesse*.

Some of Corneille's most successful comedies were set in the fashionable meeting places of Paris. *La Galerie du Palais,* presented in 1633, was such a success that he wrote *La Place Royale* in 1634 and *Le Menteur* in 1642. The latter play opens in the Tuileries gardens and moves to the Place Royale.

La Galerie du Palais includes several scenes of a shopping tour in the most fashionable shopping place for finery, books, and the so-called *"articles de Paris."* The cloth-seller offers quantities of fine silk for veils so thin that it conceals makeup. She believes that God loves her because business is good, and complains that her shop is too small. The would-be hero and heroine look over the merchandise, comment on

The galerie du Palais, by Abraham Bosse. The luxury shops in the great gallery of the Palais de Justice attracted strollers who wished to show off their clothes, converse about literature, and gossip.

the novels of Scudéry, and show off their clothes and manners. Conversation is animated and clever, filled with puns and cutting remarks. Charm and vivacity applied to Parisian life pleased the audiences. Abraham Bosse captured Corneille's scene in a superb engraving in which, though the fiction of gentility is preserved, no person is given a noble gesture or pose. Contemporaries thus knew at a glance that these were sons and daughters of judges and merchants. Bosse added:

> Icy les cavaliers les plus adventureux
> En lisant les Romans s'animent à combattre,
> Et de leur passion les amans langoureux
> Flattent les mouvemens par les vers de Théâtre.[5]

This is satire, to be sure, but even as such it reflects the unity of literature and manners.

La Place Royale is something else, more serious, even cruel. Corneille suggests that he seeks to bring out into the street the conversations usually held in bedchambers. What starts out as fun about conflicts between love and friendship ends in a morose, perverted conclusion. Alidor, the hero, is a repressed homosexual with an amiable girlfriend, Angélique, who satisfies his every desire, save that for independence. She is ready and willing to make love, but he is inadequate. His intimate friend, Cléandre, also loves Angélique, but from afar. Once Alidor discovers this, he decides to break off his courtship of Angélique and try to make her love his friend. A sordid enterprise indeed, leading to cruel attacks on the heroine, who truly loves Alidor. She finally realizes what is happening and, comprehending that Alidor is capable of neither love nor courage, accuses him:[6]

> Tu manques de courage aussi bien que d'amour;
> Et tu me fais trop voir par ta bizarrerie,
> La chimérique effet de la poltronnerie.
> Alidor (quel amant) n'ose me posséder.[7]

Frustrated, wanting to be loved, the heroine simply cannot recover. Though aware that

---

5.
> Here the most adventurous knights
> By reading novels are stimulated to fight,
> And languid lovers embellish
> The stirrings of their passion by verses from the theater.

6. At one point Alidor is confronted by a situation that would have required a challenge to duel. He backs down.

7.
> You lack courage as well as love:
> And your bizarre ways make all too obvious to me,
> The fantastic effect of your cowardice.
> Alidor (what a lover!) dares not possess me.

she is beautiful, normal, and amiable, she sees no recourse but to abandon the world. She reflects:

> Puisque de mon amour on fait si peu de conte
> Va cacher dans un cloître et tes pleurs et ta honte.[8]

Then, as she begins to hate Alidor, he in turn begins to love her; but this cannot be the basis for a proper relationship. Corneille commented, "That makes for a vicious inequality of morals."

The second couple in the play, though tainted by this painful relationship, fall in love. Cléandre is also tempted to "put friendship above love," but, owing to the urgings of his sister, he finally rejects Alidor's friendship and, in doing so, is able to fall in love. This adds to Alidor's chagrin; by now lonely, friendless, and inadequate, he stalks off the stage after a brilliant final speech in which Corneille suggests that all this has happened merely because of intense egotism. The play disturbed the Parisians at the time, so much so that Corneille commented in his introductory remarks to the published version that a poet is "never the guarantor for the fantasies he gives his actors." Moralizing all the way, yet with sympathy and poetic power, never, even in *Le Cid,* was he more perceptive about the adolescent quality and dilemmas of aristocratic life.

Anxiety is the theme of *Le Menteur.* The hero quits the "robe for the sword," begins a courtship, and, wanting to impress, lies his way into an impossible situation. Reasoning with him about what he has done, his father asks the dreaded question: "Are you a *gentilhomme*?" Lying condemns his claim to being virtuous; his robe origins cannot support his claim to be a gentleman:

> Où le sang a manqué, si la vertu l'acquiert,
> Où le sang l'a donné, le vice aussi le perd . . .
> Et dans la lâcheté du vice où je te voi,
> Tu n'es plus gentilhomme, étant sorti de moi.[9]

8.
    Since my love is so slightly valued,
    Go hide in a cloister thy tears and thy shame.

9.
    Where blood has been lacking, if virtue acquires it,
    Where blood has given it, vice likewise loses it . . .
    And in the cowardice of vice where I see you,
    You are no longer a gentleman, issuing from me.

Here Corneille says exactly the same things as Loyseau. Adopted by the monarchy and the Parisians, this jurist's commentaries had resolved, at least temporarily, the principal anxiety of the upper classes. "True" nobles became less violent, less snobbish, more refined, while the robe gradually assimilated the aristocratic style. The theatrical quality of Parisian life and the concern with clothes, polite language, and the opinions of others gave the capital a searingly refined culture. Sneering in *Le Menteur,* Corneille agreed:

> Paris est un grand lieu de marchands mêlés,
> L'effet n'y répond pas toujours à l'apparence:
> On s'y laisse duper autant qu'en lieu de France;
> Et parmi tant d'esprits plus polis et meilleurs,
> Il y croît des badauds autant et plus qu'ailleurs . . .
> Comme on s'y connait mal, chacune s'y fait de mise,
> Et vaut communément autant comme il se prise. . . .[10]

Corneille stalked Paris and its society (and perhaps Rouen's as well), describing them with the detachment of a great artist. Independent, self-confident, and frank, he was never intimidated by convention, contemporaries, or even by Aristotle, Lucan, and Seneca. Though studying the ancients and borrowing heavily, he never revered them or let their example curtail his bold imagination. When rules got in the way, he broke them. The preface to *Clitandre,* his first tragedy, was a manifesto for the moderns: "Here I take some sort of liberty to shock the ancients, in as much as they are no longer in a condition to reply. . . . Since the sciences and the arts never reach their apogee, I am permitted to believe that they did not know everything, and that from their instructions one can glean enlightenment which they did not have." Among other things, he considered the subjects of classical theater too violent for his age. He set out to refine them, and in so doing tempered the French aristocracy.

10. Paris is a great place of mingled merchants,
     The effect does not always come up to appearances:
     People let themselves be duped there as much as in any other place in France;
     And among so many of the most polished and best wits,
     Flourish as many gapers as elsewhere, and even more . . .
     As people there are not well acquainted with one another, each one dresses well
     And is commonly worth as much as he values himself to be. . . .

11. Dedicated to Richelieu.

By the early 1640s, Corneille had extended the dramatic mechanisms first developed in *Le Cid* into plays on Roman themes. In barely two years *Horace*[11] and *Cinna* were presented, and *Polyeucte* followed in 1643, demonstrating Corneille's sustained level of poetic power. He was by then thirty-four. In subsequent years he would explore the consequences and causes of violence through a panorama of Roman history. He tried medieval subjects after that, but they inspired him less than the Romans. In *Polyeucte,* Corneille brought Christian subjects to the stage, asserting that *invention,* the poetic imagination, could justifiably be used to depict the heroic life of a martyred saint. And while perhaps refusing to conclude that might makes right, not unlike Richelieu, Corneille would perceive heroic success as a sign of divine support that often, but not always, put his ethical views in accord with absolute, divine-right theory. Corneille was deeply religious. Haunted by fears that the theater was endangering his soul, he read his breviary daily during the last thirty years of his life and put years of poetic energy into a verse translation of the *Imitation of Christ.* Parisian would-be heroes were susceptible to similar religious crises.

If the theater provided a stereotype of the heroic life, the Parisian *hôtel* became the setting where the *noble homme* acted out his part. The nobility dominated the countryside, idealized hunting, and made a show of inviting hundreds of guests to parties that would go on for days. In Paris this kind of life was hardly possible, but the design of the *hôtel* sought to create the illusion of a rural setting for urban living. Not a single building, but rather an ensemble of courtyards, stables, gardens, cellars, storehouses, huge rooms, and (beginning in the 1630s) monumental staircases, the ideal *hôtel* sat on a rectangular half-acre. From the street on all four sides, nothing could be seen but the high walls, slate roofs, dormers, haylofts, and the huge, twenty-foot-high doors of the *porte cochère,* a great double doorway wide enough for a coach to pass. When these doors were closed, the *hôtel* was impregnable to bandits, police, and beggars. Walls and *porte cochère* were built out into the public thoroughfare as far as the law would allow, and often the law was violated. The streets of the *Marais* were like roofless tunnels devoid of decoration and greenery, and even of sidewalks until the eighteenth century. When horses and carriages passed, pedestrians hugged the walls, unable to escape the mud and offal thrown up by the wheels.

Just inside the *porte cochère* was a *cour d'honneur,* or great courtyard, designed and decorated to impress visitors. As in the rural château, guests were greeted here and then were taken up the monumental staircase, usually to the right, to the second or "noble" floor. The *porte cochère* and *cour d'honneur* immediately revealed the prestige of owners and residents of an *hôtel*. To give one's address as "rue de la Couleure Sainte-Cathérine, second *porte cochère* on the left," identified one as at least a *noble homme*. Lower-class Parisians identified their residences by inn signs, *passages,* or *allées,* the latter the bane of the socially inferior. *Allées* were (and are, for they still exist in old quarters) passageways, sometimes only the width of a narrow door, leading to tiny courtyards and stairways in the interior of the house. How inferior to the *porte cochère!* Left unlocked, the *allées* served as latrines for the public of a city equipped with few toilet facilities. Residents returned home to find *"pisseurs"* at their stairway or doorstep. Edicts forbade this practice, and concierges were compelled to guard *allées;* but they nevertheless remained stinking caves until after 1850.

Nor were *cours d'honneur* free of foul odors. Kitchens, pens for storing live animals to be butchered and roasted, latrines, and manure from as many as fifteen horses explain why the owners chose the second floor for their living quarters. But as in a château, residents were not embarrassed by having all this at their front doors. Not until the eighteenth century, with the rise of the cult of privacy, did the *noblesse* definitively wish to be separated from the commoners or from horses.

The noble floor was the most costly and beautifully decorated part of the *hôtel*. Bedchambers, antechambers, *cabinets,* galleries, all communicating with one another through a row of doors stretching along the inside of the U-shaped house, made it necessary to move from room to room in order to reach the staircase. Privacy was unattainable in the seventeenth-century *hôtel,* except in curtained beds and tiny *cabinets*. Above the noble floor were attics for housing servants and storing hay, or, if the *hôtel* was very large, there was a third floor of finely decorated rooms, as in the Hôtel Aubert (Salé).[12]

Ceilings were high, often fifteen to twenty feet, while rooms on the noble floor usually measured twenty by forty feet, small for a château but enormous in comparison to bourgeois houses. Rooms were generally not reserved for one particular function. The Marquise of Rambouillet's *hôtel* was avant-garde and very fashionable for several reasons, among them its *grande salle,* or multipurpose room. Here ten tapestries with woodland scenes covered every inch of the walls, setting off walnut sideboards, benches, and a long table "opening out at both ends," covered with a Turkish, geometric-design rug. Eight paintings, hung on top of the tapestries, decorated this room. Four were portraits: Catherine de Médicis, Charles IX, Henry III, and Henry IV.

12. Number 5, rue de Thorigny.

Adjoining the *grande salle* of the Hôtel de Rambouillet was an antechamber, its walls covered by six tapestries depicting the burning of Troy. Chairs, little tables, and Chinese-lacquered credenzas made it very fashionable. The chamber, or bedroom, was next in the long row of doors; it was dominated by a huge canopied bed with silk-embroidered hangings. A Turkish rug, a chandelier of rock crystal, and crucifixes and pictures of saints broke the monotony of the tapestried walls.

The next and last room in the series was the famous *chambre bleue,* the "blue room," where the Marquise held her *salons.* Blue was an innovation in the 1620s, as rooms had usually been dark red or rusty brown under the last Valois. Eight Flemish tapestries of classical figures standing in porticoes, a gift of Louis XIII, made the room appear larger than it was. A Turkish rug covered a table, while a kind of red satin daybed, Chinese and Spanish chests, and chairs and folding stools lined the walls. A gilded-copper chandelier suspended by a silk-covered rope dominated the room. Delft and Chinese vases, Venetian glass, and fresh flowers completed the décor.

Discreetly hidden behind a tapestry, a tiny *cabinet,* sumptuously decorated, provided a place for the marquise to rest with one or two intimate friends even while her *salon* was crowded with guests.

The furnishings at the Hôtel de Rambouillet strengthened the trend toward bright, glittery elegance that was to dominate Parisian interiors for the rest of the *Ancien Régime*. Masses of color, silver, gold, bright paintings, beautifully painted beamed ceilings, polished white and black checkered marble floors, ribbons, and tapestries gave upper-class Parisian life a new elegance. Color more than money separated the *noble homme* from the bourgeois, for the latter stuck to black and gray dress and somber furnishings. In his vivid, perfectly accurate scenes of Parisian life, Abraham Bosse faithfully idealized in images the typical *hôtel* which developed from that of Madame de Rambouillet.

Any *hôtel* worthy of the name also had a garden. Everyone either believed in or paid lip service to his love for gardens: in them Henry IV met ambassadors, held councils, and made love; in them the clergy prayed and nobles hunted, while ladies and servants chattered, sewed, or tended the ornate flower beds. Noble Parisians never ceased talking or writing about the reflections, perspectives, scents, flowers, herbs, designs, and freshness of gardens.

Rules for the garden were elaborate and based on the need to provide a natural setting in a minimum of space. Acres of *parterres,* or arabesques of boxwood and colored gravel, mile-long promenades, and vast reflecting pools were out of the question in the capital. The garden was the symbol of aristocratic life most difficult to construct in the city.

Walls were concealed by hedges and espalier-trained fruit trees, pruned to grow flat against walls. Mature trees were cut down, surfaces were leveled, and pipes leading to fountains were installed before small trees clipped into cubes, cones, and other geometric shapes were planted. Ten tiny trees made a garden appear far more spacious than would fewer large ones.

Gardens were laid out according to the laws of perspective; each plant added to the illusion of spaciousness. Proportions had to be in perfect harmony. Trees close to the *hôtel* were clipped a bit larger, the paths narrowed toward the far end of the rectangle, and even the water spout in the fountain had a prescribed height according to the laws of perspective. Whenever gardens had to be built near the back walls of churches or monasteries, artists covered these surfaces with murals of trees, lattices, clouds, Roman temples, and fountains so that they would not spoil the effect.

The royal gardens of the Tuileries, the Luxembourg, and the Cours la Reine became favorite spots for smartly dressed, upper-class Parisians. There one observed how to reverence a lady, bow, curtsy, carry a cane, or take off one's hat properly. Admittance depended strictly on a person's dress: an elegant, beribboned costume was all that was required. Guards rarely admitted persons garbed in the black serge of the bourgeois. In general, the same was true for the fashionable *salons,* the galleries of the really princely or ducal *hôtels,* and the Court itself. Dress and manners sufficed. Gardens painted in *trompe l'oeil,* false marble, secret stairways, doors concealed by gluing the backs of books to them, and cabinets with innumerable secret drawers and sliding panels appealed to the Parisians and were part of the theatrical quality of life.

Though there were some true connoisseurs, most purchasers bought paintings for their subject and the reputation of the artist rather than for their quality. The choice of subjects in painting and sculpture also reflected social distinctions. Yet from the really quite modest artisan household on up, religious paintings vastly outnumbered the others. Prices for works of art were low, ridiculously low, so that it was rare to find a household without engravings or paintings. An *hôtel* would contain perhaps one or two hundred pictures, and often a cabinet where the walls, doors, and ceiling were entirely painted with flowers, or with woodland or mythological scenes. Larger *hôtels* invariably contained a chapel, where again one found paintings and often sculpture.

The quality of French art sank to a new low after the civil war. The League had attacked Renaissance art as generally irreligious and heretical; hence the capital did not attract talented young artists worthy of succeeding such major artists and sculptors as François Clouet, Jean Goujon, and Germain Pilon. Henry IV was no connoisseur and was given little time to become one; Marie de Médicis recognized the power of art in international politics but lacked the taste needed to encourage young artists; and the nobility remained too preoccupied with politics and violence to be serious patrons of art until about 1630. Not quite a wasteland because of past excellence, Paris was only a cut above provincial towns, or London and Brussels, and unequal to Amsterdam in 1630. Marie de Médicis' commission to Rubens for a series of monumental history paintings glorifying the Bourbons attracted attention but did little to make Paris a capital of artists.

True, Simon Vouet returned from Rome in 1627 to do altarpieces for many of the new churches, and also received commissions from Claude de Bullion and Pierre Séguier; but here there was little leadership or sense of taste that the Parisians could grasp and make their own. Parisians who sought the pleasure and prestige that only art could give in aristocratic culture had no recourse but to buy works abroad and bring them to France. The market was usually Italy, though Flemish art remained fashionable until Poussin's conquest of the capital in about 1640.

Another reason why Paris could not attract talented artists was her citizens' failure to realize that artists were something more than artisans. Henry IV's patronage of artists in the Louvre caused resentment in the guilds. Painters and sculptors were usually from artisan or at best bourgeois families, and most Parisians seemed content to leave even the most talented among them at that level of society.

In addition, national and religious rivalries for decades worked to the detriment of Paris. Spanish and Roman influences were suspect to the Gallican-minded Parlement; only slowly did the judges realize that artists who had papal support in Rome could be free from Tridentine and Jesuitical influence. Once they had learned this and had begun to commission works of art from Roman artists, the danger was that they would be too explicit in their choice of subjects, thus restricting the artist's liberty and inhibiting his development. Without exception, the heads of state—Richelieu, Mazarin, Louis XIV—and their creatures placed far too many restrictions on the artists working for them.

Richelieu bought paintings and sculpture in Italy and encouraged the best talent he could find at home. Philippe de Champaigne, born in Brussels in 1602, became a kind of court painter to Louis XIII and Richelieu and, through the cardinal's influence, worked for nearly every serious patron of the arts in Paris from 1630 to 1660. He excelled in religious works and intimate portraits. A modified Flemish style lent grandeur to his portraits of Richelieu, Louis XIII (both in the Louvre), and Mazarin, but the grand manner strained the artist's conception of human nature and of God. Champaigne could participate in but never create a heroic style. His *Gaston de Foix* is an authentic medieval knight, not a pictorial version of the Cid.[13] Champaigne could not convey on canvas the spirit of the *grande âme*. Even so, those obsessed by *gloire* continued to honor him and ask him to paint their portraits.

Not a social climber himself, intensely devout, neither well read nor a traveler, Champaigne epitomized the bourgeois more attracted to religion than to aristocratic ideals. His portraits of Bérulle, Saint-Cyran, the Arnaulds, certain unknown bourgeois, and above all the nuns of Port Royal capture the sympathy and stern devotion of these persons and of Champaigne himself. His religious paintings are like history paintings: holiness, devotion, and divinity are conveyed by expression and gesture rather than by rays of light, angels, or other supernatural devices so dear to Baroque artists. Bourgeois taste, Jansenism, and religion—internalized, austere, without sensuality—become one in Champaigne. His own daughter, one of the nuns of Port Royal, was miraculously cured of paralysis after Mère Agnès Arnauld's declaration of a solemn novena. That Champaigne never questioned the miracle is clear by the expressions of faith that he gave Mère Agnès and his daughter in the *ex voto* of the miracle (Louvre).

During the Fronde he was commissioned on three different occasions to paint the official portraits of the *prévôt des marchands* and the *échevins.* Here again his own sober honesty enabled him to give credibility, even impart power to a group of men who no longer had any, though in their robes they seemed to. Champaigne truly respected these men; he could understand them. The minds of Richelieu or of the Duke of Chevreuse were alien to him. Emotionally incapable of reaching the heroic style, Champaigne—like Georges de Latour and the Le Nain brothers—nevertheless pleased Parisians of every social group by his great talent and refined Flemish style.

Only in Rome were there patrons and styles in paintings that would shake a lower-class provincial out of his milieu. What would have happened had Champaigne, and not Nicolas Poussin, gone to Rome? Following the work he did with Poussin at the Luxembourg Palace, Champaigne settled down; but Poussin, though handicapped by

---

13. Champaigne's portrait should be studied with Vouet's Gaucher de Chastillon (Louvre) since both were painted for Richelieu's *galerie des grands hommes*. Vouet seems to have sought the stark realism of Champaigne in this instance, since the cardinal preferred the latter's work. Cf. W. R. Crelly, *The Painting of Simon Vouet* (New Haven, 1962), 98.

Gaston de Foix, by Philippe de Champaigne. Galleries lined with portraits of eminent, courageous, knightly fighters became fashionable in the seventeenth century. Those in the Louvre and the Palais-Royal not only celebrated knightly virtues but also political ones of service to the crown—in Gaston's case, wars of conquest in Italy.

financial difficulties and illness, finally reached Rome. Paris simply could not give Champaigne what Rome gave Poussin.

Independence, sensitive friends who were freer from anxiety over prestige and social status, ancient Roman bronzes, bas-reliefs, and paintings, could only be found in Italy. Like Corneille a Norman, but of peasant stock, Poussin's break with his past was a great achievement, heroic in its own right.

He developed well in the Roman Barberini splendor of Pope Urban VIII, but then he moved into a small, intimate circle led by a learned antiquarian named Cassiano dal Pozzo. In this environment Poussin gradually attained a detachment from his origins unknown to any French artist of his age.[14] The pressure on Poussin to paint huge canvases on subjects chosen by someone else diminished after 1630. He went on to study bas-reliefs and furnishings and to read Ovid, Tacitus, and other ancient authors.

Of course he was not completely free from the influence of patrons; he probably benefited from their suggestions. Commissioned by Cardinal Barberini, about 1627, Poussin painted the *Death of Germanicus* (Minneapolis Institute of Arts). Ancient Rome and history paintings had already attracted him and he had painted ancient battle scenes, but in this work he almost naturally attained the heroic idealism that he would later refine and intellectualize. Noble gestures, expression, composition, and masculine courage; adulation of the warrior; and fascination with death make this painting heroic.

Poussin went on painting bacchanals, lighthearted mythological scenes, and some religious paintings; but in the 1630s he grew increasingly obsessed with the problem of portraying heroes. Fascinated by the superhuman, Poussin developed a synthesis of ideas and forms to portray the *grandes âmes*. In this period, violence particularly interested him: *The Martyrdom of Saint Erasmus* (Picture Gallery, Vatican), *The Massacre of the Innocents* (Chantilly), and *The Plague of Ashdod* (Louvre) all explore this theme. *The Massacre* is horrifying. A young man steps with full force on a baby, his sword lifted to cut off its head, with the mother helpless to stop him. On another plane a grief-stricken mother flees, carrying the grayish-green corpse of her baby, one of the discolored infant corpses used in a number of paintings to stir emotions. These dead babies must have shocked in an age when the eye was accustomed to seeing pictures of the rosy Infant Jesus.

Poussin's continual shifting between light, mythological subjects and noble, histor-

14. His only rival might be François Mansart. It was said that Poussin's father fought in the Wars of Religion, and that the family's fortunes had suffered from these wars. Had Poussin's father been a member of the League in Soissons before turning to farming near les Andelys?

The massacre of the Innocents, by Nicolas Poussin. As a young warrior raises his sword to kill a child, the mother desperately struggles to stop him. The woman to the right in the background expresses anguish as she lifts her eyes to Heaven.

ical, or religious ones was not unlike Corneille's vacillation between comedy and tragedy. Though commissioned in 1635 by Richelieu to paint more of the bacchanals that had earned him his reputation, the artist simultaneously worked to capture the heroic mentality in history painting. Refining his technique of reducing the source of all the violence to one single emotion by attributing different gestures to each person depicted, through varying facial expressions and gestures Poussin conveyed the different reactions to that emotion. He intellectualized every aspect of painting. Poussin expressed the guiding principle of his art, in a letter to Sublet de Noyers, Secretary of State, in 1642: "My nature forces me to search for and to love well-ordered things, fleeing confusion, which is as contrary to me as deep darkness is to light." His paintings were to be "read" for their moral, neo-stoic lessons, lessons that would edify and ennoble. Supremely intellectual, no detail, gesture, or muscle can be overlooked.

Members of Richelieu's circle implored the artist to return to Paris. They promised him honor, money, and comfortable lodgings in the Louvre. Poussin must have been tempted, for the bacchanals for Richelieu were done with extreme care and with an obvious desire to please. *The Triumph of Pan* (Morrison Collection, Sudeley Castle, Gloucestershire) was among his best in this genre. Finally arriving in Paris in 1640, Poussin discovered that while the Parisians could give honor and money, they had little conception of how to encourage an artist to do his best work. Like the popes in Rome, Richelieu loaded Poussin, who did not want a workshop filled with apprentices, with enormous programmatic painting schemes little to the artist's liking. The most important of these was the decoration of the Grand Gallery of the Louvre. Poussin soon felt himself incapable of working well, feeling that he was wasting time on *niaiseries* (silly things) and losing his independence; and annoyed by the jealousies of the Parisian artists, he left Paris in 1642, snubbing the pretentious, rich, and powerful Parisians led by Richelieu.

Poussin's departure did not mean, however, that his influence in Paris would lessen. Quite to the contrary. Already feeling inferior to Rome, and now abandoned by a Norman, the Parisians who fancied themselves art connoisseurs acclaimed Poussin all the more. The Academy of Painting and Le Brun put Poussin's work and ideas on a pedestal after about 1660 to be copied and studied for the rest of the century. Moreover, Paris may have been indirectly beneficial for Poussin, for after his return to Rome he worked more intently than ever on creating a coherent system of ideas and emotions, expressed in heroic or history painting. In Paris he had found truly sensitive and well-read admirers of his art. The Frérart brothers (one usually referred to as Chantelou),

Gabriel Naudé, and Pierre Bourdelot became his lifelong friends; through correspondence with them Poussin refined his psychology and conception of human nature. Rome had given him the techniques and models for painting, and Paris indirectly influenced his formulation of the heroic style.

Only part of Poussin's system is the theory of modes, which Anthony Blunt discovered to be an adaptation of Zarlino's sixteenth-century music theory.[15] Each mode—Ionic, Lydian, or Phrygian, for example—expressed an emotion such as joy, sorrow, or violence. But in addition to this hierarchy of genres linking emotions to expression and color, Poussin also formulated his own theory linking social status, power, courage, and other heroic qualities to composition, gesture, and iconography. By synthesizing these two theories, and by exploring their infinite combinations, Poussin created a panoramic vision of the heroic life. Like Corneille and Racine, he turned to Roman history, the Old Testament, and themes from the Early Christian era. Perhaps because he could be bolder in paint than Corneille or Racine could be in verse, Poussin depicted more sensitive religious subjects, such as the Holy Family, a monumental rendering of the Seven Sacraments, and other scenes from the life of Christ. The gestures of the kings and warriors, the Holy Family, prophets, and saints are not unlike the theatrical stances of the *grandes âmes* of Corneille.

Though Poussin did not abandon mythological subjects, he chose more solemn moments than others had chosen to depict. The titles of his paintings rarely suggest the originality that he brought to hackneyed subjects. Often avoiding the well-known moments of an episode, Poussin would change the focus or time, to add more drama and force, serenity, or joy. There is a realism in the ancients of Poussin. Never an antiquarian but always sensitive to the finest details of costume, architecture, and rank, his perception of Roman history is true. Until Poussin, there had always been something a little ridiculous or unrealistic about paintings depicting ancient Rome. This disappeared in *The Death of Germanicus*. He also joined Christianity to Rome as had

15. Delineating the direct impact of ancient sculpture, for example, on an artist's work is a formidable task, but it is easier than discerning whether the influence of ancient art theory was direct or through translation. Poussin, like Corneille and others imbued with Roman style, relied on translations of classical works made by sixteenth-century Humanists. Though often excellent, an inevitable distortion or blurring of perceptions took place as a consequence of using French words. A layer of French social values of great significance appears, for example, in the famous 1547 edition of a translation of Vitruvius' *Ten Books on Architecture,* illustrated by Jean Goujon. In Book V the *Scène Tragique* is defined: "Ceulx de la tragedie s'enchérissent de colonnes, frontispices, statues, et autres appareilz sentant leur Royaulté ou Seigneurie. . . . Ceulx de la comique representent maisons faites à la mode commune." From translations of this sort, seventeenth-century artists and men of letters could grasp the thought of the ancients without feeling a sense of anachronism or difficulty over the precise meanings of words.

never been done before. His series on the Seven Sacraments joins the heroic idealization of Rome with Christianity, particularly in *Extreme Unction* (Earl of Ellesmere, National Galleries of Scotland, Edinburgh), where the Christian's death is that of a Roman, divinely sustained warrior. Hebrew history was also bent to Poussin's rules for portraying the hero, particularly to demonstrate the attributes of kingship. While Moses was never a crowned king, Poussin chose to make him the exemplary leader of people, *par excellence*. *The Gathering of the Manna* (Louvre), chosen by Le Brun as the model for history painting, not only edifies by evoking the miracle but also demonstrates the absolute necessity for a people to have divinely sanctioned leadership. *The Triumph of David* (Dulwich College) depicts a youthful hero carrying Goliath's massive head on a pike; another picture of David (the Prado) combines the lesson of courage with the often-repeated one of divine sanction to rule. A winged victory offers both a crown and a laurel wreath to the young killer. As the heroic defender of his people, David gazes serenely on Goliath's severed head, with the armor arranged by Poussin to look like a trophy of war. The sword in David's hand replaces the sling, symbolic now of his new authority. The idealization of power in kingship reached its ultimate expression in *The Judgment of Solomon* (Louvre), which Poussin considered his finest painting. The trappings of power—silver diadem, lion-footed throne, columns, and scarlet robe—give Solomon institutionalized authority here sustained by wisdom. Poussin chose the most dramatic moment: the soldier raises his sword to halve the live child; one mother screams, a dead baby held carelessly under her arm; while the true mother lifts her eyes and arms to Solomon, imploring him to stop the soldier's blade. Solomon's hands suggest complete control; his radiant expression reveals foreknowledge. Leadership, courage in war, and justice were the attributes that Corneille chose to portray in a king. Poussin agreed.

In his mature years, Poussin kept violence out of his pictures, or offstage—for his history paintings are actually stagelike, often foreshortened as much as possible and stripped bare of superfluous personages and details. Always didactic and edifying, and never obscure, Poussin's heroic style resembles Corneille's in that rules determine every aspect of the work of art. Their psychologies are fundamentally the same, though there is less bravura in Poussin, making his mature work closer to Racine's. Poussin's definition of the hero is deeper and more subtle in expressing a single emotion, perhaps because he reached a higher level of detachment from his own society than did Corneille. Corneille would readily have accepted that a citizen of Corinth, Eudamidas, could be a hero, but it would have been unthinkable for Corneille to portray him in a humble abode, poor, and cringing with pain the way Poussin does. *The Testament of Eudamidas* (State Museum of Art, Copenhagen) owes part of its greatness to Poussin's complete fidelity to the elements used by ancient authors to demonstrate the heroic qualities of friendship. Among these was Eudamidas' poverty. One senses that Corneille would have made the same point, but through ignoring the text and adopting seventeenth-century conventions that associated the heroic with wealth. Corneille associated his own well-being almost more emphatically with money than with honor or reputation.

Unlike Corneille, Poussin was never attracted by the medieval-chivalric side of the heroic. Nor did he portray contemporary milieus. He never deigned to paint a portrait of anyone except himself, and this he did only to please his friends. If Poussin remained religious, his expression of it had little in common with that of the new saints. It was rather that of a humble, confident believer. Christianity for him was a historical religion, neither mystical nor apocalyptic. His later work is almost totally free from angels, divine *putti,* radiances, and ecstasies, the great exception being *The Annunciation* (National Gallery, London), which may have been painted for the tomb of his lifelong friend, Cassiano dal Pozzo. If this is so, this death might have caused a monumentary lapse of Poussin's historicist detachment, throwing him back upon more youthful forms of expression and perhaps also prompting him to respond to the grief being experienced by dal Pozzo's friends.

What did the Parisians understand of this, perhaps the most intellectualized painting of Western culture? The first generation of patrons, with the exception of Phélypeaux de la Vrillière, grasped little of what Poussin was trying to do. They admired him mainly because of his reputation in Rome. But this changed. By the 1660s, Poussin's achievement was not only understood; it was canonized. The intellectualization of art helped Parisian patrons and the Court to understand Poussin's achievements, because the heroic elements linking passion to expressions and the themes from Roman history had brought Poussin into the mainstream of the heroic style. Academic art under Louis XIV propagated Poussin's ideas; Le Brun's lectures on *The Gathering of the Manna* influenced a generation of artists, not only because the government now made Poussin its own, but because Le Brun was a fine artist himself. And in Poussin's paintings, wealthy Parisians finally saw in a visual medium what Corneille and Racine made come alive on the stage. Subjects and morals were essentially the same in the theater, art, and, slowly, Parisian society itself. By 1660 a tempering had taken place. Paris became a capital of art, drama, and—with Le Vau and Mansart—architecture, attracting attention all over Europe. A synthesis of aristocratic culture had risen in Paris on the foundations of anxiety and despair. The earnestness and effort of artists and the society to be "truly noble" had produced a heroic style. Edifying, monumental, and glorious, this style satisfied a need for identity and status in what were still late-medieval minds. The irony of this achievement was, of course, the complete irrelevance of this heroic style to the miserable economic conditions and the political climate of violence in which the majority of Parisians lived. The last heroes turned away from all this in the vain hope that they would become immortal through the words, manners, paint, and stone that they would leave behind.

How ironic and significant it is that this chivalric heroism arose during the reign of the suspicious and cruel, if not brutal, older son of Henry IV and Marie de Médicis. Sickly, stuttering, and shy, Louis XIII grew from an awkward boy to a warrior king whose only pleasures were hunting and singing motets with his intimate householders. If he really saw *Le Cid* performed, there is no evidence as to what he thought of it. Apart from a couple of ballets, his court was dull and very small in number. Devout, childless for more than two decades, and inclined to intense friendships with young male favorites, the king's day-to-day presence in his court counted less, from 1610 to 1643, than did the monarchical cultural image of military force and harsh justice.

The Corporate Parisians

No more than ten or fifteen percent of the Parisians in the 1640s possessed the wealth, education, and cultural horizons required for participating in the heroic style of life, yet the livelihood of many more depended on it, and on the consumerist drive that sustained it. Courtly and aristocratic consumerism propelled the rise of the Corneillian classical theater: Cardinal Richelieu merely "protected" it and added much-needed legitimation. After Florence and Venice, Paris thrived as a weak third luxury-goods-producing capital in Europe. Paintings, sculpture, household furnishings, apparel, luxury printing, jewelry, liturgical vestments and altar furnishings, fancy leather goods such as gold- and silver-mounted harness and saddles, and carriages upholstered in velvet and silk brocade with gilt bronze mountings were just a few of the luxury items made and marketed in the capital.

For the elites, town and country houses had to be furnished in such a way as to convey a sense of limitless wealth. Bequests to monasteries produced visible signs of a donor's generosity: heraldry was limitlessly inventive for all these upwardly mobile Parisians who wanted their coats of arms on every painting and chapel door donated to a church. The same arms covered ceilings in houses, carriage doors, and the townhouse doorways of the Île Saint-Louis, the *Marais,* and the Faubourg Saint-Germain—all creative, prestige-seeking, liberating expressions. An increasing awareness of the capacities of the skilled artisans in the capital extended across the elites like a domino effect. The sheer number of objects in the elite household increased enormously across the seventeenth century, and the Baroque sensibility of the Church sustained this luxury consumerism. To be sure, there were vows of poverty, and still more vows to be charitable; but in the main, the Roman Catholic Church in Paris fostered luxury for its own—that is, the high-ranking clergy—and did little to restrain the faithful.

In a similar way, the spiritual intensity of the saints might be glimpsed and felt by the typical Parisian during an occasional visit to one of the new monastic or convent communities (elite women were more prone to make such visits than men, because it was fashionable) or to participate in an intensely religious moment by watching a procession go by, with the clergy perhaps carrying a great gold and crystal monstrance. Some seventy high religious holidays were celebrated in the capital every year, in addition to Sunday services. True, as the century wore on, elite spiritual sensibilities would be fused with older, more somber habits, such as paying for masses for deceased loved ones and lighting candles in a guild chapel before the altar of the patron saint of the guild. Jesuits and Feuillants competed in organizing ever grander sung masses, accompanied by orchestras. Fashionable preachers drew crowds, perhaps as much from curiosity and snobbery as from faith.

Along with this intensified devotion came a silent, almost conspiratorial effort to exclude Huguenots from all associations and corporations to which they were entitled to belong under the guarantees of the Edict of Nantes. Royal officials declined to prosecute these infractions, almost as if they silently agreed that Protestants should be rooted out of the organizations to which they had belonged for decades. Fewer and fewer "mixed" marriages between Protestants and Catholics occurred than in the reign of Henry IV. Protestant services were only held in Charenton, some three miles from the city. Going there by boat along the Seine was therefore the usual Sunday experience for the remnant of the Huguenot community that stubbornly not only hung on to their beliefs but continued to reside and work in the capital—until 1685, when the king ordered the demolition of the beautiful church designed by de Brosse.

For some eighty percent of Parisians, life was spent within one of the approximately two hundred corporations in the capital. *Corpus* is the Latin word for body; it is the root word for their (and our) word "corporation," which for them simply meant a constituted body of persons joined together by oaths and promises to obey the rules. Nobles and clergy did not join these corporations. Though there were corporatist aspects to monastic communities, they were nonetheless different: monks and nuns lived in community under one roof and shared their meals, whereas corporation members lived in their own families.

All corporations had founding charters (some were several centuries old) specifying dues, annual feast days, the number of members to be admitted by a membership vote, the rules of work, the ceremonies for initiation and for the election of officers, and special chapel and funeral duties. Once in a guild there was little to keep an individual from developing exactly as his father. Parents did not conceive of giving their child any choice but to continue in the corporation which they themselves had known all their lives. Ideally, the son of a baker would become a baker. This was fundamental or simply taken for granted. The same was true in other artisan guilds, and for such professions as physicians or lawyers as well. Seventeenth-century French people still viewed this static way of growing up as natural, and jurists argued that it was divinely ordained. Nor did they challenge the hierarchical order of their corporations.

Though wealth and earning power doubtlessly affected the status of guildsmen, this fact was not recognized. Almost blindly, the corporate mind clung to the generally accepted Aristotelian doctrine that working with one's hands signified inferiority. Molding, manufacturing, or changing physical objects by hand rendered a person base. For this reason, the doctor of medicine never touched a patient; his assistants, or surgeons and barbers, cleaned and dressed wounds or administered enemas. Loyseau wrote: "Artisans are properly mechanics and reputed vile persons." The key word is *méchaniques:* artisans were still considered living machines that made things.

In the 1723 edition of Savary's *Dictionnaire de Commerce,* we see this rationale still underpinning the status of the major guilds. It differentiated the merchant guilds from the guilds of the artisans: "The corporation of mercers is considered the most noble and excellent of all the merchant corporations, in that those who do not work at all and who do nothing by hand except in the case of finishing things that are already made . . . rank above the other corporations." How much of this was mere lip service to an anachronistic ideal, and how much this actually shaped the corporate mind, would be very difficult to determine. It seems to have been a central, all-pervading ideal held by all members of corporations, high or low.

The artisans seem to have unquestioningly accepted a position of inferiority to the merchants, simply because "it had been that way for a long time." There were squabbles over status, but these were usually between single guilds—between the wine merchants and the mercers, for example. Rarely was there any violence, or even a challenge to the entire hierarchical system itself. Those who worked with their hands not only were inferior, but they felt inferior; and along with this inferior rank, they felt mixed pride in the skills in their hands.

As part of an attempt to have all the king's subjects pay a head tax, to some degree according to their ability to pay, state officials sought to regularize each corporation, including all the chartered bodies for Parisian artisans. The resultant list contains many guilds that were small, but it reveals the obsession with hierarchies and with the specificities of work occupations that were promoted not only by the Absolutist government but by the artisans themselves—a phenomenon not unknown in colleges and universities today, where departments jealously guard their prerogatives. The records of the law courts abound with cases of one corporation of skilled artisans suing another corporation for allegedly pirating a technique for weaving, metal finishing, or making a clock escapement. The various address books and other lists of artisan corporations all differ, but the March 1691 royal head-tax edict, which divided the corporations into four hierarchical classes, provides a sense of the whole.

In the first class were gold and silver refiners, butchers, gold and silver beaters, barbers, wig-makers, brewers, surgeons, hatmakers using flowers, hatmakers using felt, bonnet-makers, hatmakers using peacock feathers, hatmakers using gold- and silver-decorated feathers, carpenters, printers and booksellers, wine merchants, masons, weapon-makers, pavers, painters, sculptors, tanners, upholsterers, gold-wire makers, and dyers.

The second class was made up of armor- and helmet-makers, bakers, harness-makers, card and papermakers, belt-makers, leather-finishers, sausage-makers, wheelwrights, candle-makers, cauldron-makers, roofers, letter-writers, sword-polishers, secondhand-clothes dealers, clockmakers, linen merchants, cutters of precious stones, lemonade-makers, blacksmiths, cabinetmakers, weavers of gold and silk, parchment-makers, pastry-makers, skinners, plumbers, pewter-makers, freshwater-fish merchants, roasters, saddle-makers, locksmiths, wool and silk dyers, barrel-makers, glassblowers, vinegar-makers, and glazers.

The third class consisted of arquebus-makers, scale-makers, hoop-makers, purse-makers, criers (who announced deaths and wine prices and purchased old metal), shoe-makers, knifemakers, chest-makers, cooks, gilders, fan-makers, spur-makers, makers of mathematical instruments, fruit-sellers, engravers, case-makers, seed-sellers, makers of musical instruments, dancing masters, gardeners, skin-dressers, mirror-makers, earthenware potters, midwives, makers of tools with sharp edges, dyers of light colors, sheep-shearers, and basket-makers.

The fourth class, and the one taxed least, was made up of needle-makers, boatmen, button-makers, flower sellers, embroiderers, bonnet workers, carders, chain-makers, nail-makers, rope-makers, carvers, pin-makers, heavy grinders, makers of gut strings, makers of steel-point bobbins, finishers, *lupetiers,* mat-makers, bird sellers, spice-bread bakers, papermakers, makers of prayer boards in wood and horn, makers of prayer boards in jade, amber, and coral, line fishermen, net fishermen, soap-makers, weavers, ribbon-makers, whiskbroom-makers, and latrine-emptiers.

Translation of these occupations is often difficult. Sometimes the English word for the skill is no longer part of current American vocabulary. Still, the list provides a general picture of how remarkably diverse and differentiated were the crafts in a city the size of Paris. Members of both the local and the more prestigious superior courts such as the Parlement and the Chambre des Comptes were also constituted corporations, as were (and still are!) barristers, notaries, and physicians.

Historians argue about whether or not this corporatist structure weakened or stayed pretty much the same across the century. Two points must be made. First, a lot of economic activity, including manufacturing, was illegal: products were marketed that had not been made in conformity with guild wage scales and guild-supervised work sites. The thriving furniture neighborhood of the Faubourg Saint-Antoine, out beyond the Bastille, became notorious in the seventeenth century, partly because it was located beyond the area where guild rules were enforced. Second, after about 1660 state supervision of work sites and of membership rules for the appropriate guild became more strict, in conformity with Absolutist principles of order. An artisan who worked without his guild membership papers, or on a Sunday, might be turned over to the police by his neighbors, frequently as a result of a tip from someone in the same trade.

In fact, guild membership, and participation in elections and ceremonies, was largely a matter of age: the older one became, the more one participated. Officers invariably came from the oldest generation, and their sense of the history of the guild, including resistance to competing guilds, and their cautiousness with funds, made virtually all corporations conservative and sometimes difficult to tolerate for the apprentices and journeymen (day-wage workers). Guilds nonetheless remained the first line of defense for a member who found himself in dire straits of any sort, including accidents in the work place. Several stonecutters and laborers were killed in accidents while placing the huge stones of the Louvre colonnade. The king gave their widows or families small purses; certainly the masons' guild buried them with dignity.

A son born into an artisan family very likely grew up to practice the same skills as his father. Limits on the numbers of masters in each guild made it difficult to earn master rank after years as a journeyman. Sons of masters were given favorable treatment,

Cette figure vous montre Comme on Imprime les planches de taille douce,

Lancre en est faite d'huille de noix, bruslee et de noir de lie de vin, dont le meilleur vient D'allemagne. L'imprimeur prend de Cete ancre auec vn tampon de linge, en ancre sa planche vn peu chaude, les suye apres legerem/auec d'autrë linge, et acheue de la nettoyer auec la paume de sa main. Cela fait il met cette planche a lenuers sur la table de sa presse, aplique dessus vne foeuille de papier trempe et repose, et Couure cela d'une foeuille d'autre papier et d'un ou deux Langes, puis en tirant les bras de sa presse il fait passer sa table auec sa planche entre deux rouleaux

faict a l'eau forte par Bosse a Paris en L'isle du palais l'an 1642 , auec priuilege

Printing engravings, by Abraham Bosse. The roller press is being pulled by an apprentice. Engravings hang from the ceiling to dry.

including almost automatic admission to the father's guild. The apprenticeship system was contractual. Specific terms about learning the necessary skills, say over a four-year period, were accompanied by clauses about room and board. For the masters, it was possible to insist that the apprentices do much of the rough and heavy work, thus making apprenticeship quite exploitative of teenagers. There is plenty of evidence of conflict and violence in the shops over how much work was owed, and of drinking, wenching, music making, and general carousing. Arguments could become quite tense over who had the right to collect the gold filings around the jeweler's bench.

Abraham Bosse's engravings of a print shop suggests conviviality among the youthful workers who were inking, pulling the sheets, and turning the roller press that was used (and still is today) for printing engravings. The hundreds of lawsuits about breach of contract, broken tools, theft, and differences of opinion over the quality of work suggest that artisan shops were not always filled with contented journeymen and apprentices. Would Parisians have purchased engravings depicting the harsh working conditions that prevailed? The grim, distorted face of a saint in pain was commercially acceptable; that of an anguished artisan seems not to have been.

Apart from the few, but important, guilds of women—the *lingères,* linen merchants (see page 132), being a good example—which were organized pretty much along the same lines as the male guilds, spouses and daughters in the Parisian artisan world shared the labor and often kept the accounts, while also doing the household chores or supervising them. Labor was so plentiful that domestic service was to be had in an artisan household for the price of sleeping-space and board. Looms for making cloth and ribbon were sometimes so large that families virtually had to live around them and the husband, wife, daughter, or widowed aunt who was working the loom at the time. Children and women worked the shuttles of these great walnut frames with their turned knobs and solid mortises.

Artisans learned their skills while formally apprenticed to a master; but in fact it seems that the constant visiting back and forth between shops along the same street, and the frequent, almost floating character of journeymen moving from shop to shop, made learning an almost collective experience. Masters were often rivals, but when they visited one another did they hesitate to show how to hold a tool correctly or hold a piece of molten glass while the apprentice cut if off? It is impossible to answer this question. If a feud was not in the making, shops were filled with talk, for the various production stages of most crafted products required cooperation. Only the finest furniture, silver, and ironwork made in the seventeenth century has survived down to our own time, and it is of extremely high quality, not only in design but in craftsmanship. Just because something was handmade did not necessarily mean that it was well made. The mediocre pieces have long since been discarded or melted down.

The "how to make . . ." books about every skill and craft that flooded the market from the mid-sixteenth century on suggest by their variety that training apprentices remained oral and hands-on, and did not involve reading. Contradictory as this

La Marchande Lingere
Mon braue Caualier tout remply de franchise
Si vous voulez de moy quelque chose acheter
Voyez et si cela ne peut vous contenter
Je vous deployeray vne autre Marchandise

A Paris chez la veue le Camu rue St Jaques a la teste d'Or   Avec priuil. du Roy

The linen-seller. A *lingère* sold linens by the yard as well as small articles made of linen. The customer presumably seeks to buy a linen coif or handkerchief that he can give his beloved as a *faveur*.

appears, it seems that "how to make . . ." books were largely intended for buyers who did not work in the specific craft described. When Charles Le Brun began to lecture about painting in the newly founded royal academy of art, strong claims were made about the lofty status of the arts and the intellectual stature of the great exemplary painters such as Raphael and Leonardo. Almost as if influenced by Descartes' "clear and distinct ideas" and his use of the word "line" in geometry, Le Brun lectured about the "line" in Raphael's paintings, saying that his greatness lay in the contours, the "line" that is the profile of the human form. Le Brun continued on about the way Saint Michael looks down on his enemy, "showing his strength and force from God, [with] . . . his figure a vigorous male beauty." He went on to describe the disdain in the eyes and mouth: "his eyes partially open with their lids forming two perfect arcs, marks of his tranquillity," just as he kills. Clearly the first task of the master artisan or artist was to teach how to see and how to draw lines, a fundamental method pervading all the skilled crafts, and painting was still a craft. The very idea of design was of the utmost importance. Then came modeling, drawing, and modeling again, as master artisans and their journeymen sought to create and to make distinct products for the luxury market. The notarial records contain beautiful, extremely detailed drawings of silver, gold, or vermeil objects that were pinned to contracts fixing the prices and delivery dates. Many who commissioned the great luxury pieces furnished the silver and gold in the form of beautiful, but alas, dated platters and other pieces made in the sixteenth century. Competition remained keen to be appointed the king's silversmith or upholsterer, or whatever, and royal interest in and sponsorship of major craft work remained strong at least down to the 1690s. Louis XIV liked to open and close the great bronze faucets in the royal dairy, perhaps as much as he enjoyed listening to the organ in his chapel. Artisan organ-builders were frequently called upon to make the delicate pipes in the fountains that sprayed water over Neptune.

Each guild had its own special identity and history. The major ones still offered their members special honors, offices, uniforms, funeral and wedding facilities, a patron saint, a chapel, and a reception hall. The style of corporate life, be it mercantile or artisanal, was influenced primarily by the "six corps" of merchant guilds, the drapers being the oldest and therefore the most prestigious, followed in order by the *épiciers,* the mercers, the furriers, the hatters, and the silversmiths. Guildsmen were not, however, restricted to buying and selling exclusively those goods that had given the name to their corporation. The drapers and the mercers in particular dealt in the international market for all kinds of luxury goods. In addition to being guildsmen, they were *négociants,* or bankers who bought and sold letters of credit, lent money, and sponsored large-scale trading ventures. Fistfights between the apprentices of these, the wealthiest and most distinguished guildsmen, still occurred in the seventeenth century, when, for example, the *épiciers* bolted to preempt the drapers' place in a procession. No better sign of the persistence of strong corporate identities can be found than these interminable contentions and quarrels. Interguild rivalry had provided a kind of entertainment for centuries, and it would continue to do so until the Industrial Revolution.

For example, the monotonous fight between the wine merchants and the six major guilds continued from medieval times down to 1724. Desirous of recognition as the seventh major guild, the wine merchants found their claims continually opposed by the mercers. The reasons given by the mercers in the 1620s reflect their corporate mentality: "The sovereign and respectful authority of our kings has always been sustained by the characteristic attentive justice to preserve the laws and maintain the most exact order in commerce." The inference was, of course, that since the wine merchants had never been included, and since royal justice had always been good, it was best to leave things just as they were: "The distinction which that authority has judged appropriate to make among the members composing trade, and which forms that part of the State which it supports, and is a work of wisdom, must be unchangeable and must teach to everyone that he must remain in his sphere. . . . The 'six corps' of merchants in Paris are the columns of commerce and the source that upholds the capital. Their origin is almost as ancient as the city."

Having established their preeminence, the mercers turned to refuting the wine merchants' claims:

> These people, whose only purpose is to be and to fulfill an abject and servile profession . . . their cabarets and taverns have always been treated in a scornful manner, to such a point that laws have forbidden bourgeois and inhabitants to set foot in them. . . . Artifice, fraud, and deceit are the inseparable characteristics of wine merchants [and yet] they dare claim their commerce necessary to the State. . . . To make such a claim, they must needs have been drunk on the precious liquor that they themselves sell, and the fire of such a liquor must have given them a fit.

The wine merchants lost the case. Faced with a formidable array of precedents, they could think of nothing other than digging up additional precedents. The wine merchants found they had Herodotus on their side, and quoted from the first book of his *History*: "Cyrus completely forbade commerce with the Lydians after having conquered them, and in order to scorn them he ordered that they could sell nothing except wine."

Though quoted out of context and with no reference to the specific conditions in the ancient world or in the seventeenth century, Herodotus still served a purpose. If the wine merchants lost, it was not because their argument from Herodotus was thrown out of court. Quite the contrary. Be it biblical, classical, or medieval, a precedent was a precedent. Since Herodotus was much older than the medieval guilds, the wine merchants had hoped that a precedent from him would carry the day in court.

This single example of the use of Herodotus in court could be duplicated for virtually every major ancient author. These references represent the narrow obsession with precedent, that fundamental characteristic of the corporate mind. Guildsmen and men of the law—except those influenced by Humanistic studies—simply had little sense of time or of anachronism. Looking backward in a totally unhistorical fashion, guildsmen still possessed that one-dimensional view of society, language, and creation that had developed in the High Middle Ages. In man's history from Adam and Eve down to their own time, they saw no breaks or differences in character, tone, or aim.

Though the precise number of members in each guild has never been studied for the seventeenth century, a report prepared for a possible siege by the Spanish in 1637 gives some valuable contemporary estimates. Having consulted the tax rolls for street cleaning, an anonymous reporter estimated that there were 20,000 houses in Paris, asserted that on the average there were 21 inhabitants in each house, and concluded that Paris had a population of 415,000. He arrived at that figure by adding more than 300 houses to the tax rolls, an indication of the number of houses he thought had recently been built. Having defined the major guilds in a somewhat unorthodox fashion, to include apothecaries and wine merchants, he estimated that their total membership consisted of 2,725 masters and *compagnons*.

After these guilds, which he calls the "Seven Corps," he estimated the membership of the 500 artisanal guilds to be 38,000 *compagnons* over the age of twenty, and that they had 5,600 apprentices, presumably young men under twenty who were learning the *arts et metiers*. Then followed carters, porters, wood-carriers, and water-carriers, who together totaled 66,672, of whom he believed 46,000 were young, "virile," and capable of bearing arms. The last category included valets, coachmen, grooms, lackeys, clerks, and minor judicial and financial officials, who together, he believed, totaled 10,000, or more than 6,000 capable of bearing arms.

The tone of the document is one of modest confidence that Paris can withstand a siege, so the author may have made his estimates a bit high. Nevertheless, the dominance of small, independent guilds in Parisian society is demonstrated by these estimates, as is the hierarchical order in which they were arranged.

The anonymous author then went on to attempt to calculate the amount of food needed to sustain Paris during a siege. The calculations themselves are not very helpful, but the types of food mentioned give some indication of a typical guildsman's diet. The consumption of wheat was thought to be 184 *muids* daily, or 1,600 a week. (A *muid* of wheat amounted to approximately 54 bushels, or slightly more than two and a half cubic meters, the average load of a cart.) So 86,400 bushels of wheat could be considered the normal weekly consumption for Paris in the seventeenth century. This grain arrived "either by river from different places in Picardy, Brie, and Champagne . . . or by wagon from the *pays* called France [Île de France], Multien, Beauce, and the Norman Vexin."

Of this quantity, 450 *muids* went to the bakers of *petit pain,* who turned it into three different kinds of bread: *le plus blanc, chalis,* and *le pain bourgeois.* Weights and prices seem to have been prescribed by law, except for *le pain bourgeois,* which varied in weight, but not in price, depending on the price of wheat paid by the baker. Save for 1,000 *muids* consumed by the religious, the rest of the wheat was made into *le gros pain.* Here there seems to have been no control over its price and weight.

The author of the report was very aware of the political implications of wheat and bread prices. At every turn he sought to reassure his readers that if the proper political decisions were made, there would be enough bread to go around during the siege. His last remark on the subject of bread—that "twenty persons do the buying and selling of wheat"—is a hint to the Crown that the grain market might be controlled through gaining the support of this small group of merchants.

His other estimates of food consumed in Paris include: 900 cattle a week, or approximately 40,000 a year; 8,000 sheep a week, or approximately 358,000 a year—"all of which are bought by the Parisian butchers on Friday mornings at the Poissy market, to where the [animals] are driven from Normandy, Poitou, Limousin, Bourbonnais, and Champagne." Animals not sold on Fridays were held over for the markets on Mondays and Tuesdays. No fodder was thought necessary for these animals, except in cases where butchers bought them on Fridays to be killed later in the following week.

Other yearly estimates include:

The pastry baker, by Abraham Bosse. Apprentices roll out dough as the master moves the pies in the oven. His wife, who probably keeps the accounts, looks on. A servant holds the child and heir.

3,000 calves a week between Easter and Pentecost
1,200 calves a week between Pentecost and Lent[1]
25,000 pigs a year
1,456,600 dry or salted codfish
18,200 salted mackerel
23,600 white herring
360,000 red herring

---

1. The text adds that during Lent "very great quantities of veal and lamb are illegally consumed."

108,350 salmon

240,000 *muids* of wine

600 *muids* of salt

300,000 *voies*[2] of wood, plus 20,000 more from nearby bourgeois-owned private woods

18,000 *muids* of charcoal

This anonymous report represented an honest effort to estimate the population and consumption of Paris. What it suggests is that the urban diet of the seventeenth century followed the rhythm of the seasons and was probably not fundamentally different from that of the country except for the greater amount of seafood available in cities. The absence of fowl is surprising and may have been an oversight.

What is unknown, however, is whether the Parisians, owing to their greater wealth, ate more meat per capita than did the peasantry. The *gagne petits* and field hands, both at the bottom of the social scale in town and in the country, seem to have eaten almost no meat at all.

The report is probably more accurate, however, for the number of guildsmen in the capital. This total could have been determined after hasty consultation with guild members, the *consuls*,[3] and other Parisians knowledgeable about the politics of guild life. Merchants and artisans, together with their apprentices, constituted fewer than 50,000 men. This represents 15,000 fewer than those in specialized domestic service, such as the water-carriers or valets. The actual labor force connected to manufacturing in Paris was therefore quite small and exclusive. Provincials could become members of artisan guilds and servant corporations, but it is doubtful that the same would be true for the major guilds. The author of the report grouped together, and not without significance, the masters and *compagnons* of the major guilds, as if to suggest that, in prestige and wealth, the *compagnons* were better off than any of the members of the artisan guilds.

In the course of the seventeenth century, the guilds strengthened their own particular monopolies as well as their hold over members. In the late 1660s, largely at the instigation of Jean-Baptiste Colbert, the very dynamic royal minister, an extended effort was made to reform the regulations of the guilds and to strengthen their control

---

2. A *voie* equals two cubic meters of wood.

3. These merchant judges, appointed by the guilds with the approval of the *prévôt des marchands*, settled disputes between guildsmen involving sums up to 500 *livres*.

of each specific activity or practice over which a monopoly was accorded, ostensibly in order to improve the quality and quantity of goods. Seen in the general context of Colbert's social program of the 1660s, this reform and creation of new guilds appears as part of a monumental effort to bring "order" into French society. "Order" in this sense meant that every Frenchman would know and accept his status and function in the society. The inspiration for the "order" to be legislated came from medieval precedents. Royal commissions investigated the founding charters of the guilds and breathed new life into centuries-old legislation. The Crown, under Colbert's watchful eye, attempted to settle all disputes between guilds. New products and imports, always the principal sources of dispute, were assigned to a specific guild as its monopoly, and the claims of other guilds to make or sell that product were quashed. Old regulations on working conditions, quality, quantity, and selling were reinforced in a great effort to restore "order" to the entire mercantile and manufacturing sector of the French economy. The emphasis was as much moral as economic. In this program, the reforms accomplished in Paris were to serve as the model for those to be enforced in the rest of the realm. New guilds were created, particularly as a result of the general regulations of 1669, so that every Frenchman would know his place in the hierarchy of corporations that had been established to include every worthwhile enterprise. The effects of this large-scale reform are not known, but they were undoubtedly less completely applied and less disastrous than laissez-faire economists claim. The general economic crisis, not Colbert's reforms, accounted for the decline in Parisian prosperity after about 1680.

The high-spending royal Court, especially after 1660, and the attendant officials and tax administrators assured the livelihood for all these artisans. "Exports" to the *faubourgs* and to country houses also, of course, constituted the second richest market area in France, after the capital itself. As noted before, fashion in luxury clothing and in household furnishings changed more frequently than during any previous period in French history. Try as he or she might, the artisan tailor in Lyon or Bordeaux failed to capture the correct cut from the quite small and obscure engravings of the latest fashions that began to appear in Parisian magazines in the early eighteenth century. Parisian-produced clothing, hats, and furnishings commanded a premium price because of their special *cachet* of being from the capital.

Still, if we look at the furnishings that have survived in provincial châteaux and in the town houses of Dijon or Toulouse, for example, it is evident that locally made products continued to hold their own. In other words, while Paris competed with luxury products made there or imported from Italy, the market for these goods remained elite, thin, and very profitable. Did local elites fear opprobrium from their neighbors if they commissioned furnishings and clothing from Paris? It is impossible to forget the tinge of cruelty in the ridicule of Monsieur Jourdain, Molière's upwardly mobile Parisian who apes the aristocratic lifestyle.

The practice of bequeathing clothes, furnishings, and even horses and carriages to one's household servants had late medieval origins, and the usual result was that servants sold these pieces to dealers in secondhand clothes. Thousands of Parisians still barely owned a change of skirts, shirt, or blouse. But did these servants begin to wear the clothes of their deceased masters and mistresses in the seventeenth century, especially when styles began to change more rapidly? The transmission of styles across social ranks certainly occurred with increasing frequency as the seventeenth century became more and more obsessed with fashion as a result of its importance at Court, and its diffusion in engravings such as those by the Bonnart brothers, who depicted what the well-to-do should wear in the summer, in the winter, while taking coffee, and so forth.

Merchant and artisanal houses in Paris had their own unique stylistic features; and though there was some aping of the new rich, there was also a sober and more hidden "luxury." Frequently called *maisons bourgeoises,* the chief characteristic of these houses was a ground floor entirely occupied by a business, storerooms, and workshops. Viewed from the street, these houses were sober and without decoration. Iron bars and shutters covered windows that were opened on shopping days to display merchandise in the open air. Doors were thick, barred, and secured with massive locks. Low-ceilinged in comparison to the ground floor, the upper two or three stories were only accessible by very narrow stairways.

Rents remained fairly steady over the course of the century, suggesting a rough equilibrium between population growth, the construction of new housing, and the perennial subdivision of larger, older apartments into smaller ones. Only fourteen percent of Parisians owned the housing in which they lived, and of these most were not the well-to-do but artisans whose aging or single relatives frequently moved in with them and helped pay household expenses. Where artisan fathers and sons worked together in the same shop, they usually did not share eating and sleeping quarters. Housing in the seventeenth century still largely remained vertical, as it had been in the late Middle Ages, with rooms for cooking and sleeping situated above the ground-floor shop or *boutique*.

The living quarters of the house were allocated to various members of the family after long and tense negotiation. Widows had to make room for younger families; grandparents moved up and up, often to the second or third floors, just beneath the attics where hay was stored and servants and apprentices slept. A typical *maison bourgeoise* might have four or five servants to do the washing, cooking, cleaning, and to care for infants and the aged. Any vacant rooms were immediately rented. Crowded conditions prevailed, as much from the desire to earn money as from a real lack of space. Parents and their children usually occupied a single room, while cooking was done in a common kitchen. A single privy, complemented by numerous chamber pots, served the entire house. Rooms reserved for bathing were unknown in *maisons bourgeoises* until the 1770s. Bathing probably declined in frequency from what it had been during the late Middle Ages. To avoid emitting unpleasant odors, bourgeois relied on changes of underwear and perfumed waters splashed here and there.

Third floors and attics were used for servants quarters and for storing such supplies as wood or leather needed in manufacture. Extra space under a steep stairway would be partitioned off with simple rough tongue-and-groove boards and rented. The average number of fireplaces per household was two, indicating that many slept in unheated rooms enclosed in heavily curtained poster-beds. Indeed, when the valuables in a household are counted up, the bed with its curtains, blankets, featherbeds, and hemp sheets (the well-to-do used linen) was the family's most valuable possession.

The habit of decorating the walls with cheap, unframed engravings, usually religious in theme, grew apace across the century. An increasing number of middling families, celibate physicians (a large percentage), and skilled artisans added family portraits, and occasionally one of the king, to the white-washed walls. Little "looking glasses" barely four by six inches in size became a mass-market item in the Paris of the seventeenth century, allowing for the first time to see how the hair was combed or whether the wig was on straight. Only the more well-to-do artisans—silversmiths, cloth-sellers, clockmakers—could afford inexpensive Bergamo tapestries on their walls: rugs were virtually unknown in seventeenth-century Paris, but "carpets" covered tables. Bosse's engravings of domestic interiors reveal the luxurious lifestyle of elite guild families, high-ranking royal officials, and tax farmers.

In a sense, the most important corporation in Parisian life was not the guild but the family. To think of the family as a corporation is technically incorrect, because it was not thought to be a corporation in the seventeenth century. It lacked a special function, and the idea of *corps* in the seventeenth century always implied a group joined together to perform a specific function. But aside from this technical point, the family resembled the other corporations: guilds, *confréries,* courts, and *compagnies.* Encompassing grand-parents, uncles, aunts, and first and second cousins, its solidarity was often maintained by tyrannical elders who planned and directed the lives and fortunes of the younger members by establishing long-range policies about dowries, inheritances, and invest-ments. This "extended" family did not necessarily live together, for Parisian families generally had members in the provinces with whom they remained connected by financial ties. Yet these "extended" families did live under the same roof far more fre-quently than was the case after the Industrial Revolution.

Just as elders controlled the allocation of space, so they decided virtually every other aspect of the personal life of younger members of the family. The levers of control were money and withdrawal of affection. The elders' grip remained strong and final. Their tyranny cut across every social barrier (including the nobility), making a quarrel of gen-erations a fundamental characteristic of Parisian life.

The high percentage of wills and marriage contracts made by persons even of modest incomes, and their tone, suggests that family life was sordid and constrict-ing.[4] Money, furniture, apartments, business, and inheritances, not love or affection, bound the family together. Survival and some sense of well-being inevitably depended on one's family support. Whether quarrels took place in low voices or in fits of rage, in polite or in coarse language, quarrels they were nevertheless. Often they lasted for years, or for a lifetime. Though children were raised to honor their father and mother, and to respect the judgment of their elders, they soon learned about past quarrels between brothers and sisters, parents and grandparents. They grew up in a microcosmic state of nature where relationships, including those of an affectionate sort, were looked upon with distrust. Icy glances, selfishness, fawning on the elderly about to die, or seeking support from already feuding uncles and aunts were part of the family's daily life. The kiss of Brutus did not seem strange to fathers and sons who, though detesting each other, were compelled by convention to embrace.

---

4. J.-L. Bourgeon's study of the *Cité* during the Fronde (cited in the Bibliography) is a model study of French soci-ety based on notarial archives. I have relied on it heavily here because it gives a firm basis for what family life was like. Bourgeon's analysis concords with the literary evidence and suggests that life depicted by Furetière, Molière, and sermons exaggerated the unpleasant conditions of life only enough to moralize, but that the relationships described among fam-ily members reflect the reality of wills and marriage contracts. Annik Pardailhé-Galabrun's *La Naissance de l'Intime* (cited in the Bibliography) provides statistically grounded confirmation for many of the assertions to be inferred from Bour-geon—plus the startling evidence that Parisian housing in general shifted from vertical, multistory quarters to horizon-tal, single-floor lodgings.

The suffocating sentiment arising from being indebted to unloved or vindictive relatives and parents[5] blunted the careers and aims of the young. This quarrel of generations is the central theme in Molière's comedies. Elders are depicted as selfish, stingy, and overbearing toward the young. In our laughter at them we overlook the didacticism in Molière: the futility of fettering the young by not giving them money. Family life must, on the whole, have been disagreeable indeed. Withdrawal into monastic life therefore had an appeal that cannot be overlooked. It provided an escape, condoned but often not idealized by the guild family. A rebellious son's threat to become a monk or join the army might bring his parents to terms. Without money allocated by the family, a young person could not acquire what he or she desired, dowries for daughters being a major financial burden for a family. Living away from the family was out of the question, unless money was allocated for renting a room. Earning a living by getting a job was unheard of, for it was virtually impossible to find work without references or parental support. Tensions over the style, cost, and quantity of clothes demanded by the young and refused by the elders went along with arguments over the utility of education and charity. Dowries gave elders control over the selection of a husband or wife; and, in numerous cases, the policy about dowries determined that some persons would not be allowed to marry at all. Quarreling over dowries involved the entire family. Grandparents, aunts, and uncles had favorites among the younger members, and they quarreled among themselves, and with the parents, over the fate of the young. Wills, marriage contracts, and inventories of possessions made upon the death of a member of a family were the grim recordings of tensions and disputes over money. These tensions can be felt through the monotonous, formalistic notarial style. Trust among members of families must have been at a minimum if they would pay so dearly to have notaries record every financial turn in family life. Artisans of very modest means recorded their settlements with the notaries even if these involved only a few hundred *livres*. The pettiness born of insecurity and fear pervades these records, as it did the lives of those who made them.

Ideally husbands and wives were to be found within the guild to which the family belonged. Or failing that, marriage with someone of a status just slightly above or below one's own was accepted. There has been no study of the frequency of extra-guild marriage, but it would seem that the higher the status of the guild, the stricter were

---

5. *Parents* in French still conveys the meaning current in the seventeenth century. It is defined as including all one's relatives.

the parents about selecting mates for their children from the same corporation. Inter-marriage within the six major guilds was acceptable, depending on the attractiveness of the persons and their familys' wealth. Masons, carpenters, and roofers likewise were nearly on a par (though inferior to the six major guilds); thus intermarriage seems to have been frequent. At the bottom of the hierarchy, in the nearly unskilled *compagnies,* sons and daughters found mates among servants and peasant families. Admission into the major guilds remained very difficult; for though there were no provisions for restricting their memberships, members kept the entrance requirements high for all save the sons and nephews of members.

In addition to belonging to an "extended" family, and a guild, a law court, or some other corporation, a person also belonged to a parish and a quarter. Each parish had a dominant social characteristic reflecting the status of the families living within its geographical confines. For example, Saint-Eustache took its tone from the rich whole-sale merchants who lived around the church; Saint-André-des-Arts was the heart of the residences of royal magistrates; Saint-Étienne-du-Mont's proximity to the *collèges* gave it an atmosphere of learning and publishing. There is very little evidence that the law prohibiting participation in a parish if one did not reside there was violated: hence rich and poor, nobles and guildsmen, servants and judges, might all belong to the same parish. They did so in fact. Yet in each parish it was the merchant families which, with the priest (*curé*), really governed it. Noblemen rarely sat on the *fabriques,* the governing board of a parish that administered its income, ordered repairs to the church, rectory, or school (if there was one), and raised and distributed funds for char-ity. The power of the *fabrique* was enormous because its decisions about who would be allowed to donate funds for special chapels, masses, vestments, and so forth weighed heavily on the fate of a family's effort to increase its prestige through donations.

The boundaries of parish and quarter did not coincide.[6] On the *Île de la Cité* there were thirteen parishes: Saint-Barthélemy, Saint-Pierre-des-Arcis, Saint-Martial, Saint-Germain-le-Vieil, Sainte-Croix-de-la-Cité, Saint-Symphorien, Sainte-Marie-Madeleine, Sainte-Geneviève-des-Ardents, Saint-Christophe, Saint-Pierre-aux-Bœufs, Sainte-Marine, Saint-Landry, and Saint-Jean-le-Rond, plus two special parishes, Saint-Denis-du-Pas for the canons of the cloister of Notre-Dame, and inside the *Palais* the Basse Sainte-Chapelle, originally the parish established for the canons' servants. There were also Notre-Dame and a few independent chapels which, added to the parishes, pro-

---

6. Quarters, as described in Chapter 1, were sixteen in number: they were geographic units for purposes of militia defense and fiscal administration.

vided twenty-one places of worship on the island, or as many as on the entire Left Bank, and half as many as on the Right Bank. Bridges and streets were subdivided into different parishes and quarters, the unit being the house, with the little parish of Sainte-Marine extending over only twenty houses. Though each parish had a dominant social tone, parishioners included master and servant, noble and commoner, making contemporaries refer to quarters rather than parishes when they wished to delineate the prestige of a neighborhood, square, or locale.

The nobles could be influential in some parishes, such as Saint-Paul in the *Marais* and Saint-Eustache near the Halles; but even in those parishes eminent bourgeois and minor robe families controlled the *fabriques*. Often the families that held offices in the major guilds, law courts, and hospital boards also held those in the *fabriques*. With these offices passed down from father to son, or to nephew, the continuity of membership in the *fabriques* resembled that of the other corporations of Paris.

To become a member of the *fabrique*, a bourgeois had to donate heavily to the work of the parish and be sober, devout, and strictly upright in his business affairs. By being all these things, a social-climbing bourgeois could impose himself on the *curé* and the rich donors, who would honor him with membership after a decade or so of pious living and high giving. In the seventeenth century, it became customary for the members of the *fabrique* to sit in a special place of honor just opposite the pulpit during the high mass. Parishes began to vie with one another to see who could build the most costly and monumental pew, the *banc d'œuvre*, for their respective *fabrique*. The *banc d'œuvre* of Saint-Eustache, which survived the Revolution, is an excellent example of this type of monumental pew that conferred honor and status to the few members of the parish allowed to sit in it.

Other "outward signs" of grace in the church were available to a family willing to spend the money. Family chapels equipped with mortuary vaults beneath the flagstones remained very fashionable throughout the seventeenth century. In prestigious parish churches like Saint-Paul, Saint-Gervais, and Saint-Eustache, their price, negotiated with the *fabrique*, was as high as that of a fief or an *hôtel*. Never sold in perpetuity, from the time of their construction during the Middle Ages, these chapels were on the average renamed and redecorated every two hundred years. All the chapels in Saint-Gervais, for example, were apparently resold in the late sixteenth and seventeenth centuries to "new-rich" families in the law courts. On the other hand, circa 1630 those of Saint-Eustache became the elite preserve of families with royal blood or new peerages. Their arms, placed high on the keystones and pendants, survive to bear witness to what must have been a dramatic competition for honor and prestige. The serpent of Colbert, the lilies of Gaston d'Orléans, and the chevrons of Cardinal Richelieu each seem to be jostling one another for preeminence in the church's apse, the most conspicuous and therefore the most prestigious location for a chapel. Here and there, traces of paintings showing their donors kneeling piously before an altar, or their coat of arms in the window, still record for the keen eye a battle for prestige among the most aristocratic and ambitious families of France. On down through the different layers of Parisian society, similar battles were taking place.

Members of guilds and law courts proudly continued to wear their ceremonial robes for special sessions, processions, masses, funerals, and marriages. Not until the compelling force of the court style under Louis XIV did the overt manifestation of a corporate identity in dress disappear from the streets of Paris.

Guilds competed with each other in building large, beautiful chapels for their members. Their insignia were carved into the keystones and stained into the windows, to make their ownership apparent to all parishioners and competitors from other parishes. Nearly every guild paid for masses for its deceased members. In 1624 the mercers paid 84 *livres,* 10 *sols* for nineteen masses said on various holy days throughout the year in their chapel located in the Church of the Holy Sepulchre (quarter of Saint-Jacques). The price of these masses seems high, and if in fact it was, this would be just one more proof of the prestige of this, the most distinguished guild in the capital.

When Louis XIV needed funds to pay for the invasion of the Franche Comté in the 1670s and "borrowed" from the mercers (in effect, a forced loan that would not be repaid), he, on Colbert's advice, gave the mercers money for decorating their chapel. The mercers returned the compliment by commissioning the king's favorite painter, Charles Le Brun, to paint *Christ Leaving the Tomb.* Le Brun, certainly not without instructions, then painted a work rather conventional in all but one respect: he added a portrait of Colbert, dressed as a protector of the arts and commerce, holding a corner of the shroud.

The corporate identity was therefore still sustained by spiritual and moral sanctions established by the Church. How strong these sanctions were in the seventeenth century is unclear, but it is evident that those regulating economic practices were dead. The Counter Reformation had not attempted to restore the medieval prohibitions on collecting interest; nor had it led to a significant effort to reestablish the old code of laws on the quality and prices of goods. The effect of the Counter Reformation on guild life was moral and spiritual rather than economic and social. Guilds fanatically insisted that their members be of the faith, Catholic and Roman. Every attempt was made, at first legally and then covertly, to exclude Protestants from their ranks. Thus, regardless of their wealth, Protestants were barred from the prestigious positions and honors that would normally have been theirs. At every level of Parisian corporate society, they were snubbed and, if possible, ostracized from membership.

The fate of Abraham Bosse is a case in point. The Lorraine-born Huguenot had already become an accomplished artist-engraver before being appointed part-time instructor at the Academy of Painting. Bosse's genre scenes of domestic interiors and his treatment of religious and social themes were without a doubt very well received in Paris. They are precious to us as windows that look onto Parisian elite family life. Appointed to lecture on perspective, Bosse drew on the research of his good friend, the mathematician Gérard Desargues, who established the mathematics of the vanishing point while attempting to design the stonework for self-supporting stairways. There is no doubt that Bosse was a bit of an enthusiast in his teaching of Desargues' work, which was a genuine advance that could help painters construct their scenes more realistically; but Bosse ran afoul of Le Brun and his followers in the Academy who wished to maintain Leonardo's approach to perspective. The correspondence exchanged between the Academy, expressed in heavy collective authoritarian prose, accused Bosse of impoliteness and insubordination. The academicians looked down on genre painting and engraving, and they were beginning to speak and write in the courtly polite language that, as it became fashionable among the elites, was slowly invading the artistic communities most dependent on the Court and on these elites for commissions and the validation of their work. Bosse was peremptorily excluded from the Academy and forbidden to teach perspective. He appealed for support to the great Poussin, but this artist was far off in Rome and probably unable to sort out what was at stake between Bosse's presentation of Desargues' work on perspective and another academician's work on Leonardo's! The fact that Bosse was a Huguenot must also be weighed in the Academy's harsh decision to exclude him. More artisan than artist, according to the latest canons affecting the arts, and a heretic on the margins of a solidly Catholic corporation, Bosse suffered exclusion and humiliation. Looking back on the event from a distance, it is evident that the Academy's prestige would have been enhanced had it admitted Bosse to its membership, rather than keeping him as part-time assistant and then excluding him; and a more mathematically grounded understanding of perspective would have continued to be taught.

Louis XIV's revocation of the Edict of Nantes in 1685 must have been viewed by Parisian guildsmen and judges as the fulfillment of their desires. The Revocation at last sanctioned what they had been doing all along. Hence, in the context of Parisian society, Louis XIV's decision must be seen as a popular act. On this point Louis ceded to the wishes of his subjects.

Though part of the third estate and possessed of strong corporate identities, men of law, physicians, surgeons, university professors, and distinguished artists and poets held a special place in the society. No strong social ties bound these corporations together into a special group; yet their members' emphasis on education and—at least in the case of the judges and artists—their service to the state set them apart from the other commoners.

Nobles and commoners alike inveighed against the weblike, monolithic little world of the men of the law. Nobles complained that they were discriminated against because of their birth, and they attacked the practice of selling offices, which had been priced beyond the reach of many nobles' sons. Not the courts as such, or the law itself, but the legal corporations of Paris determined the spirit and often the letter of French justice. Provincials bringing a case to court in Paris found it prudent to engage a Parisian lawyer; otherwise, almost mysteriously, they found that their cases never came up before a court. Then too, in a political crisis, the legal corporations, much more than the actual courts to which the members belonged, influenced the thinking and activities of their members.

Physicians, surgeons, inspectors of weights and measures, university professors, and barbers also belonged to corporations that regulated the life and preserved the status of their members. These professions, as well as those of artists, silversmiths, and furniture makers, were in a somewhat anomalous position in the seventeenth century. For several reasons they were on the rise in status and wealth, which diminished the sense of corporate identity among their members.

The only force that pierced the exclusive, parochial identities of young men born into a corporation and raised to be like their fathers was their education in a *collège* or their calling into the Church. Without the extensive practice of sending sons to a *collège,* which developed after about 1570, it is doubtful that the aristocratic style would have become so broadly based among merchants and judges.

Life in a *collège* was bathed in an atmosphere of routine devotions and impracticality. Separated from the cares of the adult world and protected from their families, boys from the ages of seven or eight, on to the age of fifteen or sixteen, led a communal life of strict moral discipline and hard work. Nothing in the curriculum specifically denigrated their fathers' professions or guilds, but sons learned quickly from their frocked teachers that preoccupations with status, money, and pleasure were dangerously corrupting. Once inside the walls of a *collège* the boys found the celibate life held up as an ideal, not so much by precept as by example.[7] No truly secular *collège* existed; all were schools run by the religious, whose intentions were as much to restore the superior status of the life of devotion as to educate. Seen in this light, the number of prominent merchants and judges who gave money to or retired to monasteries later in life is not surprising; nor was the conflict between a son who wished to enter a monastery and his father, who had arranged a marriage and bought an office for him.

Though it is impossible to discover whether the ideals of the major seventeenth-century pedagogues were realized, the continuity and uniformity of those ideals suggests that they were. The *Ratio Studiorum,* what we call "curriculum," was in effect in all Jesuit *collèges* for over two centuries with only few modifications, and the ideals and curriculum of the other major group of new *collèges,* the Oratorians, lasted nearly as long. The pedagogues of the seventeenth century established the conception of learning, the curricula, the ideals, and the moral stance of French education that would predominate at least down to 1763, when the Jesuit Order was banned from France. Their influence was enormous, but the achievements of the founding Jesuits as pedagogues differ from those of such major thinkers as Fénelon and Rousseau who wrote on education.

Instead of formulating their own "utopian," personal theory of education, Charles Rollin, Dom François Lamy, and Father Joseph Jouvency attempted to describe the curriculum and daily life of their *collèges.* Their treatises describe existing conditions and ideals and add occasional recommendations.

Pedagogues advocated that boys be housed in a *collège* all year. Isolation from the world was considered absolutely essential for a good education. Contact with the world, even for a few moments, was believed dangerous to the moral education of boys between the ages of seven and sixteen. The world, in this case, was defined as everything outside the *collège,* including the boy's family. Though most boys were allowed to live at home because their parents could not afford to pay their board, the ideal nevertheless remained that of isolation from the world.

Once in a *collège,* sons of artisans, merchants, judges, and gentlemen were treated as near equals. Yet there were exceptions: when the Grand Condé was a student in a *collège,* a little velvet cord was placed around his own special desk. But distinctions of class and wealth nonetheless were much less marked in school than in the "outside world."

---

7. Thus the rise of monasticism may have been connected to the rise in the number of boys educated in *collèges.*

LE MAISTRE D'ESCOLE.

Cet habile Maistre d'escole, / Accoustumé parmi le bruit, / Que font les Enfans qu'il instruit, / Joint les verges à la parolle. | *Les vns d'vne estrange façon / Apprehendent la discipline ; / Et semble pleurer à leur mine, / Quand ils apprennent leur leçon.* | *Mais les autres tout au contraire, / Par vn folastre sentiment, / N'ont l'Esprit qu'au ieu seulement / Dont ils ne peuuent se distraire.* | *Toy qui te mocques de leurs ieux, / Sçache qu'ils sont pleins d'innocence, / Et souuien-toy qu'en ton Enfance, / Tu cherchois à faire comme eux.*

le Blond exerd. auec Priuilege du Roy.

A school for boys, by Abraham Bosse. The young boys on the right, still in dresses, seem to be playing as the older boys stand around a table, reading and writing. The master, switch in hand, listens to a boy who respectfully holds his hat in his hand.

A boy living in a *collège* was never left alone. All activities—learning, dining, recreation, and occasional excursions—were collective. A *préfet,* usually a young monk, was in charge at all hours of the day and night, except during lectures and masses. Classes were suspended on the frequent holy days, but the boys were only allowed to go home for the great Church festivals of Christmas and Easter. In the unreformed colleges, this strict surveillance had broken down, but in the Jesuit and Oratorian establishments it was maintained for about one-fifth of the students, the rest being allowed to live at

LA MAISTRESSE D'ESCOLE.

Ces Filles encore, petites   Quand par l'accroissement de l'âge   Alors l'énfant, dont l'exercice   Par d'estranges metamorphoses,
En leur foibles commencemens,   Se renforcera leur Ésprit ;   Est de blesser et d'enflammer .   (e Tyran des affections,
Par cette bonne Vieille instruites,   Elles en sçauront dauantage   Leur aprendra sans artifice ,   Changeant leurs espines en roses,
N'aprennent que leurs rudimens.   De viue voix et par escrit .   Qu'on sçait tout en sçachant aimer.   Contentera leurs passions .

I.D. Poilly ex-ud auec Priuilege du Roy.

A school for girls, by Abraham Bosse. The girls around the mistress seem to be asking about their reading, as the girl in the foreground reads to herself.

home. The Counter Reformation marked a revival of old rules governing student behavior; though it is impossible to document, these rules may have been more influential than the curriculum changes made by the Jesuits.

Dormitories were long, high-ceilinged halls divided into tiny cells. A corridor ran between the double rows of cells, with the *préfet*'s room located just inside the only exit from the hall. Students, awakened between four and five in the morning, began their first lessons at five or six. Next came mass, followed by a breakfast of bread and by an hour of free time; lessons continued from eight until ten. Then, before lunch at eleven, they spent an hour discussing their lessons, comparing notes, and repeating to each other what they had memorized. After a study period lasting until two in the afternoon, the boys had another hour of recreation before lessons from three to five. After a second period of comparing notes and repeating memory work, they had supper, said their prayers, and spent some time in study before going to sleep at eight (or at nine in the summer). Tuesdays and Thursday afternoons were free of classes, so with their *préfet* the boys would all go on long walks. Only in September was there a real holiday, and then only for the students who had learned their lessons well. The ideal, then, was to reduce as much as possible the students' contact with the secular world by keeping them in school all year round. Fear of the world combined with the belief that children had a "natural inclination toward evil" made devout teachers of every order strive to implant ideals in the minds of the young before experience could become their teacher. Jacques-Bénigne Bossuet, tutor to the Dauphin, expressed the pedagogue's anxiety: "The world, the world, the world, pleasures, bad advice, and bad examples."

A heavy emphasis was placed upon emulation and memorization. Through studying the lives of illustrious and devout men, and through committing to memory hundreds of precepts, psalms, and verses, the student would be edified and constrained to excel in his studies and in his subsequent career. Jouvency wrote that the student must "identify with the combatants in a battle, suffer with the vanquished, and triumph with the winners." Students in Jesuit and Oratorian *collèges* were encouraged to relive the lives of the heroes. Not so at Port Royal: Pascal opposed emulation and considered the compliment or prize given to a student who had done well to be pernicious. The desire to know had to come from within.

From the moment a student entered the gates, he was expected to speak only Latin. Harsh punishment was meted out to students caught speaking French at dinner or during study periods. Owing to the fact that boys differing in age by as much as ten years were taught together, it is difficult to conceive how the very young could have spoken at table, except to add an occasional memorized maxim. But the difference in age seems not to have affected the morale or progress of the class as much as one might expect, at least in part because the older boys were expected to help the younger ones in their grammar exercises and memory work. *Préfets* were to enter into these exercises too. Encouraged to organize competitions in rhetorical and memory exercises, the *préfet* would divide his class into two groups of nearly equal ability and rename them Romans and Carthaginians. Then entirely in Latin the class would play at being ancient soldiers locked in heated verbal battle. If one side failed to defend itself properly and was losing too quickly, the *préfet* would join it and answer the questions or recite the epigrams on behalf of the weaker side until some balance was restored, whereupon he would withdraw to the sidelines. Memorization and recitation made learning as collective an experience as possible. The teams and competitions rendered it practically impossible for a student to go off and learn on his own at his own speed.

Behind the unbelievable number of grammatical rules the boys memorized lay hidden a rigid moral code. The rules themselves were precepts, usually drawn from Cicero and selected to illustrate some point of grammar, but also to convey a moral principle. Grammar and moral philosophy became the foundation of the curriculum, inextricably connected with and unfailingly enforced through the prohibition of French. The Jesuit *Ratio* proclaims: "We will have as our aim to imitate Cicero as much as possible." Since classical works were rarely assigned in their entirety in the early years, and because the precepts were selected by the religious to present an edifying ethic, there was no possibility for students in the *collège* to find disagreement between Christian doctrine and classical letters. The Roman world was for seventeenth-century students a world of heroes, of generals, emperors, and great statesmen. "It was customary for great men in Roman times to die without leaving enough money to pay for their funerals . . . since poverty was an honor among them, and wealth was scorned." This was of course a myth, and other precepts were also mythical; but they were believed by both teachers and students. Idealized and heroic, the Roman world, as presented in the *collège,* became a coherent ethical and psychological system that offered an alternative to the corporate mentality. It was this Roman world that Corneille, Poussin, and Racine depicted and which their patrons had been prepared to understand through their years of study in colleges.

The natural philosophy (science) curriculum complemented this flight from reality. Abstract in the extreme, science as taught in Parisian *collèges* instilled not an understanding of but a hostility to physical objects. Physics in the Jesuit and Oratorian curricula still amounted to little more than commentaries on Aristotle and Ptolemy, while mathematics consisted of learning by heart Euclid's proofs. Formulas, numbers, pure forms, and essences made science a part of philosophy. Its aim was to penetrate into the "causes and first principles of things." Banned by the Church, the more recent works on astronomy were not part of the curriculum. Either heretical or suspected of being so, they could not be taught in the *collège.* How Mersenne, Pascal,

Descartes, and the other luminaries of seventeenth-century philosophy became acquainted with these works is unclear. Teachers may have discussed Copernicus, Bruno, or Galileo with advanced students in order to refute their propositions. Published refutations of heretical works often contained the heretical propositions, so students may have indirectly become familiar with the new astronomy and the new physics.

Seventeenth-century students often returned to their families as strangers. Sons of well-to-do merchants and judges may have adjusted with difficulty to the secular roles their parents assumed they would play. The evidence of this difficulty remains hard to interpret owing to the complex reasons that compelled sons to abandon their families and lead monastic, scholarly, or artistic lives. But whether for reasons of social prestige or true commitment, nearly every family in the major guilds and sovereign courts "lost" children to the life of contemplation, scholarship, and creative arts. In the aristocratic and devotional atmosphere of the seventeenth century, neither service in the government nor a career in the law was considered particularly worthy or ennobling. The moral philosophy of the *collèges* reflected this same attitude by idealizing the courtly and monastic ways of life and by teaching that making money or amassing a huge fortune was degrading and sinful.

Having spent some years in a *collège,* and having detached himself somewhat from the aims of his family, a young man of means could choose from among four ways of life: he could become a courtier and, if successful, earn through favor a career in the army or the Church; he could withdraw from society almost entirely, as did Descartes and Pascal; he could join a prestigious monastic order, such as the old Benedictine houses in Paris, and devote his time to literary and scholarly activities; or he could spend his time in the elegant, polite world of *salons* and small literary groups. None of these choices was exclusive, and several prominent men of letters in the *Ancien Régime* mixed them or moved from one to another. Though all four alternatives might involve rejecting the father's profession, they would nevertheless bring prestige and honor to the family. In many cases the family actually hoped one of these alternatives would be selected, for it did not have the means to purchase judicial offices for all the sons.

The fourth alternative, the life of letters, became attractive and separate from the others only after the foundation of the French Academy in 1635. Ever since the close association of poets with the later Valois kings, Gallican clergymen and judges had looked upon them with suspicion. Among the suspicious was Richelieu, who offered his "protection" as much in the interest of controlling the group's activities as out of a sincere desire to patronize letters.

For several years a group of bright, young, well-educated would-be courtiers, headed by Valentin Conrart, had been meeting regularly to discuss poetic and rhetorical theory, manners, and literary works. The group seems to have had no intention of forming so formidable an institution as an academy until the cardinal accidentally learned of its existence. In asking if they wished to form *"un corps,"* Richelieu, like the members, had no conscious Italian or sixteenth-century Platonic model; in fact the term *corps* suggested something much more down to earth and recognizable to sons of guildsmen and minor royal officials. The group anxiously discussed whether it wanted to be "protected" and, having recognized how impolitic it would be to refuse, accepted.

The courtly tone of the Academy was apparent from the beginning. Its members had discussed and approved Faret's *L'Honnête Homme ou l'Art de Plaire à la Cour,* a handbook on manners like Castiglione's *Courtier.* Indeed, they had slipped quietly into the polite *salons* of the capital, though their origins were anything but aristocratic. Of the first members, Conrart had refused to accept an office in a tax court offered by his father; Godeau, known as "Julie's Dwarf" in the salon of Madame de Rambouillet, did not accept his father's very lucrative but socially degrading office of lieutenant in the *eaux et forêts;* Chapelain was a notary's son; Giry was the son of an *avocat* in the Parlement; Habert, that of a military paymaster; Voiture, son of a wine merchant; and so on for the other early members. For these men the Academy was a special corporation, not unlike a guild or court of law, which would soon assure the prestige of its members. In 1667, the Academy was formally recognized as the sovereign court for judging French grammar and literature, to rank along with the Parlement and the Chambre des Comptes.

Along with preparing statutes for its members to enforce conformity of religion, morals, and dress, the Academy fixed its purpose—which was to make French the equal of Greek and Latin by ridding the language "of the garbage that it has accumulated from the mouths of the *peuple* or from the crowd in the *Palais de Justice,* and from the impurities of chicanery, or from the bad habits of ignorant courtiers." Directing its campaign for politeness of the language against every university and noncourtly group, the Academy set to work on a dictionary.

Like most corporations, the Academy spent its formal sessions listening to evidence, in this case on the meaning and use of words; then the members would by majority vote legislate the refinements of the French language. One member, Jean Sirmond, defined the purpose of the legislation as establishing that "someone who had used a word incorrectly would not have committed an error, but a sin." Their first great "case" resulted from the quarrel over *Le Cid.* Richelieu asked the Academicians to judge the merit of the play according to the classical rules of tragedy. Though inconclusive, their findings were nevertheless sensational. The Academy's investigation of *Le Cid* transformed the group into a supreme court of literary taste. By associating "his" Academy with so great a work as *Le Cid,* Richelieu inadvertently helped to synthesize and institutionalize the aesthetic canons of the heroic style.

The Academicians made François de Malherbe, a Norman poet, their great patron by attempting in their own works to follow his theories on taste and poetry. A strictly Academic style developed that can best be studied in works now largely unknown. Chapelain's epic of Joan of Arc, *La Pucelle;* Desmarets de Saint-Sorlin's *Clovis;* Giry's translations of Tertullian and Saint Augustine; and numerous verse translations of psalms and religious plays epitomized the Academic style. None of these works was scholarly or historically accurate; the translations were in fact often inordinately free since the emphasis was on style, purity of language, and the edifying qualities of the subject. Concern with genteel morality and religious conformity remained strong. As early as 1636 the Academy voted to ostracize one of its members, Mauléon de Granier, on moral grounds. It seems that some nuns had asked him to keep money for them, and that he had later refused to reimburse them.

From the beginning, then, the French Academy had the temperament of a guild or court of law. It was exclusive, limited to forty members, self-perpetuating, and possessed of a well-defined function. One important difference set the Academy apart from the traditional guilds: it could not become a preserve of a small number of select families, though this might have happened had not royal influence made it impossible.

Remaining detached from a corporation of some sort was almost psychologically impossible in the seventeenth century. Only a handful of geniuses like Poussin and Pascal, or those who sought mystical union with God, had the psychological qualities necessary for a complete break with their heritage. For those bound to the corporate heritage, the Academy fulfilled the psychological need of belonging to *"un corps."*

The academies founded under Louis XIV, largely at Colbert's instigation, were equally guildlike and traditional in spirit and practice. The Academies for Painting and Sculpture, Inscription and Numismatics, Dance, Music, Sciences, and Architecture provided a corporate identity for persons eager to separate themselves from their inferior backgrounds, and eager for recognition in some special area of knowledge. Each academy had a function in what was becoming a vast project for raising the quality of French culture to equal that of the ancients. Colbert pressed the Academicians on to finishing their dictionary by enforcing rules of attendance at sessions (he was a member himself). He also became obsessed with the problem of raising the quality of French art. In 1672, a year after its founding, he offered a prize of 1,000 *livres* to any member of the Academy of Architecture who would design a purely "French order" equal in majesty and beauty to those of the ancients. Though Colbert did more than any other single person before Napoleon to raise the status of artistic and intellectual accomplishments, he did so without realizing the psychological and social implications of his policies. His academies placed the brightest, most talented artists and savants at the service of the state; and because Colbert could only see himself as a humble servant of the king, he could only see the Academicians in the same role. For Colbert, son of a draper from Rheims, the academies were little more than guilds, whose purpose was to increase the quality and quantity of production. He wanted results—often instant results—on practical matters of technology, furnishings, and works of art. For him, knowledge, taste, and utility were inseparable. Very few artists and savants were unwilling to play the role he assigned to them, largely because the academies gave the recognition and social status that their members could never have gained alone.

Was this highly compartmentalized, increasingly consumerist, and hierarchically ordered society a stimulating and creative environment for science and art in the seventeenth century? No matter how anachronistic the question may seem, it deserves an answer, if only to confirm or refute the royal propaganda about the new "golden age" of the reign of Louis XIV. While historians have had difficulty discerning what social and cultural conditions are conducive to creative work, it is nevertheless possible, in a general way, to analyze the foundations of the much-touted Age of Greatness that poets and painters celebrated in their works. Answering such a fundamental question as "Were the principal persons known for their cultural achievements born and educated in Paris?" may shed some light on the French capital as an "environment" for creativity.

Though our concept "creativity" lacked a cognate in the French language of the seventeenth century, by harkening to the call of the muses, and by claiming that they resided along the Seine, roughly the same idea of creativity could be expressed. As a young man, Descartes wrote to a friend: "I have been cultivating the muses," his way of saying that he was working hard on mathematical and philosophical problems. Indeed, monarchical ideology had, at least since the origins of Humanism in the late fifteenth century, quite bombastically celebrated kings as the patrons of learning in Paris. Was the French capital a new Athens, Alexandria, Rome, or Florence, experiencing a golden age under Louis XIV?

The town-criers walking through the streets in 1547 to announce Francis I's death also shouted that he was the "father of arts and sciences." Dedications by poets, jurists, and philosophers to kings, queens, and other royals increased over the late sixteenth and seventeenth centuries, with local nobles and well-to-do merchants losing out as patrons. Since the Middle Ages, Paris had been touted for its learning, owing to the presence of the University, but now the state's enhanced powers permitted the capital and the Crown to come together. This rhetoric about the Crown's role in promoting arts and sciences would become standard in the high-blown charters that established the various royal academies during the 1660s and 1670s.[8]

Did this rhetoric obscure the quite mediocre Parisian cultural environment of the seventeenth century? In his famous *Siècle de Louis XIV,* Voltaire would compare Paris under Louis XIV to Athens under Pericles, Rome under Augustus, and Florence under Lorenzo de Medici; but a closer look raises doubts about the truth of this hyperbolic royalism.

When thinking of individuals who were inspired by the muses to be truly creative, the names of various writers, artists, and philosophers immediately come to mind (see table, opposite). Agreeing on a roster of the most eminent names is not easy. We all have a favorite writer or artist who, we think, belongs to the Parisian Pantheon. Leaving the roster open to additional names helps meet our current sensibilities regarding cultural inclusiveness.

Does this roster seem too long? The temptation to delete unfamiliar names is strong. Should Abraham Bosse and Israel Silvestre, remarkable artist-illustrators, be added? And there are Claude Mellan and Robert Nanteuil, the engraver-portraitists. There are also the Perrault brothers, especially Charles, author of Mother-Goose stories. The addition or the deletion of a few names probably would not alter the general conclusion that the principal creative persons of seventeenth-century France were *not* typically born and educated in Paris. If the list were pared down drastically to include only those names worthy of being carved on the façades of public libraries, as in the nineteenth century, it turns out that only two of these great creators, Molière and

8. Charles Perrault's poem, *Le Siècle de Louis XIV* (1687), prompted much reflection and evaluation of both ancient and "modern" poets, philosophers, architects, and composers. A generation later, Titon du Tillet's *Le Parnasse français* (1727) celebrated the nymph of the Seine, her muses, and French writers, composers, and muses, largely women known for their *salons*. A model of Titon's project, with all these figures standing on a mountain, has survived, dismounted and long neglected. Voltaire's *Siècle de Louis XIV* owes much to Perrault and Titon du Tillet.

Name	Birthplace	Formal Education	Creative Activity
Boileau, Nicolas	Paris	Paris	poet
Bossuet, Jacques-Bénigne	Dijon	Dijon (Jesuits)	preacher
Bourdaloue, Louis	Bourges	Bourges (Jesuits)	preacher
de Brosse, Salomon	Verneuil	Paris	architect
de Champaigne, Philippe	Brussels	Brussels	painter
Charpentier, Marc-Antoine	Paris	Rome	composer
Corneille, Pierre	Rouen	Rouen (Jesuits)	poet
Coypel, Antoine	Paris	Rome	painter
Coysevox, Antoine	Lyons	Paris	sculptor
Descartes, René	La Haye (Touraine)	La Flèche (Jesuits)	philosopher
Fermat, Pierre	Beaumont de Lomagne (Montauban)	Toulouse	mathematician
Gassendi, Pierre	Champtercier (Digne)	Aix, Avignon	philosopher
Jacquet de La Guerre, Elisabeth	Paris	family-trained	composer
de Lafayette, Marie-Madeleine	Paris	?	novelist
de La Fontaine, Jean	Château-Thierry	Château-Thierry	poet
Le Brun, Charles	Paris	Rome	painter
Le Vau, Louis	Paris	Paris	architect
Lorraine, Claude Gelée	Nancy	Rome, Naples	painter
Lully, Jean-Baptiste	Florence	Florence	composer
Malebranche, Nicolas	Paris	Paris	philosopher
Malherbe, François	Caen	Caen	poet
Mansart, François	Paris	Paris	architect
Molière, Jean-Baptiste Poquelin	Paris	Paris (Jesuits)	poet
Pascal, Blaise	Clermont-Ferrand	Clermont-Ferrand	philosopher
Poussin, Nicolas	Les Andelys	Rome	painter
Puget, Pierre	Marseilles	Rome, Florence	sculptor
Racine, Jean	La Ferté-Milon	Paris (Port-Royal-des-Champs)	poet
de Scudéry, Madeleine	Le Havre	?	writer
Sévigné, Marie de Rabutin-Chantal	Paris	?	writer
d'Urfé, Honoré	Marseille	Tournon	writer
Villedieu, Marie Desjardins	Alençon	?	writer

Mansart, were Parisian, and that they would be joined by Poussin, Corneille, Descartes, Pascal, and Racine, who were not Parisians born and educated.

The architects (except Le Vau) were Parisian by birth and/or training: their still almost artisanal craft was handed down within the family across the generations. The sense that a young painter needed to study in Rome remained strong throughout the century and was recognized by the Crown when the French Academy in Rome was founded for artists in 1666.

The great devotional writers, saints, and priests-preachers were also generally born and educated in the provinces. Saint François de Sales came from Savoy and was educated there; the Arnauld family, so influential in the development of Jansenism, was Parisian. The "Grand" Arnauld, Antoine, held a doctorate in theology from the Sorbonne. Saint Jeanne de Chantal came from a Burgundian legal family, while Saint Louise de Marillac came from a Parisian one. Saint Vincent de Paul was born in the Southwest and attended the University of Toulouse. Fénelon, preacher and author of a treatise on the education of women, came from Périgord and was educated at Cahors and then in Paris. Madame Guyon, the devout inspirer of Quietism, was born in Montargis and educated in Ursuline and Benedictine convents.

Looking at the careers of the major figures, we realize that some frequented Paris only irregularly. For a time, René Descartes thought of living in Italy, but he settled in the Low Countries and then, fatefully, went to Sweden. His contacts with the circle of learned persons around the Parisian Minim, Marin Mersenne, were infrequent but important, taking the form of a steady correspondence. It may be asserted that, while Corneille rarely made long stays in the capital, he in fact wrote for the Parisian theatergoing public and for the Court. Poussin was lured to Paris when he was already one of Europe's premier painters, but as quickly as he could, without offending the royal powers that had invited him, he returned to Rome to work (and to die). Some of his greatest paintings were commissioned by Parisians (de la Vrillière, Richelieu, Frérart de Chantelou), but he also continued to work for Italian patrons and friends. Molière and Racine traveled about in search of patronage, but for both, the Parisian theater audience and the Court were the public for which they wrote. Pascal's writings on mathematics were published for the "world" and for all time, not just for Parisian scientific circles. His *Provincial Letters,* a polemical critique of Jesuit ethics co-authored with Pierre Nicole, were written for educated Parisians. Madeleine de Scudéry's eye was frequently on Brussels, where Condé was in exile; but her sense of her readership was certainly Parisian.

Though Descartes would be by far the more influential philosopher, a comparison with another major figure, Pierre Gassendi, permits some interesting insights. Unlike Descartes, who believed that his work required a critical distance from virtually all learned circles, Gassendi circulated drafts of his philosophical works among his learned friends. After Jesuit schooling at La Flèche (near Le Mans), followed by soldiering and traveling, Descartes paid some visits to Mersenne's circle in Paris, to meet mathematicians and, in a sense, to measure their abilities before ignoring them. Since Mersenne was also a graduate of La Flèche, Descartes was remaining in contact with his former teachers, whom he hoped to convince to accept his method and to include it in the Jesuit curriculum all over France. Descartes believed that the best work was always done by a single individual, not collaboratively. He went so far as to refuse to read the mathematical papers of others (Fermat), even though he was working on related questions. Descartes also set himself up as an example to follow when learning to philosophize: the *Discourse on Method* is very autobiographical. Gassendi did just the opposite, as he carefully worked to reconstruct the life and thought of the great ancient philosopher Epicurus.

In general, philosophers working in the field of physics addressed set topics about, say, weight and mass. Then they proceeded to read all the "authorities" on the subject and would summarize their findings. Physics was therefore almost a type of learned literary criticism, until the work of Tycho Brahe, Johannes Kepler, and Galileo Galilei fundamentally altered it by an increasing use of classical and new mathematics, and measurement. Both Descartes and Gassendi would be surprised by Galileo's brilliant experimental work. Though hampered by Church censorship, Galileo very quickly managed to make his findings known to all the learned circles in Europe. While admiring Galileo's work, Gassendi remained skeptical of Galileo's claims to truth because they were mathematical rather than textual. In his country village Descartes increasingly turned to experimentation, recognizing the supreme importance of mathematics to astronomy and mechanics while continuing to dissect animals and work in pure mathematics. From his earliest work, he had sought to break away from the textual fabric and history that Gassendi not only studied but literally lived. Later in his life, Descartes was quite rude to friends from whom he had learned, claiming that he had discovered *his* method and had applied it with greater results than anyone before him, and without the help of others. Gassendi continued working on physics, and particularly on atomism, the ancient theory that everything in the universe is made up of small particles. The microscopes and telescopes made by Galileo and by Dutch master artisans were not strong enough to confirm the theory, but they were effective enough to prompt much new research in anatomy, physiology, and astronomy. The Parisian circle around Mersenne followed these studies but scarcely participated in them, other than occasionally to confirm what had already been established. Only after 1660 did Parisian savants—with the aid of foreigners lured to Paris by royal patronage—begin to undertake the laboratory or the experimental research that would contribute to these fields of knowledge.

Indeed, from what is known about domestic interiors in Paris, none included a laboratory for alchemical experiments. True, there were apothecaries and metal-founders, but no residences appear to have had the slit windows necessary for using instruments that could measure the movement of heavenly bodies. Catherine de Médicis had had a splendid column constructed upon which her astrologer-astronomer could view the heavens; but again, not until the later seventeenth century would cabinets full of natural curiosities be added to libraries. The Parisian theaters were nothing like the Globe of London, which made the cosmos into a stage, an out-of-date but still interesting model of the heavens.

Louis XIII's brother, Gaston d'Orléans, commissioned and collected very precise paintings of plants, and his cousin, the Grand Condé, read the latest scientific research, probably more from interest about its potential influence on religious beliefs than for the findings themselves. Princess Elizabeth of the Palatinate corresponded with Descartes on various subjects, but as far as it is known, none of the high aristocracy in Paris ever bothered to write him a letter or attempt to lure him back to France with honors and a handsome pension.

The unrivaled leader of the next generation of mathematician-philosophers, Blaise Pascal, appeared in Mersenne's circle when barely twelve, when his widower father left Clermont-Ferrand, moved to Paris, and began to educate the boy himself. Pascal's first work (on conic sections) was published when he was sixteen—the age at which, according to his father's plan, he should be moving somewhat away from mathematics and be studying Greek and Latin. When his father was appointed to a fiscal position out in Rouen, the son helped him keep accounts. This led to the invention of a mechanical calculator that would speed up the addition of long columns of figures. A few years later, Pascal returned to Clermont-Ferrand to attempt a verification of Evangelista Torricelli's research on the weight of air: he took measurements atop a mountain, where air pressure was lower than in the valley below. He eventually contributed to the quality of life in Paris by coming up with the idea of a bus service that would circulate through the city streets.

Pascal spent the last years of his brief life in close intimacy with his family and with his Jansenist friends. His sister, also brilliantly educated by their father, became a nun at the embattled monastery of Port Royal. Pascal's collaboration with Pierre Nicole in the *Provincial Letters* bears witness to a still possible grand synthesis between ethics, natural philosophy, and religious belief. The *Thoughts* (*Pensées*) of Pascal are profound jottings in an existential Augustinian mode that despairs of man's capacity to create social and political conditions that are truly just. Pascal remained awed by the immensity and complexity of the divine, and of man's really quite small place in it. His own devotions centered on prayer to accept God's will; his famous wager that it was better for man to bet on God's existence than to deny it or avoid taking a position (the latter views yielding no possibility for an afterlife) would haunt and comfort nonbelievers for centuries.

Through this review of the lives of Descartes, Gassendi, and Pascal, it becomes evident that the one central, indispensable meeting place for creative exchange was Mersenne and the Minim convent near the Place Royale. A graduate of the Jesuit college at La Flèche, Mersenne was not only learned, but he had a sense of well-being that prompted him to foster serious inquiry in others. The Minims were a late-medieval order that took as their patron Saint Francis of Paola, a southern Italian who had answered Saint Francis of Assisi's call. The founder and the followers of the Minims gained and kept royal protection in France from the early sixteenth century on. They were not openly hostile to the papacy, but there was some distance and a critical skepticism about the claims of the papal monarchy, especially in the reigns of Leo X and Julius II. This distance from papal ways consolidated Minim prestige in Gallican Paris, where both the University and the Parlement frequently sided with the king in the perennial disputes with popes.

The Protestant heretical impulses that were grounded in biblical exegesis and early Church history prompted the Minims to support historical research, with the Humanist presupposition that learning would always sustain the faith in Roman Catholicism. Their quite austere, nonmusical liturgies contrasted with the lavish services organized by the Jesuit Order, located in the magnificent church of Saint-Louis only a few streets away. The Minims shared in the revived Thomism that infused the Catholic Reformation, and they perceived their work as pleasing God by their learning and by their refutations of attacks on the faith by Protestants and by *libertins.*

Though a handful of minor poets and writers—the *libertins*—were irreverent rather than genuinely atheist, their ideas prompted fear within the Church. Mersenne believed that the latest astronomical discoveries would confirm the teachings of the Church. He translated some of Galileo's scientific works that would later be condemned by the commission on prohibited books. Mersenne wrote a study of the Book of Genesis and carried out pioneering research on sound.

The Minims were not reluctant to study things, as things, including the mechanics of playing musical instruments. The project on discovering "universal harmony" had Neoplatonic presuppositions, but it also produced a great deal of descriptive and illustrated information. Mersenne did not hesitate to question the relations between words and sounds. Asking whether they enter the soul separately or together was a question that could lead to heretical views.

Corresponding with virtually all the major philosophers and mathematicians of his day, and not a few historians throughout Europe, to his austere cell Mersenne welcomed Thomas Hobbes, Gassendi, Descartes, Pascal, and the geometer Desargues, plus numerous lesser luminaries. The library was one of the strongest in the capital. Having decided to build a new chapel, the Minims chose the most learned architect working in Paris at the time, François Mansart. What should be noted here, however, is that Mansart was more like Descartes than like Gassendi: he was a near loner, and a bit prickly when asked about his work. His chapel for the Minims was a quite austere, classicizing building that conformed to the asceticism of the Order. (In the nineteenth century it was pulled down to make way for a police barracks.) Mansart sought a new classicism in architectural orders that was every bit as mathematical as that of the ancients and that was free of the exaggerations that had their origins in Michelangelo's style and that opened the way toward the Baroque.

A simple comparison between the Jesuits and the Minims suggests devotional and cultural differences that marked Parisian worship services. To be sure, both orders shared the same Roman Catholic faith; but obedience to the papacy characterized the Jesuits, and the Minims kept a Gallican distance. Each vied for recognition by newly wealthy, consumerist government officials and fiscal managers, with the new Minim church becoming the most prestigious burial place in the mid-seventeenth century, despite the fact that Louis XIII, and Louis XIV willed their hearts to the Jesuit church of Saint-Louis.

PART FOUR

Urban Absolutism: The Flight from Modernity

The Frondeurs

Not every rich Parisian aspired to be a count or a courtier, but he certainly did want to become a gentleman farmer. These social aspirations were really quite different, for the drive to own land was stronger than any other in the *Ancien Régime*. It permeated every level of the society, from the artisans who dreamed of vegetable gardens to the dukes who wanted yet another forest full of deer. Land and its products remained for everyone a kind of sublime security against whatever evil might come.

Almost without exception, merchants, including the smaller ones, royal officials of every sort, judges and wealthier artisans owned land, vineyards, and country houses somewhere outside the walls of Paris. In some cases these were immense châteaux, in others modest villas or mere frame structures for summer living. The Parisians did not farm the land themselves, of course; they hired peasants and managers to see that it was done. This fact alone made the governing Parisians, those with wealth and power, at once urban and rural. Their interest remained divided between their activities and sources of income in town, and those on their farms. Unable to leave the law courts or storage houses in the winter, they quenched their thirst for country living by reading pastorals and attending the countless plays and ballets about peasants and shepherds presented in the capital.

Generally speaking, the richer the family, the more money it invested in the country. Owning land was aristocratic, and receiving revenues from it lacked the taint that came with all income from moneylending or business. In negotiating for a marriage, a Parisian with lands he could offer as part of a dowry was in a much better bargaining position than the one who could not. Land was considered a permanent investment, whereas *rentes,* town houses, and even jewels were not.

Then too, every governing Parisian strove to get away from the capital for as long as possible in the summer. Deserted by the Court, and run by a bare minimum of aspiring but not yet arrived officials and merchants from June to September, Paris resembled a city run by a government in exile. For nine months of the year, the governing Parisians were absentee landlords, and for the other two or three they usually were absentee officials or merchants. Soon after their birth, children were taken out of Paris to be raised by servants, aunts, and cousins living in country houses. Older people abandoned the capital to return to their country houses, often the place where they had been raised, to live out the rest of their lives in pious reading and in managing the farms. When the masters came into the country to join their families for the summer, they negotiated to buy more land, supervised the remodeling of their houses, installed furnishings carted out from Paris, and entertained relatives and friends. They toured their lands on horseback, hunted, and watched to see whether their *laboureurs* were cheating on plowing, harvesting, and measuring wine and other produce. The importance of this attachment to the land by virtually all the Parisians of means and political power cannot be exaggerated. From their seats in the Parlement they watched the prices of grain and wine, not only because they feared a revolt among the hungry *canaille* in Paris, but because they wanted handsome profits for themselves from their farms. How much of the Seine valley did the governing Parisians own?

This question is extremely difficult to answer, not only because land ownership has not been studied enough but also because of the problem of defining terms. When does a family implanted in the country for generations finally become "local nobility" instead of merely noble or still robe? It seems that in 1650 as much as seventy percent of the arable land in the Seine valley was owned by Parisians. This meant, of course, that the governing Parisians actually owned and in a sense controlled a prime source of the capital's food supply, its basis of subsistence. Even more significant, it is possible to state that the wealthier Parisians were the principal suppliers and profit-takers on most of the foodstuffs, chiefly grain and wine, imported into the capital. The remaining thirty percent of the arable land was mostly in the hands of the Church and the old, local nobility. The forests—held by families like the Montmorencies, by princes, and by the king himself—were almost never acquired by Parisians, either because they were not for sale, or because of social taboos that made them preserves of the upper aristocracy. The

Church seems to have owned very little land in the Paris basin. The governing Parisians were the big owners. Judges of the Parlement, Chambre des Comptes, and lesser courts, and tax officials and tax farmers had magnificent estates in the fertile *plat pays* and other parts of the Seine valley. Ormesson, Pontchartrain, Wideville, Vaux-le-Vicomte, Maisons-Lafitte, Guermantes, Grosbois, and numerous other châteaux were built in the midst of large tracts of land transformed into farms or parks. Today they are enclaves of greenery, divested of their farms that have been built up into suburbs; but in the period of the Fronde, these châteaux were noble residences representing the strong rural attachments of the most influential Parisians.[1] There was certainly nothing new about this process of urban investment in the land, but the steep climb in the rate of investment during the three decades before the Fronde catches our attention. The years from about 1620 to 1650 marked the peak of land investment for the entire century, making the prices for farms and vineyards rise to a high point that was not reached again until sometime after 1720. Many families doubled or even tripled their holdings, so that the rural interests of most Parisians increased not only in the years of economic expansion after 1620 but also in the years of depression after 1630.

Popular revolts, peasant riots, and lynchings were all parts of everyday life in the *Ancien Régime*. From a distance, these acts of violence resemble one another, as they did at the time they occurred; but a *kermesse,* or local fair, where some drunken peasants got out of hand, and the damaging of a tax collector's house were really not the same things. After a succession of crop failures, these attacks on tax collectors and estate managers, though also usually spontaneous and leaderless, would cross France like brush fires.

The pattern of events was usually the same, though the excuses and social origins of the participants varied considerably. For the absentee landlords back in Paris, these outbursts of violence, invariably directed against those whom the peasants considered the source of their misery, constituted something uncontrollable, feared, and mysterious. What caused these wanton attacks on officials and, occasionally, on the managers of their estates? How should they be stopped? The landlords did not know, but the news and rumors from the rural areas aroused anxiety for their own investments, loved ones, and possessions. Government officials in charge of provincial affairs had differing explanations for what became a crescendo of riots and murders ravaging France in the 1630s and 1640s.

---

1. Across the realm, well-to-do urban families were doing the same thing. The bourgeois of Rouen, Amiens, Beauvais, and other cities bought up to nearly forty percent of the arable land surrounding their cities.

Because of the contradictory reports sent to Paris from an area in revolt, predilections, rather than information, formed the basis for royal and what came to be Frondeur policies in Paris. Through these predilections, apparent in the mass orders for troops, hangings, and food grants, we can discern the fundamental assumptions on which the society of the *Ancien Régime* was based. First, in the minds of those having power, the military, judicial, and even religious controls for repressing violence worked effectively to transform the immediate economic causes of violence into social, moral, or theological ones. Thus, instead of viewing hunger and threatened imprisonment for debt as causes for rebellion, officials and governing Parisians alike believed that the rebels were *méchants,* given over to some devil, or, even more frequently, seduced by some evildoer who had privileges and prestige in the society. The obsession with finding a plot behind every act, or a conspiracy behind every murder, prevailed in the minds of officials, great or small, in or out of the capital.

Second, since the social structure was sustained by a hierarchy of privileges and obligations sustaining the structure of society, those invested with military and judicial powers were held responsible for the discipline of their inferiors. An inferior was like a dog on a leash: if the dog bit someone, the person holding the leash, rather than the dog, would be considered responsible for the animal's conduct. In seventeenth-century society, peasants and artisans as social groups were considered to be something like leashed animals; and when they revolted, the king, the bishops, and the nobility frequently blamed the nobles and judges of the region where the rebellion took place, for not keeping the peasantry in hand. In some cases noblemen were indeed inciting peasants to violence; but in other rebellions they were often condemned despite their efforts to keep the peace, simply because the assumptions of the society tended to blame the privileged for the acts committed by their inferiors.

What has been traditionally called the *Fronde* consisted of a series of extensive rural rebellions that eventually gained the towns and finally the capital. These rebellions ultimately became civil wars, because a large number of privileged individuals came to oppose the Crown. They were not absolutist or feudal struggles for power; nor were they class wars, or even Baroque operas come to life in Cardinal Retz or the Grande Mademoiselle.

In the years following 1630, French harvests were at best average, but they were often far inferior to those of the preceding thirty-year period. Reports came into Paris from all over the realm, including the Paris basin, describing horrible conditions of starvation, and a lack of money to buy food. But the effects of nature alone usually did not cause peasants to rebel; they were quite conditioned to accept punishments from God. But in addition to poor harvests and declining revenues, taxes of every type rose steeply each year. In region after region, royal officials raised the *taille* and the excise taxes. Town governments, estates, and guilds were forced to make "contributions" to meet the financial crisis caused by the war with Spain. From the villages and hamlets of the governing Parisians came reports of brutal tactics used by officials and troops to extort taxes from the peasants.

Knowledge that the king too was bankrupt was no source of comfort for the peasantry. In the first poor years they sold what reserves of livestock and grain they had to pay taxes; but as the depression dragged on, they were forced to sell fields, their last livestock, and even their furniture. The court records of Normandy in 1639 are filled with descriptions of how the belongings of numerous peasants were totally liquidated for tax payment. Their lords lent them money, but even the local nobility suffered from the depression because of the collapse of revenues.

After this description of the crisis in the rural areas, the reasons for the rapid increase in the purchase of lands by the Parisians become clear enough. The gentlemen farmers took advantage of the forced liquidation of peasant holdings by buying them out and taking control of the countryside. At the same time, the more ambitious Parisians bought fiefs from impoverished noblemen, assumed the noble's title, and further extended Parisian control over the rural areas in a period of grave crisis. The steep rise in the price of land after 1640 suggests that some kind of threshold of peasant subsistence had been reached, and that thoughts of selling more land were being transformed into the frustrations of rebellion. The complaints about the ruined farms and the cruel behavior of the tax collectors developed into frenzied protests to the Crown. This coincidence of poor harvests, higher taxes, and sales of land came to a climax in the Fronde.

What officials thought was happening remained confused and contradictory. The governors, dukes, and local nobility condemned the tax collectors' brutal tactics and held them responsible for the violence that ravaged the countryside. The *intendants,* however, in their reports to the chancellor, rarely mentioned these activities; rather they discussed the suffering caused by lack of food and condemned the nobility and judges for terrorizing the peasantry into rebellion against the Crown. When these reports reached the capital, the governing Parisians each believed what best suited their own social predilections. Those connected with the administration of taxes and the supporters of the war believed the newly established *intendants,* while courtiers, clergymen,

Grain prices sold at the Halles in Paris *(Yearly average prices based on harvest year, August through July)*

Source: From M. Baulant and J. Meuvret, *Prix des Céréales, extraits de la Mercuriale de Paris* (Paris, 1960).

and judges usually gave credence to the reports from older royal officials such as the *tré-soriers* and the local noblemen. Thus two camps formed: those supporting the Crown's policies of war against Spain and high taxes as a dire necessity, and their opponents, the *Frondeurs*.

The French word *fronde* means "slingshot"—not the Y-shaped tree branch type, but the long leather thong that David used to kill Goliath. A pocket in the middle of the thong holds a pebble or an acorn; the ends of the thong are held together and swung over the head in a circle. Once speed has built up, releasing one end of the thong at just the right angle causes centrifugal force to hurl the stone in a right angle to the circle. A judge in the Parlement referred to the clash of powers and wills in 1648 as the "slingshot" or *"Fronde,"* perhaps because the unarmed and lesser-armed Parisian judges, and the angry Parisians, dared to attack the royal government despite its virtual monopoly over military force. A revolution? The level of challenge to established authorities in the state and society would never become as radical as the civil war taking place during those same years in the British Isles, a revolution that culminated in the overthrow of the established government, the trial and execution of King Charles I, and the establishment of a Protectorate under Oliver Cromwell's iron hand. The British experience has often been called revolutionary; the Fronde has been more often characterized as a revolt rather than a revolution.

Attempting to compare the British and the French experiences and radical political, religious, and social disorder has often led to anachronistic conclusions. The same must be said about comparing the Fronde with the French Revolution of 1780–99:

A satire on the militia during the Fronde. Made up of merchants, valets, and artisans, the Parisian militia had a reputation for drinking—and for being afraid of the brutal firepower of regular troops.

each of these great political and social convulsions was unique, and each may be characterized as revolutionary according to the semantic and cultural significances of the word "revolution" at the time the events so characterized took place. The more elite, politically engaged Parisians felt themselves to be in a terrible storm of life-threatening power. Their own fears and hopes prompted comparisons with the situation in England, the Wars of Religion of the late sixteenth century, and the ancient Greek and Roman civil wars taught in school.

The Frondeur was not a destitute peasant or artisan but rather a member of the privileged orders who disagreed with the Crown's policies and methods for repressing rebellions. Because of their assumptions about society, the Frondeurs and the supporters of Mazarin both viewed the peasants and artisans in rebellion as animals gone mad. But when a nobleman or judge was accused of fomenting rebellion when he had not done so, the regent, Anne of Austria (1601–66), and her councillors, considered him a Frondeur! Neither antiroyalist nor pro-Spanish, and yet accused of being both, the Frondeur's own behavior remained an enigma to himself. The intellectual Frondeurs—such as Retz, then co-adjutor archbishop of Paris; La Rochefoucauld, duke, peer, and rebel, who reflected on all this in his memoirs; and Omer Talon, a royal official caught between the Council and the Parlement, and who died in despair—differed from the hundreds of rebels who supported them, in that they suffered from the frustrations of being inordinately ambitious, yet without a cause in which they could really believe.

Despite their erudition, patriotism, and articulate perception of alternative forms of government, the Frondeurs never developed a program of reforms truly subversive to absolute monarchy. Their proposals remained negative and were cast in the hope of returning to the past (often mythical), while their profound and justifiable uneasiness came from the fear that their own power and wealth would be reduced, rather than from a vision of an ideal society they sought to realize. Whom did they fear? Both the monarchy and the reformer. Their goals tended, strictly speaking, toward a restoration of an older, more corporate, and more consultative government based on noble and civic privileges.

To accuse Mazarin of treason, to claim *they* represented all Frenchmen in the Parlement, and to condemn the tax collectors for gouging the peasantry constituted the elements of a politics of fear. Like their counterparts in the Hôtel de Ville, who had also failed to cope with the problems of Paris, they offered no solution to the miserable conditions caused by war, poor harvests, and corrupt officials.

After a rebellion had been repressed, and after the public hangings, the tax collectors began going from farm to farm again, this time with new letters from the king and with more troops. Often their demands were harsher, not only because the taxes were in arrears but because of the prevailing idea that rebels were like children who had to be punished for misbehaving. The principal dynamic of social repression remained setting an example, either by hanging in the case of some serious crime or by shaming for the rest. In one rebel town the *prévôt* and *échevins* were ordered to kneel down, bareheaded, in public before a royal official, who read off a list of their crimes from "their father," the child king Louis XIV. Like children who had broken the rules, they had to be shamed and taught lessons of good behavior. In other instances, Frondeurs were clapped into prison, and months might go by before they were charged with a crime. Printers selling books and pamphlets that had not been granted royal permission to publish were arrested and sometimes were summarily tried and sentenced to death. On occasion, however, the government hesitated before ordering that the sentence be carried out, for fear of riot or that the populace would intervene to save the condemned man's life. In general, then, the innumerable acts of cruelty and the brutal punishments ordered by royal officials stemmed not from a kind of sadism but rather from the belief that these acts, as examples, would train subjects to obey. The governing Parisians observed this rhythm of revolt and repression year after year throughout the 1630s without participating. The Seine basin remained relatively quiet, and so long as Richelieu and Louis XIII lived, the governing Parisians, notably the judges, dared not rebel for fear of the harsh repression the "Just King" would mete out.

The harsh, repressive atmosphere of the later years of Louis XIII's reign prompted strong feelings of affection and support for his widow, Anne of Austria, and her two sons, Louis XIV, who was only four in 1643, and Philip, age three. Anne's understanding of politics was grounded on her astuteness at seeing and hearing little signs of disrespect or opposition. Her somewhat shrill voice, her firmness of tone, and her authority disoriented most of her male councillors, as well as the judges of the Parlement, none of whom were accustomed to dealing with a Queen Mother of courage and principle. For her sons, Anne would defend every jot and tittle of the royal prerogative, an absolutism that perhaps was not always grounded on ideology but that was nonetheless very firmly articulated and categorical. As civil war deepened, Anne knew her power rested on control of the royal signature and on the royal council. In fact, as large numbers of royal officials, including army officers, rebelled, about all that remained of royal absolutism—especially once her principal minister, Mazarin, was forced into exile—was Anne's power over the royal signature. In point of fact, the Frondeurs often sought appointments to high offices such as governorships and military commands, none of which were valid without the royal signature.

Historians have often asserted that Anne "made mistakes," but this type of assertion fails completely to characterize Anne's accomplishment of surviving in a period when French institutions and the habits of thought were being severely tested. She did not hesitate to disgrace those whom she deemed incapable of serving her and her sons well; and she doggedly fought to maintain in her service the one councillor she came to trust completely: Cardinal Mazarin.

After Richelieu's death late in 1642, and Louis XIII's a few months later, fears about royal punishment diminished. The Regency of the five-year-old Louis XIV inspired

Anne of Austria, by Robert Nanteuil. Looked upon with fondness by her subjects after the death of her husband, Louis XIII, the "Just King," Anne never lost her dignity as she defended the absolutist state during the Fronde. After 1661 she retired to a quiet life among her ladies-in-waiting at Val-de-Grâce.

little awe among the judges and princes. Moreover, Anne, the regent, and Cardinal Mazarin, her minister, made a series of decisions that aggravated the already grave tensions in France caused by war and depression. Mazarin was a cultured diplomat who could not be bothered with long and unedifying quarrels over tax laws and remonstrances. He was not a Richelieu. The latter also had been disdainful of finances, but he had survived rebellions of every type. Ever since 1630, when his victory over Marie de Médicis and the Spanish party had given him full power to ignore internal conditions and to pursue a war with Spain, Richelieu had maneuvered and used every expediency to avoid rebellion in order to defeat Spain. Reforms had been made here and there, to be sure, but for increased revenues, not for justice or prosperity. Richelieu had become obsessed with the war, especially after the Spanish conquest of Corbie in 1636.

Mazarin in his gallery, by Robert Nanteuil, 1659. Roman-born, Jesuit-educated, and a diplomat, Mazarin, once he had triumphed over the Fronde, became a passionate collector of paintings, sculpture, books, and luxurious fabrics and tapestries. He is seated in his gallery, his coat of arms above the door.

No defenses or armies stood between Paris and the Spanish infantry. Then the cardinal had thought of abandoning the capital, but Père Joseph, with his faith in divine support, had convinced Richelieu to hang on to Paris and not to flee south. After Richelieu's death the rebellions increased, gaining the Paris basin. When the destitute rose up, the *gens de bien,* either property owners or merchants, feared for their lives. The gentleman farmer's *maison* was not a château. It had no moat, gun emplacements, or drawbridges. And to a raving mob, those who managed the estates were akin to the tax collectors.

In a society where each political act and social rank is represented by an outward and exposed symbol—a ceremony, a costume, or a gesture—the first public appearance of new officials assumes an unusual importance. Anne and Mazarin were new to the Parlement after Louis XIII's death; and though they made a good first impression by freeing some of Richelieu's political prisoners, they also made mistakes. They were out of touch with the country. But the Parlement was not; nor were the princes. Both were feeling the pressure of sedition in Paris and in the provinces. Obviously, neither the Parlement nor the princes were the sincerely disinterested servants of the Crown that they claimed to be; but until Anne gave them the issues on which to oppose her, the possibility of a civil war remained remote. Without a few blunders on the part of Anne and her councillors, the Fronde would not have taken place.

Anne and Mazarin blundered when they proposed sending Antoine Arnauld's controversial Jansenist treatise, *De la Fréquente Communion,* off to Rome for examination by theologians to discover whether or not it was orthodox. Until then the Jansenist movement had been small and insignificant. As soon as Anne and Mazarin proposed sending Arnauld to Rome, however, the judges of the Parlement and the doctors of the Sorbonne raised a cry of protest. Had Anne purposely tried to unite the forces of Jansenism and the supporters of the old but still very emotional issue of Gallican liberties, she could not have done anything better than propose that Rome examine Arnauld's work. These liberties, which lay at the heart of the monarchical identity, were congeries of legal rights that assured that the French Church (called the "Gallican Church," from an adjectival form of "Gaul") would be administratively, but not doctrinally, autonomous from the papacy. Omer Talon, the eminent *avocat général,* informed Anne that there were plenty of French theologians perfectly capable of determining whether Arnauld's work on the Communion was orthodox, and that sending him personally to Rome would be throwing a French subject to the lions. He argued that the Jesuits, the Inquisition, and the papacy would put an end to Arnauld. And beyond the issue of Arnauld's work and life, would not this decision to send him to Rome reestablish the papacy's right to intervene in the affairs of the French Church?

Whether or not the picture of Rome depicted by Talon was relevant, Anne and Mazarin should have known about the judges' pathological fears over the issue of Gallican liberties. As the son of the judge who had most fervently opposed the reentry of the Jesuits into France, Arnauld must have known that he would have the Parlement's support in any case involving Gallican liberties. Anne's decision gave his Jansenist cause more support in Parisian society than he or his predecessors had ever hoped for. For the first time, the radical members of the Parlement argued that the Queen Mother was a foreigner subverting French laws, instead of defending those of her son, a minor. This charge was untenable. But by following the Jesuits' wishes and ignoring the issues of Gallican liberties, she gave the more emotionally inclined Parlementarians a lever against the Crown.

Before his death, Richelieu had often intervened to temporize or to cancel legislation that would incite rebellion; but after his death, new taxes were levied without any apparent regard for their social consequences. Then, too, Richelieu had shown considerable contempt for the tax collectors, farmers, and *traitants* who were almost overnight growing increasingly wealthy at the Crown's expense. However, neither Mazarin nor his favorite, Michel Particelli d'Hémery, the new superintendent of finance, seems to have had anything but sympathy for these rich men whose hirelings used brutal tactics in collecting taxes. Then, in 1644, among the innumerable *arrêts* passed to increase tax revenues, one stood out as an example of political ineptitude. The judges, who scorned the *hommes de finances,* had had enough.

Henry II, in an edict signed in 1548 and twice reinforced merely to collect revenues, had forbidden all the owners of land in the *faubourgs* of Paris to build houses and shops without royal permission. The ostensible purpose of the edict had been to keep the *faubourgs* from growing so large that the city's walls would no longer provide adequate defense; but like so many other edicts, this one had never really been enforced until the Crown seized upon it to make house owners pay fines.

Officials from the Châtelet went out into the *faubourgs,* that is, the suburbs of Saint-Antoine and Saint-Germain, to begin surveying and assessing almost a century of suburban growth, whereupon the inhabitants of those areas rioted and appealed to the Parlement to investigate the legality of the tax. The Parlement decided to hold a hearing on the matter. Anne, through Chancellor Séguier, made it known that Louis XIV did not want his Parlement to interfere in such matters.

Once again, as with the issue over Arnauld, a mixture of old claims and immediate circumstances threw some members of the Parlement into violent opposition to the Crown. On both the issues of Gallican liberties and the tax on the *faubourgs,* the members of the Chambers of the *Enquêtes* became much more hostile to Anne and her policies than did those of the *Grand'chambre,* where the senior members of the Parlement sat.

In the face of a revolt from the *Enquêtes* and hostility from Anne, the eminent members of the Parlement, the chief of whom was Omer Talon, had to choose between opposing the Crown and losing face before their colleagues for appearing to be lax in not defending the privileges of the Parlement. Talon went to see the Queen Mother. His speech reflects the eloquence and wisdom of the Frondeur. In warning that "it was necessary to treat the Parlement gently, or to be more precise, not to offend it, because all the other Parlements in the realm would follow the example of what happens in the one in Paris, and that the example of the capital city would be in the minds of all the others," Talon accurately predicted the course of events that would lead to a general civil war. But Anne remained firm.

The surveying of the *faubourgs* began again, this time with detachments of soldiers placed along the streets and accompanying the assessors into each house. New riots erupted. Talon again went to see Anne, this time to warn her of the general effects produced by such tactics: "Force, violence, and fear only produce refusals, and often are the seedlings of sedition. We have heard this morning the clamoring of four hundred persons assembled in the *Palais,* of every age, sex, and social status; and despite our every effort, through words and threats, to oblige them to leave, nothing worked until they learned that we had decided to go and see Your Majesty."

Why did this mob think the Parlement would defend its cause? Did members of the Parlement, for instance from the *Enquêtes,* actually excite the mob? We do not know, but it is possible. Even Talon's speech, covered with the cloak of humility, contained something of a threat. By representing the Parlement as standing between the mob and the Crown, Talon sought to gain the suppression of the tax on the *faubourgs.*

The Parlement, on receiving an appeal from the *faubourgs,* was willing to hold a hearing. There are two possible explanations for its behavior in this crisis. First, the *faubourgs* of Paris were owned in large part by distinguished families in the robe and the major guilds. Houses had been built on these lands and rented as the population of the capital increased. What were once country houses of the wealthy had become tenement houses for the poorest Parisians. Both the Faubourg Saint-Antoine and the Faubourg Saint-Germain (the area around Saint-Sulpice) were largely owned by governing

Parisians and were not far from robe quarters of the city. These *faubourgs* were over-crowded with *gagne petits* and peasants who had fled the provinces and come to Paris in search of jobs and food. They were among the most destitute of Parisians, living the closest to subsistence in rooming houses and sheds, paying weekly rents through agents to owners whom they never saw. Indeed, we know that the vast majority in these *faubourgs* were tenants, renting rooms and attics from many eminent families in Paris. The gentleman farmer of Paris was also a slumlord.

Without a detailed study, it is impossible to discover whether the *hommes de finances* owned more land and houses in these *faubourgs* than did, say, the families higher up the social scale. But even if the inhabitants of these *faubourgs* had as many tax farmers as they did judges for landlords, this would not have measurably changed the attitude of the Parlement. The Parlement remained hostile to the tax on the *faubourgs* because its members did not want to pay higher taxes; nor did they want their renters to rebel.

Second, the danger remained real that a rebellion would begin in the *faubourgs* and then extend into Paris or the countryside. Some feared such uprisings, while others favored them. The countryside around the capital was already the scene of too many "incidents," lynchings, robberies, and pillaging.

After Anne's refusal to revoke the tax, Talon went to see Mazarin. He reminded the cardinal that the immediate reason for the barricades and riots of the League on May 12, 1588, had been the presence of troops in the city. Then he went on to state that taxes should not be levied on everyone in a single area, but on different groups or goods in different areas, to avoid grounds for common protest from all classes. This was wise advice. Richelieu had known this, but it may have come as a lesson to Mazarin, preoccupied as he was, all his life, with diplomatic rather than internal affairs. Then Talon made his main point by referring to the tax on the *faubourgs*: "All the owners and renters . . . claim to be equally interested, the former from a basic interest, because they are being asked for money, and the others out of fear that the rents of the houses where they live will be increased. It is difficult under such circumstances to quiet down an entire people that is excited." Mazarin replied by reminding Talon of the successes at the siege of Gravelines, and stated that the Parlement should not oppose "all kinds of things at this time."

Talon reported back to the Parlement. The heated emotions of the judges accorded with those of the four hundred to five hundred *pauvres gens* demanding justice, "who were screaming against d'Hémery and the commissioners." The next day at about eleven in the morning "the poor folk assembled, went to the workshops, convinced the masons and laborers to leave their jobs, and, assembling in various spots in the *faubourg,* threatened to burn down Monsieur d'Hémery's house. They appeared in two or three bands, unarmed but for clubs, leaderless, and aimless, but nevertheless they generated quite a bit of fear in the city."

As the crowds grew stormy, several officials rushed to see Anne and warn her that a popular rebellion was breaking out in Paris, upon which she replied that both she and Molé, the First President of the Parlement, knew that this outbreak had been fomented by the *Enquêtes*. The officials almost immediately left the Queen Mother, who, having implied that they were responsible for the rebellion because they had not kept the *Enquêtes* under control, let them leave hungry, "without so much as a glass of water."

On the third day of the crisis, July 5, 1644, Condé, a prince of the blood and a heroically successful general, decided to force matters by insisting that more troops accompany the assessors. But when the assessors arrived in the *faubourgs* this time, the crowds so frightened them that they left without descending from their carriages, having merely approached one of the houses. The Crown had suffered a defeat. The fines were dropped, again temporarily, by the Queen Mother's councillors, who seemed as convinced as ever that the refusal to pay them was a defeat for the royal authority. When, in March 1645, the final effort to fine the builders again met with defeat, Anne accepted the advice of her stern councillors and ordered several presidents in the Parlement into exile, among them Jean-Jacques Barillon, a leader of the radicals, who had to leave Paris under military guard, while his wife was sent to their country house.

But instead of intimidating the Parlement, this merely united more of the moderate members with the *Enquêtes,* making them protest as a group against such arbitrary and illegal actions. In an effort to repair this blunder, Anne released from prison all the radicals, save Barillon, who died exiled in prison in far-off Pignerol, on the Italian frontier. If the Parlement had needed a martyr, it would have had one in Barillon; but it did not. In these years the Crown's efforts to increase taxes so angered the Parlement that its old divisions virtually disappeared. Nor did the news from England, where Parliament had taken up arms against Charles I, serve to calm spirits in the *Palais.*

Seeing that a tax on the *faubourgs* would cause a rebellion, the Crown turned to levying higher excise taxes on goods "imported" into Paris. The same storm of protest arose from the Parlement, as the divisions among its members decreased even further. This tax and others (tampering with the *rentes*) designed to fall on those who were well-off became null and void simply because the Parlement refused to register them, an act essential to making them law. After these new efforts, d'Hémery and Mazarin, in obvious defiance of the Parlement, proposed raising more money by selling offices. The Fronde of 1648, perpetrated by the judges in Paris and spreading throughout the realm, became just one more response and refusal to obey Anne and her councillors. The civil war that followed never exceeded in idealism or purpose the mixture of fears and self-interest that was at the base of the events of 1644 over the tax on the *faubourgs*.

By applying the same notions of taxation and repression to the judges that it was applying to the peasantry, the Crown turned its own officials into Frondeurs. Certainly the judges became more brazen and more demanding, but the dynamics of repression that officials employed aggravated tensions and created new ones even where there had been none before. Moreover, nothing seemed to have been solved. The war went on, the Crown's efforts to stop the Jansenist movement failed, the misery and starvation resulting from poor crops increased, and the demands of the tax collectors grew harsher.

The unwillingness of both Richelieu and Mazarin to attempt some reform in tax collection brought the absolute monarchy to civil war in a period when the *petites gens* of both the countryside and the cities were being driven down to the level of bare subsistence. Every sign of economic crisis appeared in the 1640s. And what had always been an abuse became intolerable corruption in a period of economic crisis and war. Even the lowliest day laborer was aware of the profits taken by the tax collectors; thus the outcry against them became so extensive and vehement that it reached every element in the society. In some cases, because of the very conditions from which people suffered, the charges against the *hommes de finances* were exaggerated, though these officials indisputably did reap enormous profits at the expense of both the king and his subjects. Between thirty-four and forty-five percent of the gross tax revenue collected went to the *hommes de finances* as fees for collecting taxes.

The treasurers of France, the principal tax officers in the provinces, were not unlike the judges; they served in purchased offices. Peasant resistance to increased taxes and fear of revolt had led these officials virtually to abandon their duty to collect royal revenues. However, the tax farmers, that is, those who had contracted to collect excise taxes, were willing to use force to carry out their contracts. The *parlementaires* loathed them, at least publicly. In private, the judges often invested in the lucrative tax contracts that were now causing so much disorder in the countryside.

Did the judges in the Parlement scorn the tax officials? In most cases they had ancestors or parents who, before their purchase of offices in the magistracy, had been tax officials. It was quite rare for a man and his family to climb up from being a bourgeois and merchant into the nobility of the robe without at some point being a tax official. But those who had arrived in the Parlement did not hesitate to repudiate or even condemn those below them. In fact, the men of law did everything they could to dissociate themselves from their former lucrative but socially degrading positions. Here was the principal tension and cleavage in the *Ancien Régime*. What was socially upgrading for a bourgeois and merchant could only be degrading for a man of justice. In fact, as with artisans and merchants, the tensions remained highest between the groups in closest proximity to one another.

The vain efforts to tax, the riots, the arrests, and the confusions of 1645 provided a dress rehearsal for the Fronde of 1648. D'Hémery stupidly tried once more to tax the suburbs and, failing again, challenged the Parlement to a showdown by selling additional judgeships and by tampering with the *droit annuel*. These new efforts to punish the judges only united them further and brought other royal officials who had purchased their offices into the Parlement's camp. By July 1648 the issues were clear, and economic conditions in the Paris basin had grown much worse. The peasant revolts were spreading to the Île de France. The judges, instead of going to the country that summer, stayed on in Paris to force a test of strength with Anne and Mazarin.

When the Parlement attacked the extortionate practices of the tax collectors, the *intendants,* d'Hémery, and his colleagues, it did so in response to a general demand. Peasants, nobles, judges, and clergymen all heaped scorn on the *hommes de finances*. The rebellions had weakened Anne's control and had strengthened the influence of Gaston d'Orléans, whose lack of political wisdom did not diminish his prestige as the uncle of Louis XIV and prince of the blood. Faced with Gaston's strength and with new pressure from the judges, Mazarin and Anne consented to disgrace d'Hémery and, in mid-July 1648, to remove most of the *intendants* or strip them of their power to raise taxes. This crack in the surface of "absolute monarchy" encouraged the judges to demand that the finances of the realm be investigated and the tax farmers questioned.

The Parlement appeared victorious—and self-interested, as usual—in revoking the new offices created in 1647. Yet it was clear that Anne and Mazarin were not sincere in making these concessions. Ignorant of the lessons of history, Anne ordered the arrest of several radical judges on August 26. The plot had to be postponed until that Wednesday, because Monday was Saint Bartholomew's Day, and Tuesday the feast of Saint Louis. After a *Te Deum* mass in Notre-Dame, which served as an excuse for the stationing of guards on the Pont-Neuf, Pierre Broussel, an old and respected judge known to the Parisians for his charity to the poor and his attacks on the *hommes de finances,* was kidnapped by royal officials while at his dinner table and sped out of town still wearing his slippers. Broussel's neighbors on the *Cité* tried to prevent the arrest, but guards forced them back all along the bridge. Some of his colleagues shared the same fate. Paris remained calm that night, but the following day, when Chancellor Séguier attempted to reach the *Palais* on the *Cité,* chains and barricades of paving stones and barrels barred every bridge.

Then the Parisians began to throw stones at the chancellor, driving him into the first unlocked house he could find. Later, Marshal de La Meilleraye, on horseback, fought his way into the house to bring the chancellor out and lead him to safety. The bridges and principal streets leading from the *Cité,* the seat of the Parlement, to the Palais-Royal, residence of the Queen Mother and Mazarin, were barricaded and crowded with Parisians shouting, *"Vive le Roi, Vive le Parlement, Vive Monsieur de Broussel."* Clerks and scribes from the courts, bourgeois, petty merchants, and day laborers all joined in a militant protest against Broussel's arrest.

At last the Parlement stood squarely between the crowd and the monarchy. In the afternoon its leaders crossed the barricades to be received by Anne. President de Mesmes explained: "It is a question of nothing less than the loss of the city of Paris, and, through its example, of all the others of the Kingdom. This affair involves the preservation of the State and of the Royalty."

Anne's terms were steep: Broussel could be released only if the Parlement promised "to cease meeting and working on the affairs of individuals." This vague statement served as a pretext for the judges' request for time to return to the *Palais* in order to discuss their next action. But once in the street, they were stopped by the mob. The proprietor of a cook shop put a pistol to the first president's head, blaming him for the Parlement's failure to gain Broussel's release.

The mob forced the judges to return to Anne's residence, the Palais-Royal. There they argued over details, finally agreeing to petition humbly for the release of Broussel and the others, and promising to deliberate on paying the *rentes.* The officers charged with carrying the *lettre de cachet* ordering Broussel's freedom risked their lives in getting through the mob surrounding the Palais-Royal. Though the barricades remained all evening, they quickly fell after Broussel appeared the next morning, calm and in good health. The crisis was over, but nothing was really solved. The Parlement arranged to have the *rentes* paid on the condition that the *droit annuel* be respected. Anne and Mazarin again had conceded, but only temporarily. A secret memorandum that the cardinal addressed to Anne only speaks of erasing the affront to royal authority and of blaming the judges for the insurrection. Never once does Mazarin mention the depression and popular revolts, or in any way see beyond the problems of the war. On occasion he would remark that the poor harvests would make it difficult for the peasantry to pay their taxes, but he seems not to have been very sensitive to rural society in general. He advised the queen to take Louis XIV out of Paris and to wait until things calmed down. In mid-September, Louis, Anne, and Mazarin moved to Rueil (Malmaison), leaving the judges and Gaston d'Orléans solidly in control of the capital.

Negotiations over the power of taxation continued between Anne and the judges, until the promulgation of a great reform *ordonnance* in October 1648. The Crown admitted "disorders and abuses" in the financial administration and henceforth promised to legislate and collect taxes in the customary manner and with the consent of Parlement. On the surface, the judges had won a great victory. Indeed, had Anne negotiated in good faith, absolutism in France would have been replaced by constitutionalism. But Anne and Mazarin had not negotiated in good faith. They had made concessions to the Parlement merely to gain time. The judges thought they had struck a blow for justice and for the defense of fundamental law; they thought they had ruined the financiers and cleared corruption from the state. But in reality the judges had no way of making the Crown uphold the *ordonnance*. Anne violated it before the crisis was over, and the judges were powerless to do anything about it.

The judges at this juncture owed their success to the support of Gaston d'Orléans and of public opinion—support that would continue so long as the interests of the judges concurred with the contradictory interests of the Prince and the public. But this support could not long continue. As Gaston's power increased, other princes, notably Condé, grasped control of the military power of the realm. Mazarin rightly knew that the principal enemies of the state in the long run would be Gaston, Condé, and their cohorts, and not the judges. But in losing the judges because of ill-defined political strategy and financial corruption, Mazarin also lost the Crown's strongest support against the very self-interested leaders of the aristocracy. Now that the judges were beholden to Gaston, law and order depended solely on military power and on a heroic code of honor. Both threatened the stability of the realm as the princes eagerly began a life of violence and civil war.

The judges had gained a victory on paper; the Crown had lost control of Paris. Standing momentarily between the Parisians and the Crown, the judges were soon displaced by the princes. The Parlement could not lead the "fickle, gaping Parisians," and neither could it convince the bourgeois militias to resist Condé. The mere mention of

Condé, victor of Rocroy, ended any resistance on the part of the Parisians to an "invasion" of the capital by the Prince and his troops. Received like a savior by the artisans and the *gagne petits,* Condé felt himself master of Paris. First Gaston, then Condé, La Rochefoucauld, Nemours, Longueville, Conti, and others joined in the rebellion. Ostensibly they aimed to force Mazarin's resignation; but once in control of public opinion, these princes developed an insatiable appetite for money, offices, burnt fields, and pillaged towns. In 1649 Mazarin witnessed the seizure of power by those he had most feared. For almost three years the princes would control much of France.

Just when the upheaval was at its height in 1651, Corneille presented a new tragedy on the subject of the blood feud. *Nicomède* was well received, not because it was better than Corneille's recent failures, but because it mirrored the political melee in which the Parisians found themselves. Not a *pièce à clef* any more than his early tragedies, *Nicomède* nevertheless reflected the reality of the Fronde, since Corneille always sought in tragedy to edify and instruct his audience on the behavior of the *grandes âmes.*

The blood feud in a royal family, the plots and attempted assassinations, and the fate of armies, provinces, and empires in the age of Hannibal were all familiar ground. But here and there Corneille implied explanations for popular rebellion. Laodice, queen of Armenia, plotting for the recovery of Nicomède's birthright, admits that she has encouraged a popular uprising:

> Mais pour moi qui suis reine, et qui dans nos querelles,
> Pour triompher de vous, vous ai fait ces rebelles,
> Par le droit de la guerre il fut toujours permis
> D'allumer la révolte entre ses ennemis.[2]

If the violence of the Fronde upset Corneille, he was incapable of condemning it. He does not use *Nicomède* to condemn the princes' behavior or to repudiate Laodice's justification for causing rebellions. Quite the contrary. Corneille reiterated the old conception that popular uprisings were the consequence of weakness or feuding among members of a ruling family. The play can only be considered as a near apology for the violent behavior of the Frondeur heroes.

---

2.   But for me who am a queen, and who in my quarrels,
       In order to triumph over you, have made these rebels for you,
       By the right of war it has always been permitted
       To kindle revolt against one's enemies.

Condé and his aristocratic cohorts brought extreme anarchy, violence, death, starvation, fear, and large-scale destruction of property. Not since the civil war unleashed by the Guises in the late 1580s had the Parisians suffered so much from blockades, disease, and fear. Once more the capital became the prize; the party that controlled Paris, it was believed, could impose its aims on the realm.

Again the Parlement divided into two main factions. One, a *politique* faction that opposed the princes and supported the Crown, while the detested Mazarin went into exile; and another that stayed in Paris and taxed itself and the bourgeois to support the princes, auctioned off Mazarin's library and set a price on his head, and installed a puppet regime in the Hôtel de Ville under Broussel. The majority of Parisians, including the bourgeois, generally supported the Frondeur princes throughout the period of their rebellion. All Condé had to do, it seemed, was to publish another broadside attacking Mazarin and the Parisians would rally to his banner. Retz remarked on the inability of the Court to understand or to influence public opinion. The only problem was that the princes, who certainly controlled public opinion, had no specific programs or aims to fight for. Mazarinism, as Retz called it, could be used to render mobs hysterical; but this was pointless so long as the princes did not really wish to govern, and so long as neither Gaston nor Condé understood what it meant to formulate policy, pursue the war, and actually govern France.

Armies fighting Spain and loyal to the king had to be brought home to face rebels commanded by France's most famous general. Condé loved a fight. Since he needed a large army, like the Guises he sought and received Spanish aid to support his military operations. By the law of the realm, Condé was not only a rebel but a traitor as well; yet no sovereign court would try him or sentence him to death.

Economic conditions in Paris had been hard enough in the late 1640s. The price of bread had risen steadily. But in 1651 and 1652, when wheat climbed to four times its price in the late 1640s, the Parisians faced conditions similar to those under the League. The death rate doubled in 1651 to 1653 in some if not most of the parishes circling the capital, and the birthrate dropped to a point half that of any time between 1640 and 1660. André Lefèvre d'Ormesson wrote in 1653, "Two-thirds of the villagers around Paris have died from illness, want, and suffering," a contemporary impression confirmed by recent studies.

The ceaseless marauding and pillaging by armies, both royal and Frondeur, had left Paris virtually without food. In view of the poor harvests, bread prices would have been high in any event; but the burning and dislocation caused by the war and the

AVIS QUE DONNE UN FRONDEUR AUX PARISIENS
QU'IL EXORTE DE SE RÉVOLTER CONTRE LA
TYRANNIE DU CARDINAL MAZARIN.

A Frondeur speaking from the Pré-aux-Clercs. This stylized view of political "rabble-rousing" suggests that the Frondeurs, or those curious about the rebellion, came from quite well-off groups. The Tuileries and the Louvre are in the distance.

blockades meant that the Parisians were reduced to subsistence living.[3] To make matters worse, peasants, the aged, and children fled the countryside for Paris with their belongings on their backs or in carts. The fear of the troops was greater than the fear of

3. Some bread riots did occur, but on the whole Condé's presence was enough to keep the Parisians calm under conditions of extreme hardship. Again, as had been the case in the siege against League-controlled Paris, the readiness of the Parisians to riot for food was tempered by fanatical zeal for an ephemeral cause. For his chapter on *Disettes* (food shortages),

starvation. Turenne had about ten thousand troops (including four thousand horse) under his command in April 1652, and Condé had at least seven thousand in his army. The damage this number could do even shocked Condé occasionally when he found that his army would not stop plundering long enough to engage the royal troops in battle.

Behind the ceaseless marauding and the suffering of the Parisians, the interminable intrigues between the princes and the Court continued. No significant issues divided the protagonists; the Fronde at this level was pure Court politics. Men of great power negotiated and deceived one another without any regard for the public interest. Moreover, the princes, among themselves and with Mazarin, completely ignored the rhetoric of rebellion that they had used to capture public opinion. Condé and the other princes did not really detest Mazarinism; they wanted only to weaken royal power and to remove any possibility of their being prosecuted for their violence and treason. The two worlds, that of the public and that of the Court, remained as disconnected in the mind of the princely Frondeur as in that of Mazarin. Only the violence and destruction of property would cause Condé to lose his hold on public opinion, and this would not occur until his armed attack on the Hôtel de Ville in July 1652.

In the interest of peace and Christian charity, Saint Vincent de Paul used his influence to the utmost on behalf of a settlement. He tried to shame the princes into renouncing violence; he appealed to the Queen Mother to return to Paris with the young sovereign, because his people would quiet down if he were present; and he developed and presented to Mazarin cogent and realistic political arguments for peace. The saint condemned argument after argument used by the loyalists to prolong the war. Saint Vincent de Paul knew that it was ridiculous to attempt to punish the Parisians for rebelling. He decried this fundamental tenet of seventeenth-century political psychology to Mazarin:

> Some will perhaps say to Your Excellency that Paris must be punished
> to make it behave; and I think, Monseigneur, that it is expedient that
> Your Eminence remember the behavior of the kings under whom Paris
> has rebelled; he will find that they proceeded gently, and that Charles

---

Nicolas Delamare studied the grain prices in the crucial years and discerned the relationship between high bread prices and popular disturbances. From this unpublished evidence it is clear that both Delamare and La Reynie, whom Delamare advised during the severe grain shortages of the 1680s and 1690s, had some conception of the dynamics of grain price fluctuations, public opinion, and crowd behavior in the capital. Cf. Bibliothèque Nationale, mss. fr. 21641, fols. 159–66. It is also significant that Delamare chose not to publish these findings in his great *Traité de la Police,* probably because he deemed such knowledge too inflammatory for the public.

VI, through having punished a great number of rebels, disarmed them, and removed the chains from the city, only threw oil on the fire and spread the flames to the rest, so that for sixteen years they [the rebels] continued their sedition, contradicted the king more than previously, and to this end allied themselves with all the enemies of the State, and finally that Henry III or the king himself [Louis XIV during the judicial Fronde] gained no advantage in having blockaded them.

Saint Vincent's letter proved that someone was capable of making a historical argument undistorted by myths or crude precedents. Nevertheless, Saint Vincent's peace efforts came to naught.

There was no solidarity among the rebel princes. The crimes they committed against one another in the name of honor resulted in numerous duels and murders. The princes betrayed one another by secretly bargaining with Anne and Mazarin to gain personal advantage. These secret demands seem ridiculous when compared with those made in public. For example, instead of shouting about high taxes and corrupt officials as he did before the *canaille,* Longueville, in his bargaining with Mazarin, asked to be made a prince of the blood. Intermediaries such as Retz and Chavigny, eager to play off one person against the other in order to gain power for themselves, rendered the intrigues unbelievably complex and ludicrous through want of sincerity and realism.

It was at the level of such private demands that the Fronde and Corneillian tragedy became one. The attempts made by Richelieu, and indirectly by Corneille, to curb violence in the aristocracy had failed. An evocation on stage or in art was not enough.

The princes wrote and spoke among themselves about *gloire, race,* and *devoir;* they fought one another unceasingly over love affairs with bold, sensual, and heroic-minded women. So did their followers, the admiring, insecure young sons of the nobility who sought their fortune by fighting courageously under the princes' banners. Condé fought on when he knew there was nothing more to fight for, because he did not want to disappoint his young followers. Moreover, Condé and the other princes were afraid to be accused of cowardice by these heroic adolescents. Though their motives and behavior were quite different from those of the judges who had become Frondeurs, the princes also were forced by circumstances into continuing a rebellion they knew was bound to fail. Gaston d'Orléans, older by a generation and a veteran of more plots and armed rebellions than Condé would ever witness, was labeled a coward and discredited among the young nobles. The leadership fell to Condé, who at the age of thirty could still charge into battle to stay ahead of the bravest and strongest of the wild aristocrats. Gaston lost his taste for violence; Condé did not, except when one of his princely relatives was killed or wounded. This would sadden him and then make him fight harder.

The ethics of intrigue were, however, less barbarous than they had been under Henry III. The plots on Mazarin's life were unsuccessful because they were carried out halfheartedly by individuals possessed of moral scruples. Nor did Anne and Mazarin plot the assassination of Condé. The familiar scene, that of ambushing rebels at a council meeting, was acted out in January 1650; but Mazarin had Condé, Conti, and Longueville imprisoned in Vincennes rather than stabbed to death. The effects of this imprisonment were of course the opposite of what Mazarin had hoped. The rebel cause and the loud cries of the *canaille* grew stronger as the remaining Frondeurs rallied the Southwest for the war of the princely Fronde. Anne finally had to disgrace Mazarin and free Condé. During the summer campaigns, Condé sought to keep open the supply lines leading to Paris. Turenne, of course, sought to blockade the capital and to trap Condé into doing battle with his loyal troops. Henri de la Tour d'Auvergne had slowly come over to the side of Mazarin and the Crown, at least in part as a result of his rivalry with Condé. A Protestant of illustrious birth and linked to prominent ruling families, including the House of Orange, Turenne as a general was a match for Condé.

In July 1652, Turenne finally trapped Condé just outside Paris. Condé had noted the trap and had wanted to move his army through the Faubourg Saint-Germain to safety; but Gaston had prevented him from doing so lest the troops damage his beloved Luxembourg Palace and its gardens. As Turenne closed in, Condé had no choice but to defend himself in the Faubourg Saint-Antoine just beneath the walls of the Bastille.

From the hill of Charonne, Mazarin and Louis XIV watched the preparations for battle; Anne spent the entire day in the Carmelite monastery of Saint-Denis praying for victory. At seven in the morning of July 2, the armies faced one another, ready for battle. Turenne's right charged first, commanded by Saint-Mesgrin, Mancini (a seventeen-year-old nephew of Mazarin's), and Nantouillet. Mancini and Nantouillet had sworn publicly to engage Condé in hand-to-hand combat. Their importance lies not so much in their effect on the battle as in their obsession with being heroes.

The cavalry charge they led down the rue de Charonne was successful; but then, instead of waiting for the slower infantry to clear Condé's snipers from the roofs and balconies, the young commanders led their cavalry straight into the little open place before the Porte Saint-Antoine. Condé, who had placed his reserves here, countercharged immediately.

The battle of the Faubourg Saint-Antoine. The Bastille is in the background, on the right. Smoke from its guns is evident in the middle-ground. Thus this picture captures the battle prior to the moment when the Grande Mademoiselle succeeded in having them turned toward the city instead of toward Condé's army.

In the clash of swords and horses, Mesgrin, Mancini, and Nantouillet were killed instantly *"plein de gloire,"* their cavalry was routed, and even their infantry was swept back by Condé. Turenne had gained nothing, and his right was in no position to make another charge. Nearly the same thing had occurred on the left with the same disastrous results for the loyalist army.

Turenne now had no choice but to charge right down the middle, that is, down the rue du Faubourg Saint-Antoine. He also reached the little open place before the Porte Saint-Antoine, only to be repulsed by a countercharge. Condé had become a wild man, a demigod, riding all over, shouting, killing, risking his life as boldly as possible. Twice Turenne charged down the street, and twice Condé repulsed him, each time inflicting heavy losses upon Turenne. By then it was noon and the heat had grown unbearable. Sensing that Turenne would not charge again for a while, Condé dismounted, embraced his comrades in arms, and, stripping off his armor and clothing, rolled naked in a nearby meadow in an effort to cool off.

Against his better judgment, Turenne had done battle without his artillery. Intimidated by rumors that he was a traitor, he had followed the strategy of impetuosity. Four wild cavalry charges had accomplished nothing. But by noon his artillery had arrived, enabling him to fight the kind of professionalized war he knew better than any commander in Europe. Turenne now devised a trap to draw out Condé from the little open place in a countercharge down the rue Saint-Antoine in order to cut him off between the side streets. The artillery would prevent the prince from returning to the little open place before the gates.

But Condé was too wily to be ensnared. Before it was too late he saw what Turenne was trying to do. The skirmish was intense and bloody, but Condé was not trapped. His friends, among them La Rochefoucauld, were either wounded or exhausted.

The charges ended. Turenne's maneuver had failed, but it had nevertheless permitted his artillery to advance. His cannon could now rake the little open place before the Porte Saint-Antoine. There seemed to be no escape for Condé.

Inside the capital, the Parlement and the *corps de ville* stuck to their resolution not to open the gates to Condé's defeated army. The loyalist armies now controlled the countryside around Paris, including the areas where the judges owned land; the fear of Turenne's troops and of a charge of treason dictated their stern refusal to help Condé. But the populace, as Retz called the crowds, remained hysterically attached to Condé.

Gaston d'Orléans, who had the authority to order the gates opened, had been in bed and out of touch with events most of the day. This was deliberate on his part. He feigned illness in order not to have to decide on Condé's fate. Had he gone out into the streets, the old pressure to act with bravura would have overtaken him. Gaston could have been goaded into playing the part of a hero. As it was, he avoided the public and all possibility of intimidation—save one.

The Prince of Condé. A cousin of the royal family, victor at the Battle of Rocroy, and faithful supporter of the Crown early in the Fronde, in 1651–52 the overbearing Condé led the high aristocracy's rebellion against Mazarin.

His daughter, the Grande Mademoiselle, rushed to see him when Condé's defeat appeared imminent. She pleaded with her father to sign the order that would open the gates. Finally, irresolute as he had been all his life, and desirous to please, Gaston changed his mind and signed the order.

A runner sped from the Luxembourg Palace to the Porte Saint-Antoine, and the gates were opened just in time to allow Condé and his army to escape Turenne's cannon. As the Grande Mademoiselle made her way there, she met remnants of the Frondeur army. She recounts in her *Memoirs*—with that peculiar mixture of honor and glory characteristic of the last heroes—having seen La Rochefoucauld go slowly by her, steadied in the saddle, his eyes seeming to fall out while he kept blowing to clear the blood from his face. Then she met Condé, who told her tearfully: "You behold a man in despair; I have lost all my friends." This was a prescient comment indeed, since the prince thought neither of causes nor of the lives of his troops. In the eloquent memoirs written by these Frondeurs, the only casualties mentioned are their friends, and never the hired infantrymen.

Because of the Grande Mademoiselle's heroic prank, Condé was now in Paris with his troops, but he did not control the city. Though he had the populace on his side, the Parlement and the bourgeois remained hostile. Notables from the Parlement and the *corps de ville* were called to assemble in the Hôtel de Ville on July 4.

Condé wanted to regain control of the capital. Realizing that this time he would have to use force, he decided to intimidate the notables by besieging the Hôtel de Ville. He stationed his troops, identified by a wisp of straw in their hats, in all the houses and on all the rooftops about the Place de la Grève before the Hôtel de Ville. Condé hoped to coerce the notables into naming Gaston lieutenant-general of France, Broussel *prévôt des marchands,* and himself commander-in-chief of the army.

While these preparations were going on, "everybody," says Conrart, put wisps of straw in his hair. Women, children, beggars, horses, and donkeys were decorated with Condé's insignia. Those Parisians refusing to wear this symbolic straw were labeled Mazarinists. Ridiculed and hissed by the crowd, they feared for their lives.

Aware of Condé's scheme, the notables nevertheless attended the meetings. Having kept them waiting for several hours, Condé appeared, haughtily demanding Mazarin's disgrace. The notables asked him to retire to an adjoining room that they might deliberate. Instead Condé motioned to leave; but he first stepped out onto a balcony and proclaimed to the crowd in the Grève that the notables were Mazarinists and procrastinators.

Condé had counted on his troops and on his presence to intimidate the three hundred notables, but he had miscalculated. They remained firm and eager to treat with the Crown to end the civil war. Their resolution left Condé no choice but to leave and to order his troops to open fire.

During the blaze of musket fire, the notables crouched beneath the windows and crowded into closets. Some, including a number of *gentilshommes,* bribed their way out; others disguised themselves by exchanging clothes with their lackeys before escaping. But most of the notables had no choice and had sought no other choice but to remain trapped by the musket fire. At least twenty-five bourgeois notables and two bourgeois militia colonels, including Miron de Tremblay, were killed.

Outside, the *curé* of Saint-Jean-en-Grève came forward into the square, bearing an ancient, much-reputed miraculous host "in order that the fire might be put out and the populace appeased," says the chronicler of the Company of the Holy Sacrament. But Condé's troops knocked down the *curé* "and committed violences on him unworthy of Christians and Catholics." The notables tried but could not sue for terms from Condé. They dropped little pieces of paper out of the windows, each with the word *UNION* hastily inscribed on it to indicate their willingness to govern with the princes. But Condé had gone. Once the firing had begun, negotiations or concessions were out of the question.

In the months that followed, Condé attempted to convert his military victory into effective control of the capital. Old Broussel was again "elected" *prévôt des marchands,* but the Parisians knew that Condé's authority rested solely on his guns. His attack on the Hôtel de Ville had lost him control over the populace. The horror of July 4 and the withdrawal of many judges and bourgeois from public life left Condé to control a capital without food or government. Gaston maneuvered but failed to reach a reconciliation with Anne and Mazarin. He withdrew from Paris into self-exile. Though Condé carried on the fight abroad as commander of a Spanish army, the Fronde ended in the fall of 1652 when Mazarin returned at the head of an army he had recruited himself. Mazarin and the royal family were warmly received in Paris.

The attack on the Hôtel de Ville showed that Condé did not consider seriously the interests of the Parisians. The bourgeois, and perhaps even the artisans, were growing tired of violence, for it damaged property and adversely affected business. They again turned for leadership and order to the *corps de ville* and to Mazarin. The Parlement was also eager to restore that web of authority and law that it had helped to break. And never again would Corneille's tragedies receive quite the same overwhelming approval from the Parisians.

The failure of both the judicial and princely Frondes reinforced the tradition that the *honnêtes gens*—the bourgeois and the artisans—should look to the king for law and order. But any faint hope that the Parisians could govern themselves under the medieval constitution of the *corps de ville* or that the Parlement could rule was dashed for over a century. Not until after 1750 would educated Parisians again think themselves capable of governing in their interests better than the king.

In February 1651, just as the stalemate of the princely Fronde deepened, Louis XIV made his stage debut as a ballet dancer in *Cassandre.* Though his role was not very

Louis XIV, portrait by Mignard engraved by Poilly, 1660. Still wearing the old-fashioned collar of the mid-century, the king had long before learned to gaze out with serenity and with an air of dominance. He is twenty-two in this portrait.

demanding, the king inspired awe by his self-assured steps, his leaps, his firm gestures, and the almost terrifying *gravitas* in his facial expression. Only twelve, he opened a ball by dancing a *courante* with his cousin, the Grande Mademoiselle, a difficult dance with a complex rhythm. The rules required the couple to dance alone before the entire Court.

Dancing was an art to be mastered by anyone with ambition to make a mark at Court in seventeenth-century France. There were a number of dancing masters in the capital, and virtually the entire nobility learned to dance the *courante,* the *bourée,* and the *branle.* Louis XIV was a naturally gracious dancer and a perfect student. For most of his young-adult years, he would continue to take lessons and practice. From 1651 to 1669, when he ceased dancing in public, the king would dance in some forty major ballets, performing as many as eighty roles. In 1661 he became personally engaged in founding a royal academy for the dance, and he took pleasure in rewarding and recognizing the art that his teachers and their colleagues had not only taught him to love but had made a part of his very nature and being.

The Fronde—especially under the control of the captivating and heroic rebel, Condé—had a profoundly theatrical dimension to it. His gestures and his sometimes peremptory manners fascinated contemporaries. He had defeated the Spanish army at Rocroy in 1643, when he was only twenty-one. Mademoiselle de Scudéry enhanced his heroic persona and made him bigger than life in her novel *Artamène ou le Grand Cyrus,* which appeared during the Fronde in ten volumes, in serial fashion, and totaled 13,095 pages in length. As the princely rebellion was defeated and driven back, time and again, during the death throes of the Fronde, the velvet garbed, diamond- and ruby-encrusted clothing and person of the Sun King, at once self-confident and triumphant, literally set the stage in Paris for what would be known as "the Century of Louis XIV." The king first appeared as the sun god Apollo in a ballet in 1653, in the final part of a multipart sequence danced between three and six in the morning.

A Generation of Tartuffes

The religious revival begun under Henry IV came to an end in a storm of theological controversy in 1656. The consequences of its demise were immediate and far-reaching for French society, particularly for the poor, because an ominous program of social and moral repression was born out of the failure to maintain the principles of simple Christian charity after 1656.

The religious revival had been accompanied by an extensive and quite disinterested program of charity. The work of Saint Vincent de Paul in particular had come to symbolize this charity, which, regardless of the moral condition of the needy individual, cared for his body and soul. But after 1656 the charity program changed character. It became moralistic, repressive, and politically authoritarian.

The statesmen and interest groups that destroyed the religious revival gained control of the royal agencies that administered charity, justice, the police, hospitals, and minor courts of law. Louis XIV's innovations in the Parisian administration, principally the establishment of the office of lieutenant of police, provided the power to enforce the moral and social program of the victors of 1656. Indeed, the events of that year largely determined the Crown's political, economic, and moral policies until the end of the *Ancien Régime* toward those elements of society that were repugnant to the upper classes.

As early as 1640 charities coming under the control of laymen lacked the simple devotion of the founding saints of the religious revival. Instead of Christian compassion for one's fellow man in sincere religious humanitarianism, charity to the laymen was seen as an instrument for cleansing society of "vice-ridden" persons: beggars, prostitutes, Protestants, nonconformists in thought and dress, the aged, and the insane.

The laity's gaining this control is explained by the triumph of the unreformed clergy, both secular and regular, over the leaders of the religious revival. At first this pressure was subtle; but once Richelieu sided with the unreformed clergy against the saints and their followers, it was only a matter of time before the revival was snuffed out.

Unreformed? It is paradoxical that Richelieu pressed for reform in monasteries, convents, and schools while opposing various devotional theological tendencies; but he had very strong views on all matters of religion and its relation to the state and society.

In the 1630s it became personally dangerous for clergymen to continue practicing the devotional innovations and ethical programs of the saints. The cardinal intervened to purge the leadership of both wings of the revival by undermining Bérulle's activities and by imprisoning Saint-Cyran. The followers of these revivalists, the young clergy, found themselves condemned by the state for having associated with these men. Failure to conform meant ostracism by the large body of unreformed clergy headed by Richelieu.

The cardinal's purge stifled the leadership of the revival, though it did not immediately kill the revival itself. But as the generation of reforming saints died, no young clergymen spiritually and intellectually capable of leading the revival stepped forward to replace them. Bondoise's efforts to train parish priests at Saint-Nicolas-du-Chardonnet would be strengthened by Olier's seminary at Saint-Sulpice. Jean-Jacques Olier and his Sulpicians strove to raise the educational and spiritual level of parish priests because there was a dearth of younger ordained leaders in the movement after 1640, with the result that the leadership of the revival fell to zealous laymen. Princes and dukes or prominent magistrates—Ventadour,[1] Jacques Adhémar de Monteil, and later Conti and Liancourt—joined the Arnaulds as leaders on the Jansenist side, while the Lamoignons supported the Molinist or Jesuit side of the revival.

At first the lay leaders, particularly those from the nobility of the robe, were preoccupied with founding institutions to effect their devotional and moral programs. Two particularly strong institutions were dominated by laymen. By 1640 the Company of the Holy Sacrament was a thriving, ultrasecret, ostensibly apolitical organization that

---

1. As an act of piety, Ventadour publicly announced that he would cease sexual relations with his wife.

aspired to become realm-wide, not merely Parisian. Port Royal was also growing very strong by the same date under lay leadership.

Whether inclined toward the Jesuits or the Jansenists, the *dévots,* as they were called, were similar in that their primary concern was moral reform and social conformity rather than spiritual edification. The heady controversies over the nature of grace carried on by the leaders of what were fast becoming two wings of the revival did not affect the lives or aims of the thousands of lay supporters supplying the money and political support for the religious revival. Not until 1649 did it become clear to laymen that the religious revival had split into two competing groups, so preoccupied were they with organizational matters and with what they called charity.[2]

From its beginning in about 1630, the Company of the Holy Sacrament sought to repress Protestantism and to enforce a moral code against "public sins." It also protested against usury, which it recognized as widespread, and sought to provide legal services for those who could not afford them; but as the Company grew stronger and bolder, prudish morals became its preoccupation and the principal force for attracting new members. The Jansenist moral preoccupations differed little from those of the Company, but these became obscured by the theological campaign started by Antoine Arnauld.

Owing to the failure of spiritual leadership and the declining influence of Saint Vincent de Paul and Olier over the laymen, zealots in the Company and at Port Royal allowed their own social values to become identified in their minds with Christian social action. In the Company genuine concern for the welfare of peasants who were robbed upon arriving in Paris gave way to an obsession with controlling the press so that it would not publish pornography or libelous pamphlets. The essentially medieval corporatist concern for suppressing work on holidays declined as members sought to clear all prostitutes from the streets. The members of the Company opposed allowing Jews to buy property in the countryside. They founded schools to provide instruction for those "newly converted" to Catholicism.

When Huguenots established hospitals in Paris, the Company would swing into action. Members would see to it that the hospitals were raided and closed, after which the Huguenot beds would be carted off and donated to the Hôtel-Dieu. The Company used every means at its disposal to impede Protestants from being admitted into guilds

---

2. Renty, one of the leading *dévots* of the Company, from his deathbed exhorted his Jansenist friends to abandon Port Royal. He died from exhaustion after climbing stairs to the fifth-floor lodgings of the Parisian poor in order to give them bread during the siege of 1649.

and other corporations; in 1655 the Parisian Company was reaching out to stop the admission of Protestant doctors into the *corps de médecins* in far-off Rouen. Members influential at Court and close to Chancellor Séguier pressed him to add clauses to all *lettres de maîtrise* that would require membership in the "Catholic and Roman Religion" before a guildsman could practice his trade. Other members at Court pressed for a declaration against "Bohemians"; but in the case of Bohemians, who were defined as anyone leading immoral, degraded, and corrupt lives, the Company met with little success until the Crown adopted its policy of seeking to repress all nonconformists.

As early as 1634 the Company was scandalized by the *galenterie ouverte et caquet perpetuel* that went on during mass in upper-class parishes. It took measures to stop these "disorders," as members exhorted *curés* and confessors to use the confessional as a means for repressing these activities. Then: "At that time women adopted the fashion of wearing their bosom excessively uncovered. This contributed greatly to the disorders and scandals occurring in churches. Thus the entire Company urged individuals to warn the confessors with whom they were acquainted to work at correcting this abuse, especially if [the ladies] were so imprudent as to approach the communion table in that condition." Thus began a long campaign against the wearing of low-cut dresses. Immoral in the extreme because it "greatly distracted the priests and communicants," any overt sensuality had to be repressed. This campaign would be extended to an attack on the theater, poetry, and dancing.

This modish prudery soon developed into a veritable campaign to change the manners, language, and family relationships in upper-class Parisian society. In the *dévot* family itself, this pious affectation added tensions and quarrels because invariably not every member would conform to it. External appearances preoccupied the *dévot;* ideally he was always grave, obsessed by his private devotions, confessions, and instruction in the pious life. He should never be seen at the theater. Rather, *dévots* should spend their time visiting the sick or instructing prisoners in the ways of righteousness. Denial of the flesh became the principal outward sign of grace; sex was no longer mentioned in polite society, and conversations were cleansed of all bawdy words. The glory of work was perpetually extolled.

The *dévot* affectation by 1650 had grown so strong that it was reinforcing the old claim of parents to marry off their children as they wished, regardless of the feelings of the persons involved. The law courts supported these parents by stricter legislation that required parental consent for marriage. Class distinctions were reinforced as well, for *dévots* used this moralistic piety to set themselves apart from artisans and servants.

In Molière, the head of the household vainly attempts to correct his servants' language and to punish them for any expression of overt sensuality in their speech, whether among themselves or with the children of their master. The chief objection was the *péché public,* the sin which, since others could witness it, weakened the moral conformity of the entire society.

The chief offenders were of course prostitutes, beggars, vagabonds, *gens sans aveu* (literally, persons who could not declare who they were, their work, or their residence), and libertines. Not only did these persons themselves sin, but they attracted others to everything that was "nasty and sordid." The *dévots* campaigned relentlessly against them all; and, realizing that sermons would not be enough, they developed a rationale for removing physically from society those persons who were offensive to them. Once locked up in "hospitals" for varying periods of time, beggars and prostitutes would, it was believed, correct their ways, become pious, and cease to corrupt mankind by "their bad example."

This was the theory that became the basis for a massive program for purifying or cleansing Parisian society. Saint Vincent de Paul and other members of the religious revival led the movement at first, but they withdrew as zealous laymen turned charitable undertakings into programs of social repression.

Neither the medieval Hôtel-Dieu, which was in dire need of funds, nor the Grand Bureau of the Poor were favored institutions for the *dévots.* These foundations had a tradition of caring for the sick and of giving charity without intensive moral correction. Nor did Saint Vincent's Lazarist movement provide the corrective institutions desired by the *dévots.*

The result was a campaign for a general hospital. Beginning in the mid-1630s and continuing down to the founding of the General Hospital in 1656, the *dévots* pressed persons influential in the government to have the Crown sponsor such an institution. At once prison, workhouse, hospital, house of correction, and asylum for the insane, the General Hospital was required for a morals campaign. The Company of the Holy Sacrament made the establishment of the Hospital its principal aim or "work."

At first the theological controversies did not affect lay efforts to launch the General Hospital. Indeed the theological controversy was over the heads of most *dévots;* nor were they deeply concerned about it until 1649, when Nicolas Cornet launched a covert attack on Arnauld in the Sorbonne. What had previously been simply a tendency of *dévots* to be attracted either to Jansenist Port Royal or to the Company now turned into a fierce competition between the two groups. Pope Innocent X in 1653

Visiting the prisoners, by Abraham Bosse. The biblical exhortation to visit prisoners was repeated in sermons as part of the charitable reformist program that was neither specifically Catholic nor Protestant. The subject permitted artistic playfulness about interior and exterior.

condemned the so-called *Five Propositions* attributed to Jansen, and said to be also in Arnauld's works, after which it was impossible for all but the most prominent *dévots* to continue to visit Port Royal while still remaining affiliated with the Company and supporting its General Hospital.

Just when Mazarin and Secretary of State Michel Le Tellier, who was a *dévot* himself, perceived that the social program dear to all *dévots* had become the essential element of the religious revival is unclear. But after 1653, burdened with a papal condemnation and with its greater emphasis on withdrawal from the world, Port Royal was losing its appeal. In the war of polemics, Arnauld adroitly defended Port Royal by suggesting that the *Five Propositions* could not be attributed to Jansen; but this move did not gain large-scale support for the monastery among the mass of fashionable *dévots.* The program of moral purification, emphasis on outward signs of piety, and avoidance of theological quibbles attracted larger and larger numbers of pious Parisians.

Arnauld's failure to win over the *dévots* could have been fatal to Port Royal as early as 1655 had not some accidents occurred that gave Jansenism a new basis of support. For example, the persistent Frondeur, Cardinal Retz, became archbishop of Paris at this critical juncture; and Retz refused to cooperate with the Crown. This deprived Mazarin and the Jesuits of the customary ecclesiastical authority to suppress a theological quarrel. Though not a Jansenist himself, Retz refused to do the bidding of the enemies of Port Royal. The theologians of the Sorbonne censured Arnauld and withdrew his degrees, but they alone could not deal a deathblow to the Jansenist movement. Sensing defeat, however, Arnauld sought support from the traditional ally of Port Royal, the Parlement, but this time the judges refused to become involved. Guillaume de Lamoignon, a prominent member of the Company, and other *dévot* judges blocked Arnauld's efforts to use the Parlement. Since this was not a case of violation of Gallican liberties, as had been claimed in 1640, the Jansenist cause was without Parlementary support.

Mazarin called an Assembly of the Clergy to deal with both Retz and Arnauld. After months of deliberation the Assembly finally condemned Jansenism; but, like the Sorbonne, the Assembly lacked sufficient power to silence Arnauld. The Jansenist movement was dying on its own, however, as former adherents of Port Royal joined the Company of the Holy Sacrament or simply severed their ties with Port Royal. The campaign for the General Hospital gained strength rapidly after 1653 as increasingly more *dévots* became obsessed with charity rather than with theology.

Then the anti-Jansenists blundered. Sensing victory, they overstepped themselves and gave Arnauld an issue that could be publicized to devastating effect. The Duke of Liancourt, a very prominent *dévot,* still kept his ties with both Port Royal and the Company. His great piety and prestige made him a prize for whichever party could hold his allegiance. A duke on their side was more important than the adherence of hundreds of bourgeois to these competing parties; hence Jansenists and Jesuits alike fawned on Liancourt.

With victory against Port Royal close at hand, Liancourt's confessor at Saint-Sulpice decided to refuse absolution to the pious duke until he renounced Port Royal. The confessor had consulted Olier, a prominent anti-Jansenist member of the Company, so the confessor's decision clearly was not a mere accident by a minor clergyman. The refusal to grant Liancourt absolution became a policy in the anti-Jansenist party.

Liancourt informed Arnauld, and after some negotiations Arnauld decided to rush the news of this refusal before the public. He had an issue with which to castigate his enemies. Unlike a controversy over the nature of grace, the refusal to grant a pious man absolution could be developed in order to mobilize the large *dévot* public. In his *Letter to a Duke and Peer,* and in a succeeding pamphlet, Arnauld asked by what right could a priest deny absolution to a truly penitent Christian. Overnight these pamphlets gave new life to the Jansenist cause. Then Arnauld asked for and received the cooperation of Blaise Pascal. With the help of Jansenist theologians, Pascal wrote the *Provincial Letters,* the most successful attack ever made on the Society of Jesus and the Company of the Holy Sacrament.

Beginning in January 1656, and appearing frequently throughout that year, these anonymous letters aroused a revulsion against the Jesuits and the Company. Pascal began by slashing the pronouncements of Molina and other Jesuits on the doctrine of grace; he then turned to attack the Jesuits' ethical teachings. In early December 1656, Guy Patin wrote: "All these new letters are so effective with the upright folk [*honnêtes gens*] that the poor Jesuits no longer know where they stand. One can only reply to these letters—*quae jugulum petunt,* they make such an impression upon the minds of reasonable people—that if these Master Passefins had no credit at Court, they would already be worse off than the Cordeliers." Patin was anti-Jesuit, of course, but he was correct. The Jesuits did have support at Court.

As each new letter circulated rapidly through Paris, the *dévots* began to frequent Port Royal in increasingly greater numbers. That summer, first the *curés* of Rouen and then some in Paris, began to call for an examination of the charges made in the *Letters* against the Jesuits. In the fall of 1656 it seemed that Port Royal might actually reduce the power of the Jesuits and of the Company of the Holy Sacrament by winning the public to its cause.

But the *dévots* were attracted by more than the *Letters:* miracles began to occur at Port Royal. Authenticated by pious and eminent personages, these miracles caused thousands of *dévots* to visit the little valley southwest of Paris where Port-Royal-des-Champs, the abbey's rural house, was located. Partly out of curiosity, partly out of devotion, and also in hopes of a spiritual awakening or a cure for themselves, the *dévots* went in such alarming numbers that Olier sought a royal sanction against visiting Port

Royal. Mazarin hesitated, however, in part because he himself was impressed by the sincere piety of the Arnaulds, whom he also knew to be intellectually gifted. The cardinal himself had requested some holy water from Port Royal.

Pascal, mathematician, philosopher, and scientist, had broken the web of scholastic categories that dominated Jesuit theology. Instead of hairsplitting, he boldly pointed out the contradictions, illogical assumptions, and generally weak-minded reasoning of later medieval scholasticism. There is a literalist and reductionist tone in Pascal's discussion of Christian ethics, because he insists on the validity of first, obvious principles. He evokes the mystical brotherhood of Christ and the authority of the early church fathers to demonstrate how a distortion of the first principles of faith, love, charity, and the Ten Commandments had allowed the Jesuits to condone ethical practices specifically forbidden by those first principles. The web of casuistry was broken as Pascal undermined the ethical teachings of the reformed, Tridentine Church. After discussing grace, Pascal avoided matters of doctrine; thus he could remain critical without overstepping the limits of orthodoxy.

The *Provincial Letters* circumscribe a century of ethical controversy that had gone on within the Church. From the attacks made by the later Erasmians against the Jesuits, to the *Provincial Letters,* and on to the attacks made by the Philosophes in the Enlightenment, the ethics of the Society, not its doctrines, were grounds that could be attacked most effectively. Nor did Pascal merely attack early Jesuits like Molina; he examined works published in his own lifetime by members of the Society, like Escobar, and found in them the same casuistic tendencies to distort the fundamental ethical teachings of Christ.

Instead of singling out Jesuit teaching on regicide, which had been done often enough, Pascal went deeper to examine the reasons for which one man might, according to the Jesuits, put another to death. Pascal avoided the texts that usually attracted polemicists and concentrated on the grounds for putting a man to death when he threatens the state. The result was a final blow to propositions that had served to condone regicide. But as if it were not enough to demonstrate the contradictions in the positions themselves, Pascal attacked the very method that had produced them: "For here again, Fathers, is one of the subtlest artifices of your politics, to separate in your writings the maxims that you combine in your opinions. It is thus that you have established separately your doctrine of probability that I have often explained. And this general principle having been established, you propose things separately, which though innocent in themselves, become horrible when joined to this pernicious principle."

Rigidly orthodox, Pascal could knock down the edifice whereby the Jesuits had been able to compromise Christian doctrine with contemporary political, social, and economic conventions. On the power of the state, on usury, on charity, as well as on grace, Pascal reiterated Christ's dictum: "My Kingdom is not of this World." He himself and his sister Jacqueline, who became a nun at Port Royal, were deeply devout. Pascal's answer to the question of whether or not God existed was answered in the most logical and personal way. Faced with choosing whether or not God exists, Pascal argued that it is in the individual's interest to bet that He does exist, which makes salvation possible. Wagering in favor of God's nonexistence meant, on the other hand, eliminating any possibility of life after death. And for Pascal, mathematics and physics had an absolute certainty, for they were part of the divine creation of the universe.

In the storm of 1656, the Jesuits, next to Pascal, proved to be their own worst enemies. They blundered in their attempt to refute the *Provincial Letters* by resorting to *ad hominem* attacks. Thinking they were back in the sixteenth century, and ignoring the fact that the *dévot* public was educated enough to understand the *Letters,* the Jesuits called their anonymous author a heretic, a creature of the Antichrist, and a viper. The *dévots* attracted to Port Royal now remained unmoved by these refutations. They admired the style and sheer brilliance of the *Provincial Letters.*

But public success, especially of this negative sort, meant little if it could not be converted into political force. Here Arnauld and Pascal failed. The Jansenist program of prayer and withdrawal from the world could not gain the acceptance of upper-class *dévot* Parisians. They had experienced this life in the *collège,* and those called by God to a monastery had answered the call; but Jansenism failed to appeal to those committed to a secular life.

The political force needed to change the temper of the Sorbonne, the Parlement, the upper clergy, and the court never materialized. Consequently Mazarin had no difficulty in repressing Port Royal once the furor over the *Provincial Letters* had died down. The program to purify society through the establishment of a general hospital became still more attractive to the Parisian *dévots* and the Crown. It appeared as a truly worthy, charitable cause because the presence of vice and poverty did evoke in the *dévots* a kind of Christian guilt. Moreover, the program to purify society by uplifting the sinful elements was not doctrinally suspect. Pope Alexander VII's bull *Ad Sacrum,* coming as it did in the early spring of 1657, reinforced *dévot* sensibilities against Port Royal. True to itself, the Parlement did not wish to approve the bull because it marked interference by the papacy in a French ecclesiastical controversy; but by 1657 the Jansenist cause was lost. Pascal ceased writing the *Provincial Letters* in the same month that *Ad Sacrum* was presented to Louis XIV. At the same time, the Company of the Holy Sacrament at last realized its highest aim.

The *Annals* of the Company of the Holy Sacrament recount briefly the founding of the General Hospital:

> On September 28, Monsieur de Plessis-Montbar made a report on the progress that God was granting the work on the General Hospital: he said that its letters patent had been verified, and that the directors had taken the oath in the Grand Chamber; he strongly recommended this great work to the prayers of the Company that first conceived it and that had laid its foundations by persons he had named for this purpose. That it was from it [this work] that they had gained their greatest blessing, through the success that could be seen and that had long been so universally desired.

This was brief in the extreme, and modest as well, for such a significant event. Antoine Godeau, a member of the French Academy who had marshaled the clergy in assembly to condemn Jansenism, made the dedicatory speech. He was the leading preacher of the time.

Of the twenty-six lifetime directors of the General Hospital, twelve were members of the Company. The institution was royally sponsored and governed by laymen charged with the responsibility of raising funds to administer a vast program of charity. It would administer together the Hospitals of the Pitié, Salpêtrière, Bicêtre, La Savonnerie, and Scipion to care for beggars, the aged and infirm, prostitutes, orphans, foundlings, the insane, and pregnant and nursing women. Each of these hospitals would specialize in caring for just one or two of these groups, though they would be administered collectively. In the general context of Parisian public care, they only supplemented the older hospitals, since the General Hospital was instituted primarily for those not previously considered a public burden. The local officials in the neighborhoods, known as the *quarteniers,* and the Bureau of the Poor had aided those persons who were thought of as a public nuisance, but now they were to be removed from society and either reformed or permanently sent away from the capital. Beggars, Bohemians, vagabonds or wanderers, and prostitutes had long been considered a public nuisance and had frequently been rounded up or temporarily imprisoned. Now they would be interned in hospitals because of these activities and not for reasons of health. The *dévots* firmly believed that by removing this element from society, and by informing it through sermons of God's punishments for this way of life—with said lessons reinforced with hard labor, poor food, and public shame—the population as a whole would fear and thus shun these moral failings. Those interned were used as examples to the potentially corrupt and lazy.

Beneath the rhetoric of Christian charity that served as a rationale for the General Hospital there existed a harsh moral explanation of human behavior. The *dévots* could not perceive economic or social causes for immorality, crime, and poverty. Their sole explanation for these conditions was a moral one: vice caused poverty. It led to laziness, immorality, unemployment, begging, stealing, and other crimes. The *dévots* fondly believed that persons who begged did so simply because they were too lazy to work. They also liked to believe that the wounds, ulcers, tattered clothes, and filthy, vermin-ridden style of life led by beggars were part of an act. That sound "sturdy beggars" went into the *cour des miracles* to make themselves up with putty and animal blood was *"connu de tout le monde."* The upper-class Parisians wanted to believe that those who begged were not really poor, but lazy and corrupt.

The *fainéant,* or do-nothing, was loathed by the *dévots.* Not to work was sin itself, and to beg or walk the streets marked further moral degeneration. The General Hospital undertook to instill the "Christian virtue" of steady employment into the minds of persons whose existence had always been precarious and whose lot had not been improved by work. The *fainéants,* beggars, and prostitutes were refugees from the land; the seasons had provided a rhythm of life for plowing, sowing, and harvesting. Now the *dévots* sought to adapt these persons to the rigors and work habits of urban, preindustrial society. Even in the Company there were, of course, persons who were motivated by charitable feelings toward the poor; but, in general, help for the hungry and homeless was rarely comprehended in simple humane terms.

Having fled the land in search of charity, the *fainéants* were now either told to return home or were interned in a hospital and subjected to a program in which the fear of hell and public shame provided motives for improvement. Mostly landowners themselves, the *dévots* were just as concerned with stopping the influx of laborers off their farms as with improving the moral climate of the capital. The fear that there would be no peasants to harvest the crops was the only economic motive among the otherwise stern moral considerations listed in the royal edicts after 1660. The number of *fainéants* increased steadily between 1630 and 1670. Beggars accosted pedestrians everywhere in the capital; citizens had to fight their way through crowds of them at church entrances. The number of petty crimes ebbed and flowed according to the availability of work, as *fainéants* desperate for food stole from merchants, broke into houses, and robbed citizens in the streets.

The elite Parisians saw all this in moral and religious terms. As with their attitudes toward the aristocratic life of violence, the Parisians clung to conceptions that explained poverty and misery as the consequence of sin and man's fallen nature. The results of religious fanaticism had led Henry IV to reject this conception. His social legislation reflected an awareness of quite secular and economic reasons for the well-being of his subjects and the prosperity of his realm. But once the *dévots* had revived the conception that poverty stemmed from vice, spiritual and moral factors once again predominated in social legislation. For the aristocracy and the poor, secular aims were rejected and spiritual idealism took their place. The shadow of modernity that had fallen over Paris under Henry IV evaporated in a lay-controlled religious revival.

In the first year of its activity, the General Hospital cared for about six thousand poor. Economic conditions were so grave that the very poor had to come first, which left little space for the internment of beggars and prostitutes. Moreover, the influence of radical Christian charity, represented by the disciples of Saint Vincent de Paul, had not yet altogether disappeared. But in late 1657 it seems that the special police, the "archers of the poor," began their rounds to remove beggars and other socially objectionable persons from the street. This "work" seems to have gained public support rapidly, since contributions to the General Hospital increased.

Once inside the hospitals, internees were subjected to a regular discipline of prayers, sermons, forced labor, and, if needed, floggings. Public shame played its part, for those interned had to wear special uniforms; intractable prostitutes had their heads shaved. Division of the hospitals according to the reasons for internment assured special care for persons with such different conditions as insanity and malnutrition. But eliminating mendicity and *fainéantisme* became the principal aim; and it was clearly the biggest task, since most persons after about 1670 were interned for those reasons. Laymen were expected to come to visit them, to set an example of virtue and piety for them, and to "catechise" them. Workshops were established in hospitals to keep the *fainéants* employed.

In the early years of the General Hospital, persons were interned for only two weeks; but internment was soon prolonged to from four to six weeks, probably because so many discharged were again picked up by archers of the poor for having "reverted to

The great road to the Hospital, by Jacques Lagniet. The assembled proverbs about poverty prompt ironic thoughts in the beholder, as the watchman, with his pike, pushes the poor toward the General Hospital.

their evil ways." Conditions in the hospitals were so overcrowded, humiliating, and physically dangerous that after about 1670 the fear of internment in the General Hospital may have acted as a check on the number of beggars and *fainéants* in the capital. In the 1680s the number interned rose to nearly fifteen thousand per year, but this number was not exceeded because the enormous hospitals built by Louis XIV at Salpêtrière and Bicêtre could hold no more. When the Invalides, a hospital for discharged soldiers, was opened in 1677, six thousand more indigents were removed from the streets and run-down rooming houses of Paris.

While the General Hospital was capturing the imagination and hopes of the *dévots,* the Company of the Holy Sacrament consolidated its position and bureaucratic control over charity. It had become a very web-organized corporate entity[3] with more than sixty secret cells in the realm. Its elders, treasury officials, recorders, and secret correspondents made the Company a force to be reckoned with in society. But religious sentiment remained simplistic and superstitious. When the body of Gaston de Renty, one of the founders, was exhumed in 1649, ten years after his death, so that it might be placed in a more sumptuous tomb, several members of the Company were awestruck by the fact that from the waist up his body showed no decay. His eyes, it seems, had remained well preserved, for they "were as beautiful as when he was buried." This transfer, to a contemporary *dévot,* of the venerable medieval beliefs and practices about the holiness of the saintly dead was not unique in the seventeenth century.

The secret network enabled the Company to become informed of the religious and social life of most urban centers. This successful gathering of information contributed to its downfall after bishops and royal ministers discovered that the *dévots* of the Company knew more about what was going on in the provinces than they themselves did. The upper clergy led the campaign against the Company of the Holy Sacrament. For example, Harlay de Chanvalon, Archbishop of Rouen, was known by the Company to be its enemy at Court. The *Annals* state: "The princes' jealousy of the priests in the end pushed him [Harlay] before Pilate, and the prelates animated by hatred and by resentment toward the Company, to revenge themselves for its zeal, rendered it [the Company] so suspect before the temporal power that they determined to annihilate it."

---

3. This corporate identity was clearly perceived by the members. In the *Annals* for 1660: "Cette application particulière selon les sentiments de Saint François de Sales et selon les conduites et les manières d'agir de toutes les communautés s'appelle l'esprit du corps, c'est son formel, c'est ce qui le distingue des autres corps. C'est son moyen propre pour tendre à la fin commune de la parfaite charité. Par cette connoissance de l'esprit du corps les particuliers qui en sont les membres jugent que doit être leur emploi, à quoi ils sont appellés et ce qu'ils doivent faire pour coopérer aux desseins de Dieu dans les différentes sociétés où ils se trouvent liés."

The charity hospital, by Abraham Bosse. Like visiting prisoners, feeding the sick was a charitable duty. Here Anne of Austria and her lady-in-waiting oversee the distribution of food. Children play in the ward. At the end of the ward is an altar where mass was said daily.

This suggests that the unreformed clergy opposed the Company for the same reasons that it had opposed the religious revival, though there were exceptions. Not even lay reform, when it involved large sums of money for charity, would be condoned by the bishops and parish clergy unless they could control it.

At Court, Anne of Austria—and perhaps Michel Le Tellier—at first defended the Company, but Mazarin's opposition led to the Company's suppression. Deeming it "larger at the beginning than the League," the cardinal considered it bad politics to allow such a secret and corporatist institution to exist within the state. His views about the Huguenots were influenced by the same ideas, though he generally respected the rights they had been granted by the Edict of Nantes, as diminished by the Grace of Alais (1629).

The General Hospital had drawn off the religious zeal of the *dévots;* and once the Crown stepped in to help with the "work" in 1656, it was only a matter of timing before the Company of the Holy Sacrament would be declared illegal. Mazarin decided to purge one *dévot* organization at a time, starting with the Company. In 1660 he ordered the Parlement to register an *arrêt* forbidding all secret societies, a step clearly aimed at the Company. One of its most prominent members, Lamoignon, who was First President of the Parlement, assured members of the Company that he had done everything possible to soften the blow of the *arrêt*. Yet Lamoignon may well have played the part of Judas, since the *arrêt* was accepted without a struggle, though he could have brought the Parlement to oppose Mazarin.

Only after the Company had begun to disband in 1661 did the Crown openly attack Port Royal. Jansenist strength had declined considerably since 1657. Public support had diminished because the lack of persecution had given the Jansenists little notoriety. Also, Jansenist leaders had begun to disagree among themselves on which course of action to take following Alexander VII's condemnation of Jansen's errors.

In 1661 those at Court like Anne of Austria who had winced at the suppression of the Company now pressed eagerly for the dissolution of Port Royal. Led by Chancellor Séguier, the Council of State in the spring of that year required Jansenists to sign a formulary that was deemed acceptable only to orthodox Catholics. Arnauld's efforts to condemn the formulary by arousing public opinion against it failed. The Assembly of the Clergy, which was controlled by the Crown, also supported the campaign to dissolve Port Royal.

Those living at Port Royal who were not subject to its vows were expelled in the same year. Then in 1663, after Péréfixe became Archbishop of Paris, even the nuns, including saintly old Agnès Arnauld, were dispersed to other monastic houses. Some leading Jansenists, such as Isaac Le Maistre de Sacy, were imprisoned in the Bastille.

It was also in 1663 that the Company of the Holy Sacrament held its last regular meetings. Except for a brief revival in 1664, when it was mobilized to oppose *Tartuffe,* the Company, like Port Royal, ceased to exist. The triumph of the monarchy and of the unreformed clergy over the two radical, lay-led wings of the religious revival was complete.

In precisely these same years the monarchy adopted the social program of the *dévots*. This program, the "work," had been the principal concern of laymen all along, so they were deeply pleased to have the king accept the responsibility of purifying Parisian society. Indeed, by 1661 it was becoming apparent that lay donations would never be sufficient to build and maintain hospitals large enough to intern all the indigents of Paris. The *dévots* had undertaken something beyond their means; in fact, their social program would prove to be beyond the means of the Crown as well.

By an edict signed in August 1661, begging by persons well enough to work became a punishable crime. The official view of mendicancy did not stress the concern with sin, but this concern was nevertheless there. Instead the royal councillors evoked a fuzzy historical analogy: "Begging by healthy persons has always been so odious to all peoples, that none can be found which have desired to tolerate it; and every state has ordered punishment of those who wish to live in laziness." The edict went on, after appropriate references to precedents in previous royal legislation on begging, to state that physically able male beggars would be imprisoned, whipped publicly, and sent to the galleys should they prove to be intractable beggars. Their female counterparts were ordered to be flogged and to have their heads shaved. If caught begging after three internments, women were to be banished from Paris for ten years.

This legislation was only the beginning of what would become a vast state enterprise of social repression. Hundreds of edicts would follow to extend and to refine the monarchy's program for indigents of every sort. Vast sums would be spent to turn the Salpêtrière and Bicêtre into compounds covering acres. By 1690 the French monarchy was administering and financing the largest social program for indigents attempted since Roman times.

The assumptions and aims of the program, at least at the beginning, which is the critical moment in any administrative or bureaucratic development, were never discussed and examined before they were made into law. It was rather the desires of the *dévots* and the need to compensate for the suppression of the Company of the Holy Sacrament and the religious revival that had led the monarchy to such a commitment of resources. Henceforth the medieval distinctions between hospital and prison, between crime and vice, and between charity and repression would be confused in the *Ancien Régime*. This could only have occurred as the radicalism of the revival diminished and became transformed into an obsession with social conformity and prudery. The few laymen who had been attracted to the rigors of asceticism had abandoned secular life; the others expressed religious zeal by repressing external signs of sensuality and pleasure. Like their Puritan contemporaries, the *dévots* strove to repress sex and laughter in themselves and in Parisian society.

Low-cut dresses, brightly colored clothing, pornographic literature, novels even when not pornographic, parties, dancing, gambling, the theater, and pleasure from the sex act itself were taboo to a growing number of *dévots*. Instead, reading prayers, visiting prisoners, wearing black, thriftiness, hard work, and the exhortation of one's relatives and friends to moral reform became a way of life for numerous upper-class Parisians. These mannerisms reflected harsh class prejudices, chiefly against the lower orders of society but also against the aristocratic way of life.

Prudery became the basis of self-esteem for those who neither could nor would adopt the manners of a gentleman. The *dévots* rejected the heroic style, but this was less significant than their struggle to set themselves apart from peasants and servants. The fantasy world of the *dévot* was constructed on the notion that animals—and this included peasants and servants—enjoyed free, uninhibited sexual pleasure. This was the result of their debased nature. In Molière, the servant girls remain candid, overtly sensual, and bawdy, to the consternation and frustration of their masters, who never once attempt to seduce them. The servant couples, also, while fighting because of the husband's drunkenness or laziness, remain bound together by base sexual attraction. The affected *dévot* strove desperately to repress these tendencies. Again, at least in public, religion was transformed into an obsession with social conformity and prudery. The attacks on low-cut dresses and the theater were supported by the growing numbers of *dévots* from about 1650 until 1667.

After 1661, when Louis XIV began to rule on his own, it became apparent that the *dévot* affectation posed a challenge to the heroic style. The *dévots* implicitly condemned the nobility for its licentiousness, gambling, and spendthrift manner; soon they would politely but openly attack Louis XIV himself for his sexual conduct.

After the Company and Port Royal had ceased to be a threat by 1663, this left only the *dévot* affectation itself to undermine. It is almost as if the monarchy had hired Molière to do the job. Probably in the spring of 1664, Molière prepared *Tartuffe,* a devastating satire on the *dévot* affectation. In the great fêtes of that spring, *Tartuffe* was presented before the king, after which the *dévots* both at Court and in Paris insisted that it be suppressed. In the following years the quarrel over *Tartuffe* became a test of the royal authority. Molière appealed to Louis several times to be allowed to bring *Tartuffe* before the public.

When, in 1667, the play was presented under a different name, Lamoignon, First President of the Parlement, ordered it suppressed; and Péréfixe, Archbishop of Paris, forbade anyone to perform, listen to, or read the play on penalty of excommunication.

Soup relief. Did this idealized depiction of a well-to-do woman and an elegant young priest distributing food convey how the well-to-do wanted to perceive the poor?

Parties and divisions formed to make the storm over *Tartuffe* a significant test of how far the monarchy would go in its program of purifying society. Molière's triumph was the king's as well, and the play was finally produced under its original name in 1669. The *dévot* threat seemed insignificant by then, for the power of the monarchy had been strengthened by military victories, and better crops had made the lower classes less reluctant to pay taxes. By 1669 the old generation of *dévots,* including the king's mother, was dead or dying; the monarchy was now strong enough to permit public performances of Molière's play.

Tartuffe depicted the *dévot* at his worst. Exaggerated into caricature, Tartuffe is a false *dévot* who epitomizes the moral and social proclivities of most *dévots*. Molière brushed aside the fiction that prudery is religion by making it clear that Tartuffe is not religious at all.

Tartuffe is not a fair portrait of the *dévot,* but rather that of an affected, eccentric individual who had carried the *dévot* manner to excess. His outward piety, coldness, and prudery conceal an ambitious social climber, a scheming financier, and a perverted lover. His madness derives from his lack of self-awareness. His delusion is that affectation is religion.

Molière demonstrates how the delusions of a single madman invariably become attractive to those other elements of society that are rapidly changing status. The *dévot* upsets, indeed nearly destroys, the domestic tranquillity of a solid bourgeois household. Tartuffe's madness undermines Orgon's conception of reality, first on religious and finally on social and sexual matters.

True to convention, Molière has the servant, Dorine, perceive and dare to say what is going on. Tartuffe is seducing the sturdy masculine bourgeois, Orgon, if not physically, at least emotionally:

> Mais il [Orgon] est devenu comme un homme hébété,
> Depuis que de Tartuffe on le voit entêté.
> Il l'appelle son frère et l'aime dans son âme,
> Cent fois plus qu'il ne fait mère, fils, fille, et femme.[4]

But as if this were not enough to indicate Tartuffe's perverted influence on Orgon, Dorine continues:

4.
But he [Orgon] has become like a dazed man,
Since he became infatuated with Tartuffe.
He calls him his brother and loves him in his soul,
A hundred times more than he does his mother, son, daughter, and wife.

> Il [Orgon] le choie, il l'embrasse, et pour une maîtresse
> On ne saurait, je pense, avoir plus de tendresse.[5]

Consternation reigns in the household as its head succumbs to Tartuffe's affectations. No member of the family can quite decide what course of action to take, since they have grown accustomed to look to Orgon as the head of the household and source of authority. While Orgon thinks only of Tartuffe and of marrying his daughter to him, it is Tartuffe himself who is the cause of his own undoing. Rejecting Orgon's daughter, Tartuffe makes advances to Orgon's wife.

But long before Tartuffe is discovered to be what he is, it is Dorine the servant who unmasks the *dévot*. Tartuffe, when he first appears on the stage, puts on a pious act for Dorine, saying:

> Laurent, serrez ma haire avec ma discipline,
> Et priez que toujours le Ciel vous illumine,
> Si l'on vient pour me voir, je vais aux prisonniers
> Des aumônes que j'ai partager les deniers.[6]

Dorine, to the audience, remarks:

> Que d'affectation et de forfanterie![7]

whereupon Tartuffe, pulling out his handkerchief, replies:

> Ah! Mon Dieu, je vous prie,
> Avant que de parler prenez-moi ce mouchoir . . .
> Couvrez ce sein que je ne saurais voir;

5. He pets him, kisses him, and for a mistress
   One could not have, I think, more tenderness.

6. Laurent, put away my hairshirt and my scourge,
   And pray that Heaven will always shine upon you.
   If anyone comes to see me, I am going to the prisoners
   To distribute the pennies I give as alms.

7. What affectation and boasting!

> Par de pareils objets les âmes sont blessées,
> Et cela fait venir de coupables pensées.[8]

Not only does Dorine's reply attack *dévot* prudishness, but it lets the audience infer that Tartuffe is indeed perverted:

> Vous êtes donc bien tendre à la tentation,
> Et la chair sur vos sens fait grande impression?
> Certes, je ne sais pas quelle chaleur vous monte,
> Mais à convoiter, moi, je ne suis point si prompte,
> Et je vous verrai nu du haut jusques en bas
> Que toute votre peau ne me tenterait pas.[9]

Molière charged that the *dévot* morality was not Christian, but perverted and dangerous to society. Tartuffe violates the most sacred family conventions by displaying how a socially ambitious Parisian can be sexually aroused by a servant girl and how at the same time he makes advances to the wife, instead of to the daughter, of the man who is supposedly his best friend.

When *Tartuffe* was played in 1669, it was an immense success. Though completely bourgeois, Orgon's family could clearly be seen as the microcosm of Parisian society, and indeed of the state. Orgon's triumph over Tartuffe and the restoration of order in the family was not different from Louis XIV's own success finally in bringing the Fronde to a close and, at least temporarily, sustaining the myth of the hero over that of the socially repressive religious fanatic. Louis' own less than *dévot* style of life, as much as Molière's play, defeated the affectation of the *dévots*.

---

8. Ah! Good Heavens, I pray you,
    Before speaking take my handkerchief . . .
    Cover that bosom which I cannot look upon;
    By such things are souls wounded,
    And it makes guilty thoughts come.

9. You are therefore very susceptible to temptation,
    And flesh makes such an impression on your senses?
    Surely, I don't know what passion is stirring in you,
    But I am not so quick to lust,
    And I could see you naked from head to foot
    Without your whole skin tempting me.

The intensity of religious faith and the passion for political and moral reform articulated in the League of the 1580s and 1590s culminated in an extensive effort during the 1660s to uplift and cleanse Parisian society under the aegis of the absolute state.

THIRTEEN

The New Rome

The return of Louis XIV, the Queen Mother, and Mazarin to the capital when the Fronde ended in the autumn of 1652 restored public tranquillity. Behind the polite talk at Court or in the *Palais,* Frondeurs continued to protest against Mazarin, but the tone of their arguments slowly changed from plotting to rationalizations for what had happened in the past. The judges of the Parlement wanted to forget that they had set a price on Mazarin's head. They now knew that any disorder they might cause could lead to a return of the princes in a second terrible alliance with the *canaille* not only against Mazarin but also against the Parlement and the bourgeois. The merchants and bourgeois in general may have realized after the Peace of Westphalia (1648) that France had no more able spokesman than Mazarin to negotiate with Spain, and Parisians were unanimous in their desire for a "just and lasting" peace with Spain. With the sovereign returned to Paris, local politics changed character. The physical beauty of a young and virile king, who turned fourteen in 1652, diverted their attention from the past, as did the controversy over the nature of grace, which had started up afresh immediately after the Fronde.

The decade following the Fronde was a period of slow economic recovery not only in Paris but throughout northern France. The necessary reconstruction, the shock of high mortality rates in the countryside, and the persistent political instability caused by the high taxes made recovery very slow. But the weather—and consequently the harvests—improved, causing rural incomes to rise sufficiently to diminish revolt. The basis for prosperity in the capital, as well as for public order, lay in this general agricultural recovery. Food prices, particularly the price of bread, dropped slowly not only as a result of increased production but also because the stable political climate after 1663 made hoarding less profitable. French commerce, though faced with stiff competition from the Maritime Powers, recovered gradually to become quite extensive again by 1665.

Public order and modest prosperity were thus restored under Mazarin despite his continuing commitment to the same old corrupt practices in tax administration, pensions, and ecclesiastical preferments. The Fronde, the solemn protests, and all the negotiations culminating in the ordinances that promised reform were ignored. Indeed, Mazarin's government was actually more corrupt after the Fronde than it had been before 1648. But the Parlement could no longer remonstrate or refuse to register tax legislation. The fear of anarchy was too great.

In the decade following the Fronde, Mazarin and his creatures—Le Tellier, Lionne, and Fouquet—pocketed for themselves more royal revenue than did any other group of officials in the *Ancien Régime*. Mazarin had never been wealthy; back in power, the cardinal hurriedly had to establish his own immortality in the grand manner. Before his death in 1661, Mazarin—who had returned indebted from exile nine years earlier—had accumulated a fortune unequaled in France. He arranged the richest nonroyal marriages of the century for his nieces; built and furnished a magnificent palace in Paris; bought the land, built, and endowed the Collège des Quatre Nations (Institut de France); and bought the land and strongly subsidized the construction of the Feuillants, an Italian monastic order founded during the Catholic Reformation.

The cardinal was a fanatical collector of antique sculpture, Renaissance and Mannerist paintings, bronzes, medals, jewelry, furniture, crystal, porphyry vases, books, manuscripts, clocks, tapestries, ivories, and fine cloths of silk, silver, and gold. Owner of approximately five hundred paintings at the time of his return from exile in 1652, he rapidly acquired more to make his collection unsurpassed in northern Europe.

Mazarin seems to have realized in 1652 that his *gloire* could only be attained through acquiring outstanding works of the most celebrated masters. He no longer had a lifetime ahead of him to discover talented young painters and sculptors. (He had been among the first to buy Poussin's works.) For his own immortality, Mazarin had a stroke of good luck in being able to buy some of the best paintings in Europe when Charles I's collection was put up for sale by the Puritans. Having purchased some of the best paintings of Raphael, Titian, Correggio, and Van Dyck, he also succeeded in attracting

Romanelli and Grimaldi from Italy to decorate the galleries of the Hôtel Mazarin (Bibliothèque Nationale).

While Mazarin was busy importing some of the best works of art in Europe, his last superintendent of finances, Nicolas Fouquet, undertook to support young French artists found at home. The results of Fouquet's efforts were, in the long run, far more important for the future of Parisian culture, since the young French artists whom he assembled came to dominate French taste for fifty years.

There had been some money in Fouquet's family (his mother was a Maupeou) but certainly not nearly enough to undertake the construction of the château of Vaux-le-Vicomte. Together Mazarin and Fouquet acquired millions of *livres* of public funds. With his share, Fouquet built Vaux, the most extensive, costly, and sumptuous private residence built in the *Ancien Régime*. Vaux had no equal among royal châteaux in northern Europe until Louis XIV's Versailles.

The manner in which the ministers and *hommes de finances* paid for and built the *hôtels* and châteaux in and around Paris deserves special scrutiny. Sully's château at Rosny and his purchase of the Hôtel de Sully had been modest in comparison to Bullion's expenditures on a Parisian *hôtel* and on Wideville. But the expenditures and magnificence of their successors—first Longueil at Maisons, and then Fouquet at Vaux—mark an extraordinary increase in the social pretensions of the *hommes de finances*. Before the Fronde, some great nobles had at least equaled the *hommes de finances* in their expenditures for art and culture; but after 1650 the financiers surpassed them. Nor could the prominent judges in the Parlement compete with Longueil and Fouquet in construction and in patronizing the arts. The consequences of this change were very great for the development of Paris. *Hommes de finances,* not princes or judges, became the arbiters of taste in the capital.

Located southeast of Paris on thousands of acres (three villages had to be evacuated and torn down to round out the domain), Vaux-le-Vicomte was a triumph for Fouquet and the formidable group of artists and designers patronized by this intelligent, urbane, and thoroughly ruthless *homme de finances*. Le Nôtre laid out the gardens (together nearly a mile long) and arranged the disposition of immense fountains and basins; Le Vau designed the château and the commons; while Le Brun planned and executed much of the interior decoration, including the magnificent guest apartment reserved for Louis XIV.

Vaux-le-Vicomte in the history of seventeenth-century culture was much more than just an unusually large and costly residence. It was a new, grandiose, harmonious ensemble in which all the elements of sculpture, stone, paint, shrubbery, and water were combined in a controlled magnificence. As a designer, Le Vau lacked Mansart's passion to equal the Romans. But in Vaux-le-Vicomte he produced an elegant ensemble that appealed instantly to aristocratic and would-be aristocratic Frenchmen.[1]

A fine residence was not enough for this man who took the tenets of the aristocratic life literally and applied them for his own *gloire*. He patronized the men of letters and discovered the best young writers and musicians of his age. Fouquet flattered Pierre Corneille into writing plays once more. Fouquet suggested the subject of *Oedipe* to him; he patronized Corneille's brother Thomas, who was actually a more prominent playwright in the mid-century than was the author of *Le Cid;* he hired Molière's company to perform at Vaux and encouraged this young playwright to produce his own plays for the sumptuous entertainments held there; he commissioned music from Lully to be played in conjunction with Molière's plays; and he hired such promising young authors as Pellisson and Jean de La Fontaine to write about the fêtes at Vaux.

Fouquet knew full well the power of art and culture in his society. The manner in which he asked La Fontaine to describe the famous fête in honor of Louis XIV indicates his awareness of the power of culture as a political force in a courtly society. Moreover, these men of great talent were not just occasionally in Fouquet's employ; he preempted them and controlled them through his power to give them recognition and financial support. They all flattered Fouquet in the typical fashion of artist-artisans in the seventeenth century.

Like Mazarin, Fouquet also had creatures, other *hommes de finances,* who also were profiting enormously from fraudulent tax contracts. Together Mazarin and Fouquet set the dominant political and stylistic climate of the kingdom. Had this incredible corruption continued after Mazarin's death in 1661, France would never have become the mighty military and dominant cultural power that it was in Europe by 1675.[2]

Moreover, Mazarin and Fouquet were both hostile to Paris. The cardinal was a cosmopolitan with a love for Rome, where he owned a magnificent *palazzo*. In many respects his patronage in France, his introduction of the Italian opera, and his art collections were the attempts of a lonely Roman to re-create the cultural atmosphere of that city. But Mazarin never allowed his pro-Roman sympathies to become too overt,

1. Begun in 1657, the roofs were being put on a year later, while the gardens, decoration, and furnishings were nearly completed by 1661. This was a phenomenal speed of construction for such a massive, highly decorated ensemble, and this speed must have increased what would already have been extremely high costs.

2. Colbert, Louvois, and Louis XIV's other ministers also became very rich from public coffers, but principally from gifts granted with the Sun King's knowledge and approval.

for he was wise enough to know how politically damaging this could be. Therefore his Palais Mazarin by Mansart concealed behind an austere, monumental classicism that could only be French, the rich, intricate, and soft loveliness of Roman Baroque. Nor was Fouquet attracted to Paris. His intention was to administer France from Vaux-le-Vicomte or Saint-Mandé, his country house just outside Paris, while the king resided at nearby Fontainebleau. Neither Mazarin nor Fouquet grasped the importance of Paris as a potential force for political order, centralization, and reform in the realm.

But one of Mazarin's creatures did. Neither Mazarin nor Fouquet took Jean-Baptiste Colbert seriously. He had irritated them several times by accusing them of corruption and of "stealing from the State." So long as Colbert remained unallied with great nobles or ministers, he could not be a threat: hence neither Mazarin nor Fouquet took the trouble to disgrace this hard-working son of a bankrupt draper from Rheims. But while they were ignoring him, secure in the belief that they had suppressed his complaints about corruption, Colbert became a friend and adviser to the young king. Mazarin's death would bring an inevitable struggle for the position of first minister, but Fouquet saw no threat to his power. When the blow fell, he seems honestly to have been surprised.

The consequences of Fouquet's disgrace and of Colbert's subsequent triumph upon the history of Paris cannot be overestimated. It was the boldest assertion of personal royal power since Louis XIII's help in arranging the assassination of Concini. The cultural and political climate of France changed almost overnight. Paris again became the "motor of the realm." Colbert was committed to reform and to ridding the administration of corruption. He wanted to restore royal power and to make Paris the capital of the greatest empire since the Caesars.

There were many problems, of course, for Colbert wanted to change everything at once. The Extraordinary Chamber of Justice which he had Louis establish to try Fouquet and other corrupt officials tested the Crown's power to withstand the opposition of the princes, the Parlement, and the majority of the Parisian bourgeois. These groups had favored reform, but once Colbert began suppressing fraudulent *rentes,* false titles of nobility, illegal ecclesiastical privileges, and tax-farming contracts, most of the upper-class Parisians protested. Many of the magnificent *hôtels* in Paris and the culture of the last heroes had been paid for in one way or another by corrupt practices in government. Thus the trial of Fouquet became a *cause célèbre.* Colbert had named Chancellor Séguier and First President Lamoignon to head the Chamber of Justice and to give it prestige. The Chamber investigated the tax contracts signed under Fouquet's administration and tried and sentenced a large group of *hommes de finances* who had profited by cooperating with Fouquet. The individual fines imposed upon these men, some of them prominent Parisians, ran as high as a million *livres*. Then lesser officials—the *greffiers* (clerks) and *receveurs* (tellers)—were tried and found guilty of peculation, after which some were sentenced to death, prison, or the galleys.

While these events caused an uproar in Paris, Colbert canceled *rentes* and refused to sign tax contracts that he knew now as controller-general to be oppressive and not in the interests of the Crown or of those taxed. Rich and prominent Parisians, as well as the princes, quickly exerted every possible kind of familial and financial pressure on members of the Chamber. Some members weakened, among them Lamoignon, whom Louis removed from office upon Colbert's realization that a *"cabale des dévots"* was rising to defend Fouquet.

The Chamber proceeded to investigate and to try corrupt officials from December 1661 until 1664, when it began a serious inquiry into the practices of Fouquet himself. By then Fouquet had won the support of not only the bourgeois in Paris but of the robe and the *canaille* (rabble) as well. He was depicted as a martyr fallen into the hands of tyrannical and illegal judges.

Louis and Colbert remained firm despite overwhelming pressure to cancel the trial. Having judged him guilty, the Chamber moved to vote on the sentence. Fouquet narrowly missed being sentenced to death. By this time public opinion had become so aroused that had the Chamber voted the death sentence, large-scale riots, lynchings, and pillaging would have broken out in the capital. Fouquet's trial marked the first general clash between the Crown and the Parisians over what was clearly Louis XIV's effort to reform the state.

The harmony of sinister interests that had joined to defend Fouquet made his trial as dangerous to the monarchy as were the Fronde or peasant revolts. Here Louis and Colbert were bringing before a court of law a corrupt official, an *homme de finances* without conscience for the financial difficulties and sufferings of those who paid the *taille*. Though the evidence presented against him was overwhelming, beggars, peasants, artisans, bourgeois, and probably a majority of both the Parlement and the nobility either sympathized with Fouquet openly or actively intervened to stop the trial. Indisputable evidence was discovered that Fouquet had planned extensive rebellion against the Crown. And yet Fouquet's trial brought out into the open the true sympathies of entire groups that publicly condemned the corruption of the state while privately profiting from it. In its own foolish, hysterical way, the *canaille* saw Fouquet as just another victim of the harshness and corruption of royal justice. Beggars and artisans supported Fouquet in a strange solidarity against what they thought to be general suppression by the forces of law and order.

No alliance of interests would prove more dangerous to the monarchy, for here the extent of disaffection with the regime was openly exposed. Louis and Colbert won in 1664: Fouquet's property was confiscated and he was exiled to Pignerola. But so long as he lived, there would be numerous plots to secure his return. Every minor defeat for Louis and Colbert, whether on a battlefield or in Parlement, would hearten Fouquet's supporters, not the least of whom was the poet La Fontaine. Embittered *rentiers* and tax farmers would go on calling for Colbert's disgrace from their magnificent *hôtels* built with government funds.

The monarchy's victory in 1664 was primarily Colbert's victory. Coinciding as it did with the suppression of Port Royal and the Company of the Holy Sacrament, this victory elevated the power of the monarchy in Paris to a level not seen since Richelieu. Colbert in Louis' name would have almost unlimited power to initiate and to enforce reforms in the capital and throughout the kingdom. The Parlement would balk occasionally, but Louis' power would go unchallenged in Paris for the next fifty years. So long as Louis lived, the Parisians looked to their king for prosperity, security, and general well-being. Those fifty years would be the golden age of enlightened monarchy which Montesquieu would condemn and which Voltaire would admire and yearn for in the desperate years under Louis XV, when clashes between the monarchy and the Parisians invariably led to capitulation by the monarchy.

The draper's son, Colbert, has often been pictured as a plodding, bourgeois bureaucrat, but he was in fact a visionary imbued with extraordinary creative powers and administrative genius. His vision of a well-ordered, prosperous, and monumental Paris was particularly important because it was precisely in and from the capital that he had the power to realize that vision. Paris was to be the model city for all of France.

Colbert had a naïve faith in the precepts and visions of Rome through which the *collèges* encouraged everyone to emulate the ancients and to look up to the Roman Empire as the greatest political triumph of mankind. These precepts were founded on the proposition that history does indeed repeat itself, and that if one behaves like a great Roman, or rules and conquers like one, power and immortality can be assured. This was Colbert's faith, a faith shared by many educated Frenchmen of his generation.

Jean-Baptiste Colbert, by Robert Nanteuil. Almost single-handedly, this son of a cloth merchant brought the royal finances under control and helped Mazarin become the richest man in France.

But no other Frenchman had Colbert's opportunity to act and to reform France in accordance with this faith. Risen as he had from a merchant family to become for a time the second most powerful man in France, Colbert allowed this faith to guide him absolutely in the reconstruction and administration. His predecessors had grown up with either an ecclesiastical or a judicial education. A former bishop or *parlementaire* would invariably look on France or Paris as if it were a diocese or a jurisdiction. Not so Colbert. He had accepted precepts of the *collège* in their full force, untouched by prior experiences or traditions. His secret was to recruit experts and rely on their advice, and to give the king credit for the results.

Colbert's conception of the Roman Empire was based on the simple notion that the source of power, justice, linguistic style, and cultural greatness rested within the city of Rome itself, and in the Romans. The city's laws and culture had been imposed on province after province by her conquering rulers and legions, but the greatness of Rome itself as a city had been the key to the greatness of her emperors and empire.

Similarly Paris had been and should be the source of law, order, and cultural greatness for France. French kings had carried with them, and would carry still further, the manners and laws of the capital to all parts of the realm and to conquered provinces. "Paris being the capital of the kingdom and the residence of the king, it is certain that it sets in motion the rest of the kingdom; that all internal affairs begin with it." This would be Colbert's guiding principle as well as his argument for the reform and reconstruction of Paris. The capital was a model that had to be as perfect as possible so that Paris could determine the glory and majesty of the *Imperium Francorum* "by example." Since medieval buildings, neglected guild and commercial regulations, or contradictions in French law could have the opposite effect, Colbert believed they must either be removed, renovated, harmonized, or reformed: "You know that the example set by the city of Paris should do much to assure success in the rest of the kingdom." Nor did Colbert believe even at the beginning that in his own lifetime he could make Paris the perfect model of a capital. But he wanted to provide the plans, laws, and administrative framework for those who would succeed him—his own son, he hoped—so that Louis XIV's immortality and France's greatness would be assured. Obsessive and zealous are the two words that best define Colbert's efforts to realize this vision. From the beginning, he wanted to make Paris as great as Rome.

Colbert asked architects to examine the quality of stone in the oldest churches and monuments of Paris to determine which quarries produced the most durable stone. "I am resolved," he wrote, "to give all the solidity one possibly can to the king's buildings." Similarly, his plans for arches of triumph, a pyramid, and other public monuments would, he hoped, be established for all time; though he realized that not every monument could be erected under Louis XIV.

The humanists and academicians whom Colbert patronized added considerable archeological and literary knowledge about the Roman Empire to the vague precepts he had learned in a *collège*. Though uncritical by later standards, the editions of classical texts and the very free translations were important if for no other reason than that they enabled men like Colbert to add substance to their memorized precepts. Colbert was not a Latinist, but he could and did read the ancients in translation, or study engravings or the originals of antique sculpture, medals, tools, jewelry, and monuments. This iconographical material and the collections of Latin inscriptions copied from tombs and arches of triumph directly inspired Colbert to do all he could to make Paris as much like ancient Rome as possible. The iconography of the Caesars was reproduced much more faithfully under Louis XIV than during the Renaissance.

The new knowledge of Rome reinforced already existing myths about her greatness. Never once does Colbert seem to have realized that the lofty epigrams and panegyrics on the greatness of victories were in some sense propagandistic. Nor was the boastful, lofty tone of the iconography of the Sun King's reign seen as propaganda by those who created it, but rather as objective material that would make a lasting impression on the rest of Europe. There was a shared pursuit of greatness grounded on the belief that inferiority prevailed throughout France.

At the same time, the new knowledge of Rome and the great fidelity to the Roman style in Poussin's work resulted in the almost total disappearance of the medieval-chivalric culture that had so long influenced Paris. The later seventeenth-century would witness no more *Le Cids* or medieval jousts. The fanciful world of knights so recently revived under Richelieu lost its attraction under Louis XIV. For the moment at least, France abandoned the medieval style of life. Colbert looked upon the Middle Ages as a period when the "barbarism of the Goths" had degraded architecture. Even the monarchy abandoned all but the most sacred and divine trappings of the medieval kings. Louis XIV's coronation was traditional, as was his healing of those stricken with scrofula, but neither his Court ceremonies, hunts, and dinners, or even his funeral were in the chivalric tradition. Influenced by Péréfixe's teachings, Louis XIV admired Henry IV and Saint Louis; but his French and European contemporaries did not look upon the Sun King as a medieval king or knight. He was the pagan god Apollo, or the conquering Alexander, or Caesar Augustus. Louis became for his contemporaries a supernatural being, an ancient conqueror come to life.

The official rhetoric of the monarchy also changed after 1661. Richelieu and Mazarin had prefaced their remarks about policies and hopes with the remark "God willing." This was not insincere on their part, for they and their generation believed firmly that God alone determined the harvests, the victor in battle, or the life and death of individuals. Though Louis XIV and Colbert also believed this, the belief assumed a less overt form in the political style of the reign. Official documents became more secular and affected an ancient Roman style. The evocation of what a king must do to become great or immortal tended to diminish the previous constant resort to precedents to justify a law or action. Again Colbert, in his legislation on the guilds and in his influence on the preparation of the great legal codes of the reign, was responsible for this change of tone.

To realize his vision of Paris, Colbert needed not only the support of the king but the respect of the leading guildsmen, the *prévôt des marchands,* the prominent judges in the Parlement, and humanists, painters, sculptors, and architects. In many ways Colbert's easiest task, and his most modest accomplishment once in power, was the reform of the guilds and the reestablishment of the economy. Here again strong principles—this time mercantilist—combined with a vast knowledge of social groups, legal precedents, and the jealousies and bickerings of the guilds, enabled him to "restore order." Except during the very last years of his life, the generally favorable economic conditions in the rural areas and in Paris made it easier for Colbert to win acceptance for his reforms.

Similarly, Colbert found it relatively easy as a masterful administrator to bring the tax farmers and *rentiers* under his control. He had a keen sense of the influence of public opinion and public confidence on the royal treasury. He manipulated both, to impose his will on the banking and credit operations in the capital. Colbert dealt with the *hommes de finances* from a position of strength: he had not asked them for special favors, nor had he secretly allied himself with them to share royal revenues after the manner of his predecessors. The *hommes de finances* knew full well that Colbert could not be corrupted, and that they could not rely on him or on any of his subordinates in their efforts to gain personal advantage. Competitive bidding on tax contracts was restored in a different climate of opinion. As only Colbert now knew the true state of the king's finances, the tax farmers found it difficult to increase their demands.

When public confidence was high and interest rates relatively low, Colbert would refinance notes and *rentes,* using funds he had borrowed at six percent to purchase outstanding notes paying eight percent. His predecessors, even in years of peace, had not done so. During the Dutch wars, when the Crown was pressed for income, Colbert again manipulated public opinion in order to sustain confidence in *rentes* and notes. In these early years, therefore, Colbert laid the financial and political foundations for a strong, paternalistic government that intervened steadily and forcefully in every aspect of Parisian economy and society. These reforms accustomed the bourgeois and merchants to look to the king and his ministers for solutions to their problems. There had been little disinterested initiative in Paris for centuries. Under Louis XIV, the municipal administration became what it had been under Henry IV: an agency of royal policy. The *prévôts des marchands* were in effect personally selected by Colbert until his death.

The early 1660s were propitious for Colbert's gaining control of the social and economic life of the capital. Yet the cultural aspects of political power so essential for his vision of the New Rome threatened to elude him. He needed the support of prominent artists and architects whom he could control. The result was a clash of groups and personalities. Le Vau, the key figure here, had been committed to Fouquet and to the particular group of tax farmers allied to the superintendent. Colbert tried to impose his will on Le Vau and failed, largely because the architect's prestige and support at Court remained very great. His work at the Louvre (the *Galerie d'Apollon* and the river façade of what would become the *cour carrée*), at Vincennes, at the hospital at Salpêtrière, and at the Collège des Quatre Nations had made him a leading figure who refused to be beholden to Colbert. Le Vau had the makings of an intriguer; his numerous and powerful friends were supporters of Fouquet. Colbert could do little to thwart this prominent architect, though there are signs of his wanting to do so even before Colbert's appointment as superintendent of buildings in January 1664.

By this time Le Vau had already prepared several designs for the unfinished east front of the Louvre, and construction of the entrance moat had begun. Colbert hastily intervened to thwart the architect. The king may have realized that Colbert needed to control the architectural-political aspects of royal power, especially during the final agony of Fouquet's trial. In any case, Colbert turned first to François Mansart to design a building for the very place already preempted by Le Vau's plan; but Mansart was, as usual, too intractable to be controlled. Colbert hastened to ask other architects to submit designs in what now became a competition. Colbert maneuvered by asking French architects to criticize and improve upon Le Vau's plans; then, realizing that Le Vau would always refuse to submit to his judgment on matters of taste, Colbert invited several prominent Italian architects to submit designs. This search for prestige and for control over Le Vau led Colbert to Bernini. This famous Roman, the greatest architect in Europe, submitted a design for the Louvre. Having examined it, Colbert wrote him: "It is certain that there is nothing more beautiful, more grand, more magnificent than this design, or that better reflects the grandeur of the kings for whom it is destined. One could even truly say that the ancient Greeks and Romans never invented anything that showed more taste for fine architecture and that at the same time had more grandeur and majesty." But after the flattering remarks, Colbert listed very specific complaints about the design: it neglected to consider the climate of

Paris; some apartments and stairways were not very spacious; and if built, it could not be defended against rebels or rioters. Bernini responded to Colbert's legitimate complaints by changing his designs, but after several negotiations the two men still did not agree. The plans came to a standstill in December 1664, the month in which Fouquet's condemnation freed Colbert from the threat of disgrace.

After the trial, Colbert's position was stronger; Le Vau's powerful friends hesitated. Then, at Colbert's suggestion, the king invited Bernini to come to France. Colbert probably thought he would be able to impose his will on the designs for the Louvre. Colbert's unitary conception of politics and culture held this control to be an integral part of the sovereign power. Bernini arrived in June 1665. Chantelou, Poussin's old patron, showed the Roman the modest wonders of Paris.

But things did not work out the way Colbert had expected. Bernini proved to be vain and independent. He and Colbert could not agree on a design for the Louvre. It soon became obvious that the Roman could not be used as an instrument for intimidating Le Vau since Colbert probably found Bernini's designs more objectionable than Le Vau's.

On other fronts, Colbert was more successful. By 1663 Le Brun had come under Colbert's formal "protection" through the founding of the new Academy of Painting, which at one stroke gave the painter undisputed control over the training and style of young artists and Colbert control over Le Brun himself. With so distinguished an artist as Le Brun in his camp, Colbert proceeded to found, or refound, the various royal manufactures—among them the Gobelins for tapestry manufacture and the Savonnerie for carpet manufacture—again putting Le Brun in charge. Together the Academy and the royal manufactures would become a vast, unified enterprise for the design and production of all interior furnishings. Le Brun often chose the subjects and made the initial sketches for paintings, tapestries, chairs, beds, rugs, silver, and bronzes. Through Le Brun, Colbert sponsored a large economic project that would make France independent of other countries for all paintings and art objects; but in practice, the royal manufactures barely produced enough furnishings for the royal residences.

Then Colbert allowed his creature, Charles Perrault, to cabal against Bernini among other architects and at Court. This threw further opprobrium on Bernini besides his own unerring ability to offend the French by criticizing their taste; with the result that nearly everyone, including Colbert, was pleased when the Roman left for Rome in October 1665. But the problem of selecting a design for the Louvre remained unsolved.

Collège des Quatre Nations, by Adam Perelle. Cardinal Mazarin's bequest provided for a boys' school with an enrollment of sixty, drawn from territories annexed to France during the minority of Louis XIV, and a public library. Designed by Le Vau, the Collège and Val-de-Grâce marked the creative high point of Roman Baroque on Parisian architecture. Scorned for their foreign birth, but eventually admired by the Parisians, Anne and Mazarin loved each other deeply, and perhaps physically. The fact that they shared cosmopolitan tastes in architecture is often overlooked.

After at least another year's delay, Colbert forced Le Vau, Le Brun, and Claude Perrault to collaborate on a design. Louis XIV accepted this arrangement, and by 1667 a design had been agreed upon. Though both Perrault and Le Brun were beholden to Colbert, Perrault was mainly responsible for the austere, monumental façade that was finally built. The result was very different from the domed, curved, and somewhat Roman Baroque Collège des Quatre Nations that Le Vau had designed to be built just across the Seine. The long, straight lines of the Louvre, the absence of *pots de feu,* statues,

The Louvre façade, by Sébastien Leclerc. Combining historically reinterpreted elements with bold decorative features, the new façade, shown in this engraving from 1672, is partly obscured by the scaffolding and cranes being used to raise the monolithic stone that will complete the pediment.

or trophies at the top (some had been proposed), and the utter simplicity of decoration made the Louvre a structure radically different from anything else in Paris. Moreover, design by collaboration had enabled Colbert to dominate architecture and to impose a certain style on the capital.

Colbert had won a meaningless victory. By the time the designs for the Louvre had been accepted, Louis XIV had grown bored with the palace, the designs, and with Paris itself. The king had become enamored with the idea of building a new, superb residence at Versailles. And who would be the architect? Le Vau, of course. Colbert would be nominally in charge of Versailles, but Le Vau and Louis himself designed and approved the new Versailles, begun in 1664.

Just how instrumental Colbert's stubbornness had been in causing Louis to abandon the Louvre and Paris has not been determined. But one thing is clear: the king never expressed anything but cold, polite interest in the Louvre designed by collaboration, nor did he care about its completion.

Instead of the austere, cold classicism patronized by Colbert and defined by the Perrault brothers, Libéral Bruant, and François Blondel, Louis XIV preferred something more flamboyant and less classical. Versailles had captured his imagination; he envisioned through Le Vau's designs a residence not unlike Vaux-le-Vicomte, yet still more grandiose and magnificent.

Louis was only four when he became king in the spring of 1643. He quickly learned to exude a presence and a dignified and courteous bearing. Fouquet's arrest and trial had tested the king's mettle on matters of authority. For foreign policy he deliberately created a quite bombastic, heroic, and militarist persona, something that would get him into trouble as he grew older and tended to confuse his image with reality. On cultural matters he matured slowly, but by the mid-1660s he usually made decisions quite trenchantly, on the basis of what gave him personal satisfaction. The new Louvre was in some ways a daring and unconventional building. The Le Vau design for Versailles had some grandeur but also some liveliness and warmth.

By 1665 the king was losing interest in the vision of Paris as a new Rome. This vision had at its focal point a monarch in residence, the royal presence in a capital that would serve as the "motor of the realm." But Louis turned away from this vision (Colbert's arguments and pleading notwithstanding), having wintered several times in Paris and having found the crowded quarters of the Louvre and the Tuileries unbearable. In September 1665, Colbert wrote the king rather impudently that Versailles would be a fine place for pleasure and diversions, but not for attaining *gloire*. In Colbert's mind, only monumental construction in Paris would gain the latter; but the Sun King had different ideas, and Le Vau was there to help him realize them in Versailles.

Louis XIV's decision to build Versailles was of great importance to the development of Paris. It meant the curtailment of Colbert's plans and a different political and cultural orientation for France. By 1670, Paris and Versailles were becoming two quite different centers of authority and culture. Versailles marked the definitive revival of a large Court where the commitment to country living would mingle with the *"grandes affaires"* of war and diplomacy, while Paris, especially as seen from Versailles, was a burden to be policed and taken care of.

So long as Colbert lived, the schism between the capital and the Court would remain covert. He traveled frequently back and forth from Versailles to Paris—something his successors would not do—and maintained relationships with prominent clergy, judges, merchants, and financiers. Though interest in social and economic conditions waned at Versailles, Colbert, who still wanted to make Paris a model city, persisted in his attention to these matters. To this end he established several more royal manufactures in the capital to stimulate the economy of the city and to reduce unemployment.

As Superintendent of Buildings, and aided by Nicolas de La Reynie, whom he appointed lieutenant general of the police, Colbert enforced the laws for laying out streets, quays, and markets in a way unknown since Henry IV. Land speculators and builders were not allowed to build whatever they pleased in the different quarters, for Colbert sought to reestablish Henry IV and Sully's old rulings that certain manufactures and commercial enterprises could be carried on only in specified areas. Squatters' shops hastily built on public property were cleared away, and carpenters, slaters, and masons suddenly found themselves heavily fined for storing their material on public thoroughfares where it blocked traffic. Colbert gave new impetus for the revision and enforcement of Parisian building codes to prevent fraudulent and hazardous construction resulting from the use of poor materials or inadequately insulated fireplaces.

Despite a shortage of funds, Colbert continued to build monuments in Paris in the antique style, though on a much smaller scale than he had originally planned. Most royal funds for construction were allocated for Versailles; but through his influence over the *prévôt des marchands* and the guilds, Colbert managed to raise city taxes in order to install new public fountains, street lanterns, and more paving than the king would pay for, and to construct quays along the Seine and an aqueduct to improve the city's water supply. It was also under Colbert that demolition began on the capital's walls and gates. His assistants, supervised by Louvois, completed this project so that by 1715 Paris was encircled by tree-lined boulevards instead of by walls. These boulevards became the favorite strolling place for Parisians on Sunday afternoons. Nicolas Delamare, La Reynie's assistant, announced in his treatise on the administration of Paris that Louis XIV's victories and conquests had so extended the realm that Paris no longer needed walls for defense. Indeed, the border defenses were to be the capital's principal defenses for the rest of the *Ancien Régime*.

From the boulevards the hospitals of the Salpêtrière and the Invalides rose in the distance to the east and west of the capital. There were already several large structures at the former by 1670, the year the trustees of the General Hospital commissioned

Libéral Bruant to build a central-space chapel accessible to the contagious, the poor, and the insane. Colbert was not involved in Bruant's design, but the sobriety and harmonious proportions of the heavy arching testify to the influence of Colbert's antique style. In the same year work began at the Invalides, Bruant again being the architect. Decoration on both buildings was kept to an absolute minimum. Except for the lantern at the Salpêtrière and the trophy-shaped dormers and the dome (by Jules Hardouin-Mansart) at the Invalides, both buildings evoke the monumental quality of the east front of the Louvre. Inside the Invalides, the extraordinarily high ceilings, the superior quality of the stone, the massive wooden beams, and the monumental stairways have a somber grandeur unknown in Paris before Colbert. The Salpêtrière and the Invalides were actually enormous complexes of buildings, gardens, kitchens, bakeries, and chapels. Both establishments dwarfed Henry IV's Hôpital Saint-Louis. They still inspire awe today: something about their dimensions recalls ancient Rome.

Also outside the capital were the Observatoire and the Jardin des Plantes, a garden planted to foster the sciences of medicine and botany. The Observatory was placed on a knoll beyond the Luxembourg Palace in order to facilitate the observation of heavenly bodies. Designed by Claude Perrault and begun in 1667 to house the Academy of Sciences, the Observatory also reflects Colbert's taste in buildings, since Perrault was given free rein to develop a design based on Colbert's understanding of ancient Roman architecture and mathematics.

To replace the city gates, Colbert built several monumental arches of triumph. Those of the rues Saint-Denis and Saint-Martin still survive and provide the best examples of the type of austere classicism Colbert admired. Neither slavish copies of antique arches nor Baroque in decoration, these arches have a quality about them that was more authentically antique than Le Vau's buildings either in Paris or at Versailles. The proportions and careful attention to orders, the displacement of bas-reliefs, and the use of trophies make these arches the analogues of Poussin's paintings in their powerful evocation of historical Rome. Their designers, Claude Perrault and François Blondel, had studied Roman ruins and design with a reverence unknown to Le Vau.

Ancient Rome was to evoke different things in different architects and artists; but for Mansart, Perrault, and Blondel, ancient Rome demonstrated the need for absolute obedience to the mathematical ratios governing proportions, and for faith in the ideal that one could build for eternity. Like the ancient Romans, Mansart, Perrault, and Blondel were engineers and mathematicians as well as architects. Their concern was as much for solidity as for harmony of proportions. Extensive and deep foundations,

LVDOVICO MAGNO.

A PORTE S.ᵗ DENIS a este bastie à peu prez sur les ruines de l'Ancienne l'an 1672. et acheuee en 1673. elle a 72. pieds de large et autant de
hauteur auec vne Ouuerture de 26. pieds les petites portes ont 9. pieds. elle'a ete faite pendant les Victoires du Roy sur les Hollandois. Mʳ Blondel
est l'Architecte. Cette face regarde le Fauxbourg.   A Paris chez N. Langlois rue S.ᵗ Iacques a la victoire Auec Priuilege du Roy   fait par Perelle

Triumphal arch on the rue Saint-Denis, by Adam Perelle. Separating the center of the city from the suburb
on this highly commercial street, this arch, which identified the monarchy with Imperial Rome,
extended deeply into the ways the Parisians imagined their city.

perfect "living" stone, the best lime, iron chains and bars to reinforce arches, and lead
chinking gave their buildings an immortal quality. By comparison, one senses that
both Le Vau and Bernini were concerned with surface effect, volumes and forms, and
overall impression, rather than with what is unseen but felt by a viewer with the critical powers of an engineer. Perrault and Blondel believed that if their proportions
were correct and their materials of the best, their monuments would last as long if not
longer than those of ancient Rome. Since their aspiration coincided with Colbert's
vision of Paris as the New Rome, a new immortal city, Colbert favored their designs
whenever he could.

The struggle over the control of design lasted right up to Le Vau's death in 1670. Le Vau and Le Brun had been asked to collaborate on a design for an arch of triumph to be built at the Porte Saint-Antoine; but Colbert rejected their designs in 1669 in order to choose that of Claude Perrault. A full-scale plaster model of Perrault's design was erected, but since the king ignored it and the funds of the capital were being depleted by the Dutch wars, the arch was never built in stone.[3]

Colbert's reverence for Rome, his influence upon the Academies, and his obsession with imposing "order" on every aspect of Parisian life, indirectly led him to uncover one aspect of Rome's greatness as yet ignored by humanists and antiquarians. This was the study of Roman public administration, or *police,* as Colbert and his contemporaries called it. Humanist scholars had been primarily interested in the military rather than the urban administration of the Romans.

The specific problem of law enforcement had not been recognized as something separate from the study of law or jurisprudence until Colbert sought to establish a *"bonne police"* not only for Paris but for all of France. He knew that legislation was not enough. In order to discover what were the best possible sorts of institutions and officials, and the most effective punishments or rewards leading to better law enforcement, Colbert determined to learn how the Romans had governed themselves.

Before Colbert's sponsorship of research on Roman public administration, the subject had been neglected, largely because polite conversation in a *salon* excluded remarks on Roman sewer taxes, marketing regulations, or prisons. Moreover, neither aristocratic nor royal patrons before Colbert had patronized the study of such subjects. However, he considered this knowledge of ancient public administration eminently useful. What better example for Paris than Roman *police*!

As early as 1667, Colbert reorganized the public administration, first by creating the new office of lieutenant general of police and second by installing in this new office Nicolas de La Reynie, a very hard-working *dévot* who concurred that the capital should

---

3. It was over the question of whether the inscriptions on this arch should be in French or in Latin that the quarrel between the ancients and the moderns became overt. The Perrault brothers, Blondel, and Colbert were "moderns" in that they believed contemporaries could attain the perfection of style and the immortality of ancient authors. Charles Perrault had been commissioned by Colbert to prepare the inscriptions to be carved on the arches and other monuments and engraved on medals and coins; and it was he who became head of the Academy of Inscriptions and Belles Lettres, which Colbert founded. Le Brun, an "ancient," imposed his views on the Academy of Painting despite the fact that Poussin served as his and the Academy's model. The historiographical implications of the quarrel were very significant in that the conceptions of time and anachronism as well as of changing standards of taste became more generally perceived than they had been.

become a model city of prosperity and tranquillity. The creation of a new office did not in itself significantly change law enforcement in Paris, because except for its new title, it closely resembled the old office of civil lieutenant that François Miron had held under Henry IV.

What Colbert and Louis XIV did, however, was to support La Reynie's efforts to transform the vague powers of his office into a veritable ministry of police. His administrative genius, constantly supported by Versailles, enabled La Reynie to create a more extensive and efficient institution for law enforcement than Paris had hitherto possessed. Saint-Simon judged rightly for once when he wrote of the office of lieutenant general of police: "La Reynie, Councillor of State, so well known for having been the first to lift the office of lieutenant of police for Paris from its low estate to make of it a sort of ministry." La Reynie brought a degree of law and order to Paris virtually alone. He had assistants, of course, some of whom, like Delamare, worked as hard as their chief. But La Reynie himself extended the jurisdictions of his office by personally reviewing investigation after investigation, visiting prisoners, reading libelous or pornographic novels, or negotiating with the grain merchants to stabilize the price of bread. In his more than thirty years of administration in Paris, La Reynie became a formidable presence in almost every aspect of public life in the capital.

The jurisdictions of La Reynie's office included all matters of security. He was in charge of arresting thieves, murderers, seditious persons, and the insane; of suppressing begging, fortune-telling, counterfeiting, abortion, prostitution, and gambling; and of exercising surveillance over foreigners and spies, and over habitual duelers. La Reynie was also in charge of the lighting and cleaning of streets, water distribution, fire-fighting services, and help in case of floods. The care and protection of abandoned children and the aged, as well as the general administration of hospitals and prisons were also under his control.

The strict enforcement of regulations on the kind, quantity, and quality of food brought into Paris; the enforcement of market and guild regulations; the prevention of epidemics; and the inspection of doctors, surgeons, and barbers also came under La Reynie's jurisdiction.

For all these jurisdictions there obviously were old, well-established officials—the grain measurers, for example—who did the actual work of inspecting and enforcing the law. But La Reynie directed the operations of these officials and pressed them to perform their tasks. The consolidation and reform of the public administration in Paris was long overdue. To this end La Reynie made it clear to all lesser officials that they were subject to charges of laxity or corruption if they failed to perform their duties. Since the days of Miron, there had been little attempt to force officials to perform their duties. After 1667, with a few dramatic investigations into the corruption of officials who were supposedly enforcing the law, La Reynie made royal power once more a presence in the public life of the capital. Like Colbert, La Reynie never acted in his own name but exclusively in that of the king. With Louis XIV's support, his power increased rapidly.

The basis of this power was control of the criminal courts, or Châtelet. Though La Reynie also commanded what little armed police forces the capital had—indeed, he reorganized them—it was the Châtelet that enabled him to increase respect for law and order in the capital. There were forty-eight commissioners who, robed and bonneted and accompanied by clerks, would hurry to the scene of a crime at any hour of the day or night. These commissioners would ask questions, search for weapons, and cross-examine all witnesses in the presence of the accused and of all those present at the crime. The clerk made a transcript of the investigation. If arrests were to be made, the commissioner summoned a sergeant, or armed policeman, to make them.

La Reynie had to rely on the enforcement of law and order by judicial forces. In a city with a population nearing half a million, the archers of the watch, archers of the poor, mounted sergeants, sergeant mace-bearers, process-servers, and spies in all could not have numbered more than fifteen hundred men. Then too, not all of these men were armed. Some, the sergeant mace-bearers, for example, seem to have been preoccupied with the collection and resale of confiscated property, chiefly furniture. The commissioner, or rigidly impartial justice (at least under La Reynie), rather than armed police, provided the foundation for law and order in the capital.

La Reynie himself was an extraordinarily complicated individual. By temperament a *dévot,* he was eager to eliminate from the city all such forms of vice as prostitution and begging. A loyal supporter of the *dévot* program of the General Hospital, he harassed Huguenots in the years before and after the revocation of the Edict of Nantes.

At the same time he showed great concern for individuals as such. La Reynie would personally investigate case after case where the persons involved were only of the most inferior sort, socially or morally. No person, however degraded, was refused an investigation or perhaps even a hearing before La Reynie himself. He relentlessly checked to see if his subordinates were making the mistake of treating individuals before the law as stereotypes.

La Reynie's paternalistic air toward the Parisians was not unlike Colbert's toward all the king's subjects. They were much alike in their passion for order, their total identification with the king, and their self-effacement. On the last point La Reynie's sincere religious devotion led him to an extraordinary act of self-effacement: in his will he ordered that he be buried anonymously, without a tomb, in a little cemetery just outside Saint-Eustache. La Reynie continued as undisputed master of the entire public administration in Paris until 1697, when he was relieved of his functions by younger and very ambitious ministers in Versailles eager to control Paris themselves.

Like Colbert, La Reynie also sponsored research on the *police* of the ancients in order to discover principles and precedents for efficient law enforcement. His chief adviser, Delamare, himself a commissioner for the *Cité,* was a savant who had traveled to Rome to study and who had a desire to write the history of what would later be referred to as urban public administration. Delamare's great four-volume treatise, which he never finished, was the first comprehensive history of *police* to be written in French. The *Traité de la Police* was a monumental achievement for its day in that it attempted to depict public administration since Hebrew times. Arranged topically, Delamare's work presented concisely all the evidence he could find about how the ancient Israelites, Egyptians, Greeks, and Romans, as well as the Capetians, had legislated and enforced their laws on such matters as prostitution, street cleaning, public hygiene, food shortages, fire fighting, epidemics, riots, building codes, and censorship. This might have been idle antiquarianism under someone other than La Reynie, but La Reynie was interested in Delamare's findings because they either justified decisions he had already made or opened his eyes to new possibilities of improving public administration.

Under La Reynie, absolutism would no longer merely mean sovereignty over a hierarchy of orders, corporations, and officials. It would mean the extension of royal power into the public morality of the Parisians in a way never before envisaged by a royal official. What precisely encouraged both Colbert and La Reynie to extend royal power to such questions as what Parisians could read came as much from their eagerness to assume the powers of the Church in the society as from their desire to emulate the Romans. Both Colbert and La Reynie were influenced by the *dévot* program of puritanical, ascetic morality; and as men of power they felt responsible for bringing all the power of the state to bear on realizing the *dévot* program for a morally pure society.

But neither Colbert nor La Reynie could or did use the rhetoric of the *dévots,* since that implied only the private responsibility of the Christian to assure the moral worthiness of other Christians. Instead they used the rhetoric of Imperial Rome, with all its grandiose phrases about the public good and tranquillity. But the program of urban absolutism was essentially what the *dévots* desired. In the king's name La Reynie would intervene to round up prostitutes, beggars, and vagabonds, and he would rigidly enforce censorship of all pornographic or "seditious" plays, novels, engravings, or songs. What was considered pornographic or seditious was more broadly defined than before, and of course anything considered sacrilegious was likewise suppressed by La Reynie's agents. The great machinery of censorship, which except for periods when enforcement was relaxed would run until the end of the *Ancien Régime,* was established by La Reynie with the full approval of Colbert, Louis XIV, and Chancellor Le Tellier. Committed to doing everything possible to enforce a rigid public morality, the Crown did not hesitate to censor any work that La Reynie judged unfit for the public. That Louis himself approved is beyond question. Chancellor Pontchartrain wrote to La Reynie in 1690:

> The most pressing item is that the king [has] been informed that they are to perform very soon a comedy in which all the Princes of Europe are shown leagued against France in a burlesque and ridiculous manner. His Majesty does not deem it proper to tolerate its performance; and, however, since it must not appear that His Majesty has been informed of it, nor that it is by his order that it is not being performed, it must be you who in your name, and quietly, ask some of the actors to give you the play to read, after which you yourself and on other pretexts will tell them not to perform it.

This, of course, was far from a precedent for the Crown. For centuries it had attempted to control the attitudes of the Parisians on questions of foreign policy and religion. But the extension of this practice into questions of public morality, previously the Church's domain, and the persistent, day-by-day surveillance of books, pamphlets, and broadsides, for the purpose of censorship were innovations. Under La Reynie, censorship did not mean occasional censure of a book or song; it was a rigid code enforced year after year.

The machinery of censorship was, of course, not solely the result of the desire to enforce a moral code. It also developed from an acute awareness of the importance of public opinion. Colbert used the phrase *"l'opinion publique";* he and La Reynie would take it into consideration before making major political decisions. The monarchy under Louis XIV was determined to eradicate disorders and riots. La Reynie knew that in order to do this, public confidence in the king's ministers had to be maintained.

La Reynie consciously worked to convey to Parisians of various social groups the notion that the king and his ministers were concerned for their welfare, that they had not been "abandoned by His Majesty." When a crisis developed, whether a bread shortage or an epidemic, royal proclamations were hastily printed and tacked up in markets and churches announcing the Crown's proposed remedies for the crisis, and stating that any violators of the special laws invoked for the emergency would be severely punished. Cheats and hoarders were fined, imprisoned, or publicly rebuked; commissioners were stationed in public squares, on the quays, or in other places where a riot was likely to occur; and, if any violation of the law occurred, arrests were immediate. At all levels of the society, literate or not, the royal presence made itself felt. La Reynie showed for his day considerable awareness of the psychological implications of an economic crisis or epidemic; and though this awareness was couched in the metaphor of a father raising his children, his policies were effective. Personally he was fearless. Willing to stand up and shout to an angry mob that the "king would find bread," La Reynie treated the *canaille* as if it were a group of spoiled, stupid children. Never underestimating their power, he sought to disperse that power by not allowing *"émotions"* to develop.

On another level, La Reynie fought a long and successful battle against corrupt inspectors, hoarders, speculators, and counterfeiters. There were several periods of severe food shortage in the 1680s and 1690s,[4] when the prices of the bread eaten by the *gagne petits* climbed as high as during the Fronde. During these periods the inspectors, in collusion with grain merchants, bakers, or butchers, would in return for bribes tacitly agree not to enforce price and weight regulations. La Reynie posted commissioners beside the inspectors who priced and weighed the grain on the quays and in marketplaces; and in several instances he seized the account books and arrested inspectors and grain speculators for illegal actions that tended to drive up the price of grain and thus incited *"émotions populaires."* The vigorous enforcement of price and weight regulations, combined with the confidence that the Crown was doing all it could to prevent famine, permitted La Reynie and Louis XIV's government to weather crises that could have developed into extensive riots or civil war.

In his policy of intervention into the economy in order to assure the food supply, La Reynie incurred the hostility of a series of *prévôts des marchands.* Even during severe crises, when bread was being distributed by troops in the Louvre, the *prévôts* protested

4. La Reynie wanted the *prévôt des marchands* to authorize the construction of public granaries, but the *prévôt* refused.

that La Reynie did not have the right to intervene in the economic affairs of the capi-tal. At a time when some incident over the price of a sack of grain could have started a riot among thousands of destitute and anxious *peuple,* a *prévôt des marchands* chose to defend the grain merchants and the corrupt inspectors. But with Achille de Harlay, First President of the Parlement, and the king's ministers supporting La Reynie in his quarrel with the *prévôt,* nothing was permitted to curtail Reynie's efforts to avoid a rebellion in the capital. This long quarrel is important, however, for another reason: it indicates that the old municipal government represented by the *prévôt* lacked a con-ception of the general public interest. Choosing to defend those profiteering grain mer-chants who were eager to take advantage of a crisis, it either ignored or discounted the threat of a riot.

Illustrative of an attentiveness to day-to-day living conditions in the capital and to an efficient, orderly management of resources, this account of the distribution of food, clothes, and other necessities, quarter by quarter and suburb by suburb, in the mid-1680s, is but one example of the thousands of administrative reports, accounts, and instructions generated by the royal officials in Paris. The flow of the homeless and the poor from parishes in the capital to the suburbs is at least partially recognized and taken into account, a quite modern approach that differed markedly from charitable services that were strictly limited to paupers known to reside within the city walls. The role played by the parish clergy and by female charitable orders in counting the poor and evaluating dire conditions indicates that royal administrative personnel were absent on the neighborhood level.

The report begins as follows:

> Accounts of Expenditure
> made during the winter from December 1, 1685, to April 30, 1686,
> for the help and sustenance of the poor from the suburbs of this city of
> Paris, which obeying the order that the king had the goodness to give
> to Mgr. Le Peletier, comptroller general, . . . bread, soups, firewood,
> clothes, pants, wooden shoes, and shirts have been distributed to the
> sick men and women, and remedies and food necessary for women who
> are pregnant, the recently born receiving packages of swaddling
> clothes and small linens necessary for them, and milk and flour daily
> for the older babies who are still nursing; mattresses, sheets, covers,

and bedframes for those who are sleeping on the floor, especially the poor weavers, ribbon-makers, button-makers, embroiderers, and others working inside whose work has ceased during this year.

The document then reports on the poor who have left the various suburbs and moved to the city parishes, and it gives the names of the person—a parish priest, a nun, or a woman designated by the *curé*—who is in charge of estimating the number of needy and distributing help to them. The actual sums spent over three years are provided (and are shown in table form on page 356). For example:

> Saint-Étienne-du-Mont, with the suburb of Saint-Victor, the Estra-pade *fossés* and adjacent places linked to it: there are 66 families of poor workers and day laborers, the sum of 2,294 *livres* has been granted to Reverend Father Gardeau, *curé* of the parish, based on receipts presented by him.
>
> Saint-Médard: from the Saint-Marcel suburb there are 1,180 poor families such as those described above, 40 pregnant women, 130 babies on milk and flour, the sum of 17,047 *livres, 8 sous, 6 deniers,* as presented in the memorandum of distributions certified and signed by Reverend Father Gargan, *curé* of the parish . . . and by Sister Anne de La Noe. . . .
>
> Saint-Laurent: there are 1,695 families of weavers, ribbon-makers, and other sick workers, a large number of stonecutters, laborers, day workers, water-carriers, cabinetmakers, wooden-shoe makers, and other poor—partly resulting from the six or seven companies of soldiers quartered in the parish and surrounding suburbs; the sick, the pregnant women, and 225 nursing infants, 13,193 *livres* and 10 *sous* are paid to M. Gabillon, priest, doctor of the Sorbonne.

The strident rationality (to the point of unreasonableness!) of French administration in later centuries had not reached full development, so there is no mention at all of the poor moving to the Saint-Eustache parish, which nonetheless received funds: "Saint-Eustache: . . . there are still more than 8,000 poor of all ages and both sexes, artisans, silk workers, day laborers, and others, the sick, women who are pregnant, infants on milk

Parish	1686–1687		1687–1688		1688–1689
St-Martin and St-Hyppolyte	7,919 *l.* 12 *s.*		8,102 *l.* 5 *s.*		7,520 *l.*
St-Médard	7,000		6,550		7,700
St-Jacques-du-Haut-Pas	300		650		1,600
St-Étienne-du-Mont	1,500		2,800		3,600
St-Benoît	200		250		400
St-Nicolas-du-Chardonnet	450		300		450
St-Suplice	4,435	10	3,814	10	12,200
La Ville-l'Évêque	2,000		5,106		5,850
St-Eustache	4,729	10	3,806	10	5,000
La Villeneuve-sur-Gravois	10,259	6	11,453	13	8,800
St-Laurent	13,000		14,000		12,500
St-Sauveur	1,600		1,885		2,500
St-Nicolas-des-Champs	2,595		3,380		4,440
Ste-Marguerite	3,312	10	3,626	10	5,856
Distributions by hand	1,407		840	15	1,584
Expenditures remaining for April 1688			8,611	1	
TOTAL	60,708 *l.* 8 *s.*		75,176 *l.* 4 *s.*		80,000 *l.*

Source: L. Lecestre, ed., "État de la Dépense Faite durant l'Hiver depuis le 1 Décembre 1685 jusque au 30 Avril 1686 pour le Secours et Subsistance des Pauvres des Faubourgs de cette Ville de Paris," *Mémoires de la Société de l'Histoire de Paris,* 49 (1927).

and flour . . . , the sum of 3,378 *livres,* 13 *sous,* 6 *deniers* granted to M. de Cornouailles, first vicar of the parish, and Dame Nolin, treasurer for the poor children."

While it would be impossible to draw any conclusions about royal response to the crisis of the 1680s on the basis of one set of documents, this report nonetheless provides some indications of the relations between the Church and the state, and of the latter's interest in focusing its support on skilled artisans who were destitute. The food crisis of the 1680s prompted a response by the Crown to supplement the well-established parish and monastic charitable services that had been in place for decades, if not centuries. Since the Crown as yet lacked the necessary lists of residents, their occupation, age, and marital status, it is entirely possible that the funds distributed in the 1680s were allocated quite arbitrarily, according to the efficiency and the political influence of the clergy and the prominent lay persons in each parish. A modern royal administration? Certainly not, but a modernizing one, and one that while absolutist in the definition of its authority was quite limited in practice and often still dependent on church officials and neighborhood delegates such as the *quarteniers* and the militia captains to actually minister to the needy.

After 1696, and for the rest of the *Ancien Régime,* the *prévôt des marchands* would be a powerless honorary official whose functions were exercised by the lieutenant general of police.[5] As if to demonstrate his absolute power over the capital, in 1702 Louis XIV changed the boundaries of several old quarters and added new ones, bringing the number of quarters up from sixteen to twenty. The political consequences of this reorganization permitted the Sun King to weaken the parties of opposition by adding to the *corps de ville* new municipal officials faithful to him. Urban absolutism reached its apogee under La Reynie and his successor, Marc-René Voyer d'Argenson. In the king's name the activities of half a million Parisians came under the direct surveillance of a single royal official. The chain of command over the armed forces and food supplies was simple and direct, from Louis to La Reynie and on to the commissioners in the streets. Intervention into both private and public affairs, that fundamental characteristic of absolutism in the seventeenth century, extended far beyond the old jurisdictions of feudal lord and bishop combined. This should not suggest, however, that crime, libelous literature, and moral offenses were eradicated from the capital. Quite the contrary. But until there are monographic histories of public administration and police activities, the vague evidence drawn from memoranda indicating a decline in violence and petty crimes must be accepted.

After the retirement of La Reynie and his generation of commissioners, the momentum for *bonne police* declined in Paris, but it did so slowly. La Reynie had formed the commissioners into a *corps* (they had their own chapel), had given them an ideal of service to the Crown, and had instructed them in their functions. These officials handed down this conception from generation to generation. In the eighteenth century, public administration and law enforcement would falter, not so much because La Reynie's system of commissioners had become outmoded as because later Bourbon kings and their ministers could not avoid involving the *bonne police* of Paris in the treacherous game of Court politics at Versailles. The undermining of royal authority in Paris began at the top, because of the rivalries between ministers, and then slowly pervaded the lower ranks of judicial and other officials. Charges of corruption in the *police* would become frequent as commissioners and inspectors became the object of increasing public ridicule and anger. Under Louis XV a commissioner dared not walk in some parts of the capital without a heavy guard. The *canaille* would lose the little confidence it had had in these officials under Louis XIV.

---

5. The functions of the lieutenant general of police changed little in the eighteenth century. A reading of Sartine's *Mémoire* on the *police* in 1770, ed. A. Gagier (Paris 1879), or the manuscript "Idée des Fonctions du Lieutenant de Police" in the Archives Nationales, Series K, 1021 n. 2, indicates that the institution and jurisdiction established by La Reynie lasted down to the Revolution.

But seen as a whole, Colbert's achievement through La Reynie, impressive as it is, is less impressive than his attempts to improve the general conditions of life among the poor of the capital. Colbert, along with the *dévots,* had realized by 1655 that the origins of large-scale unemployment and subsistence living in Paris lay in the provinces. Crop failures would cause an influx of destitute persons into the capital seeking employment, relief, or survival through begging, prostitution, or theft.

Through the late 1660s and 1670s, Colbert strove to force provincial cities and parishes to establish hospitals and workhouses for the relief of the poor. He and other officials hoped to reduce the influx of poor into the capital, but by Colbert's own admission, local officials remained uncooperative. The bourgeois of the towns were slow to spend the money needed for relief of the poor and no amount of royal prodding through Colbert could make them do it.

As a mercantilist Colbert shared the fear of various minor theorists that the capital would "swallow up" France, that it would outgrow its basis of subsistence. He therefore sought to enforce old legislation against new construction in the *faubourgs,* but at best this policy was erratically enforced. His decision to free the Faubourg Saint-Antoine from the rigid guild control of the *maîtrise,* or guilds, for example, actually stimulated new construction and the development of an artisan economy extremely vulnerable to any economic crisis.

In another direction, Colbert's establishment of the provincial intendancies probably did more than anything else to slow the influx of destitute persons into Paris. In many respects the duties of an *intendant* were similar to those of the lieutenant general of police, except, of course, that the *intendants* were also empowered to assess the *taille*. But like La Reynie, *intendants* had considerable police powers; they were responsible for inspecting and controlling food supplies, prisons, hospitals, and local justice in the provinces.

When the *intendance* of Paris was permanently established, Colbert chose his brother Charles Colbert de Croissi for the post. When Croissi became secretary of state for foreign affairs, Colbert gave the intendancy to his brother-in-law, Jean-Jacques Charon de Ménars in 1681. Ménars was less austere, perhaps less of a *dévot,* and certainly not as intelligent as La Reynie; but they complemented each other well during the crises of the 1680s and 1690s when the possibility of revolt threatened both the provinces and the capital. Ménars shared Colbert's obsessive desire for a *bonne police;* and, though not imaginative, he was, it would seem, quite courageous in his efforts to enforce the legislation against corruption in the tax collection and judicial administrations of the entire *généralité* of Paris. Like La Reynie, Ménars was aware of the importance of public opinion. He attempted to suppress the practice of sequestration of furniture for non-payment of the *taille,* not so much for moral reasons as because it increased the possibility of *"émotions"* among peasants and farm laborers. Though Ménars knew that some of his decisions in assessing the *taille* would cost him friends at Court, he nevertheless tried to eliminate collusion between tax farmers and prominent courtiers and judges who had arranged to have their farms exempted from the *taille.* Ménars toured villages and towns to inspect local conditions and to improve local justice and hospital facilities, just as La Reynie did in the capital.[6]

Except for correspondence about the illegal importation of Dutch books, La Reynie had little direct business with Ménars. But through the controller-general's analysis of the *intendants'* reports, and the king's own real ability to coordinate the entire royal administration, La Reynie kept informed about the conditions in the countryside. When a drought occurred, he was informed of it and would immediately place extra guards and inspectors on duty along the quays to thwart hoarders.

With the Sun King attentive to the long reports about religious, moral, and economic conditions in Paris and the provinces, officials like Colbert, La Reynie, and Ménars had some impact on the daily life of the Parisians. That impact was primarily political in the sense that the Parisians became convinced that their king was indeed concerned about their welfare.

Upon Colbert's death in 1683, his family took the precaution of holding the funeral procession and mass in the evening. There would be smaller crowds then, and consequently less danger of a riot. Guards surrounded Saint-Eustache, and others accompanied the coffin and mourners in case the *canaille* should attempt to defile Colbert's body. The death was apparently welcomed by Parisians from every social group, who held Colbert responsible for high taxes. Actually, Colbert had sought to cut expenses and to lower taxes, but Louis XIV's expansionist military policy had necessitated tax increases. For the Parisians, however, Colbert remained the object of undeserved scorn and anger.

One of the king's first decisions after Colbert's death was to give Michel Le Tellier's son, the Marquis de Louvois, the office of superintendent of buildings. Thus Colbert's

---

6. After inspecting prisons in the *élection* of Nemours in 1681, Ménars wrote Colbert: "There are no prisoners in the prisons, which are not secure, and the jailer does not know how to read or write and is 104 years old. One prisoner accused of theft escaped three months ago."

rival, the man most responsible for high taxes (after the king), was also to be in charge of royal construction in the capital. As might be expected, work on the Louvre ceased almost immediately. Some of Colbert's plans, such as the great fountain and the pyramid, would never be realized; others would not be completed until the First Empire.

Public building in the capital virtually ceased after 1683, as royal funds were diverted to war and to Versailles. To be sure, two monumental squares were built under Louvois' administration, but neither was technically a public project.

By 1680 the Duke of La Feuillade, poor in everything except noble ancestors and bravery in battle, had received numerous pensions and honors from Louis XIV. He was, it seems, sincerely grateful to his sovereign. To express his gratitude and bring still more favor, La Feuillade commissioned Desjardins, the Dutch sculptor, to carve from a single block of marble a colossal likeness of the Sun King. Desjardins' statue depicting Louis as a Roman emperor was more than twelve feet high when finished.

From the beginning, La Feuillade received subsidies from Louvois in what was to be a very costly project, since it consisted not only of a statue of the king but also of a pedestal twenty-feet high, which in turn had four more statues at the base. Louis came to see the statue and liked it very much. La Feuillade therefore gave it to the king, who ordered it placed in the newly completed Orangery at Versailles.

Then La Feuillade commissioned another statue of similar dimensions from Desjardins; only this time the Sun King was portrayed in his coronation robes. While Desjardins prepared this second colossal statue, La Feuillade bought the Hôtel de Senneterre in order to tear it down and erect in its place a square that would properly display the second statue. The Hôtel de Senneterre, located in the very fashionable new area of the *fossés jaunes* opened by Cardinal Richelieu, also had the advantage of being surrounded on all sides by streets, making considerable space available for the new square.

Through an agreement between Louvois and La Feuillade, Jules Hardouin-Mansart designed a residential square in the tradition of the Place Dauphine and the Place Royale. But for lack of space, Mansart could not make a square that was indeed square; so he designed arcs of houses with uniform façades that would form a circle around the statue of Louis XIV.

Though nominally still La Feuillade's project, Louvois had in fact arranged for Mansart's design, the acquisition of needed land, and more funds to tear down existing houses in order to build the new ones. Thus Louvois was responsible for the construction of the Place des Victoires, the third residential square in Paris. The façades were entirely of stone instead of brick and stone as in the older squares. The geometrical

The Place des Victoires. Designed by Jules Hardouin-Mansart, this circle of residences and shops framed a monumental statue of Louis XIV, atop a pedestal. Four beacons lighted this profane but almost religious "altar" celebrating the monarch.

uniformity of the older squares was lacking, since some prominent residents in the *fossés Montmartre* either refused to sell their *hôtels* to Louvois or asked exorbitant prices for them. Mansart therefore could not build a perfect circle of houses. Yet these differences between the old squares and the new one were minor, especially in view of the overall effect of the Desjardins statue.

The older squares were purely residential. The equestrian statues of Henry IV and Louis XIII complemented but did not dominate the harmonies of space and structure in the Place Dauphine or the Place Royale. But in the Place des Victoires, the colossal likeness of Louis XIV and all the trappings added to it had the effect of turning the square into a semireligious edifice.

Not merely the size alone (though the statue and base were over thirty-three-feet high) but the bas-reliefs (four slaves representing defeated European states), the high grills, and finally the addition of four beacons each thirty-five-feet high made the Place des Victoires into a temple for the adoration of the Sun King. The entire statue of Louis XIV was covered with 24-carat gold leaf, and the beacon lamps themselves, atop separate pedestals, "made the place as light as day at night." The principal inscription was brief but extraordinarily pretentious: *Viro Immortale,* to the immortal man.

The English physician Martin Lister described the Place des Victoires soon after its completion:

> The statue of the king in the Place Victoire is on foot; it is composed of brass but is gilded all over. Close behind is the statue of Victoire, that is, a female of vast size, with wings, holding a laurel crown over the head of the king and resting one foot upon a globe. Great exceptions are taken by artists to the gilding . . . but what I chiefly dislike in this performance is the *great woman* perpetually at the king's back; which, instead of expressing victory, seems to act as an encumbrance, and to fatigue him with her company. The Roman victory was of a very different description: it was a small puppet, carried in the hand of the emperor, and that he could dispose of at pleasure. This woman is enough to give a man a surfeit.

In making this comparison between the project sponsored by Louvois at the Place des Victoires with what was known about Roman custom, Lister typified not only art criticism but criticism in general in the last decades of the reign of Louis XIV. The Place des Victoires signaled a change in Parisian architecture after Colbert's death. There was less concern about conforming to the principles of the ancients. So long as the effect was stunning and the size overpowering, Louvois, Jules Hardouin-Mansart, and Louis himself would be satisfied.

As a result of Louis XIV's decision to reside permanently in Versailles, the pattern of growth in Paris changed. Construction on the eastern side of the city declined, and new construction extended rapidly toward the west. Hastened by the construction of the Place des Victoires, then of the Place Vendôme, and finally of the Faubourg Saint-Germain, this shift toward the west in the last decades of the reign created new residential areas in the capital that were almost totally distinct from the older quarters. Their residents were almost all would-be aristocrats eager to spend wealth on buildings and art that would give them status; thus they built enormous *hôtels* with large gardens, courts, and extensive stables. Western Paris became the fashionable part of the city as the *Marais* declined into the quarter of aristocratic but modestly wealthy families that it was to remain until the Revolution. When Madame de Sévigné moved to the Hôtel de Carnavalet in the *Marais,* she liked the genteel quality of the neighborhood but lamented the old-fashioned fireplaces and crowded courtyard of the old *hôtel,* the best she could afford.

In the new western quarters, *hôtel* after *hôtel* lined the streets, making them roofless tunnels. Virtually no artisans lived in the Faubourg Saint-Honoré, or in the Faubourg Saint-Germain, and there were few shops and markets. The residents in the *hôtels* either had produce trucked in or had servants purchase large quantities of supplies at the Halles. They themselves bought finery, china, and books either in the old shops of the *Palais* or in those just beginning to appear along the rue du Faubourg Saint-Honoré. The construction of the Pont Royal by Louvois begun in 1685, the first stone-arch bridge to span the Seine without support from an island, linked these new western quarters. The newly expanded and redesigned Tuileries gardens, the Cours la Reine, and the esplanade of the Invalides virtually surrounded these quarters with gardens and trees.

The Place Vendôme itself, with its immense equestrian statue of Louis XIV, conveyed the same glittery effect as Mansart's other work. Much bigger than the Place Royale, it indicates once again, as does Versailles, that for Jules Hardouin-Mansart grandeur was almost synonymous with largeness. The statue, designed by François Girardon, had to be proportionately as large. It was in fact the largest founded in France by a single pouring of molten bronze. On seeing it, Lister wrote:

La Charmante Tabagie

Dans un délicieux Séjour
Au vif éclat de tant de charmes,

Qui ne cederoit pas les armes
Enyvré de bon vin, de tabac et d'amour

The charming smokers' den. Tobacco, chocolate, and coffee became fashionable in elite Parisian circles after about 1685. The glass and decanter on the ground suggest that wine has been rejected by these card-playing experimenters in luxury products.

LA MANIERE QVE LES FRANÇOIS SON HABILLE´ SOVBS LE
REGNE DE LOVIS XIIII *en 1671 1 les Mains dans les poche et les gants Sous le*
bras. 2. la mode des Chaise roulante 3. la mode des ringraue

Courtly manners in 1671. The new male costume favored by Louis XIV, and the dancer-like postures and
gestures in fashion at Court, prompted artists and engravers to flood the French and European market
with cheap, almost popular images of the latest styles.

A view of Paris circa 1690, by Lieven Cruyl. The recently completed Pont Royal is shown in the foreground, the Pavillon de Flore and the Grand Gallery of the Louvre on the left. The *Île de la Cité* can be seen in the distance. Note the quays and roadways, very expensive public works, and the sumptuous residences along the Left Bank.

This colossus of brass . . . is astonishingly large, the figure of the king being twenty-two feet in height, the foot twenty-six inches in length, and all the other proportions of the horse as well as its rider.

In this statue the king is arrayed in the habit of a Roman emperor, and sits on the horse without either stirrups or saddle. But to confuse the whole, the head is covered with a large French periwig à la mode. I am quite at a loss to conjecture upon what principles or precedent this confusion of costume is to be justified. It is very true that in building, it is commendable to follow with precision the ancient order and simplicity, because the different orders were founded upon just principles in the mathematics; but the clothing of all emperors was arbitrary. It seems as if the people of the present time are ashamed of the style of their dress, yet no one will venture to affirm that the equestrian statues of Henry IV and Louis XIII are the less to be valued for being arrayed in the true dress of their times. . . . Now I securely appeal to all mankind, and ask, whether in representing a living prince of the present time unclothed legs and arms are even decent, and whether there is not a want of refinement in it that is very disgusting?

By the time the statue was finally placed on its marble pedestal thirty feet high, a change in taste and psychology was occurring in the capital that made the statue and the heroic idealism it represented quite out of date.

In La Fontaine's works and then in Racine's later tragedies, the forgotten problem of establishing a private morality again imposed itself on the Parisians. Corneille and the heroic idealism that had developed under Richelieu had ignored this problem by boldly asserting that a nobleman was not responsible for his actions. Reputation, *gloire,* or other persons' opinions had been the principal concern.

But in Racine, heroines and heroes are destroyed by conflicts arising within themselves. Their concern is not so much reputation as survival when faced by the awareness of their inability to control their own emotions. Jean de la Bruyère, as early as 1688, grasped this difference when he observed in his *Caractères:* "Corneille subjects us to his characters and to his ideas, Racine conforms to our own; the former paints men as they should be, the latter paints them as they are. In the first there is more of what one admires and of what one should imitate; in the second there is more of what one recognizes in others or of what one experiences within himself." La Bruyère and such memorialists and letter writers as Madame de Sévigné reflected and contributed to the demolition of the cult of the hero at the very moment of its complete articulation by the monarchy. Toward the end of the reign, this incongruity of manners and morals split the capital and the Court into two amorphous parties. Among the numerous victims of this split were Boileau and Racine, who, once commissioned to write history, were doomed to fail because of the incongruity between the heroic style now vulgarized at Versailles, which transformed Louis XIV into a demigod, and Racine's psychology, which recognized the complexity of motives in individuals and the effects of jealousy, love, hate, and lust upon their behavior. Racine's psychology was much more sophisticated than Corneille's; and though he accepted certain social definitions and conventions such as *noblesse* from Corneille, his tragedies were neither apologies for the behavior of the *grandes âmes* nor apologies for Louis XIV himself. But feeling the pressure to please at Versailles and threatened with humiliation if not imprisonment as a Jansenist, Racine attempted to write history in the heroic style and to portray Louis XIV as a great conqueror equal to Alexander and Caesar Augustus. He failed not so much because he lacked the psychology needed to write history as because he feared to use it. His psychology was appropriate for the Romans or for figures in the Old Testament, but he dared not apply it to Louis XIV.

La Fontaine's works, Racine's plays, and later the works of Boileau and La Bruyère indicate a schism between the ethical and social values of men of letters and those of the aristocracy and the monarchy. By 1670, it is true, the monarchy was adopting the heroic style uniquely for itself and was in effect undermining the aristocratic claims to heroism. But this change was less significant than the fact that outstanding men of letters ceased to be apologists for the aristocracy and the monarchy. Neither Racine's tragedies nor La Bruyère's prose works reinforced the cult of the hero or his acts of violence.

Whether contemporaries saw this schism is unclear. Louis sensed that Racine was an implicit critic if not an enemy; but he was more concerned about his Jansenist affiliation than about his conception of the heroic style of life. La Fontaine's works were censored by La Reynie, and La Bruyère took the precaution of publishing the *Caractères* anonymously (he resided in the Hôtel de Condé), but again the reasons do not seem to have been the ethical or social implications of their works. La Bruyère's *Caractères* defined a separate ethos for *Cour* and *Ville,* that is, for Versailles and Paris, but he indicated no awareness of a break between the thought of the outstanding men of letters and the monarchy. Yet the break existed—a break that would continue to widen in the eighteenth century despite and partly because of the heavy and often inconsistent policies of censorship.

For the upper-class Parisians, whether men of the robe or nobles, the attraction to the cult of heroes now preempted by Louis XIV remained as great as ever.

Despite the famine and general hardship caused by crop failures and war, the Parisians prepared a colorful ceremony in 1699 at the inauguration of the Girardon statue. The *prévôt des marchands* and the *échevins,* dressed as much like courtiers at Versailles as they dared, marched in solemn procession with the governor of Paris, his guards, and various ecclesiastics to accept officially the statue for the capital. After listening to various Latin and French eulogies and paying their respects to the relics of Saint Ovid [*sic*], which the Capuchins brought out for reasons no one quite understood, the officials attended a banquet in the Grand Gallery of the Louvre. The celebration ended with a fireworks display depicting the new equestrian statue of Louis XIV in a fiery white Temple of Glory. The official programs included, in addition to the usual number of poems on Louis' greatness, an anagram transforming *Louis de France* into *La Force Divine.* The newly installed financiers and tax farmers from the western quarters participating in these ceremonies may have felt a special pride in taking part in the adoration of this statue erected so near their own houses.

The Sun King himself, of course, was not present. From 1671 to 1693 he attended only twenty ceremonies in the capital and did not return again until 1701, after which he came to Paris only four more times in the fourteen years before his death.

For Parisians of every status, Louis XIV inevitably was seen as an object for adoration, if not worship. From the beginning he had been the "God-given" first child in a marriage barren for twenty-two years. The propaganda of poems, sermons, and history—or what was read as history by Bossuet—the gold-covered statues, the medals, and the arches of triumph presented him as a living god. The divinity of Louis XIV would be challenged by his staunchest enemies, the Huguenot exiles.

As for Louis at Versailles, his ignorance of activities in Paris and his hostility to the capital increased rapidly after about 1700. He began to insist that courtiers not go to Paris, frowning on them and grimacing at those who talked about events in the capital. When he discovered that courtiers were still going to the capital, he decided to set an example by forbidding the *fils de France,* his own son, to go to Paris. His ministers, who traveled the few miles infrequently, would admit that their reports on conditions in the capital were not based on firsthand knowledge.

But the machinery of law enforcement established by Colbert and La Reynie kept running, even after the king himself had ceased reading the detailed reports and

Louis XIV visits the Academy of Sciences, by Sébastien Leclerc (1671). Colbert describes the instruments and specimens as the king, with hat and cane, is lighted by sunlight refracted in the "burning mirror." The unfinished Observatoire can be seen in the distance. The shapes of the windows from the inside, and the view of the Observatoire windows, convey the impression that one is viewing the interior and the exterior of the same building.

making important decisions. Not wanting to upset an aging and grief-stricken old man with news of terrible suffering, poverty, and political unrest, his ministers simply acted in his name and kept from him the grim statistical evidence.

However, when riots threatened to engulf Paris in 1709, Pontchartrain, a secretary of state and son of the chancellor, decided to inform Louis of the danger. The news of the riots seemed to bother the old king only slightly. His shock was less than that experienced by the other ministers at the realization that one among them might give Louis a glimpse of the truth. Saint-Simon reported the king's reactions:

> The king was disturbed by it for several days; but, having thought it over, he understood that people who threaten and who give warnings plan less to commit a crime than to cause anxiety. What irritated him most was the deluge of the most daring and immoderate signs against him, his behavior, and his government, which, for a long time, were found affixed on the city gates of Paris, on churches, in public squares, above all on his statues, which were insulted by night in various manners, traces of which were found in the morning, and the inscriptions torn down. There was also a multitude of rhymes and songs, and nothing was spared.

D'Argenson felt it his duty to keep Paris peaceful on his own, without informing the king. So long as men as capable as he were in power, Paris could withstand terrible famines and epidemics without revolt. With the shadow of La Reynie still over him, d'Argenson gave his formula for keeping the peace:

> My practice is first to get out of my coach, to mingle with these wretches, to listen to their complaints, to sympathize with their misfortunes, to promise them help. . . . My door is open to them every day, and I try as best I can to smother the fire that is being kindled. . . . I did not have much trouble calming the common people; even the impatient complaints of an infinite number of poor women who were crying out from hunger caused me more trouble than all the rest. Nevertheless, two hours sufficed to dissipate that crowd.

Louis XIV could almost afford to ignore Paris politically so long as these capable officials had control. But in seeking to "protect" him, they did Louis a disservice, for the king still had the courage to face opposition on his own.

Instead, Louis was read d'Argenson's police reports, which deal with cases of individuals committing a crime or breaking some moral code. Saint-Simon implies that, in view of the suggestive style in which these reports were written, the king's interest in the details of crimes, sexual offenses, and violations of religious laws was prurient. These few reports must have represented a bare handful of all the similar crimes committed in a city of half a million people. The low number of crimes reported would either indicate that the commissioners had already ceased to perform their duties well or that d'Argenson merely chose a few cases at random in order to give the monarch the illusion that he was informed about conditions in Paris. Louis took these anecdotal reports seriously and gave them his full attention to assure that justice was done to the handful of prostitutes and beggars about whom d'Argenson chose to write.

This suggests that Louis XIV may have repressed his former awareness of the extent of poverty, crime, and moral violations that he had gained from reading La Reynie's hospital reports and the statistics on the number of poor. Not senility so much as the suppression of any statistical evidence that might cause him to feel guilty about high taxes and war permitted Louis to take seriously reports of five or ten crimes per week as evidence of conditions in the capital. This process of isolating the king had begun when Louis chose to live at Versailles rather than in Paris, and developed to the point that courtiers dared not mention cultural activities in the capital. The Sun King was misled by ministers and poets who coddled him and led him to accept as true the rhetoric about Paris, immortal city and New Rome.

In his final years Louis XIV was neither informed of his subjects' poverty nor allowed to see it for himself. Guards would be sent out along roads, ahead of his coach, to arrest or in some way remove beggars and maimed persons so that they might not come into the king's view as he passed by.

Few, indeed very few, of his subjects could recall when Louis XIV had not ruled France; they may unconsciously have begun to think of him as already immortal after 1700, the fifty-seventh year of his reign. Despite high taxes during the War of Spanish Succession, and extreme suffering caused by crop failures and the terrible winter of 1709, the lower-class Parisians may have rioted, but the bourgeois and judges did not join the crowds, and the barricades did not go up. The commissioners did not allow the occasional bread riots to get out of hand.

But what had made urban absolutism effective, namely, the king's own interest and his ministers' initiatives in economic and social problems, had already disappeared before Louis XIV died in 1715. The only remaining links between the monarchy and the Parisians were the ministers, the commissioners, and the monolithic image of a conquering hero equal to the Roman emperors. None of these would provide the attention to public opinion, the strict law enforcement, or even the religious awe needed to maintain order in Paris after the old king's death.

Epilogue

By 1715 London had become the fastest growing and richest capital in Europe and the leading commercial city in the world. Though Paris had never led commercially, in 1600 it had been the "greatest city" in population. This was no longer true. By the year of Louis XIV's death, Paris had not only been surpassed in wealth, but probably equaled by London's population of over half a million.

Moreover, London's growth was of a healthier sort—more diversified in commerce and manufacturing—than that of Paris. London became the center of a nascent national market, a port city strong in shipbuilding. It supplied materiel for large-scale military operations on land and sea during the global wars of the League of Augsburg and of the Spanish Succession. Though Paris continued to influence urban design and to refine culture, it slipped to second place among the cities of Europe.

The sources of growth in Paris remained the traditional ones. In 1715 the French capital was still little more than a political and ecclesiastical capital, a university town, a luxury manufacturing community, and the part-time residence of a land-bound aristocracy. Despite Colbert's efforts to stimulate large-scale manufacturing, the Parisian economy and social structure remained primarily oriented toward luxury production, political careers, and the purchase of land.

Upper-class growth in Paris occurred primarily because of the venality of offices. The monastic revival affected Paris in a similar manner. The availability of new royal and religious offices encouraged merchants and manufacturers to abandon trade for positions of higher status.

The influx of rural poor contributed greatly to Paris's growth, as it did to London's. But in the French capital, the rise of hospitals and the persistence of widespread begging and large-scale unemployment indicate that the city was less successful than London in absorbing this new labor and converting it into a source of wealth.

In Paris, the dramatic rise of the Faubourg Saint-Antoine into a manufacturing center confirms the impression that economic growth in the capital was being stifled by commercial and fiscal regulations. The new growth in this quarter resulted from Colbert's removal of some of these regulations from the Faubourg Saint-Antoine. The protests of Parisian guildsmen over Colbert's action indicate, however, that the guildsmen themselves, and not merely the Crown's mercantilist policies, sought the enforcement of the outmoded regulations even though they inhibited new growth. Moreover, unlike their London counterparts, Parisian merchants never had to face the full competition of a national and, to a certain extent, an international market. Again, the protectionist interests of the merchants and of the French state coincided, inhibiting adaptation to changing economic conditions.

More ominous than the limited sources of growth or the protectionist economy, however, was the antiquated mechanism linking Parisians to their sources of food supply. Throughout the seventeenth century, this link remained what it had been since the Middle Ages: food exchanged for taxes.

Parisians, through grain speculators and bakers, paid gold and silver for grain to the lords and peasants who produced it in the Paris basin. Then, through the *taille,* most of this same gold and silver was collected through taxation and returned to the capital. This antiquated economic system permitted a minimum of flexibility or growth. The economy of the Seine basin remained precarious and backward in comparison with the Thames-sea system, which linked London to its markets and to its sources of food and raw materials. With government approval, the Parisians continued to concentrate on the manufacture of luxury goods, which could never become a significant part of the Seine-basin economy. What manufactured goods the peasants of this region bought were made in such lesser towns as Rouen, Beauvais, Melun, and a dozen others, which were also trapped in the antiquated economy of bread-for-taxes resulting from the grain prices established by the Parisian merchants. Moreover, the Parisian merchants and royal officials, always incipient landlords if not feudal lords, actually sought to preserve this antiquated system.

This simple agricultural-fiscal structure prevented a change in fundamental living conditions in Paris. The permanent danger of famine could not be reduced, since no one knew when the price of bread might double or triple, causing hardship and death for those on subsistence incomes. Indeed, unlike their London counterparts, Parisians still lived absolutely under the laws of Malthus. A periodic rise in population, higher taxes from war, or an adverse weather cycle caused severe economic dislocation.

Parisian political and social life showed extraordinary continuity despite the violence and wars of the seventeenth century. In 1715 the structure of Parisian society was essentially what it had been in the late Middle Ages. True, the venality of offices and consumerist culture had challenged the principles underlying the medieval social structure; but by the time of Louis XIV's death, the Crown, poets, and judges had convinced all but a few diehard gentlemen that robe and sword nobility were of the same essence.

The few signs of modern crown-centered public spiritedness that appeared under Henry IV did not survive his assassination. Rule in the interest of either the public good or for the good of all the French had proved too radical for the Parisians. They preferred the religious, hierarchical, and aristocratic prejudices that the violence of the sixteenth century had led Henry IV and the *politiques* to reject. After 1610 the religious revival, the quiet strengthening of judicial, monastic, and guild organizations, and the search for order in the ideals of medieval society continued unabated through the reigns of the second and third Bourbon kings. Some tempering of the aristocratic love of violence occurred through a refinement of manners and culture, and some physical help was given to the lowliest Parisians, often accompanied by strong, moral social control. Yet the structure of Parisian society remained unchanged. Neither the Crown nor the *prévôts des marchands* made attempts after 1610 to administer the capital according to a conception of the public interest, broadly defined so as to include all Parisians.

The lesson of the *politiques* was not the only loss following Henry IV's death. Only a few Parisians in the seventeenth century understood Montaigne; these *libertins,* as they were called, kept alive some awareness of skeptical thought by reading Montaigne and the ancient Stoics. But until Pierre Bayle, the Catholic conceptions of the nature of man, of society, and of the universe would remain predominant, indeed monolithic, among literate and illiterate Parisians alike. Cartesianism prompted strong opposition from theologians in the Sorbonne, but in point of fact mind-body distinctions and ethics grounded on the analysis of human passions did not undermine the Gallican Establishment. Jansenism would have a future, but this was only a possibility when *Unigenitus,* the papal bull against it, was promulgated in 1713.

Finally, in political thought the Parisians lacked a sense of civic responsibility, pride, or virtue in their participation in the life of the capital. Late in the reign of the Sun King, La Bruyère could still describe Paris as "divided into diverse societies which are like so many small republics, which have their laws, their customs, their jargon, and their jokes." The capital lacked a public ethos that would touch the emotions and the pocketbooks of a variety of groups. Social groups were self-contained and quite willing to let the Crown administer the capital. The lack of civic initiative in the face of so many social, economic, and health problems is the most striking characteristic of the governing Parisians. Not until the Enlightenment would educated Parisians become familiar with modern conceptions of public welfare and civic responsibility; and only then could they deal with the persistent social and economic problems the capital had known for centuries.

Acknowledgments

The person who helped me the most in writing this essay was my wife, Patricia M. Ranum. She transcribed documents, worked through Blondel and other sources for me, edited, typed, and retyped the manuscript. Her quiet enthusiasm, more as collaborator than critic, was indispensable. Le Comte d'Adhémar de Panat deserves credit for interesting me in the *hôtels,* furniture, *scènes de vie,* and utensils used in daily life. Hours spent walking with him in Paris proved to be hours of lessons on the age of grills, fenestrations, door panels, and other objects rarely referred to in specialized courses of art history. He enabled me to reduce my artisan's concern for the broken or frayed condition of an object in order to imagine it for what it once was.

My teacher and dear friend, John B. Wolf, encouraged me in every possible way and helped by challenging my judgments and organization in numerous chapters. Peter Gay, who also read the entire manuscript, caught numerous stylistic blunders; those that remain I lack the talent to repair. His steady and constructive friendship along with his acceptance of the form of this essay gave me the courage to continue in what has become an unconventional way of writing history. John Elliott pointed out just how old-fashioned and impressionistic the work seemed as history, and his pleas, as well as those of David Rothman, to add more examples in the social history went unheeded. George Woodbridge, Georges Dethan, Hirmon Salomon, and Anne Harris all read chapters and caught more errors than I would like to think could ever creep into so short a book. Margaret Ross, my research assistant, helped by checking minor but important matters of fact.

In different moments, but steadily over the years in New York, Mary Mack, Willard Hutcheon, and Herbert Rowen asked about *Paris* and consented to hear me out. The Fritz Stern family kindly lent us their farm in Vermont, which proved to be an ideal place for writing, as did the Atheneum in Nantucket, thanks to the cooperative librarians. A grant from the Council for Research in the Social Sciences, Columbia University, enabled me to spend a summer in Paris, and a Chamberlain Fellowship which I received from Columbia College, provided me with half a year free from teaching which I also put to very good use in Paris. William Gum and

Nancy Lipscomb, of John Wiley and Sons, helped by being patient and friendly even when we disagreed as to how many pictures and maps the book should have.

The person who has helped me the most in revising this essay was Patricia M. Ranum, lifetime collaborator and spouse. Peter Potter's support all along has been indispensable.

Bibliography

I am particularly indebted to those historians who sought to discover connections between religious expression, morals, art, literature, social values, and economic conditions. J. Orcibal, P. Bénichou, A. Franklin, M. Dumolin, E. Chill, R. Jasinski, and M. Venard have each, and with varying degrees of awareness of what he was doing, demonstrated the necessity of looking for explanations in Parisian history without regard for the traditional fields into which historical knowledge is divided.

Since 1970, the little golden age of Anglo-American historical scholarship about Early Modern France has not generally been centered on the history of Paris. The important exceptions are the books by Diefendorf, Sutherland, Ramsey, and Ultee, cited below. Has the focus on the regions, provinces, and towns been prompted by a political-cultural impulse to sustain, by history, these identities against monarchical and more recent political and cultural centralization? This is doubtful. The call of *La France profonde* is a very deep and pervasive force in French historiography in general, and Anglo-American historians answer its appeal.

Since the 1960s, the most important works about Parisian society and culture have been by Daniel Roche, Annik Pardaillé-Galabrun, Françoise Bayard, Daniel Dessert, and Robert Descimon, all cited below. Thanks to their learning and their inspiring work as teachers and researchers, the notarial archives have been made to yield what is effectively a "new history" of the Parisians. The official history of Paris sponsored by the Mairie de Paris (Jean-Pierre Babelon, René Pillorget, and Georges Dethan, also cited below) provides brilliant overviews on every aspect of the history of the capital. Pillorget's book is remarkably "encyclopedic," yet no less erudite and historical. It has a valuable and extensive general bibliography.

The following sources and works were the most helpful in preparing this essay. The list is neither exhaustive nor systematic, since what are known to be the standard works on a subject sometimes proved to be of little value to me. I therefore chose not to include them here.

Sources

Blondel, J.-F. *Architecture Françoise*. Paris, 1752.

Boislisle, A. de. *Mémoires de la Généralité de Paris*. Paris, 1881.

——. *Le Grand Hiver et la Disette de 1709*. Paris, 1903.

Bosse, A. *Le Peintre Converty*, ed. R. A. Weight. Paris, 1965.

Botero, G. *The Greatness of Cities*, trans. R. Peterson. New Haven, 1956.

Brice, G. *Description de la Ville de Paris*. Paris, 1717.

Chantelou, P. Frérart de. *Diary of the Cavaliere Bernini's Visit to France,* ed. A. Blunt. Princeton, 1985.

Colbert, J.-B. *Lettres, Instructions et Mémoires,* ed. P. Clément. Paris, 1861–73.

Conférences de l'Académie Royale de Peinture et de Sculpture, ed. A. Merot. Paris, 1996.

Dallington, R. *The View of France.* Oxford, 1936.

Delamare, N. *Traité de la Police,* augmented by du Brillet. Paris, 1722.

Desgodets, A. B. *Traité du Toisé des Bâtiments.* Paris, 1682.

——. *Dissertation de la Compagnie des Architects-experts des Bâtimens à Paris.* Paris, 1763.

Du Breul, J. *Le Théâtre des Antiquitez de Paris,* augmented by C. Malingre. Paris, 1639.

Faret, N. *L'Honneste Homme, ou l'Art de Plaire à la Cour,* ed. M. Magendie. Paris, 1925.

Henry IV. *Recueil des Lettres Missives* (Collection des Documents Inédits). Paris, 1843–76.

La Reynie, N. *Correspondance.* Archives Nationales. Series G7, 425–28, and Bibliothèque Nationale, n. a. fr. 5247.

Lebeuf, Abbé. *Histoire de la Ville et du Diocèse de Paris.* Paris, 1754.

Lecestre, L., ed. "État de la Dépense Faite durant l'Hiver depuis le 1 Décembre 1685 jusques au 30 Avril 1686 pour le Secours et Subsistance des Pauvres des Faubourgs de cette Ville de Paris." *Mémoires de la Société de l'Histoire de Paris* 49 (1927).

Lister, M. *A Journey to Paris in the Year 1698.* London, 1699; reprint Urbana, Ill., 1967.

Louis XIV. *Mémoires,* ed. C. Dreyss. Paris, 1860.

Malingre, C. *Annales de Paris.* Paris, 1640.

Piganiol de la Force. *Description Historique de Paris.* Paris, 1765.

Poussin, N. *Lettres et Propos sur l'Art,* ed. A. Blunt. Paris, 1964.

Receuil des Anciennes Lois Françaises, ed. F. A. Isambert, vols. 16–20. Paris, 1824; reprint Ridgewood, N.J., 1964–66.

Registres des Délibérations du Bureau de la Ville de Paris, ed. F. Bonnardot, and others. Paris, 1883–1952.

Registres de l'Hôtel de Ville de Paris pendant la Fronde, ed. Le Roux de Lincy and Douet d'Arcq, 3 vols. Paris, 1846.

Renty, G. de. *Correspondance,* ed. R. Triboulet. Paris, 1978.

Saint-Simon, H. de. *Mémoires,* ed. Y. Coirault, 8 vols. Paris, 1983–87.

Sauval, H. *Histoire des Recherches des Antiquités de la Ville de Paris* (written before 1676; published in 1724).

Sully, M. B. de. *Mémoires.* London, 1778.

Talon, O. *Mémoires,* ed. Petitot. Paris, 1827.

"Une Statistique de Paris en 1649." *Bulletin du Comité des Travaux Historiques.* Paris, 1907.

Vincent de Paul. *Correspondance,* ed. P. Coste. Paris, 1920.

Voyer d'Argenson, R. *Annales de la Compagnie du Saint-Sacrament,* ed. Dom Beauchet-Filleau. Marseilles, 1900.

Works

Adam, A. *Du Mysticisme à la Révolte: Les Jansénistes du XVIIe Siècle.* Paris, 1968.

Alcover, M. *Poullain de la Barre,* Biblio 17 (PFSCL). Tübingen, 1981.

Allier, R. *La Cabale des Dévots.* Paris, 1902.

Ariès, P. *The Hour of Our Death,* trans. H. Weaver. New York, 1981.

Ariès, P., and G. Duby, eds. *A History of Private Life,* trans. A. Goldhammer. Cambridge, Mass., 1989.

Astier, R. "Louis XIV, Premier Danseur." In *Sun King: The Ascendency of French Culture During the Reign of Louis XIV,* ed. D. L. Rubin. Washington, D.C., 1992.

Auerbach, E. "La Cour et la Ville." In *Scenes from the Drama of European Literature,* trans. Ralph Mannheim. New York, 1959.

Avenel, G. de. *Histoire Économique de la Propriété, des Salaires, des Denrées.* Paris, 1912.

Ayres-Bennett, W. "Women and Grammar." *Seventeenth-Century French Studies* 12 (1990).

Babelon, J.-P. *Demeures Parisiennes sous Henri IV et Louis XIII.* Paris, 1977.

———. *Henri IV.* Paris, 1982.

Ballon, H. *The Paris of Henry IV.* Cambridge, Mass., 1991.

———. *Louis Le Vau.* Princeton, 1999.

Barbiche, B. *Les Institutions de la Monarchie Française à l'Époque Moderne.* Paris, 1999.

Barbiche, B., and S. Barbiche de Damville. *Sully.* Paris, 1997.

Baudin, M. "The King's Minister in Seventeenth-Century French Drama." *Modern Language Notes* 14 (1939).

Baumgartner, F. *France in the Sixteenth Century.* New York, 1995.

Bayard, F. *Le Monde des Financiers au XVIIe Siècle.* Paris, 1988.

Beasley, F. *Revising Memory: Women's Fiction and Memoirs in Seventeenth-Century France.* New Brunswick, N.J., 1990.

Benedict, P. *The Huguenot Population of France, 1600–1685,* Transactions of the American Philosophical Society, vol. 81. Philadelphia, 1991.

Bénichou, P. *Morales du Grand Siècle.* Paris, 1948.

Bercé, Y.-M. *The Birth of Absolutism, 1598–1661,* trans. R. Rex. London, 1996.

Berger, R. W. *The Palace of the Sun: The Louvre of Louis XIV.* University Park, Pa., 1993.

———. *Public Access to Art in Paris: A Documentary History from the Middle Ages to 1800.* University Park, Pa., 1999.

Bergin, J. *Cardinal de la Rochefoucauld: Leadership and Reform in the French Church.* New Haven, 1987.

Béguin, K. *Les Princes de Condé.* Paris, 1999.

Berriot-Salvadore, E., et al., eds. *Les Femmes dans la Société Française de la Renaissance.* Geneva, 1990.

Berty, A. *Topographie Historique du Vieux Paris* (Collection Histoire Générale de Paris). Paris, 1866.

Bitton, R. D. *The French Nobility in Crisis, 1560–1640.* Stanford, 1969.

Blet, P. *Le Clergé de France et la Monarchie.* Rome, 1959.

Blum, A. *Abraham Bosse et la Société Française du XVIIe Siècle.* Paris, 1924.

Blunt, A. *Nicolas Poussin,* 2 vols. New York, 1967.

———. *Art and Architecture in France, 1500 to 1700,* 5th edition with R. Beresford. New Haven, 1998.

Boislisle, A. de. "Notices Historiques sur la Place des Victoires et sur la Place Vendôme." *Mémoires de la Société de l'Histoire de Paris et de l'Île-de-France,* vol. 15. Paris, 1888.

Bondois, P.-M. "Le Commissaire Nicolas Delamare et le Traité de la Police." *Revue d'Histoire Moderne* (1935).

Bonney, R. *The King's Debts: Finance and Politics in France, 1589–1661.* Oxford, 1981.

Boucher, J. *La Cour de Henri III.* Rennes, 1986.

Bourgeon, J.-L. "L'Île de la Cité pendant la Fronde, Structure Sociale." *Mémoires de la Fédération des Sociétés Historiques et Archéologiques de Paris et de l'Île-de-France,* vol. 13. Paris, 1962.

———. *Les Colbert avant Colbert: Destin d'une Famille Marchande.* Paris, 1973.

Bremond, H. *Histoire Littéraire du Sentiment Religieux en France.* Paris, 1932.

Brennan, T. *Public Drinking and Popular Culture in Eighteenth-Century Paris.* Princeton, 1988.

Buffévent, B. de. "La Fabrication de la Dentelle dans les Campagnes Parisiennes sous Louis XIV." *Mémoires de la Fédération des Sociétés Historiques et Archéologiques de Paris et de l'Île-de-France,* vols. 26–27. Paris, 1975–76.

———. *L'Économie Dentellière en Région Parisienne au XVIIe Siècle.* Pontoise, 1984.

Buisseret, D. *Sully.* London, 1968.

———. *Henry IV.* London, 1982.

Burke, P. *The Fabrication of Louis XIV.* New Haven, 1992.

Carrier, H. *Les Mazarinades,* 2 vols. Geneva, 1989.

————. *Les Muses Guerrières*. Paris, 1996.

Chalumeau, R. P. *St. Vincent de Paul*. Paris, 1959.

Chartier, R. *The Cultural Uses of Print*, trans. L. G. Cochrane. Princeton, 1987.

Chartier, R., M.-M. Compère, and D. Julia. *L'Éducation en France du XVIᵉ au XVIIIᵉ Siècle*. Paris, 1976.

Chauleur, A. "Le Rôle des Traitants dans l'Administration Financière de 1643 à 1653." *XVIIᵉ Siècle*, no. 65 (1964).

Chaunu, P. *La Mort à Paris, XVIᵉ–XVIIᵉ–XVIIIᵉ Siècles*. Paris, 1978.

Chéruel, A. *Histoire de France pendant la Minorité de Louis XIV*. Paris, 1879.

Chill, E. "Religion and Mendicity in Seventeenth-Century France." *International Review of Social History* 7 (1962).

————. "Tartuffe, Religion, and Courtly Culture." *French Historical Studies* 3 (1963).

Cioranescu, A. *Bibliographie de la Littérature Française du XVIIᵉ Siècle*, 3 vols. Paris, 1965–66.

Citron, P. *La Poésie de Paris*. Paris, 1961.

Clark, D. *Pierre Corneille*. Cambridge, 1992.

Clément, P. *Histoire de Colbert*. Paris, 1892.

Cognet, A. *Antoine Godeau*. Paris, 1900.

Cognet, L. *Le Jansenisme*. Paris, 1964.

Collins, J. "The Economic Role of Women in Seventeenth-Century France." *French Historical Studies* 16 (1989).

————. *The State in Early Modern France*. Cambridge, 1995.

Cornette, J. *La Mélancolie du Pouvoir: Omer Talon*. Paris, 1998.

Coulet, H. "Le Pouvoir du Charme Féminin dans le Roman au XVIIᵉ Siècle." *XVIIᵉ Siècle* 36 (1984).

Cropper, E., and C. Dempsey. *Nicolas Poussin*. Princeton, 1996.

Cuénin, M. *Roman et Société sous Louis XIV; Madame de Villedieu* (Lille theses), 2 vols. Paris, 1979.

————. "Mme de Villedieu, ou la Gerbe Romanesque." *Littératures Classiques* 16 (1991).

Darricau, R. *Les Clercs Réguliers Théatins à Paris: Sainte-Anne-la-Royale, 1644–1793*. Rome, 1961.

Daumard, A., and F. Furet. *Structures et Relations Sociales à Paris au XVIIIᵉ Siècle*. Paris, 1961.

Davidson, H. M. *Audience, Words, and Art*. Columbus, 1965.

Davis, N. Z. "Gender and Genre: Women as Historical Writers, 1400–1820." *Beyond Their Sex: Learned Women of the European Past*, ed. P. H. Labalme. New York, 1980.

————. *The Gift in Sixteenth-Century France*. Madison, 2000.

Davis, N. Z., and A. Farge. *A History of Women*, vol. 3. Cambridge, Mass., 1993.

Dear, P. *Mersenne and the Learning of the Schools*. Ithaca, 1988.

De Boer, J. *Men's Literary Circles in Paris, 1610–1660*. Publications of the Modern Language Association, vol. 53 (1938).

Dejean, J. *Fictions of Sapho, 1546–1937*. Chicago, 1989.

————. *Tender Geographies: Women and the Origins of the Novel in France*. New York, 1991.

————. "Amazons and Literary Women: Female Culture During the Reign of the Sun King." In *Sun King: The Ascendency of French Culture During the Reign of Louis XIV*, ed. D. L. Rubin. Washington, D.C., 1992.

Des Cilleuls, A. *Des Secours à Domicile dans la Ville de Paris*. Paris, 1892.

Descimon, R. "La Ligue à Paris (1585–1594): Une Révision," and "La Ligue: Des Divergences Fondamentales." *Annales, E. S. C.,* 37 (1982).

————. "Qui Étaient les Seize? Mythes et Réalités de la Ligue Parisienne (1585–94)." *Mémoires de la Fédération des Sociétés Historiques et Archéologiques de Paris et de l'Île-de-France,* vol. 34. Paris, 1983.

————. "Paris on the Eve of Saint Bartholomew: Taxation, Privilege, and Social Geography." *Urban Society in Ancient Regime France,* ed. P. Benedict. London, 1989.

————. "The Birth of the Nobility of the Robe: Dignity versus Privilege in the Parlement of Paris, 1500–1700." In *Changing Identities in Early Modern France,* ed. M. Wolfe. Durham, N.C., 1997.

Descimon, R., and J. Nagle. "Les Quartiers de Paris du Moyen Âge au XVIIIᵉ Siècle: Évolution d'un Espace Plurifonctionnel." *Annales, E. S. C.,* 34 (1979).

Dessert, D. *Argent, Pouvoir et Société au Grand Siècle.* Paris, 1984.

————. *Fouquet.* Paris, 1987.

Dethan, G. *Gaston d'Orléans, Conspirateur et Prince Charmant.* Paris, 1959.

————. *Paris au Temps de Louis XIV (1660–1715).* Paris, 1990.

Dewald, J. *Aristocratic Experience and the Origins of Modern Culture, France, 1570–1715.* Berkeley and Los Angeles, 1993.

Diefendorf, B. *Paris City Councillors in the Sixteenth Century: The Politics of Patrimony.* Princeton, 1983.

————. *Beneath the Cross; Catholics and Huguenots in Sixteenth-Century Paris.* New York, 1991.

————. "The Huguenot Psalter and the Faith of French Protestants in the Sixteenth Century." In *Culture and Identity in Early Modern Europe (1500–1800),* ed. B. Diefendorf and C. Hesse. Ann Arbor, 1993.

————. "Give Us Back Our Children: Patriarchal Authority and Parental Consent to Religious Vocations in Early Counter Reformation France." *Journal of Modern History* 68 (1996).

————. "Contradictions of the Century of Saints: Aristocratic Patronage and the Convents of Counter-Reformation Paris." *French Historical Studies* 24 (2001).

Dorival, B. *Philippe de Champaigne, 1602–1674,* 2 vols. Paris, 1976.

Dulong, C. *La Vie Quotidienne des Femmes au Grand Siècle.* Paris, 1984.

Dumolin, M. *Études de Topographie Parisienne.* Paris, 1929.

Dunn, K. "A Great City Is a Great Solitude: Descartes's Urban Pastoral." *Yale French Studies* 80 (1991).

Dupâquier, J. *Histoire de la Population Française,* 4 vols. Paris, 1989.

Edelman, N. *Attitudes of Seventeenth-Century France Toward the Middle Ages.* New York, 1946.

Fagniez, G. *La Femme et la Société Française dans la Première Moitié du XVIIᵉ Siècle.* Paris, 1929.

Farr, J. *Hands of Honor: Artisans and Their World in Dijon, 1550–1650.* Ithaca, 1988.

Feillet, A. *La Misère pendant la Fronde.* Paris, 1868.

Finley-Crosswhite, S. A. *Henry IV and the Towns.* Cambridge, 1999.

Foisil, M. *La Vie Quotidienne au Temps de Louis XIII.* Paris, 1992.

Franklin, A. *Les Corporations Ouvrières de Paris du XIIᵉ au XVIIIᵉ Siècle.* Paris, 1884.

————. *La Vie Privée d'Autrefois, Mœurs et Coutumes des Parisiens du XIIIᵉ au XVIIIᵉ Siècle,* 27 vols. Paris, 1887–1902.

————. *Paris au XVIᵉ Siècle.* Paris, 1921.

Friedlander, W. *Nicolas Poussin.* New York, 1965.

Fumaroli, M. *La Diplomatie de l'Esprit, de Montaigne à La Fontaine.* Paris, 1994.

Gaukroger, S. *Descartes: An Intellectual Biography.* Oxford, 1997.

Gazier, A. *Histoire Générale du Mouvement Janséniste depuis les Origines jusqu'à Nos Jours,* 2 vols. Paris, 1922–24.

Gérard, A. "La Révolte et le Siège de Paris." *Mémoires de la Société de l'Histoire de Paris et de l'Île-de-France,* vol. 33. Paris, 1906.

Gibson, W. *Women in Seventeenth-Century France.* London, 1989.

Godard de Donville, L. *Signification de la Mode sous Louis XIII.* Aix-en-Provence, 1978.

Golden, R. *The Godly Rebellion: Parisian Curés and the Religious Fronde, 1652–1662.* Chapel Hill, 1981.

Goldmann, L. *Le Dieu Caché: Étude sur la Vision Tragique dans les Pensées de Pascal et le Théâtre de Racine*. Paris, 1955.

Goldstein, C. "Studies in Seventeenth-Century French Art Theory and Ceiling Painting." *The Art Bulletin* 47 (1965).

———. "Looking in the Mirror of Abraham Bosse." In *French Prints from the Age of the Musketeers*, ed. S. W. Reed. Boston, 1998.

Grand-Mesnil, M.-N. *Mazarin, la Fronde et la Presse, 1647–1649*. Paris, 1967.

Grassby, R. B. "Social Status and Commercial Enterprise Under Louis XIV." *Economic History Review* 13 (1960).

Greengrass, M. *France in the Age of Henry IV*. London, 1984.

Gutton, J.-P. *La Société et les Pauvres en Europe, XVIᵉ–XVIIᵉ Siècles*. Paris, 1974.

———. *Domestiques et Serviteurs dans la France de l'Ancien Régime*. Paris, 1981.

Hahn, R. *The Anatomy of a Scientific Institution: The Paris Academy of Sciences*. Berkeley and Los Angeles, 1971.

Hargrove, J., ed. *The French Academy, Classicism and Its Antagonists*. Newark, Del., 1990.

Harth, E. *Ideology and Culture in Seventeenth-Century France*. Ithaca, 1983.

———. *Cartesian Women*. Ithaca, 1992.

Haskell, F. *Painters and Patrons: A Study in Relations Between Italian Art and Society in the Age of the Baroque*. New York, 1963.

Hautecœur, L. *Histoire de l'Architecture Classique en France*. Paris, 1943–57.

Hibbard, H. *Bernini*. Baltimore, 1965.

Hillairet, J. *Évocation du Vieux Paris*. Paris, 1952.

———. *Dictionnaire Historique des Rues de Paris*, 2 vols. and supplement. Paris, 1963.

Holt, M. *The French Wars of Religion, 1562–1629*. Cambridge, 1995.

Houssaye, M. *Le Père Bérulle et l'Oratoire de Jésus*. Paris, 1874.

Hufton, O. *The Prospect Before Her*. New York, 1996.

Huppert, G. *Public Schools in Renaissance France*. Champaign-Urbana, 1984.

Isherwood, R. *Music in the Service of the King*. Ithaca, 1973.

———. *Farces and Fantasy: Popular Entertainment in Eighteenth-Century France*. New York, 1986.

Jacquart, J. "La Fronde des Princes dans la Région Parisienne et ses Conséquences Matérielles." *Revue d'Histoire Moderne et Contemporaine* 7 (1964).

Jacquinet, P. *Des Prédicateurs du XVIIᵉ Siècle avant Bossuet*. Paris, 1885.

Jasinski, R. *Vers le Vrai Racine*. Paris, 1958.

Jensen, D. *Diplomacy and Dogmatism*. Cambridge, Mass., 1964.

Jones, H. *Pierre Gassendi, 1592–1655, an Intellectual Biography*. Nieuwkoop, 1981.

Jouhaud, C. *Mazarinades: La Fronde des Mots*. Paris, 1985.

Joy, L. *Gassendi, the Atomist*. Cambridge, 1987.

Keohane, N. *Philosophy and the State in France*. Princeton, 1980.

Kettering, S. *French Society, 1589–1715*. London, 2001.

Klein, N. D. *Selected Writings of Madame de Villedieu*. New York, 1995.

Kleinman, R. *Anne of Austria*. Columbus, 1985.

Krakovitch, O. "Le Couvent des Minimes de la Place Royale." *Mémoires de la Fédération des Sociétés Historiques et Archéologiques de Paris et de l'Île-de-France*, vol. 30. Paris, 1979.

———. "La Vie Intellectuelle dans les Trois Couvents Minimes." *Bulletin de la Société de l'Histoire de Paris et de l'Île-de-France*, vol. 109. Paris, 1982.

Labatut, J.-P. "Situation Sociale du Quartier du Marais pendant la Fronde Parlementaire, 1648–1649." *XVIIᵉ Siècle* 38 (1958).

Lambeau, L. *La Place Royale.* Paris, 1906.

———. "Deux Hôtels de la Place Royale." *Mémoires de la Société de l'Histoire de Paris et de l'Île-de-France*, vol. 38. Paris, 1911.

Lapeyre, H. *Une Famille de Marchands, Les Ruiz.* Paris, 1955.

Larmour, R. "Corporations and Capitalism: The Grocers of Paris in the Sixteenth Century" (dissertation). Columbia University, 1963.

Laugaa, M. "Mme de Lafayette ou l'Intelligence du Cœur." *Littératures Classiques* 15 (1991).

Lavedan, P. *Histoire de l'Urbanisme.* Paris, 1941.

Lavisse, E. *Histoire de France,* ed. E. Lavisse, vol. 7, parts 1 and 2. Paris, 1906.

Lehoux, F. *Le Cadre de Vie des Médecins Parisiens aux XVIe et XVIIe Siècles.* Paris, 1976.

Lemoine, H. "Maisons Religieuses Fondées à Paris entre 1600 et 1639." *Bulletin de la Société de l'Histoire de Paris et de l'Île-de-France*, vol. 32. Paris, 1942–43.

Lemoine, Y. *La Grande Robe, le Mariage et l'Argent.* Paris, 2000.

Leroy-Ladurie, E., and P. Couperie. "Le Mouvement des Loyers Parisiens de la Fin du Moyen-Age au XVIIIe Siècle." *Annales, E. S. C.,* 25 (1970).

Lougee, C. *Le Paradis des Femmes: Women, Salons, and Social Stratification in Seventeenth-Century France.* Princeton, 1976.

Lux, D. *Patronage and Royal Science in Seventeenth-Century France.* Ithaca, 1989.

Mabille de Poncheville, A. *Philippe de Champaigne.* Paris, n.d.

MacLean, I. *Woman Triumphant: Feminism in French Literature, 1610–1652.* Oxford, 1977.

Magendie, M. *La Politesse Mondaine et les Théories de l'Honnêteté en France au XVIIe Siècle.* Paris, 1925.

Magne, E. *Paris sous l'Échevinage au XVIIe Siècle.* Paris, 1960.

Major, J. R. *Representative Government in Early Modern France.* New Haven, 1980.

Mandrou, R. *Introduction à la France Moderne.* Paris, 1961.

———. *Magistrats et Sorciers en France au XVIIe Siècle.* Paris, 1968.

Mariéjol, J.-H. *Histoire de France,* ed. E. Lavisse, vol. 6, parts 1 and 2. Paris, 1904.

Martin, H.-J. *Livre, Pouvoirs et Société à Paris au XVIIe Siècle (1598–1701),* 2 vols. Geneva, 1969.

———. *The French Book, Religion, Absolutism, and Readership (1585–1715),* trans. P. and N. Saenger. Baltimore, 1996.

Martin, H.-J., and R. Chartier, in collaboration with J.-P. Vivet. *Histoire de l'Édition Française*, vol. 1. Paris, 1982.

Massip, C. *La Vie des Musiciens de Paris, au Temps de Mazarin, 1643–1661.* Paris, 1976.

Maugis, E. *Histoire du Parlement de Paris.* Paris, 1916.

McGowan, M. *Le Ballet de Cour en France de 1581 à 1643.* Paris, 1963.

McKenna, R. J. "The Personal Religious Life in the Thought of St. Francis of Sales" (dissertation). Union Theological Seminary, 1963.

Mesnard, J., et al. *Précis de la Littérature Française du XVIIe Siècle.* Paris, 1990.

Meuvret, J. *Le Problème des Subsistances à l'Époque de Louis XIV,* 2 vols. Paris, 1988.

Mignot, C. *Le Val-de-Grâce: L'Ermitage d'une Reine.* Paris, 1994.

Miron de l'Espinay. *François Miron.* Paris, 1885.

Montgrédien, G. *La Vie de Société aux XVIIe et XVIIIe Siècles.* Paris, 1950.

Moote, A. L. *The Revolt of the Judges: The Parlement of Paris and the Fronde, 1643–1652.* Princeton, 1971.

———. *Louis XIII, the Just.* Berkeley and Los Angeles, 1989.

Morrissette, B. A. *The Life and Works of Marie-Catherine Desjardins (Mme de Villedieu).* St. Louis, 1947.

Motley, M. *Becoming a French Aristocrat: The Education of the Great Nobility.* Princeton, 1990.

Mours, S. *Le Protestantisme en France au XVIIe Siècle, 1598–1685*. Paris, 1959.

Mousnier, R. *La Stratification Sociale à Paris aux XVIIe et XVIIIe Siècles*. Paris, 1976.

Nelson, R. J. *Corneille, His Heroes, and Their Worlds*. Philadelphia, 1963.

Neuschel, K. B. "Noblewomen and War in Sixteenth-Century France." *Changing Identities in Early Modern France*, ed. M. Wolfe. Durham, N.C., 1997.

Newton, W. R. *Sociologie de la Communauté de Port-Royal*. Paris, 1999.

Olivier-Martin, F. *Organisation Corporative de la France d'Ancien Régime*. Paris, 1938.

Orcibal, J. *Jean Duvergier de Hauranne, Abbé de Saint-Cyran et son Temps*. Paris, 1947.

Pardailhé-Galabrun, A. *La Naissance de l'Intime*. Paris, 1988.

Parmentier, B. *Le Siècle des Moralistes*. Paris, 2000.

Pekacz, J. T. *Conservative Tradition in Pre-Revolutionary France: Parisian Salon Women*. New York, 1999.

Pillorget, R. *La Tige et le Rameau: Familles Anglaises et Françaises, XVIe–XVIIIe Siècles*. Paris, 1979.

———. *Paris sous les Premiers Bourbons, 1594–1661*. Paris, 1988.

Pitts, V. J. *La Grande Mademoiselle at the Court of France, 1627–1693*. Baltimore, 2000.

Poëte, M. *Formation et Évolution de Paris*. Paris, 1910.

———. *La Promenade à Paris au XVIIe Siècle*. Paris, 1921.

———. *Une Vie de Cité, Paris de Sa Naissance à Nos Jours*. Paris, 1927.

Poisson, J.-P. *Notaires et Société*. Paris, 1990.

———. *Études Notariales*. Paris, 1996.

Pouvoirs Féminins au XVIIe Siècle, XVIIe Siècle, 1984.

Quilligan, M. *The Allegory of Female Authority: Christine de Pisan's "Cité des Dames."* Ithaca, 1991.

Radouant, R. *Guillaume du Vair, l'Homme et l'Orateur*. Paris, 1907.

Ramsey, A. *Liturgy, Politics, and Salvation: The Catholic League in Paris and the Nature of Catholic Reform, 1540–1630*. Rochester, 1999.

Ranum, O. *The Fronde: A French Revolution*. New York, 1993.

Ranum, Patricia M. "A Sweet Servitude: A Musician's Life at the Court of Mlle de Guise." *Early Music* 15 (1987).

———. "Feindre des Poutres pour Faire Simmetrie aux Vrayes: La Rénovation de l'Hôtel de Guise, 1666–1667." *Histoire et Archives* (Société des Amis des Archives de France), no. 10 (July–December 2001).

Rebelliau, A. *La Compagnie Secrète du Saint-Sacrement. Lettres du Groupe Parisien au Groupe Marseillais, 1639–1662*. Paris, 1908.

Reinburg, V. "Hearing Lay People's Prayer." In *Culture and Identity in Early Modern Europe (1500–1800)*, ed. B. Diefendorf and C. Hesse. Ann Arbor, 1993.

Robiquet, P. *Histoire Municipale de Paris*. Paris, 1880–1904.

Roche, D. *The People of Paris*, trans. M. and G. Evans. Chicago, 1987.

———. *The Culture of Clothing*, trans. J. Birrel. Cambridge, 1994.

Rodis-Lewis, G. *Descartes: A Biography*, trans. J. M. Todd. Ithaca, 1995.

Rosenberg, P. *France in the Golden Age: Seventeenth-Century French Paintings in American Collections*. New York, 1982.

Roupnel, G. *Histoire de la Campagne Française*. Paris, 1932.

Salmon, M. *La Portefeuille d'Achille de Harlay*. Paris, 1909.

Salomon, H. *Public Welfare, Science, and Propaganda in Seventeenth-Century France*. Princeton, 1972.

Salomon, H. P. *Tartuffe devant l'Opinion Française*. Paris, 1962.

Sawyer, J. K. *Printed Poison: Pamphlet Propaganda, Faction Politics, and the Public Sphere in Seventeenth-Century France.* Berkeley and Los Angeles, 1990.

Sayce, R. A. *The French Biblical Epic.* Oxford, 1955.

Schiffman, Z. S. *On the Threshold of Modernity.* Baltimore, 1991.

Scoville, W. C. *The Persecution of the Huguenots and French Economic Development, 1680–1720.* Berkeley and Los Angeles, 1960.

Sedgwick, A. *Jansenism in Seventeenth-Century France.* Cambridge, Mass., 1997.

————. *The Travails of Conscience and the Arnauld Family.* Cambridge, Mass., 1998.

Sellier, C. *Anciens Hôtels de Paris.* Paris, 1910.

Sippel, C. "The Noblesse de Robe in Early Seventeenth-Century France: A Study of Social Mobility" (dissertation). University of Michigan, 1963.

Snyders, F. *La Pédagogie en France au XVIIe et au XVIIIe Siècles.* Paris, 1965.

Stroup, A. *A Company of Scientists.* Berkeley and Los Angeles, 1990.

Stuurman, S. "From Feminism to Biblical Criticism: The Theological Trajectory of Poullain de la Barre." *Eighteenth Century Studies* 33 (2000).

Sutherland, N. *The Massacre of St. Bartholomew and the European Conflict.* London, 1973.

Taton, R. *Les Origines de l'Académie Royale des Sciences.* Paris, 1966.

Thuillier, J. *Nicolas Poussin.* Paris, 1988.

Timmermans, B. "The Originality of Descartes' Conception of Analysis as Discovery." *Journal of the History of Ideas* 60 (1999).

Timmermans, L. *L'Accès des Femmes à la Culture (1598–1715).* Paris, 1993.

Truant, C. *The Rites of Labor: Brotherhoods of Compagnonnage in Old and New Régime France.* Ithaca, 1994.

Ultee, J. M. *The Abbey of Saint Germain des Prés in the Seventeenth Century.* New Haven, 1981.

Van Baelen, J. R. "Tragédie et Moralité chez Rotrou" (dissertation). University of California, Los Angeles, 1963.

Van Deursen, A. *Professions et Métiers Interdits: Un Aspect de l'Histoire de la Révocation de l'Edit de Nantes.* Groningen, 1960.

Venard, M. *Bourgeois et Paysans au XVIIe Siècle.* Paris, 1957.

Viala, A. *Naissance de l'Écrivain.* Paris, 1985.

Viguerie, J. de. *Une Œuvre d'Éducation sous l'Ancien Régime: Les Pères de la Doctrine Chrétienne en France et en Italie, 1592–1792.* Paris, 1976.

————. *L'Institution des Enfants: L'Éducation en France, XVIe-XVIIIe Siècles.* Paris, 1978.

Watson, E. C. "The Early Days of the Académie des Sciences." *Osiris* 7 (1939).

Wells, C. C. *Law and Citizenship in Early Modern France.* Baltimore, 1995.

Wildenstein, L. *Le Goût pour la Peinture dans la Bourgeoisie du Début du Règne de Louis XIII.* Paris, 1959.

Wolf, J. B. *Louis XIV.* New York, 1968.

Wolfe, M. *The Conversion of Henry IV.* Cambridge, Mass., 1993.

Yates, F. A. *French Academies in the Sixteenth Century.* London, 1947.

————. *The Valois Tapestries.* London, 1959.

Illustration Credits

Pages 22–23: Bibliothèque nationale de France, Paris (hereafter cited as B.N.F.). Page 30: B.N.F. Page 31: B.N.F. Page 34: B.N.F. Page 46: B.N.F. Page 64: B.N.F. Page 71: B.N.F. Page 74: The Metropolitan Museum of Art, New York City, Fletcher Fund, 1927 (27.59). Photograph © 1983 The Metropolitan Museum of Art. All rights reserved. Page 85: B.N.F. Page 94: B.N.F. Page 95. B.N.F. Page 97: Author's collection. Page 99: Author's collection. Page 101: B.N.F. Page 113: Author's collection. Page 115: Author's collection. Page 124: Evergreen House Library, The Johns Hopkins University. Page 133: B.N.F. Page 134: Arlette Lebigre. Page 138: The National Gallery, Washington, D.C. Page 140: Librairie Farfouille. Page 149: B.N.F. Page 161: B.N.F. Page 169: B.N.F. Page 180: Author's collection. Page 182: Author's collection. Page 184: B.N.F. Page 185: Louvre, Paris. Page 186: B.N.F. Page 188: Author's collection. Page 202: B.N.F. Page 203: B.N.F. Page 207: B.N.F. Page 208: Author's collection. Page 211: B.N.F. Page 221: Musée historique de Versailles. Page 223: Musée de Chantilly. Page 234: B.N.F. Page 236: B.N.F. Page 241: B.N.F. Page 254: B.N.F. Page 255: B.N.F. Page 277: B.N.F. Page 280: Author's collection. Page 281: Georges Dethan. Page 293: B.N.F. Page 297: B.N.F. Page 299: Author's collection. Page 302: Author's collection. Page 310: B.N.F. Page 318: B.N.F. Page 320: B.N.F. Page 324: B.N.F. Page 336: B.N.F. Page 342: B.N.F. Page 343: B.N.F. Page 347: B.N.F. Page 361: B.N.F. Page 364: B.N.F. Page 365: B.N.F. Page 366: B.N.F. Page 370: B.N.F.

Index

Italicized page numbers indicate either an illustration or an item in a caption. Discussions of literary works are included in the entry for the author.